Essays in Derivatives

Essays in Derivatives

Risk-Transfer Tools and Topics Made Easy

Second Edition

DON M. CHANCE, Ph.D., CFA

Louisiana State University

WILEY

John Wiley & Sons, Inc.

Published by John Wiley & Sons, Inc., Hoboken, New Jersey.

Published simultaneously in Canada.

For general information on our other products and services or for technical support, please contact our Customer Care Department within the United States at (800) 762-2974, outside the United States at (317) 572-3993 or fax (317) 572-4002.

Wiley also publishes its books in a variety of electronic formats. Some content that appears in print may not be available in electronic formats. For more information about Wiley products, visit our web site at www.wiley.com.

Library of Congress Cataloging-in-Publication Data:

Chance, Don M.
  Essays in derivatives : risk-transfer tools and topics made easy / Don M. Chance. – 2nd ed.
    p. cm.
  Includes bibliographical references and index.
  ISBN 978-0-470-08625-4 (cloth)
  1. Derivative securities.   2. Risk management.   3. Investments.   I. Title.
  HG6024.A3C475   2008
  332.64′57–dc22

                                                                          2008008489

Printed in the United States of America

10 9 8 7 6 5 4 3 2 1

Contents

Preface to the New Edition

Those who are familiar with the first edition know that the book was a compendium of essays I wrote and posted on the Internet, back at a time when the Internet was just a toddler. Having labored over these essays and then given them away, I got this crazy idea to put them into a book and charge people money. Needless to say, the free essays were more popular than the book, but the publisher and I have been satisfied with the success of *Essays in Derivatives*, enough so that we have undertaken to update this book.

The first edition was published in 1998, and here we are about 10 years later. The derivatives business has gotten older, smarter, and more sophisticated. I have changed universities and at least gotten older. A lot of what I said in 1998 just won't cut it today. And there are a lot of topics that aren't quite as interesting today as they were in 1998, plus some that are important today that were not so back then. Thus, an updating seemed like an important thing to do.

My primary objective in a book like this is to create something about derivatives that is easy to read. Derivatives can be a painful subject to learn, and many legal pads are used up, sometimes frustratingly, in working through some of the principles covered in technical derivatives books. This book is different. While I do not advise that you curl up with it by a warm fire, a loyal dog, and a loved one, I do think you can relax in an easy chair and read it without pen and paper at your side. To that extent, this book is unique. Rarely will you find a derivatives book without equations. (OK. Technically there *are* some equations, but they are mostly buried within sentences and don't jump out at you like those big offset monstrosities you see in most derivatives books.) Of course, the absence of equations comes at a cost. You cannot get yourself up to a sophisticated level in derivatives by reading this book, but you can make a great deal of headway. Learning derivatives entails climbing a steep learning curve. Getting at least part of the way there with the minimum amount of mental anguish is a major accomplishment and provides encouragement for taking the next and somewhat harder step.

For those who have read the first edition, I hope you will use this version as an opportunity to brush up. I have removed a few essays that seemed outdated, combined a few others, and added essays on why derivatives are used, volatility derivatives, weather derivatives, forward and futures pricing, risk management in organizations, worst practices in derivatives, and best practices in derivatives. Every essay has been at least partially polished if not substantially rewritten. In addition, at the end of each essay I have now provided a few practice questions so you can see if you remember what you read. (The answers are at the back of the book.) In addition, the seven major sections of the book now contain short overviews to alert you to what's coming up. Reading lists have been updated to include material that has emerged in the last 10 years.

If you are already an expert in derivatives, this book will not teach you much. It is quite elementary. But if anyone has ever asked you where to get started (and I have certainly gotten that question many times), this book should be a good answer. Take it for what it is intended to be: an easy-to-read introduction. No more, no less. For those trying to learn the topic for the first time, read it and see if you don't agree: A basic understanding of derivatives need not be hard, and it can be fun to read about. (OK. Maybe "fun" isn't the word. Maybe it's "enjoyable.") And if it isn't, you will at least have saved some money over the monster tome you probably would have bought if this book hadn't come along.

As usual, many people contribute to the production of a book. I want to thank the Wiley folks: Bill Falloon, Emilie Herman, Laura Walsh, Pamela van Giessen, and Christina Verigan. I also want to thank Frank Fabozzi for his publishing of the first edition of this book and his encouragement for this revision. I also thank my family: Jan, Kim, Ashley, Michael, Joel, Kurt, Sadie, and Hunter. (Note: Some of these are dogs, and they do get credit. Writing a book is hard enough without a little laughter.)

As always, I invite your comments and suggestions. Send them to me at dchance@lsu.edu. With enough praise for encouragement or complaints to fix, maybe there'll be a third edition. But give me another 10 years, please.

DON M. CHANCE, PH.D., CFA
Baton Rouge, Louisiana
March 2008

Preface to the First Edition

This book had its origins on a sleepless night when I discovered that the Internet was a great place to convey ideas.[1] I had found the UscNet group misc.invest.futures, which was the only user group whose discussions were focused on derivatives. Misc.invest.futures struck me as a group whose conversation was largely dominated by someone selling a new futures trading service, a discount brokerage firm, or someone with an opinion about whether a commodity had "bottomed out" according to some technical indicator. Even worse were those people offering astrological advice for futures trading. Amid all of this commercialism and hype, it appeared to me that the readership had a thirst for knowledge of another sort: simple, to the point, and not motivated by a big sale. I am, of course, as profit-oriented as anyone else, but being new to the Internet, I decided to make my entry on a pro bono basis, with the hope that down the road there might be some profits, however modest they are likely to be.[2]

Thus was born my weekly column on derivatives, which later was called Derivatives Research Unincorporated or DRU.[3] Over the next 52 weeks, I posted a total of 41 essays to the misc.invest.futures group, simultaneously depositing them into an electronic filebox where they were available for downloading. The feedback I received was surprising, overwhelming, and, above all, gratifying. Virtually every week I received a new e-mail from a reader somewhere around the world, many asking how to obtain personal subscriptions, which I would not do. I was even getting requests for topics, making me feel somewhat like a disk jockey, spinning the platters of derivatives.

Soon others began placing pointers to DRU on their home pages, and DRU began to be mentioned in articles about sources available on the

---

[1] Maybe this is because almost everything on the Internet is free or very inexpensive, and it's hard for people to complain that they're not getting their money's worth.

[2] If you're reading this at a book store or library, please go out and buy the book. In fact buy an extra copy for a loved one. (Just kidding, unless you're in love with a derivatives person.)

[3] I cannot legally tell you what it was originally called, but many of you already know and others can guess.

Internet in the area of derivatives. My readers ranged from individuals seeking a little extra knowledge, to technically skilled personnel of major financial institutions, to college students and professors. I seemed to have developed something of a cult following like the *Rocky Horror Picture Show*! People e-mailed to complain if I disappeared for a couple of weeks.

The second year I wrote another 20 or so essays. I finally quit writing them when it was taking too much time, I was getting too many e-mails from people with questions, and I was running out of topics that could be written up in simple, nontechnical language. When I posted my last essay in September 1996, I thought DRU had come to an end. The phone calls and e-mails continued to the point that I was beginning to feel like the Ann Landers of derivatives. Repeated efforts to discourage people from contacting me were mildly successful. What I wanted was that people would read the essays, perhaps refer to my main home page (www.cob.vt.edu/finance/faculty/dmc), and take advantage of any other writings, documents, or links that I had posted but, generally, leave me alone. At around the same time, I had reached an agreement with a major business publishing group to have the essays published in hard-copy form. A long and complicated story later, we broke off the arrangement. Since that time, I continued to be contacted by individuals and firms who enjoyed the essays.

About a year later, Frank Fabozzi found my web site. Frank and I had enjoyed a productive business relationship a few years back but had not talked in several years. One thing led to another, and Frank agreed to publish these essays in his own publishing venture, Frank J. Fabozzi Associates (www.frankfabozzi.com). I believe you will agree that Frank has done an excellent job with his own publishing venture, and I am pleased to now be a part of it.

The original essays all sounded like a conversation with an unidentified person, namely the Internet surfer. There were no charts or graphs, with the exception of a few figurelike tables necessary to illustrate binomial trees. There were no complex equations, and the number of simple equations was kept to an absolute minimum. The tone was informal and written in fairly nontechnical language. People told me repeatedly how beneficial this approach was to them. In this book version, each essay has been rewritten, maintaining the basic qualities that made them attractive, while simply polishing the language and removing references that suggested that this was a posting on an Internet site.

The level of knowledge I assume in the reader is pretty low. I would say that one should already know the definitions of options and futures. That's about it. I have been told that the essays appeal to individuals at all levels of expertise. Beginners will particularly find them useful, and experts seem to appreciate the simple manner in which such seemingly complicated subjects can be presented. They have been used in college classes as well as in corporations, financial institutions, and government agencies in training employees, executives, and clients. With all of this given freely to the rest of the world, don't you think I deserve to earn at least one hour at minimum wage?

In the original versions, the essays were written and posted in whatever order a topic came to me. Now they have been grouped into logical sections. In addition, 10 new essays have been added to fill in some gaps. In some of the essays there is a list of articles called *For More Reading*. I chose these articles very carefully. Any article mentioned in an essay is included. Otherwise, I tried to include only classic articles, articles that are pretty much standard references for these topics, and articles that are exceptionally well written and at a slightly higher level than that of these essays. Obviously some of you will disagree, especially with omissions. To this I say, you're probably right, but you'll have to write your own book.

At the end of this book is a reading list of books in derivatives, arranged in various groups, with some commentary about each group and a selected few of the titles. After reading these essays, this collection of books is where I would go next.[4]

Also be aware that I maintain a large collection of materials and links at my web site (www.cob.vt.edu/finance/faculty/dmc). Clicking on the "Courses" menu choice gives you free access to an extensive collection of lecture notes and a set of materials called "Teaching Notes," which to some extent are more advanced versions of some of the essays in this book. You might also enjoy a site called DerivaQuote, which is a collection of quotations about derivatives, with a few others on finance in general. As with most sites, this one is dynamic, with new quotes added as I stumble on them. There is also a dynamic bibliography of all published articles I can find on modeling the term structure and pricing interest rate derivatives. Who knows what else there will be by the time you're reading this.

Please send me your feedback on this book by e-mail (dmc@vt.edu) or snail mail (Department of Finance, Pamplin College of Business, Virginia Tech, Blacksburg, VA 24061), or give me a call at 540-231-5061 or a fax at 540-231-3155. Maybe there will be a second edition someday, and your input would be useful.

There is still a long way to go before people understand and appreciate derivatives as well as they do stocks and bonds. I hope these essays will

---

[4] Don't forget to get my other book *An Introduction to Derivatives*, 4th ed., the Dryden Press (1998), ISBN 0-03-024483-8, which you can have ordered by any book store, or through www.amazon.com or by calling Harcourt Brace at 1-800-782-4479. It's expensive, but so is everything else on this subject.

contribute to the general knowledge level and help dispel the myths about derivatives. But please don't send me your questions on how to solve your personal or corporate derivatives problems. I just cannot respond to all of the requests I receive of this type.

And please, don't ask me to write any more articles for the Internet.

DON M. CHANCE, PH.D., CFA
Blacksburg, VA
1998

One

Derivatives and Their Markets

A derivative is a contract between two parties that provides for a payoff from one party to the other based on the performance of an underlying asset, currency, or interest rate. The payoff of the derivative is said to be "derived" from the performance of something else, which is often called the underlying asset or just the "underlying." As noted all derivatives have two parties, who are typically known as the "buyer" and "seller" or sometimes the "long" and "short." The short is even sometimes referred to as the "writer." Derivatives almost always have a defined life. That is, they typically expire on a specific date. The payments made on a derivative are sometimes made partially at the start, sometimes made during the life of the derivative, and sometime made at the expiration. Some derivatives can be terminated early. Some derivatives have their payoffs made in cash and some have their payoffs made in the underlying or even in another asset. Derivative contracts can be informally negotiated between two parties or can be created on a derivatives exchange. Some types of derivatives are regulated and others are essentially unregulated.

The four basic types of derivatives are forward contracts, futures contracts, options, and swaps. Other types of derivatives can be created by blending some of these derivatives with the underlying. Some people also refer to asset-backed securities as derivatives and we will cover these in this book.

Understanding derivatives requires an understanding of what their payoffs would be given the payoff of the underlying. Options, for example, pay off either a given amount of money that is determined by the underlying or they pay off nothing. Forwards, futures, and swaps on the other hand almost always pay off something. Their payoffs are driven nearly one-for-one by what the underlying does. Understanding derivatives also requires an appreciation for the circumstances under which a derivative would be appropriately used. That is, why would someone use a derivative and if they would, why would they use one type of derivative instead of another? Finally and perhaps most importantly, understanding derivatives requires an understanding of how they are priced. If you pay $5 for an option on a stock or enter into an interest rate swap promising to pay a fixed rate of 6%, why $5 and 6%?

Grasping the basic ideas behind derivatives is not too difficult. I predict that you will have little trouble understanding the four basic types of derivatives and will know the kinds of situations in which one might be used and preferred over another. The hardest part is indeed understanding the pricing. All of this material is covered in this book. We work you up to it slowly and (hopefully) painlessly.

This first section covers the basics. Essay 1 describes how the derivatives markets are organized. The second essay is an update of paper I wrote years ago on the history of derivatives markets that proved to be very popular. It takes you from ancient times to today. The third essay explains why derivatives exist and what they are used for. Essays 4–6 introduce the four basic types of derivatives. Essay 7 then explains the types of risks that these instruments are designed to protect against.

The Structure of
Derivative Markets

It has been said in the past that derivatives are kind of a sideshow, where the main event takes place in the money and capital markets. You could attend the sideshow without taking part in the main event and vice versa. With respect to derivative and money/capital markets, that is simply not true today. Derivatives are so widely used that even if you have no intention of using them, it is important to understand how they are used by others and what effects, positive and negative, they could have on money and capital markets.

As you probably know, the money market consists of the over-the-counter markets for various short-term securities, such as Treasury bills, bank certificates of deposit, and commercial paper. The capital market consists of organized stock exchanges, such as the New York Stock Exchange, the American Stock Exchange, the Philadelphia Stock Exchange, and the Midwest Stock Exchange, to name a few. In addition there is the well-known National Association of Securities Dealers, otherwise known as Nasdaq, which is the principal over-the-counter market for securities. A small amount of corporate bond trading occurs on the New York Stock Exchange and the American Stock Exchange. By far, however, the preponderance of corporate bonds and all government bonds and asset-backed securities trade on the over-the-counter markets, which are simply dealers who stand willing to trade on either side of the market.

From around the middle nineteenth century until around 1990, it was probably correct to say thought that the center of the derivatives industry was Chicago. This belief from 1973 on, was due to the futures trading at the Chicago Mercantile Exchange and the Chicago Board of Trade and, the options trading at the Chicago Board Options Exchange. From the early 1990s on, however, the explosive growth in the global markets for swaps and other over-the-counter derivatives created new centers in New York,

London, and Tokyo. The over-the-counter derivatives market is quite simply any firm willing to do either side of a derivatives transaction. These dealers stand ready to buy and sell derivatives with a spread between their bid and ask prices. By hedging their remaining exposure, they would, with sufficient volume, generate a profit. The competition in this market grew, however, reducing profit margins to paper thin, but few players exited the market. Today it remains a large and active market.

On the other side of derivatives transactions are the parties called *end users*. These are primarily corporations that face certain types of risks. For example, firms engaged in multinational business nearly always have foreign exchange risk. Firms that use various commodities as raw materials, such as airlines using jet fuel, face exposure to price changes. Virtually all firms borrow money and are thus exposed to the risk of interest rate changes. Most end users are corporations hedging one or more of these types of risks. A typical corporation does not use derivatives heavily but selectively chooses to hedge a particular risk with which it feels uncomfortable. Such transactions typically come out of the corporation's treasury department. Some corporate treasurers, however, engage in speculative trading, sometimes due to pressure to make money or reduce costs by trading. We will hear this point again in Essay 72.

In addition, investment managers face interest rate risk, foreign exchange risk, and the risk of stock price movements. Although investment managers are much more in the business of dealing with financial market risks than are corporate treasurers, derivatives are more widely used in the corporate world than in the investment world. This point is probably true because so many investment managers are either pension fund or mutual fund managers whose charters restrict their use of certain types of instruments like derivatives and require them to adhere to well-accepted fiduciary guidelines. Corporations, however, have far fewer restrictions placed on them by their shareholders and are not considered fiduciaries in the sense that a pension fund manager is.

Some state, local, and foreign governments are also active users of derivatives. The United States government, however, does not directly engage in derivative transactions. Some of its agencies, such as the Postal Service, have used derivatives. In addition the U.S. government at one time issued callable bonds, which are ordinary bonds with an embedded derivative.

The derivatives industry also consists of software and consulting firms. The financial software industry has grown rapidly from a few small firms to at least 50 firms, but in recent years has consolidated through mergers and acquisitions. Consulting firms perform studies and give advice on firms' derivatives operations, typically with an eye toward ensuring that adequate controls are in place. When problems occur, consulting firms often assist firms in sorting out the problems and dealing with the fallout. In some cases these consulting firms are well-known public accounting firms.

Finally, whenever an industry grows as rapidly as has the derivatives industry, combined with the fact that the amounts of money at stake are large, a concomitant growth in the number of lawyers and law firms involved in derivative transactions can be expected. In the early stages of the growth of the exchange-listed derivatives industry, law firms primarily dealt with the occasional law suits between clients and brokers. As the over-the-counter industry grew, the legal aspects of derivatives came to include the importance of proper documentation of each contract. Lawyers were increasingly called on to assist those organizations experiencing derivatives losses in transactions with dealers to sue the dealers, claiming that they were misled and that they had viewed the dealers as advisors and not adversaries. And while all derivatives dealers have their own legal staff, most use outside attorneys to defend themselves when they are sued. Today derivatives attorneys continue to do this kind of work but also perform more due diligence and compliance work, meaning that they attempt to prevent legal problems before they occur rather than deal with them afterward.

Thus, we see that the derivatives industry has a diverse group of participants. It is a dynamic and exciting industry that has grown rapidly but still has much potential for becoming even larger and more diverse.

TEST YOUR KNOWLEDGE

1. Explain the difference between a dealer and an end user.
2. Why are derivatives used more by corporations than by investment funds?
3. How does the U.S. government use derivatives?

A Brief History of Derivatives

The history of derivatives is quite colorful and surprisingly a lot longer than most people think. A few years ago I compiled a list of the events that I thought shaped the history of derivatives. That list is published in its entirety in the Winter 1995 issue of *Derivatives Quarterly*, the full citation of which is at the end of this essay.[1] What follows here is a snapshot of the major events that I think form the evolution of derivatives.

I would like to first note that some of these stories are controversial. Do they really involve derivatives? Or do the minds of people like myself and others see derivatives everywhere?

To start we need to go back to the Bible. In Genesis Chapter 29, believed to be about the year 1700 BC, Jacob purchased an option costing him seven years of labor that granted him the right to marry Laban's daughter Rachel. His prospective father-in-law, however, reneged, perhaps making this not only the first derivative but the first default on a derivative. Laban required Jacob to marry his older and notably less attractive daughter Leah. Jacob married Leah, but because he preferred Rachel, he purchased another option, requiring seven more years of labor, and finally married Rachel, bigamy being allowed in those days. Jacob ended up with two wives and 12 sons who became the patriarchs of the 12 tribes of Israel, and a lot of domestic friction, which is not surprising. Some argue that Jacob really had forward contracts, which obligated him to the marriages, but that does not matter. Jacob did derivatives, one way or the other. Around 580 BC, Thales the Milesian purchased options on olive presses and made a fortune off a bumper crop in olives. So derivatives were around before the time of Christ.

---

[1] This article is out of print, but please do not ask me for a copy unless you are engaged in serious professional research on the history of derivatives. For anyone else, the high points are covered in this essay, and I would suggest that you do not spend a lot of time on the details of derivatives history. It's not that important.

The first exchange for trading derivatives appeared to be the Royal Exchange in London, which permitted forward contracting. The celebrated Dutch tulip bulb mania, which you can read about in *Extraordinary Popular Delusions and the Madness of Crowds* by Charles Mackay, published in 1841 but still in print, was characterized by forward contracting on tulip bulbs around 1637. The first "futures" contracts are generally traced to the Yodoya rice market in Osaka, Japan around 1650. These were evidently standardized contracts, which made them much like today's futures, although it is not known if the contracts were marked to market daily and/or had credit guarantees.

Probably the next major event, and the most significant as far as the history of U.S. futures markets, was the creation of the Chicago Board of Trade in 1848. Due to its prime location on Lake Michigan, Chicago was developing as a major center for the storage, sale, and distribution of midwestern grain. Due to the seasonality of grain, however, Chicago's storage facilities were unable to accommodate the enormous increase in supply that occurred following the harvest. Similarly, its facilities were underutilized in the spring. Grain prices rose and fell drastically.

To help stabilize prices, a group of grain traders created the "to-arrive" contract, which permitted farmers to lock in the price and deliver the grain later. This mechanism allowed the farmer to store the grain either on the farm or at a storage facility nearby and deliver it to Chicago months later. These to-arrive contracts proved useful as a device for hedging and speculating on price changes. Farmers and traders soon realized that the sale and delivery of the grain itself was not nearly as important as the ability to transfer the price risk associated with the grain. The grain could always be sold and delivered elsewhere at another time. These contracts were standardized around 1865, and in 1925 the first futures clearinghouse was formed. From that point on, futures contracts were pretty much of the form we know them today.

In the mid-1800s, famed New York financier Russell Sage began creating synthetic loans using the principle of put-call parity, which is discussed in more detail in Essays 22 and 23. Sage would buy the stock and a put from his customer and sell the customer a call. By fixing the put, call, and strike prices, Sage was creating a synthetic loan with an interest rate significantly higher than usury laws allowed.

One of the first examples of financial engineering was by none other than the beleaguered government of the Confederate States of America, which issued a dual-currency optionable bond. This instrument permitted the Confederate States to borrow money in sterling with an option to pay back in French francs. The holder of the bond had the option to convert the claim into cotton, the South's primary cash crop.

Interestingly, futures/options/derivatives trading was banned numerous times in Europe and Japan and even in the United States in the state of Illinois in 1867, though the law was quickly repealed.

In 1874 the Chicago Mercantile Exchange's predecessor, the Chicago Produce Exchange, was formed. It became the modern-day Merc in 1919. Other exchanges had been popping up around the country and continued to do so.

The early twentieth century was a dark period for derivatives trading, as bucket shops were rampant. Bucket shops are small operators in options and securities that typically lure customers into transactions and then flee with the money, setting up shop elsewhere.

In 1922 the federal government made its first effort to regulate the futures market with the Grain Futures Act. In 1936 options on futures were banned in the United States. All the while options, futures, and various derivatives continued to be banned from time to time in other countries.

The 1950s marked the era of two significant events in the futures markets. In 1955 the Supreme Court ruled in the case of *Corn Products Refining Company* that profits from hedging are treated as ordinary income. This ruling stood until it was challenged by the 1988 ruling in the *Arkansas Best* case. The *Best* decision denied the deductibility of capital losses against ordinary income and effectively gave hedging a tax disadvantage. Fortunately, this interpretation was overturned in 1993.

Another significant event of the 1950s was the ban on onion futures. Onion futures do not seem particularly important, though that is probably because they were banned, and we do not hear much about them. But the significance is that a group of Michigan onion farmers, reportedly enlisting the aid of their congressman, a young Gerald Ford, succeeded in banning a specific commodity from futures trading. To this day, the law in effect says, "you can create futures contracts on anything but onions."

In 1972 the Chicago Mercantile Exchange (CME), responding to the now–freely floating international currencies, created the International Monetary Market, which allowed trading in currency futures. These instruments were the first futures contracts that were not on physical commodities. In 1975 the Chicago Board of Trade (CBOT), created the first interest rate futures contract, one based on Ginnie Mae (GNMA) mortgage-backed securities. While the contract met with initial success, it eventually died. The CBOT resuscitated it several times, changing its structure, but it never became viable. In 1975 the Merc responded with the Treasury bill (T-bill) futures contract. This contract was the first successful pure interest rate futures. It was held up as an example, either good or bad depending on your perspective, of the enormous leverage in futures. For only about $1,000, and later less than that, you received the price volatility of $1 million of T-bills. In 1977 the CBOT created the T-bond futures contract, which went on to be the highest-volume contract for about 200 years. In 1982 the CME created the Eurodollar contract, which has now surpassed the T-bond contract to become the most actively traded of all futures contracts. In 1982 the Kansas City Board of Trade launched the first stock index futures, a contract on the Value Line Index. The CME quickly followed with their highly successful contract on the Standard & Poor's 500 index.

Now let us step back to 1973, which was a watershed year for the derivatives industry. Early in the year, the Chicago Board of Trade created the first options exchange, which was named the Chicago Board Options Exchange (CBOE). Prior to this time, options had been traded only in an over-the-counter market conducted by a handful of dealer firms. The CBOE provided the first organized options market. It created a set of standardized options on 16 individual stocks that would be offered by a group of dealers who would make markets in these options. Thus, investors could buy and sell options as easily as they bought and sold stocks. Also, during that year, the *Journal of Political Economy* published an article written by MIT economists Fischer Black and Myron Scholes that contained a formula for valuing an option. At almost the same time the *Bell Journal of Economics and Management Science* published a paper by Robert Merton that contained the same formula. The model initially became known as the Black-Scholes model, but given the significance of Merton's contribution, I will call it the Black-Scholes-Merton model. It is covered in Essay 27. At the time of its publication, the model seemed a relatively minor contribution to academic discussions. It quickly became clear, however, that the model would be useful to those who trade options. In particular, the CBOE market makers could use the model not only to price options but to also hedge the transactions they were obligated to do as providers of liquidity.

Soon thereafter, options began trading at the American Stock Exchange, the Philadelphia Stock Exchange, and the Pacific Stock Exchange. The New York Stock Exchange also got into the act, but a little too late and eventually sold its small options business to the Pacific Exchange, which eventually sold it back to the New York Stock Exchange, where it operates today under the name of Arca-Ex.

In 1983 the Chicago Board Options Exchange (CBOE), decided to create an option on an index of stocks. Though originally known as the CBOE 100 Index, it was soon turned over to Standard & Poor's and became known as the S&P 100, which for many years was the most actively traded exchange-listed option.

The 1980s marked the beginning of the era of swaps and other over-the-counter derivatives. Although over-the-counter options and forwards had existed previously, the corporate financial managers of that decade were the first to come out of business schools with exposure to derivatives. Soon virtually every large corporation, and even some that were not so large, was using derivatives to hedge and, in some cases, speculate on interest rate, exchange rate, and commodity risk. New products were rapidly created to hedge the now-recognized wide varieties of risks. As the problems became more complex, Wall Street turned increasingly to the talents of mathematicians and physicists, offering them new and quite different career paths and unheard-of money. The instruments became more complex and were sometimes even referred to as "exotic."

In 1994 the derivatives world was hit with a series of large losses on derivatives trading announced by some well-known, and highly experienced firms.[2] These and other large losses led to a huge outcry, sometimes against the instruments and sometimes against the firms that sold them. While some minor changes occurred in the way in which derivatives were sold, most firms simply instituted tighter controls and continued to use derivatives.

But everything that happened in 1994 was not bad. JP Morgan Co. launched an innovative Internet-based service called RiskMetrics. RiskMetrics evolved out of the company's own efforts to manage its risk. Several years earlier JP Morgan chairman Sir Dennis Weatherstone had asked his subordinates to create a report that would appear on his desk at 4:15 every day that would give an indication of the money that the bank could lose in its trading positions. This report, which came to be known as the "4:15 Report," is said to have launched the use of a concept called "Value at Risk," which is covered in Essay 66. Value at Risk or VaR requires an extensive amount of data on historical interest rates, exchange rates, commodity prices, and stock prices. In 1994 the bank made a bold decision to publish the data on its web site every day, thereby giving the data away for free. Many people criticized the bank, and others thought it had lost its notion that bank services do not come free. But the bank responded that giving the data away would encourage others to practice good risk management. Moreover, the bank would benefit from the consulting services it could provide to users of the data. The concept worked, and RiskMetrics was so successful that the company created another service called CreditMetrics and eventually spun off the operation from the bank into its own successful entity.

In 1995 Fischer Black died. He had been one of the first academics to leave the ivory towers and go to Wall Street, setting the stage for a large

---

[2] We cover some of these stories in Essay 72.

flow of academics to Wall Street. His death precluded him from receiving the Nobel Prize in Economics that was awarded in 1997 to Scholes and Merton.

The year 1998 was a rough one for financial markets. A financial crisis related to Russia and several Asian countries led to the default of a large hedge fund, Long Term Capital Management (LTCM), which had been started by Scholes and Merton along with a former Federal Reserve governor and a veteran Wall Street bond trader. The Federal Reserve negotiated a large bailout from the fund's creditors, a group of Wall Street banks, but the damage had long-term implications for derivatives markets. LTCM was a big user of derivatives, and its demise left everyone wondering once again if derivatives were tools that could be abused to the detriment of more than just the user. Other large derivatives losses occurred in 2002 with the National Australian Bank, in 2004 with China Aviation Oil Company, and in 2008 with Société Générale. But in comparison to the problems of the early 1990s, large and uncontrolled derivatives losses were much less common.

In the year 2000 the Financial Accounting Standards Board issued its rule FAS 133 that for the first time forced U.S. companies and companies listed on U.S. exchanges to record derivatives on the balance sheet and income statement. The international community responded with its own version of the rule, IAS (International Accounting Standard) 39, but this rule did not go into effect until 2005.[3] The year 2000 also saw the creation of a new options exchange, the International Securities Exchange (ISE), which is a completely electronic exchange. The ISE has been a remarkable success and in a few short years, its volume of options on individual stocks surpassed that of the CBOE.

Several notable events occurred in 2002. The Chicago Mercantile Exchange became a publicly traded company, leading to a wave of new such conversions by derivatives exchanges. The CBOT and ISE went public in 2005. The large European exchanges of LIFFE (London International Financial Futures Exchange) and EuroNext merged to become a very large exchange that would threaten the competitive edge held by the three Chicago exchanges.

Futures on individual stocks had existed outside of the United States for a number of years, but in 2002 they began trading in the United States. Although two markets opened up, a consortium of the CBOT, CME, and CBOE called OneChicago is the only one that survived. Volume in single stock futures, however, has never lived up to expectations in the U.S.

---

[3] Accounting for derivatives is covered in Essay 71.

In the fall of 2006 one of the most important announcements in the history of derivatives markets occurred. Crosstown rivals the Chicago Board of Trade and the Chicago Mercantile Exchange announced a $25 billion merger. The two exchanges had begun joint clearing several years earlier and had flirted with merger talks from time to time. But the marriage of these two mega-exchanges was the termination of a long history of rivalry and ushered in a new era for the derivatives industry.

As a final note, one of the most talked-about events in the derivatives business is the new set of bank capital regulations. Because banks are so heavily into derivatives market making, banking regulators have always been concerned about the risk to the banking system from the use of derivatives. The Basel Committee on Banking Supervision, which is sponsored by the Bank for International Settlements in Basel, Switzerland, first issued a set of advisory guidelines for global banking regulators in 1988, which was amended in 1996. These guidelines are an attempt to harmonize banking regulations around the world. In 1999 the Committee began work on new regulatory guidelines, which culminated in a document known as Basel II that went into effect in 2007. Although the guidelines are not mandatory, Basel II is considered to be a major improvement over the original guidelines, but it does remain controversial and will likely be scrutinized and amended in future years.

These stories hit the high points in the history of derivatives. Even my aforementioned "Chronology" cannot do full justice to its long and colorful history. The future promises to bring new and exciting developments. Stay tuned.

FOR MORE READING

Bernstein, Peter L. *Against the Gods: The Remarkable Story of Risk*. New York: John Wiley & Sons, 1996.

Bernstein, Peter L. *Capital Ideas: The Improbable Origins of Modern Wall Street*. New York: The Free Press, 1992.

Black, Fischer, and Myron Scholes. "The Pricing of Options and Corporate Liabilities." *The Journal of Political Economy* 81 (1973): 637–653.

Chance, Don M. "A Chronology of Derivatives." *Derivatives Quarterly* 2 (Winter 1995): 53–60,

Derman, Emanuel. *My Life as Quant: Reflections on Physics and Finance*. Hoboken, NJ: John Wiley & Sons, 2004.

Mackay, Charles. *Extraordinary Popular Delusions and the Mdness of Crowds*. New York: Harmony Books, 1841; reprint 1980.

Merhling, Perry. *Fischer Black and the Revolutionary Idea of Finance*. Hoboken, NJ: John Wiley & Sons, 2005.

Merton, Robert C. "Theory of Rational Option Pricing." *Bell Journal of Economics and Management Science* 4 (Spring 1973): 141–183.

Tamarkin, Bob. *The Merc: The Emergence of a Global Financial Powerhouse.* New York: HarperBusiness, 1993.

TEST YOUR KNOWLEDGE

1. How did futures contracts begin in the United States?
2. What two events occurred in 1973 that revolutionized the options industry?
3. What were the first futures contracts not on commodities?
4. On what exchange and when was the first stock index futures contract created?
5. What landmark decision did JP Morgan Co. make in 1994 that facilitated greater transparency in risk management?

Why Derivatives?

In this essay we shall take a look at why derivatives exist. No, this is not some existentialist Monty Python "What is the meaning of derivatives?" treatise. It's not really that profound. What we want to know is why derivatives exist, which is to say, why people use them and why they are not dominated by other instruments.

To understand this question, we must first look at what derivatives *really* are. Yes, we know they are instruments in which the performance is *derived* from some other instrument or asset. But more fundamentally, we need to see derivatives as instruments that permit the transfer of risk from one party to another. Each derivative transaction has two parties, a buyer and a seller. Typically the buyer pays to transfer the risk to the seller. The seller accepts payment to compensate for the assumption of risk.[1] A description of this sort would apply to an insurance contract, and indeed derivatives should be viewed like insurance. One party pays or gives up something to get another party to accept the risk.

Derivatives are not the only means of transferring risk. For example, an investor could purchase a put option to protect a stock or portfolio against downside loss, a strategy known as a protective put, which we cover in Essay 39. As an alternative, the investor could just liquidate the portfolio and put the money in some other stock, index, bond, or a risk-free asset. In other words, transactions in the actual assets that are exposed to the underlying risk are possible. But transactions in assets can be extremely expensive. The cost of liquidating stocks and bonds is not terribly high, but moving the money to other assets does add another layer of cost. And then at a later date, you might want to reverse the transaction and return to the original

---

[1] This description is basically that of an option. Forwards, futures, and swaps do not involve a direct payment from buyer to seller, but they can be viewed as having indirect payments in the form of the buyer promising to give up potential future gains.

position. And transacting in some assets can be quite expensive. Picture the owner of a million barrels of oil selling them. It is not just a matter of signing a few pieces of paper. That heavy oozy stuff has to be moved somewhere. But cost is not the only factor.

Derivatives are generally a much more efficient means of transferring risk. Because derivative markets require so much less capital than do spot markets, they are usually more liquid. Higher liquidity means more efficiency such that prices change more rapidly in response to new information, which is a good thing. Derivatives are also a much easier mechanism with which to sell short. There are significant regulatory impediments to short selling stocks. For some large and heavy assets such as oil and gold, it is very difficult if not impossible to sell short. Yet derivatives on these assets are as easy to sell short as are derivatives on stocks, which are much easier to sell short than are the stocks themselves.[2] Taking a short position can be the only possible way for some to hedge a risk, so this feature of derivatives is a very valuable one.

Thus, derivatives should be viewed primarily as instruments for transferring risk. Given their advantages as noted, we could possibly stop at this point and say that we have now justified why derivatives exist. But we have not answered the more fundamental question of why you would want to transfer risk. Is there some advantage to transferring risk? If there is not, then there is either no justifiable reason for derivatives or risk transfer is not what derivatives are all about.

Let us recall that in competitive markets, you are rewarded for bearing risk. If all capital is invested in the risk-free asset, that capital earns only the risk-free rate. If capital is invested in risky assets, returns fluctuate from period to period, reflecting the fact that the asset is risky. Over the long run, the average returns from risky assets should exceed the risk-free rate.[3] Clearly if the holder of a risky asset decides to engage in a complete hedge

---

[2] "Short selling" is a term primarily used with stocks and bonds and means to borrow the asset and sell it in hopes of buying it back at a later date at a lower price. The short seller then returns the borrowed asset to the lender. In derivatives markets, no one actually borrows anything and in fact, the term "short selling" is rarely used. You simply "sell" or "go short" a derivative, which is nothing more than taking the opposite side of the contract from the buyer, thereby guaranteeing to do whatever is obligated by the contract at the later date. This not to say that short selling is not without risk. Most short positions have considerable risk, but the point is that it is much easier to enter into a short position in a derivative than in the underlying asset.

[3] There is no magic wand that makes this happen. Indeed, some investments in risky assets over somewhat long periods of time are outperformed by the risk-free asset. For example, in September 1963 the Standard & Poor's (S&P) 500 was around

of all risk using a derivative, the investor can expect to earn only the risk-free rate. That begs the question of why anyone would want to hedge. If the risk-free rate is all that you want, then you should simply invest in the risk-free asset.

Well, that is theory and we must acknowledge that theory and reality are not always in line. Some investors want to take risks at certain times and not at others. Some investors want to take certain types of risks and not others. Sometimes certain undesirable risks must be taken in order to take certain risks that are desired. For example, an airline must bear the risk of fuel prices in order to engage in its principal line of business, transporting passengers. The risk of transporting passengers is the risk that airlines should be taking. This risk is one in which airlines should be able to exploit to their advantage. Transporting passengers and their baggage safely and on time is what airlines are good at.[4] Forecasting the price of oil is not. Thus, airlines ought to hedge the price of oil, a risk for which they have no competitive advantage, and take the risks of which they have a competitive advantage. Of course, all airlines do not always hedge. Most hedge a little and some, like Southwest Airlines, hedge a lot. It is probably not a coincidence that the hedgers tend to do better.

Also, a risk taker could feel that there are periods of time in which the risk is much greater than normal. During those periods of time, a hedge would be in order. For example, consider a portfolio manager holding a portfolio during the last few weeks of an election when the market is expected to be especially volatile. If the end of the election period corresponds to a critical period for the portfolio, the manager might want to hedge.[5]

Another common portfolio use of derivatives is in asset allocation overlays. Consider a portfolio allocated 75% to stock and 25% to risk-free assets. These two portfolios are managed by separate and independent money management companies. The overseer of the fund decides that the 75–25 allocation is a bit much for stock, so she would like to sell stock and buy bonds. She would much prefer, however, that the two independent fund

---

84. In September 1974 it was around 64, a loss of about 24% in 10 years. Risky assets should outperform the risk-free asset over a rather vaguely defined period known as the long run, though that would probably entail several decades. Otherwise, investors would wise up and not invest in the risky asset.

[4] I have a feeling at this point that you are thinking "He must be joking." Maybe I should restate it as "...what airlines *should be* good at."

[5] As an example, a pension fund manager might be looking at a critical date on which a portion of the portfolio will need to be liquidated to pay out claims. If this date occurs during an especially volatile period, the manager might consider hedging.

managers continue to operate without having to buy and sell additional securities. They are doing a good job of achieving target performance. But the overall portfolio has too much risk for the manager's comfort level. By using derivatives that reduce the stock risk and increase the allocation to the risk-free asset, the overall desired asset allocation can be achieved without disrupting the two individual portfolios. Naturally if the risk needs to be increased later, derivatives can be used to alter that allocation as well.

Finally, let us note that we have been referring to hedging as if it eliminates the risk, leaving only the expectation of a risk-free return. This notion is somewhat theoretical and academic. Complete risk elimination is rarely seen or even desired for it is often far too costly. As humans we generally do not like risk, but we often willingly take it when we could eliminate it.[6] Usually risk takers are willing to accept a small amount of risk. An old saying goes, "The only perfect hedge is in a Japanese garden." Likewise, perfect hedges in the financial world are rare. Risk takers usually view these hedging transactions as attempts to reduce the risk to a tolerable level.

In addition to all of this talk about hedging, we ought to acknowledge that derivatives can enable us to easily *increase* risk. After all, everyone cannot reduce risk at the same time. This is like everyone wanting to dance but no one wanting to partner up. It takes two to tango, as they say. Someone has to be willing to increase risk. These parties are often referred to as *speculators*, but we should be careful about what we call them. In fact, they have been called some pretty bad and unfair names. Many regulators and politicians believe that speculators are bad for markets. They believe that speculators are greedy investors who care nothing about anyone but themselves. Speculators are thought to be very short-term investors who "steal" profits from others. Their actions are often viewed as destabilizing the market.

Speculators are vital to the survival of the market. As noted, everyone cannot reduce risk at the same time. Diversifiable risk is the only risk that everyone can eliminate. If a market is in equilibrium and one investor attempts to reduce his risk, at least one other investor has to increase hers. If hedgers are somehow the "good guys" and speculators are somehow the "bad guys," how is it that good guys are forced to accept risk higher than they desire if the bad guys refuse to dance?

---

[6] Let me offer an example. We could in all likelihood completely eliminate the risk that a terrorist would hijack an airplane if we forced every passenger to be strip-searched and all items be removed and inspected from all luggage. I feel pretty certain we would consider the financial and nonfinancial costs of such a policy to be far in excess of the benefits.

A party that increases risk need not even remotely be considered a speculator. Consider a pension fund with $100 million invested in stock and a $100 million allocated to risk-free bonds. This is a 50–50 allocation, which is a common target. Such a portfolio has risk of about half that of the market as a whole, which under no stretch of the imagination would make it one of those evil speculators. Suppose the stock market falls in value by 20% while the risk-free portfolio returns 5%. The portfolio now consists of $80 million of stock and $105 million of bonds, a 43% allocation to stock and 57% allocation to bonds. The risk of this portfolio has, therefore, fallen below the desired exposure of 50–50. To get back to the target allocation, the portfolio manager needs to sell some bonds and buy some stock. As noted earlier, this can be quite costly. It is much cheaper to do so with derivatives. The derivatives would have to increase the stock market risk, therefore, and in some eyes, that would make this adjustment a speculative one.

Using derivatives to manage risk is nothing more than engaging in transactions that align the actual level of risk with the desired level of risk. Academic theory often touches little on the practical impediments to doing this alignment. It mostly assumes that all portfolios are properly positioned at the desired level of risk. In the absence of these practical impediments, derivatives might well not exist. After all, virtually anything that can be done with a derivative can be done using the underlying assets and no derivative. But practical differences do matter. As we have noted, derivatives are usually cheaper, much more liquid, and easier to sell short.

Opponents of derivatives are quick to argue that hedging or the more broadly defined "risk management" is just a type of financial transaction. The celebrated Modigliani-Miller (M&M) theory of capital structure says that a firm cannot increase shareholder wealth, the ultimate objective, by rearranging its capital structure. They argue that value is created only by the investments that firms make in their assets. Capital structure, the mix of debt and equity, simply divides up the claims on the assets but cannot make the value of the claims any higher.

The problem with this argument is that it assumes away the same impediments, which economists refer to as "market imperfections," that make derivatives valuable. Moreover, derivatives can make investments in assets more valuable. Remember how an airline can create value by flying passengers and their baggage safely and timely to the desired destinations.[7] But airlines cannot be expected to create value by forecasting energy prices. Thus, energy hedging makes sense for airlines. Other firms can hedge raw

---

[7] It does happen on occasion.

material prices and use those raw materials to create value by providing products and services.

The M&M arguments also provide a safe haven for derivatives to exist when we consider market imperfections. M&M show that if corporate taxes are considered, debt is preferred over equity because of the tax deductibility of interest. But debt is preferred to equity only to the extent that the expected costs of bankruptcy do not exceed the value of the interest tax deduction.[8] By hedging, a firm can reduce the likelihood of bankruptcy, thereby reducing the expected bankruptcy costs, while using more debt and benefiting from the interest tax deduction.

Hedging also makes creditors and potential creditors happy. Lenders always prefer that borrowers take as little risk as possible. Typically more credit is available to those companies that keep their risks low. Access to credit is considered a valuable thing to have. Companies with unexpected needs or cash deficiencies rely heavily on short-term unplanned loans.

Most companies turn first to internally generated cash flows to finance growth.[9] Indeed, some pharmaceutical companies finance their research and development (R&D) exclusively with cash flows from their foreign operations. When their domestic currency increases in value, their foreign cash flows generate fewer units of their domestic cash, thereby forcing them to reduce R&D. For pharmaceutical companies, that means a slowdown at the beginning of a very long and costly pipeline. So you can figure that 10 years or so later, some new drugs will not be on the market and some people will die. OK, I know I am overdramatizing this point, but it is not far from the truth. If cash flows are needed to fund R&D, then R&D will suffer when cash flows are down, and that definitely means some drugs will not come to the market as early. Infer what you want about life and death.

Fortunately, most pharmaceutical firms recognize this problem and wisely hedge this risk. They reason that they cannot forecast exchange rates, so they should not take these kinds of risks. So in this manner, firms can use derivatives to make their assets more productive and that, according to M&M, is where value is created.

---

[8] The "expected costs of bankruptcy" refers to the costs that firms incur paying the legal system to adjudicate a bankruptcy process. The legal system effectively has a claim on firms without putting any capital at risk. Recognizing expected bankruptcy costs in the M&M framework means that companies take on as much debt as possible to benefit from the tax deductibility of interest but only to a point where the benefits do not exceeds these costs.

[9] Corporate finance theory refers to this priority as the pecking order. Internal equity is the first choice of financing, followed by debt and then by external equity. See any corporate finance text for an explanation.

Hedging also makes financial planning much easier. Recall again the airlines that hedge the price of fuel. It is much easier for them to plan for the next year if they know what their fuel costs will be. Suppose an airline is planning to add a new international route. It cannot add the route overnight. Plans must be made a year or so in advance. The airline would like to do some advance promotions featuring their attractive fares. It can do this much easier knowing what its costs will be. There are surely other benefits, however hard to quantify, of being able to plan with more certainty.

Hedging and risk management, if conducted on a broad basis, promotes a greater awareness of risk within a firm. This "risk culture," as we might call it, can permeate the organization at all levels and lead to a greater recognition of what risks every employee should take and what risks it should eliminate. Risk taking is, after all, everywhere within a company. Of course, it is hard to quantify these benefits, but they too are surely there.

Risk management and hedging also facilitate the measurement of risk so as to incorporate risk into performance evaluation. Divisions of a company that take varying degrees of risk must be evaluated on a risk-adjusted basis. Companies that make an effort to identify risks and take only those risks they are comfortable with are far more likely to be able to adjust for risk in performance evaluation.

Some academics believe that hedging has certain tax advantages. It has been noted that the progressive tax schedule in the United States and most other countries penalizes companies with volatile income. When a company has a good year and is in a high tax bracket, it pays a lot of taxes. When it has a bad year and is in a low tax bracket, it pays a small amount or no taxes. Because of the progressive tax rate, the low taxes in a bad year do not offset the high taxes in a good year. Consequently, the firm pays a higher tax rate over time than it would pay on its average level of income. In addition, income in bad years, such as years in which there is a loss, cannot always be used to offset future taxes. In principle, hedging by stabilizing income can be used to alleviate this problem. By keeping income at a low level of volatility, firms do not jump back and forth into different tax brackets. This argument has much appeal, but, unfortunately, it does not hold up well in practice. There is only a small degree of progression in corporate tax rates. The income of most firms does not fluctuate much over the different tax brackets. Empirical evidence shows that taxes are not a major issue in hedging decisions.

Finally, we have to acknowledge somewhat reluctantly that there are some not-so-good reasons for hedging. As we know, the boards of directors of companies constantly strive to align the interests of managers with that of shareholders. While some progress can be made on that front, I believe we have to recognize that this is somewhat the old case of forcing a square peg into a round hole. *Managers are not shareholders, even if they are shareholders.* I know that sounds weird. Let me explain.

With the exception of a few incredibly ignorant or stupid shareholders, we can assume that shareholders hold diversified portfolios. Managers, however, hold highly undiversified portfolios. Even newly hired managers with broadly diversified personal portfolios will soon have rather undiversified portfolios. They will receive stock and options in large enough quantities that it will skew their portfolios so that they are more highly exposed to the employer firm than they should be. In addition, the managers' wealth accounted for by their human capital—that is, the present value of all of their expected future earnings from the firm—will be exclusively concentrated in that one firm. Finally, the managers bear a high degree of reputational risk. If the company performs poorly while they are at the helm, their ability to obtain attractive future employment is jeopardized.

Thus, managers do not bear the same type of risk as investors. Managers hold highly undiversified portfolios, especially after accounting for human capital and reputational risk. To reduce this risk, managers will naturally want to make the company less risky. Wouldn't you? Hence, we often observe companies engage in diversifying mergers. Why did a company like General Electric buy a stockbroker named Paine Webber, then an entertainment company named RCA, and eventually be called a conglomerate? Now you know.

Managers also will tend to hedge to reduce risk. In fact, hedging is surely a much easier way to reduce risk than buying another company. Thus, we can reasonably surmise that managers do a great deal of hedging to help themselves. Shareholders, however, should want their managers to focus on taking the risks they should be good at taking. If investors wanted a hedge, they would do it themselves.[10]

This conflict between managers and shareholders can be alleviated somewhat by the awarding of stock options, a topic we take up in Essay 65. The holder of a call option will naturally benefit if the underlying has more risk. Hence, options should induce managers to get their companies to take more risk, although it does not always work that way. And stock options have their own problems, as we shall see in Essay 65.

---

[10] This is the essence of the M&M argument: If a company cannot do anything for its shareholders that they cannot do for themselves, then no value is created. Hedging is certainly something that shareholders can do for themselves, but again we have to recognize the practical impediments. Shareholders of airlines can hedge the price of fuel, but it is difficult for the shareholders to obtain the information they need, such as how much fuel the airline needs and when it is needed, to be able to implement effective hedges.

Let us end this essay with a short recap. Derivatives are tools for transferring risk. They generally work well and at low cost. Risk transfer, if done properly, is nothing more than an alignment of the risks taken with the desired risks. Sometimes that means reducing risk by hedging and sometimes it means increasing risk, which means speculating or whatever nasty or benign term you want to use. Although there are a variety of reasons why derivatives are good instruments and risk management is a worthwhile activity, the most important one encapsulates all of the others. *Taking the amount of risk you are comfortable with is more important than anything else.* Using a derivative to do this is an easier and cheaper way than transacting in the underlying asset.

And to paraphrase Martha Stewart, "That's a good thing."

FOR MORE READING

Smithson, Charles W. *Managing Financial Risk: A Guide to Derivative Products, Financial Engineering, and Value Maximization*, 3rd ed. New York: McGraw-Hill, 1998, chap. 20.
Stulz, René. *Risk Management and Derivatives*. Mason, OH: Thomson South-Western, 2003, chap. 3.

TEST YOUR KNOWLEDGE

1. What is the primary reason for using derivatives?
2. If a hedge is put in place and the risk is completely eliminated, the hedger earns the risk-free rate. Why would a hedger do this when it could earn the risk-free rate by investing directly in the risk-free asset? Why go to so much trouble to put on a hedge?
3. What role do speculators play in derivatives markets?
4. Why does risk management not always involve hedging?
5. For what personal reason do managers sometimes make their companies hedge?

Forward Contracts and Futures Contracts

Let us start out by gaining an understanding of the concepts and differences between forward and futures contracts. To most individuals, futures contracts are more familiar, but forward contracts are more fundamental and simpler instruments. To understand futures is to first understand forwards and then to appreciate the features that the exchanges put into the contracts that make them similar to but still distinct from forwards.

First off, let us define a forward contract. It is a contract between two parties in which they agree that on a future date, one party, the buyer, will pay the other party, the seller, a sum of money and will receive something in return. That "something" could be an asset, a currency, an option, or just another sum of money representing the value of such an instrument. As is often done in the derivatives business, this underlying instrument will be referred to as the underlying.

The parties to a forward contract reach their agreement by direct negotiation between each other. They set the terms and conditions to whatever suits them. They must carefully define the underlying, both in terms of its identity and its quantity, state the fixed price at which the future transaction will take place, and specify the terms governing the delivery of the underlying.

In a forward contract, the buyer is obligated to pay cash and accept delivery of the underlying. The seller is obligated to obtain the underlying and make delivery. Either party could be financially unable to carry out his part of the bargain. In the event of one party not doing what it is supposed to do, that party is in default. Thus, when the two parties agree to the contract, each must assess the credit risk of the other. Each party brings credit risk to the transaction. Consequently, one party's risk is partially offset by that of the other. In the extreme case, of course, it might be that a counterparty will not enter into a forward contract with a party of unacceptable credit risk.

Alternatively, the party with the weaker credit might be required to post collateral or obtain a standby letter of credit. Some forward contracts will stipulate that the parties will settle up any gains or losses prior to expiration. This form of credit enhancement is very similar to what is done in futures markets, which we turn to in a few more paragraphs.[1]

When first established, a forward contract is neither an asset nor a liability. It is simply an agreement. Neither party pays anything to the other. This means that its value at the start is zero. Once established, forward contracts are not generally designed to be tradable in the market. That is, there is essentially no secondary market. Let us say, however, that in July I go long one September gold forward contract at a price of 391. Assume that it is now August 1 and that new contracts that would require delivery on the same date as my existing contract are going for 393. I could go short a new contract, and I would have locked in the purchase of the gold in September at 391 and its sale at 393. This guarantees a profit of 2, which has a discounted value of slightly less than 2. Thus, my forward contract now has a value equal to the present value of 2. I could then view it as an asset, but a later drop in price could turn it into a liability.

The price at which the two parties agree to exchange the underlying asset at expiration, called the *forward price*, is obtained by taking the spot price and adding to it the cost of carry, which is the storage cost and the interest forgone minus any convenience yield or dividend/interest paid on the underlying. We cover this point in more detail in Essay 21.

The forward market is a nonstandardized market wherein parties engage in fixed-price contracts for future delivery of an underlying asset or currency. The contracts are intended to be held until the delivery date and are subject to default. Contract sizes tend to be large, and the market is dominated by large financial institutions and corporations.

Futures markets arose to permit greater access to forward trading for parties whose credit would not be as strong as the large firms and institutions that dominate forward markets, which would not be as well known, and which would not deal in sizes as large as in the forward market. Futures markets accomplish this result by standardizing the contracts and guaranteeing against default by means of a clearinghouse that stands between buyer and seller, guaranteeing each to the other. Standardization means that most of the terms, but not the price, of the contract are set by the exchange. This means that the exchange precisely defines the underlying asset or currency, the settlement date, and the manner in which delivery is made. Consequently, you can trade only contracts that are authorized by the exchange.

---

[1] The credit risk of derivatives, including forward contracts, is covered in Essay 68.

In contrast, on the forward market, you can create any set of contract terms that another party will agree to. This standardization reduces costs to the exchange and facilitates the creation of a liquid market, wherein a party having purchased or sold a contract can reenter the market and sell or purchase the identical contract to offset or erase the original obligation. Although the futures exchanges generally speak as if these are liquid markets, there is no guarantee that there will be a large number of other parties willing to trade a particular contract. Consequently, bid-ask spreads can be quite high. For actively traded contracts, bid-ask spreads are usually the minimum price change permitted.

The futures exchange, by means of a clearinghouse, intervenes between buyer and seller and guarantees to each that if the other defaults, it will pay off. To provide this guarantee, participants in the market must meet minimum capital standards, must deposit cash or acceptable collateral in a margin account, and must submit to having their accounts updated daily. The latter procedure, called the *daily settlement* or *marking-to-market*, results in the paper gains and losses that have accrued since the previous day, being paid out from the losing parties to the gaining parties on a daily basis. This system has worked perfectly. Although there have been some defaults by individuals and firms, clearinghouses always paid the other party.

We should also note that forward contracts are private transactions and are essentially unregulated. Futures transactions are public. You can observe their prices, though not the names of participants. They are also highly regulated at the federal government level.

We say more about forward and futures contracts when we get into understanding their pricing in Essay 21. At this point, you should just know the essential differences, which relate to the issue of customization versus standardization and the daily settling of futures gains and losses.

FOR MORE READING

Chance, Don M., and Robert Brooks. *An Introduction to Derivatives and Risk Management*, 7th ed. Mason, OH: Thomson South-Western, 2007, chap. 8.

Hull, John C. *Options, Futures, and Other Derivatives*, 6th ed. Upper Saddle River, NJ: Prentice-Hall, 2006, chap. 2.

McDonald, Robert L. *Derivative Markets*, 2nd ed. Boston: Addison Wesley, 2006, chap. 2.

Smithson, Charles W. *Managing Financial Risk: A Guide to Derivative Products, Financial Engineering, and Value Maximization*, 3rd ed. New York: McGraw-Hill, 1998, chaps. 4, 6.

Stulz, René. *Risk Management and Derivatives*. Mason, OH: Thomson South-Western, 2003, chap. 5.

TEST YOUR KNOWLEDGE

1. What is meant by the difference between customization of forward contracts and standardization of futures contracts? What is the advantage of each?
2. Why is a forward contract neither an asset nor a liability when it is created, and when does it become an asset or liability?
3. Why is the daily settlement feature used in futures markets?

Options

An option is a contract between two parties in which one party, the buyer, pays a sum of money, the *option price* or *premium*, to another party, the seller, and receives the right to buy or sell an underlying asset or currency at a fixed price during a specified period of time. As noted, the option either grants the right to buy, which we refer to as a *call option*, or the right to sell, which we refer to as a *put option*. The fixed price at which the asset or currency can be bought or sold is called the *exercise price*, and sometimes the *strike price*, the *striking price*, or just the *strike*. The date on which this right terminates is called the *expiration date* or just the *expiration*. Options that permit exercise on any day during the option's life are called *American options*, while options that permit exercise only at the time at which the option is expiring are called *European options*. These terms have nothing to do with where the options exist.[1]

While options are considered to be financial contracts, there are a wide variety of options all around us. For example, when you go to a baseball game and the game is rained out, the team gives you an option to return in the form of a rain check, which guarantees you a ticket to a future game. When you clip a coupon from a newspaper, it specifies that a particular item can be purchased at a fixed price or a fixed discount up to an expiration date. The right to cancel a contract or drop a course in school is also an option. The right to change an airline ticket is also an option, one for which you may have to pay an additional price.

Financial options are created either directly between two parties in the form of nonstandard, over-the-counter options or options standardized on an exchange on which options trade. The latter have their exercise prices

---

[1] I like to think that the terms "American" and "European" with respect to option are like "French," "Italian," and "Russian" with respect to salad dressings. There is no connection between the product and these nationalities, and no one would assume that they are used primarily in the countries associated with their names.

and expiration dates set by the exchange. In the United States, standardized options are available on the International Securities Exchange, the Chicago Board Options Exchange, the Boston Options Exchange, and the American, Philadelphia, and Boston Stock Exchanges.

These option markets are made liquid by the trading activities of dealers who stand ready to buy or sell these standardized contracts. Consequently, when an individual purchases or sells an option, that person can reenter the market at a later date and sell or purchase that option, thereby offsetting the two positions and leaving the party with no further right or obligation to buy or sell the asset. Although the exchanges guarantee a market in each option, there is no guarantee of high liquidity, so the bid-ask spreads can be quite wide in less actively traded options, which tend to be those in which the price of the underlying stock or index is far away from the exercise price and the expiration is more than a few months.

An important feature of standardized options is that the performance of the seller is guaranteed to the buyer by the exchange, through its clearinghouse. The seller must deposit sufficient margin to ensure to the clearinghouse that it can perform its obligation, should the holder of the option exercise it. Although some sellers have defaulted, in all cases the holder of the option was paid. Because the holder of the option does not have to exercise it, she has no obligation, so there is no reason for the clearinghouse to guarantee the buyer to the seller.

As noted, the options on organized exchanges are primarily options on stocks and stock indices. The organized exchanges have also had options on bonds and foreign currencies, but these instruments have not been very actively traded. There is, however, an extremely active over-the-counter market for options. These are typically transactions between corporations and financial institutions or between two financial institutions. The financial institutions serve as dealers, making markets in these customized options, which might be on stocks, indices, currencies, bonds, or commodities. In these options, the buyer or seller typically specifies the desired underlying asset, exercise price, exercise terms, and expiration. The dealer then willingly takes the opposite position, usually hedging its risk with another transaction elsewhere. There is no credit guarantee, so the buyer does have to be concerned about the seller fulfilling its part of the obligation. This problem might be managed by having the seller deposit collateral or post a letter of credit.

Customized options are more commonly of the European style, meaning that they specify exercise only at expiration. They are typically meant to be held until expiration. If a party having purchased or sold a customized option wants to offset the position, he can do a new transaction that is opposite his original position. This will reduce the market risk remaining over the life of the option, but the party still faces the possibility that the seller will default on one of his options. In some cases, the party will go back to the original dealer from whom he bought or sold the option and arrange an offset, meaning that the parties will settle and cancel the rest of the contract, thereby eliminating any remaining market and credit risk.

In many cases customized options provide that exercise is done by cash settlement, meaning that instead of one party delivering the underlying asset or currency and the other paying the exercise price, the parties simply exchange an equivalent sum of cash. This procedure is also used by the organized exchanges on stock index options.

FOR MORE READING

Chance, Don M., and Robert Brooks. *An Introduction to Derivatives and Risk Management*, 7th ed. Mason, OH: Thomson South-Western, 2007, chap. 2.

Hull, John C. *Options, Futures, and Other Derivatives*, 6th ed. Upper Saddle River, NJ: Prentice-Hall, 2006, chap. 8.

McDonald, Robert L. *Derivative Markets*, 2nd ed. Boston: Addison Wesley, 2006, chap. 2.

Smithson, Charles W. *Managing Financial Risk: A Guide to Derivative Products, Financial Engineering, and Value Maximization*, 3rd ed. New York: McGraw-Hill, 1998, chap. 10.

TEST YOUR KNOWLEDGE

1. What is the difference between an American option and a European option?
2. How do clearinghouses of options exchanges serve to guarantee a standardized option against credit risk?
3. How is a customized option terminated or offset before expiration?

Swaps

Swaps are extremely popular financial transactions that have come to be the most widely used derivative. Of course, most people would not do one in their personal financial transactions, but believe it or not, most people have almost surely already done something similar to a swap. We shall get to that in a later paragraph.

Why should an investor care about swaps? Let us say that an investor traded futures. If that were the case, then she would need to know who some of the major players are in the futures markets, particularly the Eurodollar futures markets, and what they are doing. That investor would probably know that Eurodollar futures volume has grown tremendously in the last few years. The reason is not because everybody discovered Eurodollars all of a sudden. It is because swap dealers are hedging their risk with Eurodollar futures. When you have millions of dollars of principal value on which you have to make interest payments at a fluctuating Eurodollar rate, a Eurodollar futures hedge is an obvious choice.

A swap is a contract between two parties in which the first party promises to make a series of payments to the second while the second party promises to make a series of payments to the first, with both sets of payments occurring on a set of scheduled dates. The two sets of payments are determined according to different formulas. On at least one set of payments the dollar amount is not yet determined. We call these the *floating payments*. The other set of payments can be fixed or floating but determined by another formula.

The most common type of swap is the *interest rate swap*. Usually an interest rate swap involves one set of payments being determined by a floating interest rate such as the Eurodollar rate (LIBOR), while the other set is fixed at an agreed-on rate. This instrument is typically called a *plain vanilla swap*. Other types of arrangements are possible: Some interest rate swaps have both sets of payments tied to floating rates, oftentimes one being LIBOR and the other being the Treasury bill rate. This instrument is called a *basis swap*. Interest rate swaps involve only the exchange of interest payments based on a face value, called the *notional principal*, but the notional principal itself is never exchanged. At each payment date, the party who owes more to the other makes a net payment so only one party in fact makes a payment. Interest rate swaps are covered in more detail in Essay 9.

There are several other types of swaps. *Currency swaps*, covered in more detail in Essay 10, involve one party making payments in one currency and another making payments in another currency. Notional principal is usually exchanged at the start and at the end of a currency swap. At the start, the two parties are exchanging equivalent values in different currencies. At the end, the reverse transaction occurs. Depending on movements in the exchange rate over the life of the contract, one party gains at the expense of the other. This is consistent with the objective of the swap.[1] There also are *equity swaps*, which involve one party paying the other a rate based on the rate of return on an equity index like the S&P 500 or the DAX. The other party makes a payment based on something else say a fixed rate, LIBOR, or another equity index. Although equity swaps are used much less than interest rate and currency swaps, equity swaps have considerable growth potential because they make it very simple, easy, and inexpensive to reallocate a portfolio to a different equity sector. Equity swaps are covered in more detail in Essay 13.

Another kind of swap is the *commodity swap*, where one party makes a payment based on the price of a particular commodity. The other party typically makes a fixed payment, but other payment structures are possible. Oil is a good example of a commodity on which a great deal of swap trading is done. An airline might enter into a swap in which it agrees to pay a fixed price times a certain number of barrels of oil on a series of future dates and on those dates, the counterparty will pay the airline the price of the oil on that date times the number of barrels. It is common, however, in these types of swaps that the oil price is based on the average price of oil over a period of time since the payment. Averaging smooths out price volatility and reduces the effect of a sharp price movement at expiration. Commodity swaps are covered in more detail in Essay 15.

There are a number of variations of swaps, some of which make the swaps quite exotic and complex. Some swaps have options attached. Others have a notional principal that varies during the life of the swap. In addition, credit derivatives, covered in Essay 18, also include a type of swap, the credit default swap.

---

[1] Some currency swaps specify an exchange of notional principal due to the objectives of the parties.

The Bank for International Settlements estimates that the notional principal outstanding swaps as of June 30, 2007 was over $315 trillion, but this number is not particularly meaningful except to indicate the level of usage. Because notional principal is usually not exchanged and only the net payments are made in most swaps, the amount of money changing hands is nowhere near the notional principal. Swaps are susceptible to default since they are not guaranteed by any third party. Parties are sometimes required to post collateral or mark to market periodically, as in the futures market. Speaking of futures, swaps can be shown to be virtually identical to a strip of futures contracts with different expirations, which is why Eurodollar futures hedges work well for dealers.

To conclude, recall that I said you had probably done a swap before. My favorite analogy to a swap is an apartment lease. You enter into an agreement to make a fixed payment on each of a set of prespecified dates and the other party agrees to grant you the use of a service, which clearly has some value, however indeterminate it may be to you. That value can change over time as your needs change. Thus, a swap resembles an apartment lease or any other contract in which you agree to exchange a series of payments or services on a set of dates.

FOR MORE READING

Chance, Don M., and Robert Brooks. *An Introduction to Derivatives and Risk Management*, 7th ed. Mason, OH: Thomson South-Western, 2007, chap. 12.

Hull, John C. *Options, Futures, and Other Derivatives*, 6th ed. Upper Saddle River, NJ: Prentice-Hall, 2006, chap. 7.

McDonald, Robert L. *Derivative Markets*, 2nd ed. Boston: Addison Wesley, 2006, chap. 8.

Smithson, Charles W. *Managing Financial Risk: A Guide to Derivative Products, Financial Engineering, and Value Maximization*, 3rd ed. New York: McGraw-Hill, 1998, chap. 8.

Wilmott, Paul. *Derivatives: The Theory and Practice of Financial Engineering*. Chichester, UK: John Wiley & Sons, 1998, chap. 32.

TEST YOUR KNOWLEDGE

1. How does a plain vanilla swap differ from a basis swap?
2. Why is notional principal exchanged in most currency swaps but not in interest rate swaps?
3. What feature of most commodity swaps is somewhat different from most other swaps?

Types of Risks

Any book about derivatives will invariably find itself focused on risk. Derivatives are, after all, the tools used to manage risk. But to understand how to use the tools, we have to have a good understanding of what the actual risks are.

Risk, of course, is all around us. We identify risks at all times, often subconsciously, and take corrective actions to manage it. For example, I have an extreme aversion to being caught in the rain without a raincoat or umbrella. Attached to my soft canvas briefcase is a holder for a small umbrella. Another small umbrella is in my car, and I usually carry another and even smaller one in my luggage. A fourth and larger umbrella is in my home office, and another large one is in my work office. OK, OK. I may sound paranoid, but I have virtually eliminated this risk. The important point, however, is that the risk is eliminated at a cost that is far less than my expected cost of being drenched. In fact, the cost of eliminating this risk is trivial. In particular, the umbrella attached to my briefcase adds virtually no weight and is almost never seen.

While I must confess that I made no conscious and formal effort to assess the risk and the cost of risk elimination, I nonetheless subconsciously engaged in the activity of risk management. To practice good risk management, organizations must do so in a more formal manner. They must identify their risks, define their tolerance for risk, assess the costs of risk management, and take action to align their desired risks with their actual risks, subject to benefits exceeding costs. In this section, we look at what types of risks exist.

Experts usually classify the risks faced by an organization into *market risk*, *credit risk*, *operational risk*, and *other risks*. Market risk is usually further subdivided into the risk associated with interest rates, exchange rates, commodity prices, and stock prices. Virtually all organizations face interest rate risk. Those that borrow money, which is almost every company, are exposed to gains and losses from rising interest rates. Even the few firms that do not borrow, however, face the risk associated with interest rates. For examples, using equity or retained earnings for financing during a period when interest rates are falling is an opportunity cost. Most businesses are also influenced by the state of the economy or industry, which usually is sensitive to interest rates. Home builders, for example, might borrow no money but will find the demand for their services down during periods of rising interest rates.

Exchange rates are also a source of risk to many businesses. Those that have foreign subsidiaries have the obvious problem that their cash flows are denominated in foreign currencies but will be converted back to their domestic currency. If the domestic currency increases in value, their foreign cash flow will return fewer units of the domestic currency. Even businesses that do not have foreign operations will find themselves in competition with foreign companies. As the domestic currency strengthens, their customers could find it more attractive to buy from foreign companies.

Commodity prices influence all businesses to some extent. The most critical commodity is oil, and virtually all businesses are influenced by oil, though some much more than others. Other commodities, such as gold, silver, and certain agricultural crops, are also key determinants of the performance of some businesses.

Stock prices are the fourth source of market risk, but, strangely, this risk is not all that important for most businesses. Clearly financial firms, which hold stock market investments, are influenced by the performance of stocks, but most firms are nonfinancial. While their pension funds are likely to be affected by the stock market, their operations are not directly related to it.[1]

Besides market risk, most firms are exposed to credit risk. At a minimum, most firms lend money to their customers who pay later. Many firms make loans directly to other companies and individuals. Hence, there is the possibility of not being repaid. Credit risk is, however, quite unlike market risk. Whereas market risk can often be observed on a day-to-day basis in the interest rate, exchange rate, commodity, and stock markets, credit risk is somewhat harder to see. Defaults occur somewhat infrequently, and it can take a long time to determine how often defaults should occur. While some debt securities trade in an open market and prices reflect changing credit risk, most debt securities do not trade openly. They trade only when someone wants to trade, and that is not as often as stocks are traded. Assessing credit risk is difficult. Fortunately, the derivatives business has made great

---

[1] Naturally the stock market is a reflector of expectations about the overall economy, but the sensitivity of a business to the overall economy is the actual risk. The stock market just provides information about the economy.

strides in helping us gain an understanding of credit risk. We will take up this topic again in Essay 18, when we discuss credit derivatives, and in Essay 68, when we discuss the credit risk of derivatives.

The third category of risk is operational risk, which basically refers to the kinds of bad things that happen to a company's operations. Computer hackers, terrorist attacks, fraud, and assorted disasters are the obvious examples. We will take up operational risk in Essay 69.

Finally, we mention the ubiquitous "Other" category. Risk experts have identified a handful of these miscellaneous categories of risk. They arise from changes in regulations, accounting rules and taxes, as well as problems related to the payments system, wherein money is sent in anticipation of money being received. In addition, liquidity is a common source of risk, reflecting the inability to buy or sell when you need to. Also, most large financial institutions face a constant threat of being sued, which is called legal risk.

For a good treatment of the myriad of risks, see the "Galaxy of Risks" on the web site of a risk management consulting firm called Capital Market Risk Advisors (www.cmra.com).

Of course, identifying a risk does not mean that you can or should eliminate it. For example, if a financial trading firm eliminates all market risk, what is it left with? The risk-free rate. It can hardly expect to impress its shareholders by earning the risk-free rate. They can do just as well on their own. If an energy company hedges the price of energy, its shareholders may question why they invested in the company. Good companies identify the risks on which they feel they have a competitive advantage and reduce if not eliminate those on which they feel they have no competitive advantage. For example, an airline might hedge the price of oil because it knows that it cannot forecast the future price. But the airline willingly accepts the risk of the demand for air travel, because this is its area of specialization.

Of course, risk management has a cost, and that cost can be too high. Complete risk elimination, or perfect hedging, is seldom done in practice. Consider, for example, the risk of a terrorist getting himself or a bomb onto a plane. Following the attacks on the World Trade Center in 2001, governments instituted a series of risk controls that have exacted a price on all air travelers. Although no further events have occurred to date, it is unclear if the risk is lower and if the cost is justified. The absence of a risk event does not mean the absence of risk, so clearly the risk has not been eliminated.

Most people constantly monitor and measure risk, often subconsciously, and take actions that align the desired risk with the actual risk, subject to those actions not costing more than the benefits they bring. Risk management is such a natural process that even animals do it. Some do it quite well and some, particularly those with short life spans, often do it rather poorly. Animals differ in their risk tolerances as well. Observe how one dog that does not know you will immediately come up to you, perceive no risk, and practically beg for petting, while another will shy away until it is more comfortable.

In short, identifying and managing risk is not a financial activity. It is a natural part of life.

FOR MORE READING

Smithson, Charles W. *Managing Financial Risk: A Guide to Derivative Products, Financial Engineering, and Value Maximization,* 3rd ed. New York: McGraw-Hill, 1998, chap. 1.

TEST YOUR KNOWLEDGE

1. What are the four categories of risks?
2. Why can exchange rates be a source of risk to a business that does not have any international business?
3. Why is the stock market not a direct source of risk to most companies?

Two

The Basic Instruments

Now that you know what options forwards, futures, and swaps are, you need to dig a little further. This section goes into more detail on the basic types of derivative instrument. These 13 essays cover FRAs, interest rate options, interest rate swaps, currency swaps, structured notes, securitized instruments (also known as asset-backed securities), equity swaps, equity-linked debt, commodity swaps, swaptions, credit derivatives, volatility derivatives, and weather derivatives. We also cover a particular distinction that is important in understanding options: whether the option is American style or European style.

Wow! This seems like a lot to absorb. Trust me. It is. But you decided that you wanted to learn derivatives so don't quit now. Unless you already have some of this knowledge or you find yourself breezing through the essays, I suggest you do not read more than one or two essays a day. Take it slow and easy. You really do need to grasp the differences between these types of instruments before we get to the next section on pricing.

Interest Rate Derivatives: FRAs and Options

You might already be familiar with derivatives on bonds. Options, futures, and options on futures where the underlying asset is a bond are commonly traded. When the derivative expires, the price of the bond at that time determines the payoff of the derivative. In contrast, when the derivative is on an interest rate, the payoff is not based on the price of a bond but rather on the interest rate. This causes a few problems in pricing, but mostly the problems are just in understanding the basic structure of the instrument. For example, the notion of bullishness and bearishness can be somewhat confusing. For example, if you are bullish on interest rates, it usually means that you expect interest rates are to decrease. Then you might want to buy a call option on a bond. In the case of interest rate derivatives, however, you would buy a put.

Most interest rate derivatives denominated in dollars are based on the London Interbank Offer Rate, called *LIBOR*, which is also called the Eurodollar rate. A Eurodollar is a dollar deposited outside the United States. LIBOR is the rate London banks charge when they lend each other dollars. Other currencies have comparable rates. The euro, for example, has two rates, Euro LIBOR which is traded in London and Euribor, which is traded in Frankfurt. There are LIBORs associated with different maturities, such as 90-day LIBOR and 180-day LIBOR, which refer to the rates on 90-day time deposits and 180-day time deposits, respectively. When a bank or corporation borrows at LIBOR or LIBOR plus a spread, it typically pays interest in the amount of the rate times the number of days in the period divided by 360. Thus, a 90-day $10 million LIBOR loan where LIBOR is 8% will require an interest payment of $10,000,000 (0.08)(90/360) = $200,000 in 90 days along with the principal repayment.

Let us start by examining a very basic type of interest rate derivative, the *forward rate agreement* or *FRA*. This instrument is a contract between two parties in which one party promises to make an interest payment at an agreed-on (fixed) interest rate on a future date and receive from the other party an interest payment based on a rate that is yet to be determined.

Suppose a corporation is planning to take out a single payment loan on a future date, say six months from now. In this kind of loan, the corporation will receive a discounted amount from the lender and will pay the full face value back at the maturity date. The rate of discount will be LIBOR plus a fixed number of basis points. Fearing an increase in interest rates, the corporation enters into an FRA with a derivatives dealer in which the corporation will pay the dealer interest on a given notional principal at a rate agreed on today. The corporation will receive from the dealer the interest on that same notional principal based on LIBOR. The date on which LIBOR is determined is the date the corporation issues the loan. In that way, if interest rates are up on that day, the corporation pays more on the loan but receives a boost from the higher interest paid by the dealer. The net effect is that the corporation is able to lock in a fixed rate equal to the FRA fixed rate plus the spread on its loan over LIBOR.

On the expiration date of the FRA, the amount of the payment is determined and payment occurs that day or technically a couple of business days later. This procedure contrasts, however, with the practice in most interest rate derivatives in which payment does not occur until after the expiration. For example, on most interest rate derivatives, if the underlying is 90-day LIBOR, payment will not occur until 90 days after expiration. This procedure is due to the convention in the structure of floating-rate loans wherein a loan based on 90-day LIBOR would have the rate set at the beginning of the quarter and the interest would be paid 90 days later. The difference between that method and the one used in FRAs is only a present value adjustment made by discounting the FRA payment at the current rate.

In simple terms, an FRA is a forward contract that can be used to lock in the rate on a loan. If used by itself—that is, without a loan—an FRA is simply a speculative position in LIBOR. The holder of the long position has agreed to make a fixed interest payment, which has been agreed on when the contract is signed, and receive a floating interest payment. It is a pure speculative position on a future interest rate with the potential for large upside gains from rising interest rates and large downside losses from falling interest rates.

Since it is possible to construct a forward contract, it is also possible to construct an option. An interest rate call option is an option on an interest rate, such as LIBOR. The buyer of the call pays a premium, usually expressed in basis points, and obtains the right to make a fixed interest payment at a future date and receive a floating interest payment. The fixed payment is determined by the strike rate, corresponding to the strike price or exercise price for options on assets. The holder exercises if the underlying rate in the market ends up higher than the strike rate. As noted earlier, the actual payment occurs one period after the expiration.

As an example, suppose you buy a call option on three-month LIBOR, expiring in six months with a strike rate of 8% and a notional principal of $10 million. The premium is paid today. In six months, if LIBOR exceeds 8%, you exercise the call, making a payment of 0.08(90/360)($10 million) and receiving a payment of LIBOR(90/360)($10 million). If LIBOR ends up less than 8%, the option expires worthless.[1] In either case, the premium is lost because it was paid at the start. A put option would work the other way; that is, exercising if LIBOR ends up less than 8%. The actual payoff is made 90 days after the expiration. This procedure corresponds to the fact that on a loan, the rate is set at the beginning of the interest payment period with the interest paid at the end of the period.

An interest rate call is useful to hedge a situation in which a party will be damaged by an increase in a specific interest rate on a specific day. An interest rate put is useful when a party will be damaged by a decrease in a specific interest rate on a specific day. Of course, an FRA can be used in either situation, but with an FRA, the benefits of a move in the opposite direction are lost. The advantage of giving up the gains from favorable moves is that there is no cash paid up front.[2] An option preserves the gains from favorable moves but at the expense of having to pay a premium up front.

In many cases, a party is subject to the risk of interest rates on a series of dates. A typical situation is when a firm borrows or lends at a floating rate and makes semiannual interest payments.

The firm could buy a series of interest rate calls if borrowing, or puts if lending, with expirations corresponding to the dates on which the loan interest rates are reset. Derivatives dealers offer a portfolios of these options in a package deal called an *interest rate cap* for calls and an *interest rate floor* for puts. Thus, a cap is a series of interest rate calls and a floor is a series of interest rate puts. The individual component options are called *caplets* and *floorlets*.

Since either a cap or a floor will cost the premiums of a combination of options, some parties choose to save some of the up-front cost by entering

---

[1] I have occasionally been criticized for using the expression "ends up," when I am referring to where the underlying is. It is just an alternative way of saying "at expiration is" or something similar. I place a premium on not using the same phrases again and again.

[2] See the previous footnote. I have also been criticized for using the expression "up front," which just means "at the time the contract is initiated." Doesn't "up front" Sound better? It is certainly more economical.

into an *interest rate collar*. A typical collar involving a borrower would entail the purchase of an interest rate cap with a given strike and the sale of an interest rate floor with a lower strike. It is possible to set the strikes such that the premium on the floor offsets the premium on the cap, resulting in no net cash outflow at the start. The result is that the borrower will effectively have a maximum and a minimum interest rate it pays. At a rate in between the cap and floor strikes, the borrower will pay a rate that moves directly with the level of the underlying rate. In short, the gains from potentially lower rates beyond a point are given up to pay for the avoidance of potentially higher rates beyond a point.

When the cap and floor premiums offset, this transaction is often referred to as a *zero-cost collar*. This term is misleading however, because there is no such thing as zero cost. From an accounting or cash flow standpoint, there may be no cost but the cost is incurred in an economic sense by giving up the gains from lower interest rates. The fact that this cost does not show up as a cash outlay does not truly make it any less real.

Collars are just variations of the bull and bear spreads that have been used for many years by option dealers. Using the principle of put-call parity, there are several ways to construct a collar.

Further treatments of related transactions are found in Essays 42 and 50.

Pricing interest rate derivatives is complex and requires a good arbitrage-free model of the term structure. It is critical that a dealer price these options in relation to each other. Otherwise, the dealer would find itself potentially quoting prices that enable customers to execute arbitrage against the dealer. In Essays 58 and 59 I discuss models of the term structure and interest rate derivative contract pricing and illustrate them for FRAs and options in Essay 62.

The most widely used derivative on an interest rate is the interest rate swap, which is covered in the next essay.

FOR MORE READING

Chance, Don M., and Robert Brooks. *An Introduction to Derivatives and Risk Management*, 7th ed. Mason, OH: Thomson South-Western, 2007, chap. 13.

Hull, John C. *Options, Futures, and Other Derivatives*, 6th ed. Upper Saddle River, NJ: Prentice-Hall, 2006, chap. 6.

Jarrow, Robert A., and Stuart M. Turnbull. *Derivatives Securities*, 2nd. ed. Mason, OH: Thomson South-Western, 2000, chap. 13.

McDonald, Robert L. *Derivative Markets*, 2nd ed. Boston: Addison Wesley, 2006, chap. 7.

Smithson, Charles W. *Managing Financial Risk: A Guide to Derivative Products, Financial Engineering, and Value Maximization*, 3rd ed. New York: McGraw-Hill, 1998, chap. 5.

Stulz, René. *Risk Management and Derivatives*. Mason, OH: Thomson South-Western, 2003, chap. 14.

Wilmott, Paul. *Derivatives: The Theory and Practice of Financial Engineering*. Chichester, UK: John Wiley & Sons, 1998, chap. 35.

TEST YOUR KNOWLEDGE

1. What is the primary rate used as the underlying for most interest rate derivatives?
2. How is an FRA like a typical forward contract, and how is it different?
3. What characteristic about the payoff of an interest rate option is different from the payoff of a typical option?
4. What do interest rate caps and floors consist of?

Interest Rate Derivatives: Swaps

We introduced swaps in Essay 6. In this essay we cover a specific type of swap, the interest rate swap, which is the most widely used of all derivatives. An interest rate swap is a contract between two parties in which each party agrees to make a series of interest payments to the other on scheduled dates in the future. Each interest payment is computed using a different formula. For example, let us take the simplest interest swap, called the *plain vanilla or fixed-for-floating rate swap.* Let us say that on June 19, XYZ Corporation agrees to make payments to a swap dealer, which we shall call ABC Bank, each December 19 and June 19 for the next three years. The interest payments will be based on a dollar principal amount of $20 million, which is called the *notional principal*. The payment dates are called *settlement dates*. Let XYZ promise to pay ABC interest at a fixed rate of 9%. ABC promises to pay XYZ Interest at the LIBOR (London Interbank Offer Rate), in effect exactly six months prior to each settlement date.

Today we observe LIBOR and consequently XYZ and ABC know what the first payment will be on December 19. Normally only the net payment—that is, the net amount that one party owes the other—is made. On December 19 we shall observe LIBOR, and that will determine the payment on the following June 19. Thus, while the first LIBOR-based or floating payment is known, all of the remaining floating payments are yet to be determined. You can see that XYZ in effect buys a claim on a series of interest payments at LIBOR by agreeing to make a series of interest payments at 9%. The actual payments are computed as (LIBOR – 9%) × (Number of days in six-month period/360)(Notional Principal) The parties can agree to use the assumption of 180 days in the six-month period instead of the exact day count. They can also agree to use 365 days in the year. The terms are simply set at whatever the two parties agree to which is usually dictated by convention in the market for the underlying rate.

Some people find it a bit confusing that LIBOR at the beginning of the period sets the rate paid at the end of the period. We have briefly touched on this in Essay 8 when we covered FRAs and options, but let us look at it again a little closer. Consider why XYZ could have entered into the swap. Suppose XYZ was currently engaged in a loan with three years left with payments reset every six months on June 19 and December 19 according to LIBOR. XYZ will probably pay LIBOR plus a spread of a fixed number of basis points. Thus, at the beginning of each six-month period, XYZ finds out its new interest rate and makes its interest payment six months later. Consequently, XYZ is highly exposed to interest rate risk. By entering into the swap, XYZ's exposure is eliminated. Any increase in the interest it owes is offset by an increase in the interest it receives on the swap. In effect, XYZ has converted a floating-rate loan to a fixed-rate loan at 9% plus the spread over LIBOR.

Why did XYZ do this? Perhaps it could have obtained a fixed-rate loan in the first place, but that is not always possible. Perhaps XYZ sees this as a more attractive deal. That is possible, but if XYZ did not do the swap, it would be a debtor and face no credit risk, With the swap, it assumes the risk that ABC will default. So maybe it saves a little for taking on the risk that the bank will default. Perhaps XYZ took out the floating-rate loan earlier, thinking rates would fall. Now it thinks rates will rise. The swap allows it to change the loan to a fixed-rate loan. Moreover, the swap is a very efficient instrument. It can be constructed at extremely low cost and is cheaper than taking out a new fixed-rate loan and using the proceeds to buy an offsetting floating-rate security paying LIBOR. Technically this alternative would accomplish the same thing, but it would surely be much more costly and time consuming to set up.

The term structure of interest rates and the forward rates implied by the relationship between short- and long-term rates, which is covered in Essay 55, are critical to the valuation of a swap. When initiated, the swap has no value to either party. It is neither an asset nor a liability. The present value of the fixed payments equals the present value of the floating payments that are implied by the forward rates in the current term structure of interest rates.

If the term structure does not change, neither party will gain nor lose at the expense of the other on the swap. If, however, interest rates rise, XYZ will gain on ABC because XYZ pays fixed and receives floating. The swap will have positive (negative) value to XYZ (ABC) and can then be thought of as an asset (liability), The actual numerical value is computed by determining the present value of the floating payments implied by the new term structure minus the present value of the fixed payments.

The bank, acting as a dealer in interest rate swaps, determines the fixed rate that it is willing to pay against LIBOR. This rate, as noted, equates the present value of the fixed payments to the present value of the floating payments, given that the floating payments are set at the forward rates implied in the current term structure. Then the dealer adds and subtracts a fixed number of basis points so that it quotes a higher rate to accept if paying LIBOR and a lower rate to pay if receiving LIBOR. The actual quote is stated in terms of a fixed number of basis points over the rate on the U.S. Treasury note with maturity closest to the swap maturity, This convention protects the dealer in the event that it makes a quote just before interest rates make a sharp move.

The specifics of swap pricing and valuation are covered in Essays 37 and 63.

The dealer will, of course, do numerous derivative transactions, including interest rate options and various other options, forward contracts, futures, and swaps. The dealer will attempt to hedge its overall position, and if successful, if will earn the spread between the rates it asks to receive and the rates it offers to pay.

FOR MORE READING

Buetow, Gerald W., and Frank J. Fabozzi. *Valuation of Interest Rate Swaps and Swaptions*. New Hope, PA: Frank J. Fabozzi Associates, 2001, chaps. 1, 2.

Chance, Don M., and Robert Brooks. *An Introduction to Derivatives and Risk Management*, 7th ed. Mason, OH: Thomson South-Western, 2007, chap. 12.

Hull, John C. *Options, Futures, and Other Derivatives*, 6th ed. Upper Saddle River, NJ: Prentice-Hall, 2006, chaps. 7, 30.

Jarrow, Robert A., and Stuart M. Turnbull. *Derivatives Securities*, 2nd ed. Mason, OH: Thomson South-Western, 2000, chap. 14.

McDonald, Robert L. *Derivative Markets*, 2nd ed. Boston: Addison Wesley, 2006, chap. 8.

Smithson, Charles W. *Managing Financial Risk: A Guide to Derivative Products, Financial Engineering, and Value Maximization*, 3rd ed. New York: McGraw-Hill, 1998, chap. 8.

Stulz, René. *Risk Management and Derivatives*. Mason, OH: Thomson South-Western, 2003, chap. 16.

Wilmott, Paul. *Derivatives: The Theory and Practice of Financial Engineering*. Chichester, UK: John Wiley & Sons, 1998, chap. 35.

TEST YOUR KNOWLEDGE

1. How is a plain vanilla interest rate swap used to change a floating-rate loan to a fixed-rate loan?

2. Why is it possible for a floating-rate loan and a swap to be a cheaper source of fixed-rate financing than a fixed-rate loan?
3. The fixed rate on a swap is the one that assures what condition at the start of a swap?
4. Why is the fixed rate on a swap quoted as a Treasury fixed rate plus a spread?

Currency Swaps

A currency swap is an agreement between two parties in which one party promises to make payments to the other in one currency and the other promises to make payments to the former in a different currency. Currency swaps are similar to yet notably different from interest rate swaps and are often combined with interest rate swaps.

Let us say that a firm in the United States needs euros to fund a construction project in Germany. It can issue a fixed-rate bond in euros or issue a fixed-rate bond in dollars and convert those dollars to euros. Let us assume it does the latter. There are several ways to convert the dollars into euros. One way is to construct a dollar/euro currency swap. At the start of the transaction, the firm takes the dollars received from the issue of the dollar-denominated bond and pays them to the swap dealer who pays our firm an amount of euros. These amounts of dollars and euros represent the notional principal of the swap. Note that the notional principal is exchanged up front in a currency swap in contrast to the procedure in an interest rate swap, where an exchange of equivalent notional principals would be meaningless.

Then at each scheduled coupon payment date, the firm makes the normal dollar interest payment on its bonds. At the same time, the firm pays an agreed-on amount of euros to the swap dealer and in turn receives dollars. As is traditional in most foreign exchange transactions, the amounts are not netted.

The receipt of the dollars on the swap can offset the payment of the dollar coupon interest. If the amounts do not offset, the difference is a known spread that poses no additional risk. When the bond matures, the firm pays its bondholders in dollars but receives an equivalent amount of dollars from the swap dealer to which it paid an agreed-upon amount of euros. Thus, the notional principal is also exchanged at the end of the life of the currency swap.

The net effect is that the firm converted a dollar-denominated loan into a euro-denominated loan. The firm can take a loss or gain on the swap transaction alone, but its overall position of the swap plus the dollar-denominated bond is that it is exposed as a borrower to the euro. If the euro weakens, the firm gains on its overall position, though we should not forget that it may have additional exposure to the euro elsewhere in its assets and liabilities.

By issuing the dollar-denominated bond and the pay-euros, receive-dollars currency swap, the firm may find that it gets a significantly better rate than had it issued a euro-denominated bond in the first place. This result can arise because the firm has an advantage borrowing in its own currency. If it has a sufficiently good relationship with the dealer bank and qualifies for the swap, the dealer bank will view the firm as a better credit risk on the swap than would foreign bondholders had it issued the foreign bond. Note, however, that the firm has taken on one risk that it would not have had if it had issued the euro-denominated bonds. It now faces the risk that the dealer will default. Any savings it generates could simply be compensation for taking on this additional credit risk.

Note that the interest rates that determine the swap payments are fixed. Some swaps mix currency and interest rate risk by varying the coupon interest rate. These are called *cross-currency swaps*. In this kind of swap, one or both interest payments are floating. For example, suppose the firm wanted to borrow at a floating rate in euros. Then it could structure the swap so that its euro payments were made at the floating rate of euro LIBOR. If it had been forced to borrow at dollar LIBOR, it could have structured the swap so that it received dollar LIBOR and then paid either a fixed rate or euro LIBOR.

Thus, there are four types of swaps it could have entered into:

1. Pay dollars fixed, receive euros fixed.
2. Pay dollars fixed, receive euros floating.
3. Pay dollars floating, receive euros fixed.
4. Pay dollars floating, receive euros floating.

Many of the important characteristics of interest rate and currency swaps are the same. Pricing the swap at the start involves finding the interest payments and exchange rate that gives the swap a zero initial value. This topic is covered in Essay 37. Valuing the swap later in its life means finding the present value of the payments in each currency, converting to a common currency, and netting the difference, which makes the swap either an asset or a liability to one party and the opposite to the other. Dealers price and trade these swaps in essentially the same manner as interest rate swaps.

There is, however, one major difference: Because the principal is generally exchanged at the start and at the termination of the swap, the potential for default at the end of the swap gives an additional element of credit risk to the transaction.

Note further the relationship between interest rate and currency swaps. Suppose we enter into these swaps:

1. Pay dollars fixed, receive euros fixed.
2. Receive dollars fixed, pay dollars floating.

The first swap is a fixed-fixed currency swap. The second swap is a plain vanilla interest rate swap. The combination of the two is equivalent to a single currency swap in which we receive euros fixed and pay dollars floating. It should be easy to see that we could construct any of the currency swaps by combining another currency swap with a plain vanilla swap.

In understanding currency swaps, it is important to see that they are equivalent to two other types of transactions. Consider our pay-euros-fixed, receive-dollars-fixed swap. It can be viewed as the issuance of a euro-denominated bond wherein the proceeds are used to purchase a dollar-denominated bond. Of course, the payment dates and terms on the swap and the bonds must correspond. In addition, the swap can be viewed as a series of foreign currency forward transactions in which the party has agreed to make a series of euro payments and receive a series of dollar payments.

An interesting variation of an interest rate and currency swap is the *diff swap*. A typical diff swap would be this: Pay dollars at the U.S. interest rate, usually LIBOR, and receive dollars at the euro interest rate. In other words, the payment based on the euro interest rate is not made in euros but rather in U.S. dollars. This type of swap is a pure play on the difference between U.S. and euros interest rates and has no currency risk whatsoever. Clearly it is a type of currency swap with the currency risk hedged.

FOR MORE READING

Brown, Keith C., and Donald J. Smith. *Interest Rate and Currency Swaps: A Tutorial.* Charlottesville, VA: Research Foundation of the Institute of Chartered Financial Analysts, 1995.

Chance, Don M., and Robert Brooks. *An Introduction to Derivatives and Risk Management*, 7th ed. Mason, OH: Thomson South-Western, 2007, chap. 12.

Hull, John C. *Options, Futures, and Other Derivatives*, 6th ed. Upper Saddle River, NJ: Prentice-Hall, 2006, chaps. 7, 30.

Jarrow, Robert A., and Stuart M. Turnbull. *Derivatives Securities*, 2nd. ed. Mason, OH: Thomson South-Western, 2000, chap. 14.

McDonald, Robert L. *Derivative Markets*, 2nd ed. Boston: Addison Wesley, 2006, chap. 8.

Smithson, Charles W. *Managing Financial Risk: A Guide to Derivative Products, Financial Engineering, and Value Maximization*, 3rd ed. New York: McGraw-Hill, 1998, chap. 8.

Stulz, René. *Risk Management and Derivatives*. Mason, OH: Thomson South-Western, 2003, chap. 16.

TEST YOUR KNOWLEDGE

1. Explain how a company can borrow in one currency and use a swap to convert the loan to a loan in another currency.
2. In doing the transaction in question 1, explain why a company might get a better rate doing the loan in a foreign currency and swap rather than in its domestic currency.
3. Explain how two currency swaps can combine to produce a plain vanilla interest rate swap. Use the dollar and yen as the two currencies and make the two swaps result in paying dollars fixed and receiving dollars floating.

Structured Notes

Structured notes have been in the center of many of the stories of organizations that suffered large losses trading derivatives. A structured note is a derivative in one sense but not in another. A structured note is a debt security in which the interest payments are determined by some type of, occasionally complex, formula. A pure floating-rate security or "floater," in which the interest is tied to LIBOR, is a kind of plain vanilla structured note that has been around for many years. Thus, unlike a derivative, a structured note is a debt security. Like a derivative, however, the interest on a structured note is determined by how another security, rate, or price moves, sometimes determined by a complex formula. In the last few years, issuers have made the formulas more complex to meet the needs of users who want to take more specific positions on interest rates, such as anticipating a twist in the term structure.

As an example, consider a basic floating-rate security. Let us set up a two-year floating rate security in which the interest is paid semiannually at the rate of LIBOR plus 200 basis points. The rate is set at the beginning of the six-month period and the interest is paid at the end of the period. Now suppose we add the following feature: Interest will be at 150% of LIBOR plus 200 basis points. We now have now increased the volatility of the interest payments by 50%. This type of security, while still called a structured note, is really not a derivative at all.

Recall that in Essay 8 we discussed interest rate caps and floors. Some structured notes have a cap on the maximum interest. Suppose that the holder of the note sells a cap where the underlying is LIBOR and the strike rate is 10%. The expiration dates of the component caplets correspond to the interest rate reset dates on the note. Thus, on any of these dates, if LIBOR exceeds 10%, the seller of the cap, who also holds the note, must pay LIBOR − 10%. It receives LIBOR plus 200 basis points on the note, for a total receipt of LIBOR + 200 basis points − (LIBOR − 10%) = 12%, if LIBOR exceeds 10%. If LIBOR is less than 10%, the holder of the note receives LIBOR + 200 basis points from the note alone, because the caplet expires unexercised. Thus, a structured note with these terms is equivalent to an ordinary floating-rate note with a coupon of LIBOR plus 200 basis points and a short cap struck at 10%. So the issuer of such a note has effectively issued an uncapped note and purchased a cap. If the note had a minimum rate, the option would be a floor.

There are a wide variety of structured notes. One in particular that has received a lot of unfounded negative publicity is the *inverse floater*. This security is simply a floating-rate instrument with an interest rate that moves inversely with market interest rates. This type of instrument can be created from a standard floating-rate note by adding a swap. For example, suppose a firm issues an ordinary floating-rate note, with the interest rate set at LIBOR + 200 basis points. Then suppose it enters into a swap in which it pays a fixed rate of F and receives a floating-rate based on LIBOR, with the reset dates corresponding to the dates on the note and with the notional principal equal to twice the par value on the note. Then the interest payment will be LIBOR + 200 basis points $- 2 \times$ LIBOR $+ 2F = 2F + 200$ basis points $-$ LIBOR. Note now that the interest payment moves inversely with LIBOR. Consequently an inverse floater can be viewed as an ordinary floater attached to a swap based on a multiple of the notional principal. Note that when LIBOR exceeds $2F + 200$ basis points, the interest rate becomes negative. In most cases, there is a floor placed on the total interest, which is achieved by having the borrower sell a cap struck at $2F + 200$ basis points. Thus, when LIBOR exceeds $2F + 200$ basis points, the borrower makes a payment amounting to LIBOR $- (2F + 200$ basis points). This payment offsets the negative interest, that is, the interest paid from lender to borrower. Thus, issuing an inverse floater with a minimum interest rate of zero is equivalent to issuing a standard floater, entering into a pay-fixed, receive-floating swap on twice the notional principal, and selling a cap struck at twice the fixed rate plus the floating rate spread.

An inverse floater, as you see, moves opposite to market interest rates. Consequently, it can be used to hedge a position in any ordinary security whose value moves inversely with LIBOR. As long as the holder of such a security understands that, unlike most debt securities, its value moves directly with interest rates, the instrument itself should cause no problems. Unfortunately, financial reporters have some times made the inverse floater sound like an out-of-control financial monster, behaving in a counterintuitive way. Just because the coupon moves down when interest rates move up and vice versa does not make this instrument dangerous. There must be something about the way "inverse floater" sounds to the naïve ear that suggests that it is a piece of complex exotica dreamed up by a crazy mathematician at a Wall Street firm.

Many structured notes, and particularly inverse floaters, do have an element of increased embedded leverage not commonly found in standard notes. This leverage comes from the use of a factor by which the rate adjusts by a multiple, such as 1.5 times LIBOR. This effect does give the instrument an extra kick that increases the risk, but it does not take a rocket scientist to multiply LIBOR by 1.5 to see the potential effect. A small number of structured notes have leverage embedded in a clever and misleading way, however, which is by stating the leverage factor as a fractional divisor. For example, suppose the interest rate is: (LIBOR + 300 basis points)/0.05. Of course, dividing by 0.05 is the same as multiplying by 20, but to most people, this effect is not obvious. Thus, the interest is paid as if the notional principal is 20 times the stated notional principal.

Another class of structured notes is called *range notes*. These instruments typically pay interest at an above-market rate if LIBOR stays within a specific range, which may change according to a schedule. If LIBOR moves outside of that range, these notes may revert to a lower interest rate or no interest at all. This instrument is easy to construct. Suppose the terms were that the interest rate would be LIBOR if LIBOR is between 8% and 10% and zero otherwise. The issuer can replicate this instrument by issuing an ordinary floating-rate note and adding some exotic options called barrier options, which we cover in Essay 44.

Other types of structured notes pay a promised rate but allow additional payments based on the movement of a commodity price or stock index. This instrument, however, is more commonly known as commodity-linked debt or equity-linked debt, the latter of which we cover in Essay 14.

Given the complexity of these payment formulas, you may wonder why structured notes are used. The answer is that they provide investors with an opportunity to take advantage of views not only about the direction of interest rates but also the volatility, the range, and shape of the term structure. Many of these notes are not used for hedging, but the trading they generate does provide liquidity as dealers hedge their positions in other markets that are widely used by other parties. In addition, some of these notes have at times permitted firms to take advantage of favorable tax and accounting treatment, although those advantages usually disappear over time. Suffocating regulations are often an impetus for structured notes and, in fact, many derivatives. Structured notes sometimes provide a way to get around regulatory treatment. Also, some of these notes provide a natural hedging device. The structured note market is essentially buyer-driven, meaning that the securities are created to meet the needs of buyers with specific outlooks or positions in which a payoff of the sort just described would solve a problem or exploit an opportunity.

Structured notes are but one of a number of instruments that contribute greatly to the efficient functioning of our markets. Do not let reporters lead you to believe that these complex securities are in some way so bizarre that they are nothing but gambling. Many of these securities are no more speculative than ordinary stocks and bonds, and they serve a very useful purpose. They are often complex, however, and do require careful examination before entering into a transaction. You must be fully aware of and comfortable with how the interest formula is computed as well as the principal. But, of course, this is true of any investment in a debt security.

FOR MORE READING

Chance, Don M., and Robert Brooks. *An Introduction to Derivatives and Risk Management*, 7th ed. Mason, OH: Thomson South-Western, 2007, chap. 14.

TEST YOUR KNOWLEDGE

1. How can a debt security be constructed to provide a floor on the amount of interest paid?
2. How are inverse floaters differ from ordinary floaters?
3. Why are structured notes used?

Securitized Instruments

An important innovation in the financial markets has been the securitization of assets. Securitization is the process of combining a group of debt securities into a portfolio and issuing new securities that have a claim on the portfolio. Of course, by that definition, you would include mutual funds as securitized investments, but in practice, mutual funds are never thought of in that way. Rather, securitized investments commonly distinguish themselves by the fact that they alter the priority of payments to the holders of the securities according to some specified procedure. Usually this procedure takes into account default and early payments on the underlying debt securities. The individual claims that make up a securitized investment are referred to as *tranches,* and the tranches differ according to the priority of payments they receive. For example, some debt securities, such as mortgages, often pay off prior to maturity. These early payments must then be allocated to the tranches according to a schedule or priority. Some debt securities default. The tranches must then bear the loss from default according to a schedule of priority.

The first type of securitized asset was the residential mortgage in 1969. The first nonmortgage asset securitization was lease receivables in 1985. Since that time, credit cards, bonds, loans, and many other types of debt instruments have been securitized. The claims issued against these securities are generally called *asset-backed securities.* When the underlying assets are mortgages, the asset-backed securities issued against the mortgages are called *mortgage-backed securities* (MBS). Within the MBS family are *collateralized mortgage obligations* (CMOs). A general family of instruments referred to as *collateralized debt obligations* (CDOs) has arisen and encompasses the securitization of bonds and loans. These instruments are referred to as *collateralized bond obligations* (CBOs) and *collateralized loan obligations* (CLOs). We will first talk about the MBS market.

There are MBS whose principal and interest are guaranteed by a U.S. government entity or a government-sponsored enterprise. These securities are called agency MBS and do not expose an investor to credit risk. For nonagency MBS, issuers usually employ various vehicles for enhancing the credit of the security to obtain a targeted investment-grade rating. Investors in MBS are exposed to the uncertainty about the future cash flow because the borrower has the right to prepay the loan, in whole or in part, prior to the scheduled maturity date. This risk is called *prepayment risk* and is a major factor in understanding MBS.

Consider the prepayment risk that an investor faces in the basic mortgage-backed instrument, the pass-through security. When interest rates fall, homeowners will begin prepaying their mortgages, leaving mortgage holders receiving principal repayments earlier than planned. These cash flows then have to be invested in a lower interest rate environment. The returns on mortgage pass-throughs are thus quite volatile, much to the surprise of many investors who sometimes are not properly informed by their brokers of this risk.

Some variations of the instrument are created in the form of *interest-only strips*, sometimes called IOs, and *principal-only strips*, sometimes called POs. The former entitle the holder to only the interest payments while the latter entitle the investor to only the principal payments. The investor in the PO earns a return based on the speed at which the principal is repaid. The faster the prepayment speed, the greater the return. A PO investor benefits from a declining interest rate environment because prepayments can be expected to increase. The prepayment risk faced by a PO investor is that interest rates will rise and prepayments will slow down. In contrast, an IO investor benefits from a rise in interest rates because prepayments will slow down and therefore the mortgages will be outstanding for a longer period of time. The prepayment risk faced by an IO investor is that interest rates will fall and that prepayments will accelerate. In fact, the prepayment rate might be so high that the investor will not receive enough interest to recover the amount invested.

Now let us look at the collateralized mortgage obligation (CMO). Some CMO tranches receive principal only, some receive interest only. Some are paid off in a specified order, meaning that principal and interest payments are applied to certain tranches only, while others generally receive either nothing or only the interest. When the first layer of tranches is fully repaid, the next tranche then steps in line to receive its principal and interest. Some have a limited degree of protection against principal repayments, meaning that principal repayments are applied to other tranches. Another has a claim on any residual value after all tranches are paid off. There are numerous other types of tranches, some of which have complex payoff formulas.

Financial reporters have described the CMO market as one where nefarious rocket scientists working away in labs late at night carve up the mortgages of innocent homeowners and sell them in complicated little pieces at exorbitant prices to unsuspecting individual investors. There is no question that some of these instruments are indeed complicated. Others are quite simple. The tranches bear different types of both interest rate and prepayment risk. For example, a tranche with low priority will receive only interest payments until the principal is repaid on higher-priority tranches. This feature gives the tranche protection against prepayments while generating interest in the interim. Later the prepayment protection is removed. The main point is that these tranches offer widely divergent risk-return profiles. Hence, investors interested in holding mortgage securities need not bear too little or too much risk. You simply buy the tranche that fits your degree of risk tolerance.

Unfortunately, due to some unscrupulous brokers, some investors suffered painful losses by investing their liquidity in high-risk tranches. The brokers capitalized on the fact that many of these securities had interest payments guaranteed by a government agency. Due to the risk, the expected returns were more attractive than those of otherwise comparable government and corporate bonds. Thus, the securities were advertised as "government-guaranteed" with very attractive returns. Of course, the government guarantee was nothing more than insurance in the event that a homeowner defaulted. The holders of these tranches still bore interest rate and sometimes prepayment risk, which is the reason why the expected returns were so high. Brokers should, of course, not put individuals with a low tolerance for risk into these securities, and it goes without saying that those individuals should always know what they are investing in.

Now let us look at the CDO market. It arose as financial institutions realized that just as mortgages could be securitized, so could virtually any type of loan or bond. Hence, they began packaging loans into CLOs and bonds into CBOs. The technical differences are minor. CDOs in general are instruments whose returns are primarily driven by the credit risk of the underlying instruments. Each tranche is specified as being positioned in an order of priority that defines how defaults are allocated. A CDO contains one or more debt tranches and a single equity tranche. The equity tranche bears the most credit risk, because it typically incurs the first losses. Subsequent losses are then allocated to tranches in the specified order. The seniormost tranche bears the least credit risk.

Naturally there are many variations of this basic theme. For example, there are CDOs with a single tranche (only equity) levered by the use of outside credit and *synthetic CDOs* in which the credit risk exposure is obtained indirectly by selling credit derivatives, a topic we take up in Essay 18, on certain loans or bonds rather than holding the loans or bonds directly. There are CDOs in which the underlying securities are purchased and held to maturity and without any buying or selling and others in which the securities can be sold and replaced by other securities. In the latter case, a collateral manager is paid a fee to attempt to buy and sell to avoid defaults. There are CDOs in which an arbitrary percentage, called a *haircut*, is applied to the portfolio to provide a margin of safety to protect the investors from defaults. If the equity value falls below the haircut, the manager must sell some securities and pay the holders of the debt tranches an amount sufficient to bring the equity value to above the haircut level.

ABSs have also been constructed with packages of receivables, especially credit card receivables, and these have somewhat less of a prepayment problem though they can certainly default. Also, credit card receivables represent nonmaturing debt so they are somewhat different from other ABS.

Asset-backed securities are an important financial innovation for one principal reason: They provide investors opportunities and access to markets they would not otherwise have. For example, it would not be practical for individuals to invest in mortgages. Yet individuals commonly hold MBS, oftentimes through mutual funds. Those who want to minimize prepayment risk can hold senior MBS securities. Investors can easily engage indirectly in lending money to corporations by purchasing CDOs, and the choices vary widely with respect to the risk. Of course, many investors will own these securities through mutual funds, but in any case, the ABS market opens up what would otherwise be fairly illiquid securities to a broader group of investors. Although ABS can be quite complex and are not suited for every investor, they make a positive contribution to financial market efficiency. As always, an appropriate matching of investor needs and risk tolerance to the characteristics of the instrument is of the utmost importance.

FOR MORE READING

Chance, Don M., and Robert Brooks. *An Introduction to Derivatives and Risk Management,* 7th ed. Mason, OH: Thomson South-Western, 2007, chap. 14.

Fabozzi, Frank J., Anand K. Bhattacharya, and William S. Berliner. *Mortgage-Backed Securities: Products, Structuring, and Analytical Techniques.* Hoboken, NJ: John Wiley & Sons, 2007.

Hull, John C. *Options, Futures, and Other Derivatives,* 6th ed. Upper Saddle River, NJ: Prentice-Hall, 2006, chap. 29.

Lucas, Douglas J., Laurie S. Goodman, and Frank J. Fabozzi. *Collateralized Debt Obligations: Structures and Analysis,* 2nd. ed. Hoboken, NJ: John Wiley & Sons, 2006.

Neftci, Salih N. *Principles of Financial Engineering.* San Diego: Elsevier Academic Press, 2004, chap. 18.

TEST YOUR KNOWLEDGE

1. Explain the general structure of an ABS.
2. What is prepayment risk, and how is it allocated in a CMO?
3. How is default risk allocated in a CDO?
4. What is the principal advantage is offered by ABS?

Equity Swaps

An equity swap is an agreement between two parties for each to make to the other a series of payments in which at least one party's payments is based on the return on a stock or index. The other party makes a payment that can be computed any other agreeable way. It could be based on a floating interest rate, it could be on a fixed rate, or it could be on the return of another stock or index. In other words, at least one payment has to be based on an equity return.

Consider an investor with a portfolio consisting of all U.S. stocks. He decides to diversify internationally by allocating 20% of the portfolio to foreign stocks. To keep things simple, let us say he wants the foreign component to be exclusively German stocks and primarily the stock of German blue-chip companies. Of course, he could sell some domestic stock and buy foreign stock, but these transactions would incur significant transaction costs. In addition, dealing with foreign stock can be extremely burdensome because of different legal systems, lack of sufficient information, custodial fees, and, in particular, the dividend withholding tax. The latter arises out of treaties between countries that require a country to withhold a portion of the dividends in the event that the investor is liable for taxes. In some cases, these withheld dividends can be recovered, but doing that incurs some additional costs and delays.

The equity swap was primarily developed to deal with these problems in cross-country investing. Suppose our investor enters into a swap in which he agrees to pay the Standard & Poor's (S&P) 500 return to the swap dealer based on a notional principal equal to 20% of the market value of his portfolio. The dealer will pay the return on the German index, the DAX, based on an equivalent notional principal. He has, in effect, sold the U.S. stock and bought German stock. The payments can be made at any interval desired but quarterly would be common.

An important distinction, however, between equity swaps and interest rate swaps is that the equity return, unlike an interest rate, can be negative.

Thus, if one market goes down and the other goes up, one party will be responsible for both sides of the payments. In general, equity swap payments will appear to be quite volatile, but this phenomenon reflects only the normal volatility of the markets. The same results would be obtained by trading the securities directly.

In this type of equity swap, the payments determined by the DAX could be structured so as to be made in dollars or in euros. If the payments were in dollars, the transaction would be equivalent to selling the U.S. stocks, buying the German stocks, and hedging the currency risk. For example, suppose our investor wanted only to participate in any growth in the German stock market but did not want to bear the currency risk. He would then structure the swap so that the payment is based on the DAX return applied to a dollar notional principal. If he wanted the currency risk, the payment would be based on euro notional principal though possibly converted into dollars at the current exchange rate before being paid to him. Then he would receive or make an additional payment to reflect the effect of the currency rate change on the notional principal. In other words, if the notional principal were € 20 million and the DAX went up 5%, he would receive € 1 million, converted to dollars at the current exchange rate, less the payment he makes on the S&P 500. If, at the same time, the euro rose 1 % against the dollar, he would receive an additional € 200,000. This result would reflect the fact that he gained from both the German stock market and the euro currency. Of course, he could lose either or both ways as well.

Other types of equity swaps could be used, for example, when a firm wishes to sell large-cap securities and buy small-cap securities. An equity swap would be set up so that the firm makes payments based on the return on a large-cap index and receives payments based on the return on a small-cap index.

There are numerous ways to structure an equity swap. The notional principal can be fixed or variable. The former would replicate the position of a portfolio that is rebalanced periodically so as to maintain the same dollar allocation to a particular asset class. The latter would reflect a portfolio that is not rebalanced and grows or recedes due to normal changes in the relative market values of the asset classes.

Equity swaps can also be structured so that they are based on specific industries or market sectors, or even individual stocks, though the latter is not common. An equity swap to synthetically sell a single common stock would be used primarily when an individual is highly exposed to the risk of that one stock and has no other way to reduce that risk. This situation occurs, for example, for an executive of a firm. The executive holds numerous shares of stock as well as options on the firm's stock. Some executives have resorted to entering into swaps with a swap dealer. The executive simply agrees to pay the swap dealer the return on the stock and any dividends. These payments can be done either quarterly or accumulated and paid at the end of the swap's life. The dealer agrees to pay the executive the return on another stock, an index, a fixed interest rate, or a floating interest rate. This arrangement accomplishes the objective of removing the exposure to the stock while maintaining legal ownership of the stock, thereby preserving the executive's voting rights and deferring the taxes. It might appear that the executive could convert an accumulated short-term capital gain to a long-term capital gain, but the Internal Revenue Service has closed that loophole.

Equity swaps are not used as widely as interest rate swaps, primarily because equity portfolio managers simply do not tend to use swaps as much as do fixed-income portfolio managers. This observation could primarily reflect the fact that swaps originated in the fixed-income and currency areas. While there remains considerable potential for growth in the use of equity swaps, these instruments have not been as widely used as other swaps.

FOR MORE READING

Chance, Don M., and Robert Brooks. *An Introduction to Derivatives and Risk Management*, 7th ed. Mason, OH: Thomson South-Western, 2007, chap. 14.

Hull, John C. *Options, Futures, and Other Derivatives*, 6th ed. Upper Saddle River, NJ: Prentice-Hall, 2006, chap. 30.

Jarrow, Robert A., and Stuart M. Turnbull. *Derivatives Securities*, 2nd ed. Mason, OH: Thomson South-Western, 2000, chap. 14.

TEST YOUR KNOWLEDGE

1. When an investor enters into an equity swap to pay the return on a stock or stock index, what form can the other payment take?
2. Explain how an equity swap involving a foreign stock index may or may not involve currency risk. Why would someone choose one structure over the other?
3. What purpose does a fixed or variable notional principal serve in an equity swap?

Equity-Linked Debt

Equity-linked debt is a security that is structured so as to pay off a fixed return, like a bond, plus a potentially greater return arising from the performance of an equity index. It offers the assurance of a bond but appeals to investors who also want to take a position on a specific movement in the stock market.

As a typical example, consider a two-year note promising a 2.5% return, paid completely at maturity (although interim payments could be structured). This note might also pay 50% of any increase in the Standard & Poor's (S&P) 500 over the life of the security. If the S&P decreases over the security's life, the holder receives no equity return but gets the guaranteed 2.5% fixed return. The actual equity payoff is normally determined as the percentage increase in the index multiplied by the participation rate, which is the percentage of the gain or loss that the holder will receive times the notional amount. For example, suppose at the start the S&P 500 is at 1,500.00. Let the holder receive 50% of any increase in the S&P 500 during the two years. The notional principal is $100,000. Suppose at maturity the S&P 500 is at 1,793.54. The holder receives $100,000(1.025)(1.025) = $105,062.50, the guaranteed interest plus return of principal. The percentage increase in the S&P 500 is (1,793.54 − 1,500)/1,500 = 0.1957. Thus, the holder also receives 0.5(0.1957)($100,000) = $9,785. If the S&P ended up at maturity at less than 1,500, the holder would receive only the $105,062.50.

To my knowledge, these securities first appeared around 1986 or 1987 under the name of market-index certificates of deposit (CDs). There were about 20 major banks offering these CDs at the retail level. They were thought to appeal to individual investors who were dissatisfied with the rates they were getting on CDs and who were missing out on a strong and prolonged bull market. The CDs were also marketed with the attractive feature that they were insured as in any other bank deposit, although the insurance covered only the guaranteed or fixed rate of interest and the principal. The equity return was not guaranteed. It was also possible to buy these CDs with a downside return. In other words, the holder could get the guaranteed return plus a certain percentage of any decrease in the S&P 500, but of course no equity return if the S&P increased. In either case, the security had only one-way risk, and it was thought that this feature would be particularly appealing to investors. As it turned out, however, the retail market just did not bite. To make matters worse, there was the stock market crash of October 19, 1987. That event pretty much killed the interest in market-index CDs, and not surprisingly, investor activity in CBOE call options on market indices decreased as well.

A new instrument surfaced a few years later, marketed primarily at the institutional level, and these appear to have been successful. They offer many attractive and unusual features. Some pay off based on the average of the index over a period of time. Others make interim payments just like a bond. Even some foreign governments got into the act. For example, the Republic of Austria raised some cash selling these securities with payoffs tied to the S&P 500. There are also securities tied to numerous foreign indices, such as the Nikkei, which can either pay off in the foreign currency or in the domestic currency at a fixed rate, meaning that the currency risk is hedged. It is quite easy to find instruments with downside equity returns so as to pay off in a bear market. It is also possible to have the equity payment be positive when the market goes up and negative when the market goes down.

Another reason that these instruments have been successful in the institutional market is that some firms can use them as debt instruments and get around restrictions on the holding of equities. This explains why many insurance companies hold equity-linked debt. They can hold these instruments, which qualify as bonds and yet give them equitylike returns. This feature exemplifies another reason why derivatives are popular, which is to get around regulations that do not account for the different ways in which instruments can be combined and structured to produce other instruments.

Decomposing these securities reveals that they are a combination of a bond and an option. Assuming that the guaranteed interest payment does not occur until maturity, the bond component is simply a zero-coupon bond. Letting the equity component be a fixed percentage of the increase in the S&P 500 means that it can be represented by a given number of European call options. If the payoff is on the downside, the underlying equity component is like a put option. If the payoff applies in both directions, the underlying equity component amounts to a forward contract on the index itself.

Pricing the issue correctly is very important to the seller of the instrument. There is no actual "price" in the traditional sense of a dollar amount. The "price" or value of the transaction is reflected in both the guaranteed interest payment and the participation rate with the higher the one, the lower the other. Option pricing theory can be used to compute the value of the implicit call or put. Various combinations of the guaranteed rate and participation rate will set the value of the combined fixed income and option components equal to the notional principal, which is the amount the investor pays at the start. The issuer must also take into account any hedging costs. Since the issuer is short an option, it will have to hedge by buying an option. The holder of the security should take into account the possibility of the issuer defaulting.

These instruments are available from many banks and dealers, and some have a liquid secondary market. The American Stock Exchange has been particularly active in this segment of the market. These instruments have also been quite popular in Europe and Asia, building a solid base of retail customers.

Variations of this instrument have arisen in the form of commodity-linked debt, but the equity-linked instruments have been more successful. Equity-linked debt is, in my view, one of the great innovations in the derivatives markets. Such instruments are generally quite simple and meet a variety of needs.

FOR MORE READING

Chance, Don M., and Robert Brooks. *An Introduction to Derivatives and Risk Management*, 7th ed. Mason, OH: Thomson South-Western, 2007, chap. 14.

Kat, Harry M. *Structured Equity Derivatives*. Chichester, UK: John Wiley & Sons, 2001, chaps. 1, 4, 9, 13.

McDonald, Robert L. *Derivative Markets*, 2nd ed. Boston: Addison Wesley, 2006, chap. 15.

TEST YOUR KNOWLEDGE

1. Describe how equity-linked debt is a form of debt and a form of equity.
2. Now describe how equity-linked debt is a form of debt and a form of an option.
3. How would an issue of equity-linked debt be hedged if the debt paid off a fixed rate plus any decrease in a market index?

Commodity Swaps

A commodity swap is an agreement between two parties in which each party promises to make a series of payments to the other—the standard definition of a swap—and in which at least one set of payments is determined by the price of a commodity. Though the payments could be made by delivering actual units of the commodity, the typical arrangement is that there is simply a cash payment determined by the commodity price.

Commodity swaps are quite common in the oil industry. Heavy users of oil, such as airlines, will often enter into contracts in which they agree to make fixed payments, say every six months for two years, and receive payments on those same dates determined by an oil price index. Computations would be based on a specific quantity of the oil. This arrangement locks in the price the airline pays for that quantity of oil, purchased at regular intervals over the two-year period. The airline will buy the actual oil it needs in the spot market.

This kind of hedge, while likely to be reasonably effective if properly designed, will still probably contain some basis risk. The exact type of oil the airline uses may not be represented perfectly by the oil price index on which the swap payments are made. More important, however, the quantities and the timing of its spot market purchases might not correspond to the swap payments. There is often considerable uncertainty as to the timing and amounts of a company's spot market purchases, so the hedge will often be far from ideal. But these considerations do not mean the company should not be hedging. On the contrary, hedging is likely to play a major role in keeping it alive in days of turbulent oil prices.

One interesting feature in commodity swaps is the manner in which the variable payment is calculated. In most standard interest rate, currency, and equity swaps, the variable payment is based on the price or rate on a specific day. In oil swaps, it is fairly common to base the variable payment on the average value of the oil index over a defined period of time. For example, let us say the next settlement date is August 15. Then the variable payment owed on August 15 might be based on the average of the daily index values for each business day from August 1 to August 14. This feature removes the effects of an unusually volatile single day and insures that the payment will more accurately represent the value of the index in the first half of August. High single-day volatility could arise from a number of sources, including the possibility of manipulation by a large institution, country, or trader. Such volatility—though not necessarily from manipulation—often characterizes markets dominated by a small number of large and powerful participants. Oil is one such market.

Another way in which the averaging could be done is over the entire period between settlements. The averaging could be done daily, weekly, monthly, or quarterly. This feature would ensure that the payment would be representative of an average price over the period. For an airline purchasing oil steadily over the entire period, this is often an acceptable, if not preferable, arrangement.

These average-price payoff structures are found in other derivatives, especially in options. They are called *Asian options*, a topic we cover in Essay 48. It is not widely known, but the Chicago Board of Trade's federal funds futures contract is based on the average of the federal funds rate over the last month of the contract's life, giving it an Asian-style payoff.

You might reasonably wonder why standard forward or futures hedges would not be preferable. Without rehashing the debate over which is preferable, let us simply note that swaps are equivalent to a series of forward contracts that each have the same fixed price. The swap structure could be far more efficient than a package of individual contracts. Also, as it can be difficult to determine which futures settlement dates to use, an average-price commodity swap can serve to hedge reasonably well at possibly lower cost, delivering at settlement a price that is representative of the price of the commodity over the life of the contract.

FOR MORE READING

Chance, Don M., and Robert Brooks. *An Introduction to Derivatives and Risk Management*, 7th ed. Mason, OH: Thomson South-Western, 2007, chap. 12.

McDonald, Robert L. *Derivative Markets*, 2nd ed. Boston: Addison Wesley, 2006, chap. 8.

TEST YOUR KNOWLEDGE

1. Why are average price swaps often used in oil markets?
2. Identify two types of derivatives other than commodity swaps in which the payoff is based on an average price or rate.

American versus European Options

A European option can be exercised only at expiration. An American option can be exercised any day prior to expiration.[1] Thus, an American option is a European option with the additional right to exercise it any time prior to expiration. This feature naturally raises the interesting question of whether this right is worth something and, if so, how much. In what follows, I shall ignore taxes, transaction costs, market liquidity, and the possibility that investors might be irrational. I shall use options on stock as the example.

It turns out that for call options, the right to exercise early can be quite trivial. If there are no dividends on the underlying stock, then there is no reason to exercise an American call early. The call could never sell for less than the exercise value. For most people who hear this statement for the first time, it sounds impossible to believe. The tendency is to think that a call that is deep in-the-money on a non-dividend-paying stock that is not expected to go any higher should be exercised. But exercise is simply not the best thing to do. If you are not optimistic on the stock, there is no reason to hurry up and exchange the option for the stock. You would not be any happier holding a stock that is going nowhere, and to make matters worse, you would be out the interest on the money spent to buy the stock with the option.

The reason the call will always sell for no less than its exercise value is that regardless of how high the stock is, it can always go higher. An exercised call is a dead call, and the investor can benefit no further from leveraging the stock price increases; nor can she benefit from the downside protection of the call.

If you are still not convinced, consider this example of a call with a strike of $100. Let us say you are at expiration and the stock is worth more than

---

[1] As I noted in Essay 5, these names have nothing to do with America and Europe.

$100. If you had not exercised it early, you would exercise it now, paying $100 and acquiring the stock. If you had exercised it early, you would now be holding the same stock, but you paid out the $100 to acquire it at an earlier date and you would be out the interest on $100 from the day you exercised it until today.

In the alternative outcome where the stock is worth less than $100, consider what would happen. If you had not previously exercised it, you would now let it expire. If you had previously exercised it, you would be holding a stock worth whatever its price is today plus you would have paid out $100 earlier and would be out the interest on the $100. If the current price of the stock is less than $100, then the current price of the stock is definitely less than $100 plus the interest you have lost. So in either case, you are worse off having exercised the call early. In short, why pay the exercise price early? When you get to expiration, you will be absolutely no better off. It is like paying a bill early and throwing away the right to decide whether you actually want to keep the merchandise.

Not exercising early does not mean that you should do nothing before expiration. An option on a stock that you expect to go no further should be sold or offset.

If, however, there are dividends on the stock, it might pay to exercise the call early. Exercising it early would leave you in the same position as in the preceding example, but now you would also have a dividend plus the interest on it, which could be enough to make up the difference. You never exercise early to capture the dividend except at the last instant before the stock goes ex-dividend. Otherwise, you are paying the exercise price out earlier than necessary. In short, the known stock price drop that occurs at the ex-dividend date can be avoided by exercising early. This does not mean that you always exercise early at the ex-dividend instant. Whether to exercise early is determined by, among other things, how large the dividend is and how much time remains or, more specifically, how much time value remains in the option's price. Exercising throws away the time value component of the option's price.

Of course, in practice, there could be other reasons for exercising early. Some large institutions with deep-in-the-money calls could choose to exercise early rather than take a large illiquid transaction to the floor where the trade will tell others about their position or result in a decline in the price. Also, the transaction cost of exercising an index option early can be lower than the cost of liquidating the options. Call options granted to employees and executives that cannot be sold or offset with a short sale of the stock might reasonably be exercised early.

American puts on stocks without dividends always have some possibility of being exercised early. For example, suppose you owned an American put on a stock that went bankrupt. By bankrupt, I mean that the company is dead and will not come back to life. Thus, I am ruling out a reorganization of the company or restructuring of its debts. Consequently the stock is worth zero. In that case, you are holding an option to sell the stock for the exercise price, and there is absolutely nothing gained by waiting until expiration to exercise it. The bankruptcy case is one obvious situation, but bankruptcy is not required to justify early exercise. Let us look at a more likely case.

Suppose you are holding an American put at expiration. The exercise price is $100. Let the stock be worth less than $100. You exercise the put and pick up the difference between the stock price and $100. Had you exercised it early, you would be better off because you would have gotten the $100 earlier and could have picked up the interest on it. You could have shorted the stock at that time and covered the short position at expiration. In other words, if you had known the put would end up in-the-money, you would have been better off to have exercised it early.

Suppose the put ends up out-of-the-money. Had you exercised it early, you would have picked up the $100 early, invested it to earn some interest, and you could have shorted the stock at whatever its price was at that time. Now at expiration you cover the short position. If the stock price now at expiration exceeds the exercise price plus the interest you earned on it, you would end up with a deficiency and you would wish you had not exercised it early. Thus, if the stock price ends up above the exercise price, it is possible that you would have been better off exercising early, but it is also possible that you would have been better off waiting. As noted, if the stock ends up below the exercise price, you would definitely be better off having exercised early. Of course, all of this is after the fact and proves only one thing: You could conceivably be better off exercising early.

Finding out exactly when to exercise early is a difficult task and can be accurately computed only with an American put option pricing model or procedure like the binomial model, which we cover in Essay 28. Some approximation methods, however, are available. It is easy to say that you exercise when the market price is driven to the exercise value, but then you are just following the market, which had to have used an option pricing model to establish that the current market price is the exercise value.

Dividends complicate things quite a bit. When a company pays a dividend, it helps put option holders because it works to constrain the stock's growth. Consequently, early exercise is less likely to occur the higher the dividend. When early exercise is justified, it will nearly always be the case that exercise should occur immediately *after* the stock goes ex-dividend. That is, if you are going to exercise the put early, you might as well do it after the stock price drops. Again, an option pricing model is necessary to tell you the optimal time to exercise early.

The exact manner in which the right to exercise early is factored into the option's price is taken up in Essays 35 and 36.

FOR MORE READING

Hull, John C. *Options, Futures, and Other Derivatives*, 6th ed. Upper Saddle River, NJ: Prentice-Hall, 2006, chaps. 9, 11.

Jarrow, Robert A., and Andrew Rudd. *Option Pricing*. Homewood, IL: Irwin, 1983, chaps. 5, 6.

Jarrow, Robert A., and Stuart M. Turnbull. *Derivatives Securities*, 2nd ed. Mason, OH: Thomson South-Western, 2000, chap. 7.

McDonald, Robert L. *Derivative Markets*, 2nd ed. Boston: Addison Wesley, 2006, chaps. 9, 10, 12.

TEST YOUR KNOWLEDGE

1. Why would you not exercise an American call early when there are no dividends on the stock and you believe the stock has reached its maximum price?
2. Why does a dividend make an American call potentially attractive for early exercise?
3. What makes an American put (assume no dividends) attractive for early exercise in contrast to an American call?
4. Why do dividends make American puts less attractive for early exercise?

Swaptions

Just as there are options on various assets, so too are there options on various derivatives. When the underlying is a swap, the option is called a swap option or *swaption*.

Because it is an option, the swaption has all of the traditional optionlike features. It grants the right to buy or sell an underlying instrument, which in this case is a specific swap, at a fixed price or rate, for a period of time. The buyer of the swaption pays the seller a premium and obtains the right to enter into the underlying swap. A swaption has the characteristics of either a call or a put.

When the underlying is an interest rate swap, the swaption grants the right to enter the swap as either a fixed-rate payer, floating-rate receiver or a fixed-rate receiver, floating-rate payer. The underlying swap has a specific maturity. For example, consider a firm that purchases a swaption expiring in one year that grants it the right to enter into a three-year pay-fixed, receive-floating swap at a rate of 10.5%. The swaption must be specified as either European, meaning it can be exercised only at expiration, or American, meaning that it can be exercised at any time up to expiration. A swaption granting the right to pay a fixed rate is called a *payer swaption*, while a swaption granting the right to receive a fixed rate is called a *receiver swaption*. Payer (receiver) swaptions are also sometimes referred to as put (call) swaptions, since they are purchased when interest rates are expected to go up (down) and bond prices are expected to go down (up).

At the expiration date, the holder of the swaption makes an exercise decision based on the current rate for the swap on which the option is written. Using our example, suppose at expiration the market rate on three-year swaps is 10.9%. We shall assume that this is the rate that a dealer offers to pay. In other words, any qualifying firm can go into the market and enter into a three-year swap, paying a floating rate and receiving a fixed rate of 10.9%. This result is independent of the existence of the swaption; it is simply the rate on the underlying instrument—a three-year swap—at expiration. In this case, the holder of the payer swaption will definitely exercise it. The swaption gives the holder the right to enter a three-year swap paying a fixed rate of 10.5% and receiving LIBOR (London Interbank Offer Rate), while that same swap could be obtained in the market by receiving a fixed rate of 10.9% and paying LIBOR. Upon exercise, however, there are several things the firm could do.

If it truly wanted to enter into the swap at that date, it could simply hold the swap on its books. It would then mark it to market at that point and show it as an asset. In Essay 64 we show how swaptions are priced. Alternatively, if the firm did not necessarily need the swap, it could enter into a new three-year pay-floating, receive-fixed swap at the market rate of 10.9%. The firm would then hold two swaps, one paying 10.5% fixed and receiving LIBOR and the other receiving 10.9% fixed and paying LIBOR. The LIBOR payments offset, leaving the firm with a three-year annuity of 0.4%. If the swaption were written by the dealer with which it took out the new swap, the firm could probably arrange for both swaps to cancel or offset, and the value of the swap at that point, the present value of a three-year annuity of 0.4%, would be paid to it as a lump sum. If both swaps remain alive, the attendant credit risk of both swaps remains. Some swaptions can be structured so as to settle automatically at expiration in cash.

A payer swaption is like a call option on an interest rate. Recall from Essay 8 that an interest rate call is the right to make a fixed interest payment and receive a floating interest payment. The only difference is that an exercised interest rate call normally results in only one interest payment. A combination of interest rate calls, which is a cap, is somewhat similar to a swaption but still has some differences. A cap is a combination of calls with the same strike in which an independent exercise decision is made at each of the expiration dates of the component options. A swaption permits exercise at only one date. Exercise combined with the creation of an offsetting swap at the market rate creates a series of fixed payments and receipts, with each equal receipt larger than each equal payment. Thus, while there are technical differences in the streams of cash flows between a payer swaption and an interest rate call, the concepts are still quite similar. Both grant the right to make a fixed (or series of fixed) payment(s) and receive a floating (or series of floating) payment(s). This comparison is most helpful in remembering what a fixed-pay swaption is really like and when it is exercised, namely when interest rates go up sufficiently by expiration.

A receiver swaption is like an interest rate put because it will be exercised when rates go down by a sufficient amount. The principles discussed earlier for payer swaptions apply with obvious changes to the terminology for receiver swaptions. Many people, however, liken swaptions to options on bonds. While we said that a payer swaption is like a call on an interest rate, we must note that it is like a put on a bond. Rising interest rates will result in exercise. Likewise, a receiver swaption is like a call on a bond. Falling interest rates are necessary to induce exercise. Some people prefer the bond analogy because an option on a bond when exercised results in the purchase of the bond and thereby the generation of a stream of fixed payments. A swaption, however, does not result in the lump-sum payment of the price of the bond at the start, nor is the face value repaid at maturity. It generates only a series of net interest payments.

If the swaption is American style, it is quite possible that it will be exercised early. The decision to exercise early is not simple, however, and is much like the decision of when to exercise an American put. An analytical model is needed to determine whether the swaption should be exercised early. We cover this topic in Essay 64. Other exotic features, such as barriers, lookback provisions, Asian-style settlements, and the like, can be easily incorporated into the swap terms, but these magnify the pricing complexity.

Swaptions have a variety of applications. The obvious one is pure speculation on interest rates. The swaption is a leveraged play on interest rates at a particular point in the future. There are a number of ways to make such a play, and a swaption is not necessarily the best way. But this is the same question as whether a futures or forward is better than the other or whether long a call and short a put is better than a forward. We could argue all day about the merits of equivalent or roughly equivalent derivative combinations without getting anywhere. The coexistence of numerous similar derivatives is proof that certain instruments better fit the needs of some users and certain instruments better fit the needs of others.

Beyond speculation, it is not hard to visualize why a firm might want to buy a swaption. It is necessary only to remember why a firm might want to enter into a swap. For whatever reason, suppose a firm feels that it will need to enter into a pay-fixed swap at a future date. It worries that interest rates will rise. It might be willing to pay a premium to lock in the maximum rate it will pay in the future. If it thinks it will need to engage in a receive-fixed swap, it may be worried that rates will fall so it might be willing to pay a premium to lock in the minimum rate it will receive.

It should also be noted that a firm might wish to buy a swaption to give it some flexibility to terminate a swap already held. For example, suppose a firm engages in a 10-year swap but believes that it might need to terminate the swap after 4 years. Let the swap be a pay-fixed swap. Then the firm might purchase a receiver swaption on a 6-year swap that expires in 4 years.

The swaption would allow the firm to do an offsetting 6-year swap in 4 years at a rate known today. It might also be able to structure the swaption so that exercise cancels the original swap. It is also easy to see here the potential benefit of an American swaption. The firm might have no idea when during the original swap's 10-year life it might like to cancel it. The American swaption would give it that right, but, of course, it would be more expensive than its European counterpart.

Some investors also use swaptions in conjunction with callable bonds to obtain a seemingly better rate. For example, a callable bond is a combination of a noncallable bond and a written call option on the bond in which the issuer has the right to exercise. The issuer of the callable bond might sell a receiver swaption, which as noted is similar to a call on a bond. If the bond is called, the receiver swaption presumably gets exercised on the firm, which then enters into an offsetting swap in the market. The net effect is that the new lower interest payments are increased to leave the firm approximately back where it was, paying the higher interest rate before the call, but having earned the option premium up front to offset the higher rate it had to pay for issuing a callable bond. It has effectively converted the callable bond into a noncallable bond and could get a more attractive rate this way. Of course, such a swaption should be American style so that it is exercised whenever the issuer calls the bond. A similar procedure, buying a receiver swaption, can be used when a firm wishes to convert a noncallable bond to a callable bond. The timing of the swaption exercise is not perfectly matched, however, with the calling of the bond, so this strategy is somewhat imprecise.

Swaptions also exist on other underlyings such as currencies, commodities, and equities, but these markets are much smaller than that for interest rates.

Since there are options on swaps, it is not surprising that there are other derivatives on swaps. Forward swaps contractually obligate two parties to engage in a swap at a future date at a rate they agree on today. The futures exchanges have offered futures on swaps, but the market for these instruments has not developed much depth.

In Essay 64 we look at how swaptions are priced using a binomial structure tree.

FOR MORE READING

Chance, Don M., and Robert Brooks. *An Introduction to Derivatives and Risk Management*, 7th ed. Mason, OH: Thomson South-Western, 2007, chap. 13.

Neftci, Salih N. *Principles of Financial Engineering*. San Diego: Elsevier Academic Press, 2004, chap. 18.

TEST YOUR KNOWLEDGE

1. Explain what happens when a payer swaption is exercised and offset.
2. How is a swaption like an interest rate cap or floor, and how is it different?
3. Why might a company use a swaption, other than to speculate on interest rates?

Credit Derivatives

For all over-the-counter instruments, there is reason to be concerned that a counterparty will default. Indeed, default could be the oldest risk that humans have ever attempted to manage. This essay takes a look at a relatively new family of derivatives designed to reduce if not eliminate the credit risk: credit derivatives. The market for credit derivatives is rapidly growing, and rightly so. These instruments strip the credit risk off a loan or derivative and trade it separately.

Actually, instruments of this sort have existed prior to now in the form of credit insurance, but these policies have had a somewhat limited market and have been very specialized. Moreover, any product called "insurance" automatically falls under a heavy umbrella of regulation in the United States. Each state regulates the insurance industry, and political battles and red tape are rampant. Calling these new instruments credit derivatives avoids these problems.

Consider an ordinary bond issued by a party that could default. Regardless of how low that probability of default may be, the holder of the bond is taking a position based on interest rate movements and changes in the credit quality of the issuer. A derivative tied to the credit quality of the issuer can be constructed and would allow the lender to execute a hedge on the credit risk, holding on to only the interest rate risk. Likewise, a party so desiring could speculate on a borrower's credit risk without the interest rate risk. It may seem like no one would want to do so, but obviously those who hold low-grade bonds are doing so already. A credit derivative would allow them to speculate only on the credit risk without worrying about the interest rate risk.

Like any derivative, a credit derivative must have a well-defined payoff. It can be based on a specific credit event, such as a default. Other possible credit events are bankruptcy, a specified price or yield change in the issuer's debt, or a downgrade by one of the credit-rating companies. In the case of a default, a reference asset, such as a particular bond of the issuer, would be priced a specified period after the default. Any loss in value from the default date until the pricing date then becomes the "value of the underlying" and is used to determine the credit derivative payoff. Like all other derivatives, credit derivatives can take the form of forwards, swaps, or options. Interestingly, however, it is possible to construct a credit derivative with just a slight modification of a plain vanilla swap.

Suppose a party held the bonds of company A and wished to maintain only the interest rate risk while eliminating the credit risk. The party could arrange a *total return swap*, in which it agrees to pay a dealer all of the price changes and the interest on the reference bond. The dealer would pay it a fixed or floating rate, the latter usually based on LIBOR (London Interbank Offer Rate). Since any credit problems would be reflected in the price changes, any change in value due to credit quality, would be passed on to the dealer. In turn, the party holding the bond would receive payments based on market-determined interest rate movements that would be uninfluenced by the credit of the reference bond. This is a very simple transaction, differing only slightly from a standard swap.[1]

The most widely used credit derivative is the *credit default swap* (CDS). This instrument is identified as a swap, but it more closely resembles a simple insurance policy. Of course, the reason for that is, as mentioned earlier, calling something "insurance" is asking for a heavy dose of regulation, but calling it a credit derivative renders it a transaction that needs only to conform to standard commercial law.

Anyway, a CDS is a transaction in which one party, the credit protection buyer, agrees to make a series of annual payments to the other, the credit protection seller. If the underlying credit event occurs, the credit protection seller pays the credit protection buyer an amount to compensate for the credit loss. For example, if the underlying credit event is a default on a bond, the credit protection buyer will usually tender the bond to the credit protection seller and be paid par value. Thus, as noted, this instrument is much like insurance. The annual payments are analogous to the insurance premium. In the event of a loss, the credit protection seller, acting just like a traditional insurer, compensates the credit protection buyer. Some CDSs provide for a cash settlement rather than a tendering of the underlying, and there are a handful of other variations. Credit default swaps have proven to be tremendously successful, indeed the most successful of all credit derivatives, and rightly so. They use a relatively simple instrument—the swap—to strip off the credit risk and do so without layer after layer of regulations.

---

[1] As noted, a total return swap pays the total return, consisting of price changes and interest. A slight variation is an asset swap, which pays only the interest and then at expiration pays the principal.

Two other forms of credit derivatives do exist. The credit spread option is an option in which the underlying is the yield spread on a bond that is subject to default. The yield spread is the difference between the yield on the bond and the rate on a default-free security, such as a U.S. Treasury note. The spread reflects a handful of factors but mostly credit risk. The spread widens as investors perceive greater credit risk. Hence, you can purchase or sell puts and calls in which the underlying is the credit spread.

The last form of credit derivative is the credit-linked note. This instrument is a promissory note issued by one party in which repayment of the principal is contingent on the repayment of a debt by another party. For example, let us say that Party A issues such a note to Party B, contingent on the credit of Party C. Party C has a particular obligation due on or before the obligation of Party A to Party B. If Party C defaults, Party A can legally and without any consequences reduce the principal payment it owes to Party B. Hence, Party B is lending money to Party A but accepting the credit risk of Party C.

Note that the parties to the credit derivative contract are not the ones whose underlying credit is of concern; however, there is credit risk in the credit derivative contract itself, arising from the possibility that the counterparty required to pay off based on the credit of a third party could itself default. In most cases such risk would be very low, because two independent defaults would have to occur for there to be a credit loss.

Pricing credit derivatives should theoretically be based on the standard rules for pricing other derivatives but where the "underlying" is modeled as the stochastic process driving the party's credit risk. The rule of no arbitrage applies as usual, but the pricing procedure is more problematic than pricing market risk. Modeling credit risk is much more difficult, starting with the fact that the normal probability distribution does not apply to credit risk. It is difficult to assess the possibility of a credit loss, primarily—and fortunately—because credit events are not very common. There are literally thousands of companies in the market that have never defaulted, and yet you cannot assume that the probability of any of them defaulting is zero. Default for a given party typically occurs only once. This problem makes it difficult to observe and gain experience with the credit risk of a particular company.

Pricing credit risk, however, has made great strides due to the Black-Scholes-Merton model, which we cover in Essay 27. That model provides a framework for viewing default as an option held by the stockholders and granted by the creditors. As such, the stock price will behave to reflect the value of that option. One company, KMV Corporation, took this concept and applied it to build a credit risk model. The KMV model uses the prices of publicly traded stocks to deduce the likelihoods of default and the appropriate credit risk premiums. Judging by its widespread use and the sale of the company to Moody's, the model has been highly successful. The ideas behind this model are covered in Essay 67.

Other methodologies for measuring and managing credit risk have been developed by Credit Suisse First Boston and RiskMetrics. Suffice it to say that the information and techniques for measuring and managing credit risk have accelerated in recent years and have helped fuel the enormous success of the credit derivatives market.

It would seem that anyone entering into a transaction with a party whose credit risk is of concern might be interested in using credit derivatives. These, however, are not the main users. Banks often purchase credit derivatives for the purpose of reducing their credit exposure to segments of the market. Credit derivatives based on sovereign debt are among the most popular for obvious reasons. The opposite party is betting on the creditworthiness of another party. Anyone wishing to take such a position can do so with this kind of instrument. The opposite side is often taken by parties wanting exposure for brief periods in markets where traditional cash market securities do not exist. Oftentimes these parties are hedge funds or other speculators.

Credit derivatives, being customized to the credit risk of a particular borrower or group of borrowers, are likely to be relatively more expensive than are most derivatives. This is because derivatives on market risks are typically tied to an index or commodity, whose risk is much more generic and widely faced. In contrast, a credit derivative is based on the credit risk of one specific borrower or group of borrowers; thus, there is not likely to be a large market for an instrument in which the risk is so narrow and specific. Some companies have created indices of the premiums on credit default swaps. These indices have also been constructed as tradable portfolios, thereby creating some standardized combinations of credit derivatives for trading.

Credit is one of the oldest forms of risk. The ability to trade risk is what risk management is all about. Credit derivatives, though still new and quite complex, are an increasingly popular tool for transferring the credit risk from one party to another.

FOR MORE READING

Anson, Mark J. P., Frank J. Fabozzi, Moorad Choudhry, and Ren-Raw Chen. *Credit Derivatives: Instruments, Applications, and Pricing.* New York: John Wiley & Sons, 2000.

Das, Satyajit. "Credit Derivatives." *The Journal of Derivatives* 2 (Spring 1995): 7–23.

Das, Satyajit. *Credit Derivatives and Credit Linked Notes.* New York: John Wiley & Sons, 2000.

Howard, Kerrin. "An Introduction to Credit Derivatives." *Derivatives Quarterly* 2 (Winter 1995): 28–37,

Jarrow, Robert A., and Stuart M. Turnbull. *Derivatives Securities*, 2nd ed. Mason, OH: Thomson South-Western, 2000, chap. 18.

McDonald, Robert L. *Derivative Markets*, 2nd ed. Boston: Addison Wesley, 2006, chap. 21.

Neal, Rob S. "Credit Derivatives: New Financial Instruments for Controlling Credit Risk." *Federal Reserve Bank of Kansas City Economic Review* 91 (2nd quarter 1996): 15–27.

Neftci, Salih N. *Principles of Financial Engineering*. San Diego: Elsevier Academic Press, 2004, chap. 18.

Smithson, Charles with Hal Holappa. "Credit Derivatives (1)." *Risk* 8 (December 1995): 38–39.

Smithson, Charles with Hal Holappa and Shaun Rai. "Credit Derivatives (2)." *Risk* 9 (June 1996): 47–48.

Stulz, René. *Risk Management and Derivatives*. Mason, OH: Thomson South-Western, 2003, chap. 18.

TEST YOUR KNOWLEDGE

1. For what purpose do credit derivatives exist?
2. Identify and explain the most widely used type of credit derivative.
3. Why is pricing credit derivatives difficult, at least in comparison to pricing derivatives based on market risk?

Volatility Derivatives

We will come to learn in later essays that volatility is a critical factor in pricing options. All else being equal, a more volatile asset will have more expensive options. Greater volatility gives the option more potential to gain. Of course, greater volatility also opens up the possibility of more large undesirable moves in the underlying. But with options, the loss is limited, so the impact of volatility is beneficial for the holder of the option.

Because volatility affects the value of an option, it is one of the factors that must be incorporated into the process of valuing the option. Assigning a value to an option is a matter of inserting these variables—volatility being one of them—into a formula. If there is any doubt about the inputs that go into the formula, there is some risk simply from using the formula.[1] But even if volatility can be measured accurately, there is a risk associated with the possibility that the volatility will change.

A veteran trader of options on commodity futures once told me that one of his biggest concerns in trading was the fact that volatility would be greater around the harvest date of the commodity, and he did not know how to incorporate that factor into his pricing. Now, if you know what the future volatility would be, then the volatility is variable but not random. That problem is not hard to solve. You can incorporate it into a binomial tree, which is a model that we cover later. But more often than not, you do not really know what the future volatility will be, any more than you know the future value of the underlying.

That conversation with the trader was my first exposure to the concept of volatility risk, and I spent some time trying to figure out how to help him. I quickly realized that volatility risk was not going to be an easy factor to get your hands around. Little did I know that the derivatives industry would take on volatility risk in a big way a decade or so later, and it would struggle with the concept too.

---

[1] Experts refer to this risk as *model* risk.

Volatility is a quantifiable factor and is usually captured by the standard deviation. Standard deviations can be measured by inferring their values through the prices of options, a topic we take up in a Essay 34, or by statistically estimating it over a period of time using observed prices of the underlying. Whenever something is quantifiable, it lends itself to research and analysis. A lot of quantitatively oriented people have invested a great deal of time into getting a handle on the notion of random volatility. Unfortunately, the progress to date is not impressive, at least not to me. But let us see what we do know.

As a prelude to what we shall cover later, consider that option value is a function of volatility, time to expiration, the price of the underlying, the exercise price, and the risk-free rate. An option valuation model typically assumes that only the price of the underlying and time can change. The risk associated with the price of the underlying is usually eliminated through hedging by holding a position in the underlying. Time itself, while constantly changing, poses no problems in option pricing, because time is not probabilistic. An option with 30 days to expiration today will—with 100% certainty—be an option with 29 days to expiration tomorrow. Hence, the effects of the only two changing variables, time and the underlying, are either unimportant or can be neutralized. While interest rates do change, the effect is fairly small, so it poses no major problems. Except for certain types of exotic options that we will cover later, the exercise price does not change. Volatility is the only remaining variable, and it is a critical one. Option prices are highly sensitive to volatility, and volatility is the only variable that is not directly observable. Thus, the estimate of volatility we insert into the model itself can be wrong. When we add the fact that volatility can change in a random manner, we have more problems than Jack Bauer can solve in 24 hours.[2]

Since the Jack Bauer problem-solving techniques would not lead to an answer,[3] we must address the question of how to neutralize the volatility risk. One method is to trade another instrument whose price is driven by the same volatility. For an option, we could simply use another option on the same underlying to hedge the risk. This approach could lead to a formula for pricing and hedging the option when volatility is random, but it would enable us only to price the option relative to the other option. Thus, we would have to know one option price in order to know the other. Pricing an option off of another option is a most unsatisfactory approach. How can

---

[2] Well, OK, I should back off on that. The number of problems Jack Bauer can solve in 24 hours is ∞.

[3] Torture would not be particularly helpful to us here.

we call it an option valuation model if we already have to know the values of other options? We want to be able to price the option relative to the underlying. To truly solve this problem, we have to have either one of two things: the risk premium associated with volatility or the ability to hedge volatility with another instrument. The first is an important issue in a whole different branch of financial economics, but there are no simple answers and the controversy is quite heated. We'll return to the second later. It is, of course, why volatility derivatives were invented.

If volatility changes in a known manner, we can, of course, insert the new volatility into the formula and obtain a new option price. But to do so is to violate the model's assumptions. And if volatility is one value now and likely to be some unknown value later, well, that's the Jack Bauer problem. We have no idea how to incorporate this effect into the model. There are some models that incorporate changing volatility, called *stochastic volatility*, finessing it by either implying the volatility risk premium from other instruments or assuming that the volatility risk premium is zero. These approaches lead to fancy models, but in all honesty, these models have been of much more use to their academic authors in writing equation-laden articles and getting tenure than in actually solving a real-world problem.

Thus, changing volatility poses a special *risk* to users of options. Note the operative word: risk. For where there is risk, there is usually an opportunity to trade and manage that risk. As such, financial institutions have created derivative products based on volatility itself. For in principle, any factor that can be measured fairly objectively can be traded. Consider a stock in which the volatility is currently 30%. You could create an option on the volatility of that stock. Assume a call option expiring in three months in which the underlying is the realized annualized standard deviation of the daily return on the stock over that time period. Let the buyer choose an exercise rate of 35%. When the option expires, the realized standard deviation over the life of the instrument is computed. Let us say it is 37%. Then the option expires in-the-money (37% is more than 35%). The call holder exercises, receiving a cash payment of 2% times some underlying notional chosen when the contract is created. If the realized volatility is 35%, the call expires out-of-the-money. In a similar manner, you could create swaps and forward contracts.

Exchange-traded derivatives on volatility have also appeared. In 1993 the Chicago Board Options Exchange (CBOE) in conjunction with Professor Robert Whaley of Duke University created an index of the implied volatility of options on the Standard & Poor's 500. This index came to be called the VIX (for "Volatility Index"). In 2004 the CBOE launched a futures contract on the VIX, and in 2006 options on the VIX were introduced. Since that time, more indices on volatility have been traded. The contracts have not been hugely successful, although the options have done much better than the futures and appear to have long-term viability.

Nonetheless, volatility derivatives have not solved the problem of managing volatility risk. They have merely transferred the problem to dealers who are better equipped to manage it. But because changing volatility is so difficult to build into option models, pricing and hedging these instruments is quite challenging for even sophisticated dealers. Their counterparties should thus be aware that the prices offered in the market are unlikely to be very attractive. These prices will reflect the complexity of these instruments and the difficulty for the dealers of pricing and hedging. Of course, there is nothing wrong with that. If a particular surgery is difficult, the surgeon should charge a premium.

Lest I appear to be critical of volatility derivatives, I would like to end on a more positive note. Volatility derivatives are one of the more creative innovations to come out of the derivatives world in the last 10 years. They attempt to solve what is clearly a serious problem, how to manage the risk of volatility. That they have not fully succeeded is not a reason to throw the baby out with the bathwater. More research is needed; hopefully someday these instruments will be easier to price and hedge.

FOR MORE READING

Demeterfi, Kresimir, Emanuel Derman, Michael Kamal, and Joseph Zou. "A Guide to Volatility and Variance Swaps." *The Journal of Derivatives* 6 (Summer 1999): 9–32.

Detemple, Jérôme, and Carlton Osakwe. "The Valuation of Volatility Options." *European Finance Review* 4 (2000): 21–50.

Grunbichler, Andreas, and Francis A. Longstaff. "Valuing Futures and Options on Volatility." *Journal of Banking and Finance* 20 (1996): 985–1001.

Neftci, Salih N. *Principles of Financial Engineering*. San Diego: Elsevier Academic Press, 2004, chap. 14.

Whaley, Robert E. "Derivatives on Market Volatility: Hedging Tools Long Overdue." *The Journal of Derivatives* 1 (Fall 1993): 71–84.

TEST YOUR KNOWLEDGE

1. If you were asked to describe the concept of the "volatility of volatility," what would you say?
2. How are volatility derivatives constructed to pay off?
3. What is the VIX?

Weather and Environmental Derivatives

As you probably know by now, the study of derivatives entails understanding risk. We have covered a lot of different types of risks, the main ones being market risk arising from interest rates, exchange rates, commodity prices, and stock prices, and also credit risk, which of course is when someone fails to pay what is owed. We also discussed volatility risk wherein one of the important parameters of option valuation is itself uncertain. In this essay we introduce derivatives on one of the most interesting and important sources of risk: the weather.

It is not difficult to think of the types of businesses that benefit or are hurt by the weather. Even a child's lemonade stand benefits from hot weather while the kid with the snow shovel offering to clear off your driveway benefits from heavy snowfall. On a more professional level, we can imagine beer and soda companies benefiting from hot weather and companies that sell hot chocolate and cocoa benefiting from cold weather. Ski resorts, vacation properties, the travel industry, and clothing manufacturers are good examples of companies whose business is partially and in some cases primarily driven by the weather. On a larger scale, public utilities and airlines are heavily influenced by the weather. Although all of these risks could be thought of as essentially market risks, the notion of weather as a source of risk aims to connect the risk with its fundamental origin, which can facilitate managing that risk. The derivatives industry has recognized the importance of weather by creating a class of products known as *weather derivatives*.

Weather is an excellent variable on which risk can be measured. Weather is typically a highly quantifiable variable. In fact, we are inundated with information on weather, and virtually every adult and many children have a modest understanding of it. Statistical information is abundant, and lengthy series of historical data exist on temperatures and precipitation for localities all over the world. With the advent of such sites as www.weather.com and weather.yahoo.com, it is a simple task to obtain qualitative and quantitative information on weather anywhere on the planet. Insurance companies, which have provided policies against weather-related damage for a long time, have extensive information about the historical consequences of severe weather. As such, it is easy to identify weather as a source of risk, and therefore, it ought to be feasible to create a derivative that pays off based on some measure of weather.

Let us take one common measure of weather: the temperature. The derivatives industry uses temperature as the underlying of various contracts by means of two related concepts: the *heating degree-day* and the *cooling degree-day*. A heating degree-day is the number of degrees the average temperature in a given day is below 65 degrees Fahrenheit. A cooling-degree day is the number of degrees the average temperature in a given day is above 65. If the average temperature in a day is 63 degrees, the weather is measured as two heating degree-days. If the average temperature in a day is 67 degrees, the measure is two cooling degree-days. A heating-degree day is, thus, a rough proxy for the necessity to provide heat to obtain a comfortable temperature, while a cooling degree-day is a rough proxy for the necessity to provide coolness to obtain a comfortable temperature. Of course, further details are necessary to define how the average daily temperature is measured, but there are industry standards.

The notion of a heating or cooling degree-day provides a reasonable underlying for weather derivative contracts. Consider one six-month call option on cooling degree-days. Let us say the buyer expects that the average temperature over the next month (assume 30 days) will be 72 degrees, which is 7 cooling degree-days on average. Then as a rough choice for the exercise price, the buyer chooses $30*7 = 210$. The buyer pays the premium and receives a call option that will pay at expiration a certain amount of money, call it m, for every cooling degree-day over 210. If the total number of cooling degree-days is less than 210, the option expires out-of-the-money. If the buyer is interested in benefiting from lower-than-expected temperatures, she would buy a put on heating degree-days and benefit if the number of heating degree days is lower than the chosen strike.

Of course, determining m is the really difficult part. The option buyer needs to know what financial loss she expects on her business for each degree above 65 is the average temperature. These estimates, however, should be fairly well understood by anyone in business. Indeed, the child with the lemonade stand probably knows to make a few more quarts of lemonade on those hot days and a few less on cooler ones.

Other forms of weather derivatives have been created on such measures as rainfall and snowfall. Dealers that make these markets typically have an expertise in these markets. Often this expertise is purchased by buying another company or by hiring personnel, such as weather experts.

While most weather derivatives contracts are over the counter, exchange-traded weather derivatives have existed since the first ones were launched in 1999 at the Chicago Mercantile Exchange (CME). These futures and options on futures are based on average temperatures in 18 U.S. and 15 non-U.S. cities. The CME has also offered futures and options on futures on an index of hurricane intensity, the number of days of frost, and the number of days of snowfall. In spite of great efforts, however, the CME contracts have not garnered much volume. A few years ago the Chicago Board of Trade offered derivatives on insurance claims arising from hurricanes and earthquakes. These contracts drew a great deal of acclaim and attention, in particular from academics keen on deriving pricing formulas. But after all was said and done, these contracts did not draw much actual trading volume.

A family of related instruments makes up what I refer to as *environmental derivatives*. These instruments are based on the prices of claims on pollution output. For example, sulfur dioxide is a principal pollutant in industry. For many years firms have been granted allowances for certain amounts of sulfur dioxide that they can emit. Firms that invest in pollution control often find that they have more permits to pollute than their actual pollution. Thus, they can sell the excess. Firms with shortages can buy excess. In this way, total pollution remains the same but is allocated more efficiently. Likewise, in this day and age with such discussion of global warming, carbon dioxide is often referred to as a principal contributor. Carbon dioxide credits can be bought and sold in the same manner as described for sulfur dioxide. It should be no surprise then that when spot markets exist for an instrument, so too can derivatives. In the United States, the Chicago Climate Exchange and Chicago Futures Exchange were created for trading these types of instruments. These contracts have met with some limited success, but their long-term viability is not clear yet.

While some tout the weather and environmental derivatives markets as innovative and successful, I can agree only on the first point. They certainly are innovative, striking at the very heart of certain significant risks encountered by many businesses. Nonetheless, their innovative nature has in some sense been their bane. Weather derivatives may be innovative, but they are completely out of the traditional box of derivative products and therein lie some problems.

As we will determine later in this book, understanding derivative products requires an ability to determine their prices. Traditional derivatives such as options, futures, and swaps have well-defined formulas for their prices. These formulas rely on the principle of arbitrage, whereby the derivative price prohibits either party from locking in a risk-free profit off of the other. Unfortunately, weather derivatives cannot be so easily priced. In a conventional arbitrage transaction, it is necessary for a party to be able to own the underlying asset. Thus, you might buy a bond and sell an option on a bond, which can eliminate the risk, leading to a risk-free return, which can be benchmarked to the risk-free rate. But no one can buy the weather and sell an option on it. A party can be exposed to the weather, but that exposure cannot be easily isolated and traded for pricing purposes. For example, a large northeastern airline, such as U.S. Airways, is highly exposed to winter weather in the northeast corridor. U.S. Airways stock can be considered as being partially driven by the weather, but it is difficult to isolate how much of the stock performance is driven by the weather. Even if you could, it would be impossible to trade only that exposure.

Pricing weather derivatives typically occurs in a much more challenging manner. Usually the underlying variable and its financial consequences are forecasted, and a price is based on a discounting of the expected payoffs. As we discuss in later essays, however, the discount rate is a critical component of the process. Where hedging is available, the risk-free rate can be used. Otherwise, you must estimate a risk premium. My impression is that much of weather derivatives pricing ignores the problem of estimating a risk premium, thereby assuming that investors are neutral to weather risk, which clearly is not the case.

Similar problems exist in pricing environmental derivatives. In short, success in this business seems more like a distant and barely visible star in space but one that could burn out before reaching our universe. Perhaps in the next edition of this book I can tell a more optimistic story.

FOR MORE READING

Cao, Melanie, and Jason Z. Wei. "Pricing the Weather." *Risk* 13 (May 2000): 67–70.
Geman, Hélyette. *Insurance and Weather Derivatives*. London: Risk Books, 1999.
Hull, John C. *Options, Futures, and Other Derivatives*, 6th ed. Upper Saddle River, NJ: Prentice-Hall, 2006, chap. 23.

TEST YOUR KNOWLEDGE

1. Why is weather a good variable on which to base derivatives?
2. In spite of your answer to question 1, why have weather derivatives not been successful so far?
3. How are heating- and cooling-degree days used as the underlying in weather derivatives?
4. How are derivatives based on emissions designed?

Three

Derivative Pricing

The day is finally here. This is what I told you will challenge you. Understanding how derivatives are priced is probably the most difficult part of learning about derivatives. To help you get started, let me try to teach you something right here in this introduction.

Suppose you find that unleaded 89 octane gasoline sells for 3.01^{99} at one station, while across the street, it sells for 3.03^{99}. Both are convenience stores operated by major oil companies. They offer virtually identical products and services. Their gas prices are posted and easily visible from all angles. Assume that both stations are equally accessible and the traffic flow from both directions is approximately equal. Thus, a customer would have no difficulty choosing one station over another. It should be apparent that the station with the cheaper gasoline will get most if not virtually all of the business. Hence, it is quite rare to see a widely used and nearly homogeneous product like 89 octane gasoline selling for different prices. One store would drive the other out of business, but of course, competition forces the other store to adjust its price. Now, we are not arguing that the same product will *always* cost the same. Wal-Mart, Target, and Macy's may have different prices for the same product, but customers are typically not able to switch easily and costlessly from one seller to another. In the financial world, nearly costless switching is quite easy. It is as simple to buy a bond from Merrill Lynch as it is to buy it from Goldman Sachs.

Suppose you find that a stock is selling for $50 on one exchange and for $53 on another exchange. It is possible to buy the stock on the cheaper exchange and sell it on the more expensive exchange and net a profit, provided your costs are not more than $3. This situation is called an *arbitrage opportunity* and the transaction is referred to as *arbitrage*. In an arbitrage, someone is able to earn a profit by taking no risk and investing no money. It is essentially manufacturing money out of nothing. Financial markets work very well, and you are very unlikely to see a stock selling for two prices on two different markets.

So how does this work for derivatives? Remember that a derivative "derives" its value from the underlying. As such, the derivative behaves much like the underlying. It is possible to use the derivative to replicate the underlying and vice versa. Likewise, it is possible to combine the derivative and the underlying to eliminate all of the risk in which case, the position should return the risk-free rate. On that basis, it is possible to determine the appropriate price of the derivative, which will be the price that guarantees that the derivative replicates the underlying and that no one can earn more than the risk-free rate on a risk-free transaction. In other words, if the derivative is correctly priced, arbitrage should not be possible.

Does it always work this way for derivatives? Well, not exactly. There are very few instances in which a clean arbitrage profit is even theoretically possible, what more in reality. Some of the models require information that is not easy to get and figures on which people would disagree. Thus, a lot of what goes on in the market and may be called arbitrage is really not arbitrage. But those are technical issues you can think about at a more advanced stage. For now, I suggest you take the rule of no arbitrage as the truth as it will serve you quite well in helping you to understand derivative pricing.

This section consists of 17 essays covering a variety of topics. I will not list them all here, but suffice it to say that we will cover how to price options, forwards, futures, and swaps. We will also learn something about how the risks from these instruments is hedged, which plays an important role in how these instruments themselves serve as tools for hedging.

Forward and Futures Pricing

In Essay 4 we introduced forward and futures contracts. Forward contracts are the simplest of all derivatives. Recall that they represent an agreement between two parties in which one party commits to purchase an underlying asset at a fixed price at a later date. The other party commits to sell the underlying asset at the fixed price at the later date. A forward contract is a customized, over-the-counter agreement and is subject to the possibility of default by the party that ends up owing the other the greater amount. A futures contract is essentially a standardized version of a forward contract in which a futures exchange has assigned a fixed set of terms and conditions concerning the identity of the underlying, the number of units of the underlying, the expiration date, and delivery procedure. The futures exchange provides a market for trading of the contract and also a clearinghouse for transferring all payments and providing a credit guarantee that assures each party that it will incur no credit loss. To manage the credit risk, futures exchanges provide for a daily settling of gains and losses that requires that parties with accumulated losses during the trading day pay parties with accumulated gains during that day. Minimum margin requirements assure that adequate funds are on hand. In this essay we look at how these contracts are priced.

The first principle of forward and futures pricing is that the contract price at expiration is the price of the underlying. Consider a forward or futures contract that expires in one month. Now consider that contract when it has one week to go. Then consider that contract with one day to go. Continue to shorten the life of the contract until its expiration is instantaneous. At that point the contract is essentially an ordinary transaction to purchase the asset. Thus, the forward or futures price of a contract at expiration is the price of the underlying. That result is, hopefully, obvious. The less obvious task is to price the forward or futures contract prior to expiration. Let us start with forward contracts for they are simpler.

Suppose an investor holds one unit of an asset. This asset is traded in a market and has an observable price S, which is commonly known as the *spot price* or *cash price*.[1] We do not question whether S represents the true value of the asset. We simply take S as given.[2] Now suppose the investor enters into a forward contract to sell the asset at a fixed price at a specific later date. This investor is taking the short position, which is balancing or *hedging* his long position in the underlying. The counterparty is taking the long position in the forward contract, thereby agreeing to buy the asset at the fixed price at the later date. All terms and conditions are agreed upon by the two parties. The fixed price, called the forward price, is denoted as F.

It should be easy to see that the owner of the asset is now engaged in a riskless transaction. He owns an asset worth S and has contracted to sell it at a later date at a price F. So his return is guaranteed. In well-functioning markets, that return has to be the risk-free rate. Thus, F has to be the value of S compounded at the risk-free rate. When S is converted to F by compounding S at the risk-free rate, the forward price accounts for the cost of financing S. That is, the investor who owns the asset has money tied up in the asset and, therefore, incurs an opportunity cost.[3] If the investor sells the asset at F and F reflects the growth of S at the risk-free rate, then the opportunity cost of the investor's money has been properly accounted for in the model.

If the forward price in the market is not equal to S compounded at the risk-free rate, an opportunity for arbitrage is possible. If the forward price in the market is too high, an arbitrageur can buy the asset and sell the forward contract, which would lead to a risk-free position that earns more than the risk-free rate. If the forward price in the market is too low, an arbitrageur can sell the asset and buy the forward contract. This transaction is the opposite of the other one and creates an initial cash inflow that the arbitrageur must pay back later with interest, making it an implicit loan. If the forward price is too low, however, the implied interest rate is lower than

---

[1] Even more common is the reference to this price as simply the *price*. That is, we say that something has a price, without qualifying that it is a spot or cash price versus a forward or futures price. When covering forward and futures contracts, however, we need a clear distinction between the different types of prices.

[2] This is one of the common and indeed most important aspects of derivatives pricing. The price of the underlying is taken as given. We do not determine this price. Then, given that price, we price the derivative off of the underlying.

[3] The cost of financing can be viewed as the direct costs of borrowing money to pay for the asset or the implicit costs associated with investing one's own funds in the asset, and thereby losing the interest on the funds.

the risk-free rate. One could, therefore, invest the proceeds from the sale of the asset at the risk-free rate, which would more than cover the cost of paying back the implicit loan. To engage in this transaction, however, requires that the arbitrageur either already own the asset or be able to borrow it so as to engage in a short sale.

So we have seen that the forward price equals the spot price compounded at the risk-free rate. In most cases, however, some other adjustments are needed to correctly arrive at the value of F.

Suppose the asset is one that incurs costs to hold. These are called *carrying costs*. Heavy physical assets such as oil and gold incur extensive storage costs. Assets that can be destroyed, such as bushels of soybean that could be burned, must be insured. These costs in total are the carrying costs, sometimes referred to as the *cost of carry*. The investor engaged in this risk-free transaction will not earn a net return of the risk-free rate if the carrying costs are not considered. Thus, F must not only reflect the value of S compounded at the risk-free rate but also any costs incurred to hold the assets. These costs should be adjusted for the time value of money so that when factored in to determine F, they reflect the costs plus the accrual of any interest on these costs. If the forward price reflects these values, it will be higher than without. Because the forward price would be high enough to compensate for the costs incurred, it would a return of the risk-free rate.

Some assets generate income while being held. The classic example is stock and bonds. Some stocks pay dividends and some bonds pay interest. These dividend and interest amounts are usually known at the time of the transaction. The investor who holds the asset would receive these payments and would therefore earn more than the risk-free rate. Thus, the forward price should be adjusted downward to reflect these cash payments. The investor holding the asset would receive a return less than the risk-free rate from selling the asset at the forward price, but these cash payments would augment the return to bring it up to the risk-free rate.

Some forward contracts, however, do not trade at values that imply a risk-free rate. This puzzling phenomenon has been formalized into a theory called the *convenience yield*. It is believed that certain assets offer non-pecuniary benefits to their holders. The convenience yield captures this notion. It is said to arise from the advantage of having an asset in possession during a shortage. Suppose for example that there is currently a shortage of a particular asset. Obviously the price would be quite high. For simplicity let us assume no carrying costs and cash flows from the asset. Then to obtain the forward price, we compound the asset value at the risk-free rate. But we might observe the actual forward price in the market to be lower than this amount. This differential, which is referred to as the convenience yield, reflects the added benefit of owning the asset during a shortage. The owner avoids the costs of not having the asset on hand during shortages or under conditions of unexpected increases in demand.[4] Convenience yields are frequently seen in oil markets, where shortages and market instability are common. They are also likely to be a function of the difficulty of short selling.

Admittedly the notion of a convenience yield is somewhat murky. In some sense it is like a plug-figure, a number that makes things balance. But it clearly exists in the marketplace and arbitrage is unable to exploit it. My own inclination is to believe that short-selling restrictions preclude the arbitrage that would drive away the convenience yield, but I have no proof. In any case, this factor exists so we have to acknowledge it in any pricing models. Consequently, the forward price can be lowered from its otherwise theoretically correct value by the amount of the convenience yield or whatever you want to call it.

Thus, we see that the theoretical forward price is the spot price compounded at the risk-free rate, increased by the cost of carry and reduced by any explicit cash payments on the asset and any convenience yield. Any deviations from this relationship can be exploited by arbitrage. The costs of engaging in arbitrage, however, create a band around the theoretical forward price. Thus, the actual forward price can deviate from the theoretical forward price within the band created by the costs of arbitrage.

As noted previously, forward contracts are subject to credit risk. We discuss the credit risk of derivatives in Essay 68, so we shall leave out any detailed coverage here. Suffice it to say that the effect of credit risk on a forward contract would be to nudge the forward price up or down a little depending on the credit quality of the two counterparties and which one is the better credit.

Virtually every treatment of the pricing of futures contracts covers them as if they were the same as forward contracts. In fact, almost everything known about the convenience yield and carrying costs comes from observations of futures prices. Futures contracts essentially have no credit risk, so the forward price treatment without incorporating credit risk is correct. The primary difference between forward and futures contracts lies in the daily settlement. Recall that at the end of each day, the futures clearinghouse determines which positions have gained in value and which have lost. It then charges the losses to the margin accounts of the losing positions and credits the corresponding gains to the margin accounts of the winning positions.

---

[4] These costs can come in the form of angry customers, such as what would happen if a customer walked into McDonald's and found that the store had no beef. Those customers might go to Burger King and never return to McDonald's.

All parties must maintain minimum margin balances, so the losing investors could be forced to deposit additional funds or close out their positions.

These daily settlements create a slightly different cash flow pattern from forward contracts. For example, suppose someone goes long a forward contract at the price of $100. Another person goes long an otherwise identical futures contract at a price of $100. Let the contract expire in two days. At the end of the first day, the futures price is $101. The holder of the futures contract receives a credit of $1. The holder of the forward contract receives nothing because the contract has not expired. Now let us move one day later at which time the contract is expiring. Assume that the spot price is $104. As described earlier, the forward and futures price at expiration is the spot price. Thus, the futures price would be $104, and the holder of the futures contract would be credited the change in the futures price from the previous day, $104 − $101 = $3. The holder of the forward contract would buy the asset worth $104 for a price of $100, thereby netting a gain of $4.[5]

Now both the forward trader and the futures trader have $4, but the futures trader received it in the form of $1 at the end of the first day and $3 at the end of the second day. The forward trader received it in the form of $4 at the end of the second day. In this case the futures trader is better off because of the interest on $1 for one day. But if prices had fallen and both parties showed a loss, the forward trader would be better off, because the futures trader would have incurred the loss over time while the forward trader would not have realized the loss until expiration.

The important question is whether futures prices should be higher than forward prices. The answer lies in the relationship between futures prices and interest rates. If futures prices and interest rates are positively related, then futures prices will increase when interest rates increase. In that case, futures contracts are preferred over forward contracts. Increasing futures prices will lead to daily settlement profits that can be invested in an environment of rising interest rates. Of course, this is good. Decreasing futures prices will lead to daily settlement losses that can be financed in an environment of falling interest rates. This too is good. Thus, if futures prices and interest rates are positively related, then investors would prefer futures contracts, which would push futures prices above forward prices. A negative relation between futures prices and interest rates would, by opposite arguments, lead to a preference for forwards over futures and, thus, make forward prices be higher than futures prices. If there is no relation between futures prices and

---

[5] This gain can be realized by selling the asset. Some forward contracts settle in cash, in which case the holder of the short position would simply pay $4 to the holder of the long position.

interest rates, then there is no preference for one type of contract over the other, and their prices should be the same.

In reality, the differences between futures and forward prices are fairly small and at least some of the difference can be explained by the difference in credit risk. As such, most pricing models of forwards and futures in theory and in practice are the same. That means that the daily settlement used in futures contract is generally disregarded and futures contracts are priced like forward contracts. Given the short-term nature of futures contracts and the likely small impact of the interest on daily profits, this is probably a safe assumption. If contracts were being priced with long-term expirations, however, there is the potential for a notable difference in forward and futures prices.

If one does want to incorporate the daily settlement feature into futures contracts, a formula is usually not feasible. Numerical approaches such as finite difference methods and binomial models can usually accommodate this feature. These methods are covered in Essays 28 and 29.

FOR MORE READING

Chance, Don M., and Robert Brooks. *An Introduction to Derivatives and Risk Management*, 7th ed. Mason, OH: Thomson South-Western, 2007, ch. 9.

Hull, John C. *Options, Futures, and Other Derivatives*, 6th ed. Upper Saddle River, NJ: Prentice-Hall, 2006, ch. 5.

Jarrow, Robert A., and Stuart M. Turnbull. *Derivatives Securities*, 2nd ed. Mason, OH: Thomson South-Western, 2000, ch. 2.

McDonald, Robert L. *Derivative Markets*, 2nd ed. Boston: Addison Wesley, 2006, ch. 5.

TEST YOUR KNOWLEDGE

1. Explain in general terms how a forward contract price is determined, given that the underlying incurs costs of storage, makes cash payments, and offers a convenience yield.
2. For the simple case of no cash payments or convenience yield, explain how arbitrage would be conducted to take advantage of the situation that a dealer quotes a forward price that is too high.
3. How does the relationship between futures prices and interest rates determine the differential between forward and futures prices?

Put-Call Parity for European Options on Assets

Put-call parity is probably the most important principle to understand in option pricing. It is truly one of the most elementary principles, and yet it provides extremely valuable insights into the factors that are most important in pricing options. In this essay we look at put-call parity for European options. We discuss put-call parity for American options in Essay 23.

Let us start off with some symbols. Let S be the current price of the underlying asset, X be the option's exercise price, c be the price of a European call, and p be the price of a European put. Let $PV(X)$ be the present value of the exercise price, calculated by discounting the exercise price at the risk-free rate. We shall assume no cash payments on the underlying, but it is easy to add dividends by simply replacing the asset price, S, by the asset price less the present value of the cash payments.

There are numerous ways to learn the basic relationship expressed by put-call parity. Probably the most familiar is $p = c - S + PV(X)$. The reason this formula is so popular is that we often take the call price as given, and we then need to find the put price. Alternative ways of expressing put-call parity are: $c = p + S - PV(X)$, $S = c - p + PV(X)$, and $PV(X) = p - c + S$. My favorite and the absolute easiest to remember is $p + S = c + PV(X)$. Let us look at how put-call parity is derived and see why this is the easiest formula to remember. Once you remember it, the rest is simple.

First learn this statement: protective put = fiduciary call. A *protective put* is a put plus a stock. A *fiduciary call* is a call plus a risk-free bond. Now we demonstrate why this is true. Suppose you buy the asset and insure it with a put to form a protective put. This position will require an initial outlay of $S + p$. At expiration, consider the case where S^*, the asset price at expiration, is less than or equal to X. Then the asset is worth S^* and the put is worth $X - S^*$ for a total of X. Suppose S^* ends up greater than

X. Then the asset is worth S^* and the put is worthless. Your overall position is, therefore, worth the greater of S^* or X.

Now let someone else simultaneously do a fiduciary call. That will require an outlay of c dollars for the call and $PV(X)$ dollars for the risk-free bond that has a face value of X. At expiration, if S^* is less than or equal to X, the call will be worthless and the risk-free bond will have a value of X. If S^* ends up greater than X, the call will be worth $S^* - X$ and the risk-free bond will be worth X for a total of S^*. The fiduciary call is, therefore, worth the greater of S^* or X.

Obviously the two transactions will produce the same result at expiration. Thus, it should cost the same to establish each position up front. This means that $p + S = c + PV(X)$. If this were not true, it would be possible to go long one side and short the other and earn an arbitrage profit. For example, suppose $p + S$ were less than $c + PV(X)$. This means that the put and asset are underpriced relative to the call and the risk-free bond. The appropriate transaction is to buy the underpriced combination of put and asset and sell the overpriced combination of call and risk-free bond. At expiration the short call and risk-free bond will offset the long asset and put, leaving you with zero cash inflow or outflow at expiration, but the cash received up front from the sale of the call and the risk-free bond is more than the cash paid for the asset and put. This means that money comes in risk-free and never goes out. Everyone doing this would force prices to align by the put-call parity equation. The call price and risk-free bond values would tend to fall and the put and stock values would tend to rise until parity is reached.

Earlier we said that this version is the easiest of the put-call parity formulas to learn. Notice that in each of the other formulas listed earlier, there were some positive signs and some negative signs. This version is the only one with all positive signs. To remember the basics, just learn "call plus risk-free bond equals put plus stock," or "fiduciary call equals protective put."

The various put-call parity formulas are useful for learning which combinations are equivalent. Take any of the variations of put-call parity. Whenever you see a plus sign, interpret that to mean buying; whenever you see a minus sign, interpret that to mean selling, or borrowing if you are talking about $PV(X)$. For example, $p = c - S + PV(X)$ means buying a put is equivalent to buying a call, selling the asset, and buying the risk-free bond. The formula $c = p + S - PV(X)$ means buying a call is equivalent to buying a put, buying the asset, and borrowing the present value of X or selling short the risk-free bond. The formula $S = c - p + PV(X)$ means buying the asset is equivalent to buying a call, selling a put, and buying the risk-free bond. The formula $PV(X) = S + p - c$ means that buying the risk-free bond is equivalent to buying the asset, buying a put, and selling a call. Note that reversing the signs means that borrowing is the same as selling the asset, selling a put, and buying a call. If any of these arguments do not sound convincing, just look at the payoffs at expiration from the position on the left-hand side and those of the position on the right-hand side. They will be equivalent.

Put-call parity can also be tied in with the cost of carry model, which is how you price a forward or futures contract. Assuming no cash payments on the asset, we know that the forward/futures price, F, is equal to the asset price compounded at the risk-free rate, that is, the future value of the asset price: $F = FV(S)$. This result is obtained by assuming that you can buy the asset and sell a forward or futures contract to form a risk-free hedge. The return would be the risk-free rate only if $F = FV(S)$. Alternatively, $S = PV(F)$. Substituting into the put-call parity formula, we obtain $p + PV(F) = c + PV(X)$. A more common way of stating this is as $c - p = PV(F - X)$. In words, this means that buying a call and selling a put is equivalent to buying a forward or futures contract and lending the present value of $F - X$. Of course, X can be set at any level so $PV(F - X)$ can be negative, meaning that instead of lending $PV(F - X)$, you are borrowing.

Put-call parity for European options is extremely important. Fortunately it is a simple concept, easily and quickly learned and hopefully not forgotten.

FOR MORE READING

Chance, Don M., and Robert Brooks. *An Introduction to Derivatives and Risk Management*, 7th ed. Mason, OH: Thomson South-Western, 2007, chap. 3.

Hull, John C. *Options, Futures, and Other Derivatives*, 6th ed. Upper Saddle River, NJ: Prentice-Hall, 2006, chap. 9.

Jarrow, Robert A., and Andrew Rudd. *Option Pricing*. Homewood, IL: Irwin, 1983, chap. 4.

Jarrow, Robert A., and Stuart M. Turnbull. *Derivatives Securities*, 2nd ed. Mason, OH: Thomson South-Western, 2000, chap. 3.

McDonald, Robert L. *Derivative Markets*, 2nd ed. Boston: Addison Wesley, 2006, chap. 9.

TEST YOUR KNOWLEDGE

1. What is a fiduciary call and a protective put?
2. Suppose the components of a fiduciary call cost less than the components of a protective put. What transaction would an arbitrageur do, and how would it make money at no risk?

3. Suppose short selling is outlawed. Explain how put-call parity can be used to create a synthetic short position in an asset.
4. Show how options and risk-free bonds can be used to create a forward contract.

Put-Call Parity for American Options on Assets

In Essay 22 we covered put-call parity for European options. This time we look at how put-call parity changes if the options are American.

First, let us review the basics of American options. An American call option is the same as a European call option if there are no dividends, coupons, or other cash payments or yield on the underlying asset. This statement is true because there is no incentive to exercise early. Exercising early just gives up the interest on the exercise price and makes the decision to buy the asset earlier than necessary.

If the option is a put, there is always a possibility of exercising early, since the underlying asset price can go sufficiently low that it is not worth holding for any additional gain. In the case of puts, dividends/coupons and the like reduce the probability of that happening, because they drive the asset price down for sure.

Let us start off by assuming there are no dividends or other payments on the underlying asset. We shall use the uppercase C and P for the American call and put prices, respectively. Consider portfolio A, which consists of an American call and a risk-free bond with a current value of the exercise price, X. This bond will mature to a value of $X(1+r)^T$. The call will not be exercised early because the underlying asset makes no dividend or other payments during the life of the call. Portfolio B consists of an American put and a unit of the asset. Suppose at some time prior to expiration, the holder of the American put in Portfolio B exercises it. She delivers the asset, receives X, and reinvests it to accumulate a value of $X(1 + r)^{T - j}$ where $T - j$ reflects the time from the date of exercise to the expiration.

If, at expiration, the asset price ends up below X, the holder of Portfolio A ends up with $X(1 + r)^T$. The holder of B ends up with $X(1 + r)^{T-j}$. Portfolio A is better because it reflects the accrual of interest over a longer period. If the put were not exercised early, Portfolio B would be worth X at expiration, which is clearly less than the value of A at expiration.

Now suppose at expiration, the asset price ends up above X. Then the holder of Portfolio A would end up with $S^* + X[(1+r)^T - 1]$. If the put were exercised early, the holder of B would end up with $X(1+r)^{T-j}$, whereas if the put were not exercised early, B would end up worth S^*. In any case, Portfolio A dominates Portfolio B in the sense that the holder would always end up with more money with Portfolio A. Consequently, the cost of A up front, $C + X$, must exceed the cost of B up front, $P + S$. This result establishes an upper bound on the value of the put and the asset.

A lower bound can be easily established. Since the European call price equals the American call price if there are no cash payments on the asset, the value of a European put plus the value of the asset must equal the value of the American call plus the present value of the exercise price, $p + S = C + PV(X)$, where p is the price of a European put option. Because an American put must be worth at least the value of a European put, we can now say that $P + S > C + PV(X)$.

Thus, American put-call parity can be written as $C + X > P + S > C + PV(X)$. Technically, we must use the $\geq$ sign since equality is possible in some extreme cases, so we shall state it as $C + X \geq P + S \geq C + PV(X)$.

Once we introduce cash payments on the asset, things become a little more complicated. We must incorporate the fact that the American call might now be exercised early. Assume the asset is a stock, so the cash payments are dividends. We then adjust the stock price by subtracting the present value of the dividends, $PV(D)$, paid over the life of the options. Suppose we modify the risk-free bond in Portfolio A such that its current value is $X + PV(D)$. For the time being, make the call in A a European call and use a lowercase c for its current value. By a similar argument as earlier, we can show that A dominates B, meaning that $c + X + PV(D) > P + S$. Because an American call cannot be worth less than a European call, we have $C + X + PV(D) > P + S$. Without dividends, we had another inequality, $P + S > C + PV(X)$. If we add dividends, we know by intuition that this adjustment increases a put's value and decreases a call's value. Thus, that inequality must still hold.

Putting these results together, we see that put-call parity for American options is written as $C + X\ PV(D) > P + S > C + PV(X)$. The trick in demonstrating the proof with or without dividends is to treat one option as European, develop the result, and then in the last step, change the European option to an American option. The latter will have a value that will be at least that of the former. This trick preserves the correct result.

How can put-call parity be used when the options are American? Let us reexamine the result $C + X + PV(D) > S + P > C + PV(X)$. Suppose the first inequality is violated. In other words, $C + X + PV(D) < S + P$. The left-hand side is too low and/or the right-hand side is too high. This means to execute the transactions on the left-hand side and reverse the transactions on the right-hand side. So you would buy the call and the risk-free bond with current value of $X + PV(D)$. You would then sell short the asset and the put. These transactions would generate cash up front and would guarantee no cash outflow at expiration. With everyone doing the same thing, prices would adjust until the inequality held as required by the rule. If the condition is that $S + P < C + PV(X)$, you would buy the asset and the put, sell the call, and borrow the present value of the exercise price. These transactions would generate a positive cash flow up front with no possibility of a cash outflow at expiration. Everyone doing this would force prices to realign.

Differences in opinion about the present value of the dividends or other cash payments could produce some disagreement over whether the put-call parity relationship holds for a given case. In fact, nearly all of derivative pricing theory assumes that the dividends or other cash payments are known over the life of the derivative. If this assumption is not true, then the pricing models and arbitrage relationships might not hold. Also, any arbitrage would require that the risk-free profit earned exceeds the transaction costs. Subject to these caveats, put-call parity, whether an equality or inequality, imposes a stringent relationship on put and call option prices relative to the price of the underlying asset, the exercise price, and the interest rate. This relationship must hold or profitable arbitrage can be executed. It is one of the most basic of all option relationships, and any professional option trader will be as familiar with it as with his or her own name.

FOR MORE READING

Chance, Don M. and Robert Brooks. *An Introduction to Derivatives and Risk Management*, 7th ed. Mason, OH: Thomson South-Western, 2007, chap. 3.

Hull, John C. *Options, Futures, and Other Derivatives*, 6th ed. Upper Saddle River, NJ: Prentice-Hall, 2006, chap. 9.

Jarrow, Robert A., and Andrew Rudd. *Option Pricing*. Homewood, IL: Irwin, 1983, chap. 5.

Jarrow, Robert A., and Stuart M. Turnbull. *Derivatives Securities*, 2nd ed. Mason, OH: Thomson South-Western, 2000, chap. 3.

McDonald, Robert L. *Derivative Markets*, 2nd ed. Boston: Addison Wesley, 2006, chap. 9.

TEST YOUR KNOWLEDGE

1. Given American put-call parity as $C + X \geq P + S \geq C + PV(X)$, what would an arbitrageur do if $C + X < P + S$?
2. Repeat question 1 but assume that $P + S < C + PV(X)$.
3. Suppose that the violations in both questions 1 and 2 occur. Which would be more profitable to do?
4. If the underlying is a stock, how would dividends affect American put-call parity?

Call Options as Insurance and Margin

In this essay we are going to take apart the call option and reveal some insights that do not appear obvious on the surface. First, let us recall put-parity for European options, which we covered in Essay 22. Suppose you buy the asset and a put and borrow funds equal to the present value of the exercise price, promising to pay back the exercise price at the option's expiration. Suppose at expiration, the asset ends up above the exercise price. Then the put expires worthless, and you end up holding the asset and paying the lender an amount of money equivalent to the exercise price. If the asset ends up below the exercise price, you exercise the put and end up selling your asset for the exercise price, which is then passed on to the lender to pay off your loan. This strategy is identical to holding a call.

If a call is equivalent to owning the asset, owning a put, and borrowing the present value of the exercise price, then you can say that a call is a protective put plus a loan that helps pay for it. Another way to look at a call is to say that it is like an insurance policy (the put) and a long position in the asset combined with a loan. Thus, the long asset plus loan is like a margin transaction. Therefore, a call is equivalent to a margin transaction plus an insurance policy on the asset.

Viewed from that angle, a number of interesting insights are offered. For example, as you probably know, you can buy stock on margin but you have to conform to the margin requirements, which are 50% initial margin and maintenance margin of usually 25% to 30%. The same effect can be accomplished without the inconvenience of the margin requirements by buying a call. This approach creates a margin transaction that is also downside insured. If you do not want the downside insurance, just sell a put, which will offset the implicit put that is part of the call. Thus, a long call and a short put on a stock is like a margin transaction, which is why it also makes a good substitute for futures or forward transaction, which are also "margin-like" transactions.

Notice how the call gets you completely around the margin requirements. Consider an out-of-the money call where the stock price is substantially below the exercise price. Not only will the transaction involve implicitly borrowing more than 50% of the purchase price of the stock, but it will also involve borrowing some of the insurance premium.

For example, consider a one-year call with volatility of 0.35, stock price of $100, strike of $120, and risk-free rate of 5%. The call would be worth $8.84 and the put would be worth $22.99.[1] Your $8.84 call premium would represent the purchase of stock for $100, the purchase of a put for $22.99, and the borrowing of $114.15 with a promise to pay back $120 in one year. Thus, your $100 stock was purchased by borrowing all $100, meaning you had no equity whatsoever in the stock, and you had $14.15 of borrowing that was used to help pay the $22.99 price of the put.

Another interesting insight from this approach is that we always tend to say that volatility helps a call by giving it the advantage of upside moves without any downside penalty. In other words, if volatility increases, your upside potential is greater but your downside potential is the same because if the call ends up out-of-the-money, you do not care how far out-of-the-money it ends up. There is not much harm in this interpretation, but frankly, it is not completely correct. Remembering that the call is a margin transaction plus a put, let us look at the effects of volatility on each component.

First take the insurance. Does volatility affect the price of a put? Of course. A put will be worth substantially more if the volatility is higher. The insurer will demand a greater premium to accommodate the greater risk. Thus, the holder of the call pays a higher price because the downside risk is greater.

What about the margin transaction? Does volatility affect it? We tend to think that the asset value will decrease with higher volatility, but in the option framework we are using here, we see that higher volatility increases the value of the long call and short put. These effects offset, so volatility does not appear to affect the value of the call, even though intuition says that it does. We must remember, however, that the positive effect of volatility on a call and a put is based on the assumption that the underlying does not change.

If a call option consists of margin plus insurance, and a volatility change has a positive effect on insurance and no effect on margin, we get a new

---

[1] These values are obtained using the Black-Scholes-Merton model, which is covered in Essay 27.

perspective. The impact of volatility on a call cames strictly from the insurance. So let us set the record straight. A call is worth more when the volatility is higher because it contains a limit on the downside loss. The upside effect of volatility is, at best, neutral and, at worst, a negative.

Things are not always as they seem, which is verified when we look at a call option under a microscope.

FOR MORE READING

Chance, Don M. "Translating the Greek: The Real Meaning of Call Option Derivatives." *Financial Analysts Journal* (July-August 1994): 43–49.

Galai, Dan. "Characterization of Options." *Journal of Banking and Finance* (1977): 373–386.

TEST YOUR KNOWLEDGE

1. Explain why a call option consists of margin plus insurance.
2. How does the answer to question 1 reveal a way of getting around margin requirements?
3. Why does the benefit of volatility on a call come from the downside and not the upside?

A Nontechnical Introduction to Brownian Motion

This essay starts a series that looks at the topic of option pricing. We start with a piece on the concept of *Brownian motion*, which has a long history in the physical sciences and a surprisingly long history in the field of finance. Readers with a strong mathematical background, however, are likely to be disappointed. Consistent with the other essays in this book, the material will be presented with a minimum of mathematics. This approach makes it accessible to more people, some of whom will then go on and study it in more detail. Many mathematicians and economists have often demonstrated to me that they cannot communicate what they are doing in simple terms, but if the technical person cannot explain a technical concept to a nontechnical person, the technical person does not understand the problem, it is not a very important problem, or, as is usually the case, the technical person cannot communicate with words.

Let us start with the assumption that the prices of assets evolve in a random manner. I do not care what the technical analysts who waste the time and money of investors say, stock prices, currency rates, and interest rates are largely unpredictable. But unpredictability does not mean you should not attempt to understand the probability process driving the numbers. Estimates of the expected returns and volatilities are essential in investing. The manner in which asset prices fluctuate through time according to the laws of probability is known as a *stochastic process*, where the word "stochastic" essentiality means "governed by the laws of probability."

A stochastic process is a sequence of observations from a probability distribution. Rolling dice at regular time intervals is a stochastic process. In this case the distribution is stable because the possible outcomes do not change from one roll to the next. Rolling a 6-5 three times in a row, while highly unlikely, in no way changes the probability of rolling another 6-5. A changing distribution, however, would be the case if we drew a card from a deck without replacing the previously drawn cards. Real-world asset prices probably come from changing distributions, though it is difficult to determine when a distribution has changed. Empirical analysis of past data can be useful in that context—not to predict the future but to know when the numbers are coming out according to different probability parameters.

Around 1827, the Scottish scientist Robert Brown observed the random behavior of pollen particles suspended in water. This phenomenon came to be known as Brownian motion. About 80 years passed before Albert Einstein, surprisingly unaware of the work of Brown, developed the mathematical properties of Brownian motion. I do not mean to suggest that no work was being done in the interim, but scientists did not always know what other work was being done, especially in those days of primitive communications. It is not surprising that it was Einstein who received most of the credit.

Let us start by assuming that a series of numbers is coming out of a standard normal (bell-shaped) probability distribution. This assumption means that the numbers on average equal zero and have a standard deviation of 1. Just as a reminder or if you are not aware: A standard deviation of 1 means that about two-thirds of the time, the numbers will be between $+1$ and -1, that is, one standard deviation around the average of zero. About 95% of the time, the numbers will be between two standard deviations around zero, and 99% of the time, they will be between three standard deviations around zero.

Numbers like this have very limited properties and in this form are not very useful. Let us transform these numbers into something more useful. Suppose we are currently at time t. Take any number you would like, call it $Z(t)$, and make this is our starting point. Now move ahead to time $t+1$ and draw a number from the standard normal probability distribution. Call it $e(t+1)$. A very simple transformation of the standard normal variable into the Z variable would be to add $e(t+1)$ to $Z(t)$ to obtain $Z(t+1)$. Another simple transformation would be to multiply $e(t+1)$ by a term we call t, which is the length of time that elapses between t and $t+1$. If that time interval happened to be one minute, t would be $1/[(60)(24)(365)]$, or in other words, the fraction of a year that elapses between t and $t+1$. One reason we like to multiply $e(t+1)$ by a time factor is that we would like our model to accommodate various time intervals between t and $t+1$. These statistical shocks that are the source of randomness might be larger if they were spread out over a longer time period; hence, the need to scale them by a function of time.

In fact, to model asset prices that evolve continuously, we need the interval between t and $t+1$ to be as short as possible. Mathematicians say that "in the limit," meaning almost there but not quite, t will approach zero. When t is so small that it is almost but not quite zero, we use the symbol dt. Unfortunately, the model $Z(t+1) = Z(t) + e(t+1)dt$ will give us a problem when dt is nearly zero, because the variance of $Z(t+1)$ will be nearly zero and zero variance means the complete absence of randomness. This result occurs because dt is very small, and to obtain the variance, we have to square it, which drives it even closer to zero. Thus, the variable Z will have no variance, which takes away its randomness. We cannot even call it a "variable" anymore. The problem is best resolved by multiplying $e(t+1)$ by the square root of dt, that is, $Z(t+1) = Z(t) + e(t+1)(dt)^{1/2}$. Then when we need to square the expression to take the variance, we have no problems squaring $(dt)^{1/2}$, which is just dt.

This model has many convenient properties. Suppose we are interested in predicting a future value of Z, say at time s. Then the expected value of $Z(s)$ is $Z(t)$, because the expected random change in the process is zero. If you start off at $Z(t)$ and keep incrementing it by values that average to zero, you would not expect to get anywhere. The variance of $Z(s)$ is $d(s-t)$ or, in other words, the amount of time that elapses between now, time t, and the future point, time s.

This statistical phenomenon is the process called *Brownian motion*. Now let us take the difference between $Z(t+1)$ and $Z(t)$, which will be $e(t+1)(dt)^{1/2}$. We write this as $dZ(t) = e(t+1)(dt)^{1/2}$. This process, the increment to the Brownian Motion, is called a *Wiener process*, named after the American mathematician Norbert Wiener (1894–1964) who did important work in this area. In pricing options, we are more interested in the process $dZ(t)$ than in the process $Z(t)$. We shall transform $dZ(t)$ into something more useful for modeling asset prices, but that is a topic covered in Essay 26.

It is perhaps important to note that the mathematics necessary to define the expected value and variance require the mathematical technique of integration. The ordinary rules of integration, however, do not automatically apply when the terms are stochastic. Fortunately, work by the Japanese mathematician Kiyoshi Itô proved that this integral, defined as a "stochastic integral," does exist through a modified definition. Consequently many of the rules of ordinary integration apply.

One interesting property of the Wiener process is that when you square it, it becomes perfectly predictable. This statement seems counterintuitive. How can you generate perfectly random numbers, square them, and find them to be perfectly predictable? Well, do not try any barroom bets on this one yet. No human can draw numbers fast enough to make this happen. But let us take a look at what this statement means. Given that $dZ(t) = e(t+1)(dt)^{1/2}$, we draw a value of $e(t+1)$. Of course it is unpredictable, and we already know that its expected value is zero and its variance is the square of $(dt)^{1/2}$, that is, dt times the variance of $e(t+1)$, which is 1, so the variance is simply dt. Note that this result uses the statistical rule that the variance of a constant, $(dt)^{1/2}$, times a random variable, $e(t+1)$, is the constant squared times the variance of the random variable.

Now suppose we square the value drawn, which gives us $e(t+1)^2$ times dt. Now we want to take the variance of this term. Again, to take a variance involves squaring. Once we square dt, we obtain zero, as discussed a few paragraphs back. Thus, the square of $dZ(t+1)$ has a variance of zero, which means that it is perfectly predictable and will in fact equal dt. The only problem with doing an experiment to see if you can predict this variable is that it relies on your ability to make dt very small. You would have to draw values of e faster than the speed of light. You are operating in a discrete-time setting, when the model is based on continuous time. You can, however, do a reasonable replication of this phenomenon in a spreadsheet simulation with time intervals as long as a full day. Putting things into words, however, means that this noisy series of numbers is so small that when squaring them, we obtain an even smaller series of numbers that converges to a constant value, dt.

So why do these things matter? They are the foundations of the most fundamental model used to price options. We shall need to progress a little further, however, and I reserve that material for the next essay.

Brownian motion as a basis for modeling assets on which options trade was evidently discovered by the French doctoral student Louis Bachelier in 1900. Bachelier's dissertation at the Sorbonne under the direction of the famed mathematician Henri Poincaré was at that time considered uninteresting. It was discovered more than 50 years later by an American economist, James Boness, who had it translated and reprinted. Although Bachelier solved the option pricing problem only for a very limited case, he pointed others in the right direction.

FOR MORE READING

Bachelier, Louis. "Theory of Speculation." In *The Random Character of Stock Market Prices*, ed. Paul H. Cootner. Cambridge, MA: MIT Press, 1964, chap. 2.

Chance, Don M. "The ABCs of Geometric Brownian Motion." *Derivatives Quarterly* (Winter 1994): 41–47.

Dimand, Robert W. "The Case of Brownian Motion: A Note on Bachelier's Contribution." *British Journal of the History of Science* 26 (1993): 233–234.

Jarrow, Robert A., and Stuart M. Turnbull. *Derivatives Securities*, 2nd ed. Mason, OH: Thomson South-Western, 2000, chap. 4.

Maiocchi, Robert. "The Case of Brownian Motion." *British Journal of the History of Science* 23 (1990): 257–283.

Merton, Robert C. "On the Role of the Wiener Process in Finance Theory and Practice: The Case of Replicating Portfolios." *Proceedings of Symposia in Pure Mathematics* 60 (1997): 209–221.

Wilmott, Paul. *Derivatives: The Theory and Practice of Financial Engineering.* Chichester, UK: John Wiley & Sons, 1998, chap. 3.

TEST YOUR KNOWLEDGE

1. How was the phenomenon of Brownian motion discovered?
2. Why is the Brownian motion stochastic process specified to have increments that are related to the square root of the time interval and not the time interval itself?
3. Why is the square of a Brownian motion a predictable value in continuous time but not in discrete time?

Building a Model of Brownian Motion in the Stock Market

This essay is the second in a series on the mathematics of option pricing. In Essay 25 we looked at the statistical model called Brownian motion. We saw that Brownian motion characterizes a random variable, which we called $Z(t)$. The basic property of $Z(t)$ is that it moves according to a drawing from a standard normal probability distribution, which has mean zero and standard deviation of 1, times the square root of the amount of time that elapses from one drawing to another. To be technically correct, the time increment should be very small, that is approximately zero. The difference between $Z(t)$ and $Z(t-1)$, which is the standard normal variable times the square root of the time increment, is called a Wiener process. To be more precise, we say that the Wiener process is $e(t)(dt)^{1/2}$.

With the ultimate objective of pricing an option on a stock, in this essay we look at how this process can be used to model stock price movements. We know that stock price fluctuations have several important characteristics:

1. Over the long run, stock prices go up. They are said to "drift" upward. This characteristic represents the return from bearing risk. The Wiener process does not drift, but as I show later, it is easy to make it drift either upward or downward.
2. Stock prices are random. We know that Wiener processes are random, though we cannot use the basic Wiener process for every stock because different stocks have different volatilities. We can, however, transform the basic Wiener process to give it different volatility.
3. It should be more difficult to forecast stock prices farther into the future than nearby. This statement does not mean that stock prices are very predictable but that the margin of error, which is related to the variance

of the future stock price, should be greater when predicting far into the future than when predicting near into the near future.

4. A stock price should never be negative.

The properties of a stock's return can be described by its mean and variance. While other properties such as skewness might be relevant, we ignore them for this model. Let E be the expected return on the stock and σ^2 be the variance of the return on the stock over a period of a year. It is common to express expected returns and variances on an annual basis, but other time periods are possible. Let σ be the standard deviation, which is the square root of the variance. Our model needs to be consistent with these chosen values. Let R be the return on the stock, which is the change in price divided by the base price, across the holding period h. We assume no dividends. Let the return over holding period h be defined by the expected return plus a noisy error term, g. In other words, $R = Eh + g$. We do not yet know what g is, but since it is noisy, it is reasonable to assume that it is influenced by the variance.

Now let us force the expected value of the left-hand side to be Eh. This is E times h, not a slangy Canadian expression. It means that the expected value of the right-hand side has to be Eh. Because the expected value of Eh is Eh, we can obtain the desired result by making sure that the expected value of g is zero. We must keep this constraint in mind as we look for a way to model the noise, g.

Now let us force the model to have the correct variance. If the variance over a year is σ^2, then the variance over the holding period h is $\sigma^2 h$. The variance of the left-hand side can be set to this value by setting the variance of the right-hand side to this value. There are two terms on the right-hand side, Eh and g. The first term Eh is the expected value, which is a constant and thus has no variance, which also means that it has no correlation or covariance with the g term. Thus, we can set the variance of g to $\sigma^2 h$. So we simply require that the variance of g be $\sigma^2 h$.

One model that has this variance is $\sigma e(h)^{1/2}$, where e is a standard normal random variable. You should recognize this model since it is just the Wiener process, which we covered in Essay 25, multiplied by the stock's standard deviation, σ. We let h be dt, a very short time increment. Remember our requirement that the expected value of g must be zero? The expected value of g is indeed zero, because it is just a Wiener process, which has zero expected value, times σ.

Now we have a model in which the expected return and variance equal what we want it to be. That model is $R = Edt + \sigma^* e^*(dt)^{1/2}$. Does this model have the other properties we want it to have? If S is the current stock price, then the stock price after the period h is $S(1 + Edt + \sigma e(dt)^{1/2})$. What is the variance of this future stock price? Without getting into the technical details, which are really not all that difficult, the variance will be larger if dt is larger. That is probably easy to see. Just picture random values of e coming out. If dt is larger, the future stock price will be more variable. In other words, the farther out you are forecasting, the greater is the variance.

Finally, the model must not permit the stock price to go below zero. From the previous paragraph, we have the future stock price as $S(1 + Edt + \sigma e(dt)^{1/2})$. Subtracting the current stock price, we have that the change in the stock price is $SEdt + S\sigma e(dt)^{1/2}$. Thus, if the stock price reaches zero, our formula tells us that the change in the stock price will be zero, and in fact, the stock price will be stuck at zero. It cannot recover, meaning that the state of bankruptcy has occurred. It might appear that the stock price could be slightly above zero and the next change might be large and negative, allowing the stock to go below zero, but that is not possible if dt is truly small enough. The rules regarding Brownian motion allow only very tiny movements to occur over a given instant in time. The stock price cannot go crashing through zero, because it will become stuck at zero.

Thus, our model allows us to replicate the behavior of the stock over a short holding period. We have taken the basic Brownian motion process and converted it into a form that models stock price movements. This model has many convenient and reasonable properties. We refer to the process as *geometric Brownian motion*. It is "geometric" in the sense that the *proportional change*, which is what we mean by the percentage change, in the stock price follows this stochastic process.

Without providing the mathematical details, we can say that the returns on stocks follow a lognormal distribution. This distribution is not the normal, or bell-shaped, curve. A lognormal distribution is skewed toward positive returns in contrast to the normal distribution, which is symmetric. A lognormal distribution, however, does imply that the logarithm of the returns comes from the normal or bell-shaped distribution.

These properties are all desirable and fairly realistic. Of course, no model will reproduce perfectly the process in which stocks returns are generated. The real world can rarely be reduced to a set of mathematical equations. But as is nearly always the case, if a set of mathematical equations can reproduce the basic manner in which a real-world phenomenon occurs, it can have many uses. One of these uses is in pricing derivatives on assets that follow the process described by the mathematical model covered here, which we address in Essay 27.

FOR MORE READING

Chance, Don M. "The ABCs of Geometric Brownian Motion." *Derivatives Quarterly* (Winter 1994): 41–47.

Jarrow, Robert A., and Stuart M. Turnbull. *Derivatives Securities*, 2nd ed. Mason, OH: Thomson South-Western, 2000, chap. 4.

Merton, Robert C. "On the Mathematics and Economics Assumptions of Continuous-Time Models." *Financial Economics: Essays in Honor of Paul Cootner*, ed. William F. Sharpe and Cathryn M. Cootner. Englewood Cliffs, NJ: Prentice-Hall, 1982.

Osborne, M. F. M. "Brownian Motion in the Stock Market." *Operations Research* (March–April 1959): 145–173.

Wilmott, Paul. *Derivatives: The Theory and Practice of Financial Engineering*. Chichester, UK: John Wiley & Sons, 1998, chap. 3.

TEST YOUR KNOWLEDGE

1. Identify the four desirable characteristics of a model of stock price movements.
2. How is the Brownian motion process used to model stock price volatility when each stock has a different volatility and Brownian motion has a specific volatility?
3. How does the model of stock prices covered in this chapter prohibit the stock from going below zero?
4. What is the difference between a normal distribution and a lognormal distribution?

Option Pricing: The Black-Scholes-Merton Model

This essay deals with the celebrated Black-Scholes-Merton model for pricing European options. The model first appeared in a 1972 article in the *The Journal of Finance* in which Fischer Black and Myron Scholes published an empirical study testing whether the prices of over-the-counter options conformed to the model. Strangely, the actual article that presents the derivation of the model was not published until 1973 in *The Journal of Political Economy*, which is a story I shall tell later in this essay. At around that same time, Robert Merton was working on the same problem and obtained the same formula with some new results. His paper was published in *The Bell Journal of Economics and Management Science* in 1973. Twenty-four years later, the Nobel Committee awarded their Economics Prize to Scholes and Merton; with Black, having died in 1995 being ineligible.

First off, let us call the model BSM, and when referring to the individuals, we shall call them Black, Scholes, and Merton. BSM is a formula that relates the price of a European call (or put) to the variables that should affect its price. Intuition tells us that the stock price, exercise price, risk-free interest rate, volatility of the stock, time to expiration, and dividends, payouts, or carrying costs on the underlying asset should affect the option's price. Interestingly, before BSM there was a widespread belief that the expected growth of the asset price ought to affect the option price. BSM demonstrates that this belief was not true, though it is not obvious on the surface why this is not true. I shall touch on that point in a later essay. In short, BSM like any good model, tells us what is important and what is not important. It does not promise to produce the exact prices that show up in the market, but it does a remarkable job of pricing options that meet all of the assumptions of the model. In fact, it is safe to say that virtually all option pricing models, even the extremely complex ones, have much in common with the

BSM-based models. The model has had as much impact as any other model in economics or finance, which is why the Nobel Prize was awarded for its discovery.

Let us describe the model with reference to a call option on a stock. Black, Scholes, and Merton start by specifying a simple and well-known equation that models the way in which stock prices fluctuate. This equation, called geometric Brownian motion and which we covered in Essays 25 and 26, implies that stock returns will have a lognormal distribution, meaning that the logarithm of the stock's return will follow the normal (bell-shaped) distribution. Black, Scholes, and Merton then propose that of the variables that determine the option's price, only two can change: time and the underlying stock price. Time poses no problem because it is deterministic. A 20-day option today will be a 19-day option tomorrow. It is the uncertainly of the stock price that causes problems.

Black, Scholes, and Merton propose that the call price will move deterministically with the stock price over a very short interval. This statement means that, while we do not know where the stock is going, we know that given a change in the stock price, we can say precisely where the option price will go. This point holds only over the very shortest time period. It is, of course, the basic calculus concept of a first derivative. Given knowledge of the first derivative, you can then form a portfolio consisting of a long position in stock and a short position in calls that eliminates the risk. This hedged portfolio is obtained by setting the number of shares of stock equal to the approximate change in the call price for a change in the stock price, or, of course, the first derivative of the option price with respect to the stock price. This mix of stock and calls must be revised continuously, a process known as *delta hedging*, which I shall cover in Essay 30.

Black, Scholes, and Merton then turn to a little-known result in a specialized field of probability theory known as *stochastic calculus*. This result defines how the option price changes in terms of changes in the two factors that determine it, the stock price and time to expiration. Then they reason that this hedged combination of options and stock should grow in value at the risk-free interest rate. Otherwise, a trader could engage in profitable arbitrage, which would induce similar trading by others, the combined effects of which would be to drive the return of the hedged portfolio to the risk-free rate, at which point the arbitrage trading would stop. They then show that from this result you obtain a partial differential equation or PDE, which is a fairly complicated expression containing first and second partial derivatives of the option price with respect to the stock price and a first derivative with respect to time. The solution of a differential equation is the original function whose derivatives are specified by the equation. In this case, that solution is the formula for the option price. Often, however, there are numerous candidates for the solution, and the correct solution is the one whose value equals a given condition that you know must hold. In the case of the option pricing formula, the option price must be worth the exercise value of the option at expiration. Imposing this condition, called a boundary condition, on the solution leads to the correct formula for the option.

Black and Scholes actually had some difficulty solving this equation. Though Black had a Ph.D. in applied mathematics from Harvard, he was not a specialist in differential equations, and Scholes was only a financial economist who specialized in empirical testing of financial models. Solving differential equations is often a matter of making educated guesses and taking advantage of prior knowledge of what the final solution might possibly look like. Black and Scholes benefited from the fact that previous researchers had almost found the elusive formula. Their predecessors' solutions looked remarkably similar to what we know as the correct formula. As it turned out, Black obtained the solution with a different approach, using the celebrated capital asset pricing model in which the expected returns of all assets must equal the risk-free rate plus a risk premium determined by the asset's covariance with the market. Upon obtaining the formula, Black took the derivatives, inserted them into the differential equation, and by that was able to verify that the solution was correct. Black eventually discovered that the differential equation could be transformed into one that was equivalent to one well known in physics as the heat transfer equation, for which the procedure for finding the solution was already known. Interestingly, Merton solved the equation himself using a different approach.

Strangely, Black and Scholes had trouble getting the publishers of academic journals to care about their result. They were originally rejected by one distinguished economics journal, then another. Fortunately, Merton Miller, another financial economist who won the Nobel Prize himself years leter, asked the editors of the original journal, *The Journal of Political Economy*, to take another look at the paper, and the article was then finally accepted. In the meantime, Black and Scholes tested their model. The paper reporting the results was published before the paper deriving the model was in print. Merton held up publication of his paper in deference to Black and Scholes, and his paper eventually appeared at around the same time as their did. The publication of these papers was fortuitously timed in that it coincided with the creation of the world's first organized options market, the Chicago Board Options Exchange.

The rest was history. I would be surprised if there were many discoveries in economic and financial research that have had greater impact. It has taken many years but the offspring of the BSM model are now generating the prices of trillions of dollars of options and other derivatives. Though Black, Scholes, and Merton became famous and wealthy, I think it is safe to say that had they been practitioners instead of academics primarily interested in pushing forward the frontiers of knowledge, they might have made even more money, keeping their formula to themselves for a long time.

Although these essays are meant to use a minimum of technical notation, the Black-Scholes formula is worth stating in its entirety. It is

$$c = S N(d_1) - X e^{-rT} N(d_2)$$

where

$$d = \frac{\ln(S/X) + (r + \sigma^2/2)T}{\sigma \sqrt{T}}$$

$$d_2 = d_1 - \sigma \sqrt{T}$$

and $N(d_1)$, $N(d_2)$ are cumulative normal probabilities.[1]

Here c is the call option price, S is the current stock price, X is the exercise price, r is the risk-free rate, T is the time to expiration, and σ is the standard deviation or volatility of the stock.

FOR MORE READING

Black, Fischer. "Fact and Fantasy in the Use of Options." *Financial Analysts Journal* 31 (July–August 1975): 36–41, 61–72.

Black, Fischer. "How to Use the Holes in Black-Scholes." *Journal of Applied Corporate Finance* 1 (Winter 1989): 67–73.

Black, Fischer. "How We Came Up with the Option Formula." *The Journal of Portfolio Management* 15 (Winter 1989): 4–8.

Black, Fischer, and Myron Scholes. "The Pricing of Options and Corporate Liabilities." *The Journal of Political Economy* 81 (1973): 637–654.

Black, Fischer, and Myron Scholes. "The Valuation of Option Contracts and a Test of Market Efficiency." *The Journal of Finance* 27 (1972): 399–417.

Chance, Don M., and Robert Brooks. *An Introduction to Derivatives and Risk Management*, 7th ed. Mason, OH: Thomson South-Western, 2007, chap. 5.

---

[1] A personal story will help you appreciate why I published the formula in this nontechnical set of essays. On the day on which Scholes and Merton won the Nobel Prize, a newspaper reporter from on unnamed major network called to ask me to explain why Scholes's and Merton's work merited the prize. After doing so, the reporter asked me to read the formula to him over the telephone. Take a good look at the formula and imagine trying to "read it" to someone over the telephone. I asked for his fax number to which he said, "Never mind."

Chriss, Neil A. *Black-Scholes and Beyond: Option Pricing Models*. Chicago: Irwin Professional Publishing, 1997.

Cox, John C., and Mark Rubinstein. *Options Markets*. Englewood Cliffs, NJ: Prentice-Hall, 1985, chap. 5.

Hull, John C. *Options, Futures, and Other Derivatives*, 6th ed. Upper Saddle River, NJ: Prentice-Hall, 2006, chap. 13.

Jarrow, Robert A., and Andrew Rudd. *Option Pricing*. Homewood, IL: Irwin, 1983, chap. 9.

Jarrow, Robert A., and Stuart M. Turnbull. *Derivatives Securities*, 2nd ed. Mason, OH: Thomson South-Western, 2000, chap. 8.

McDonald, Robert L. *Derivative Markets*, 2nd ed. Boston: Addison Wesley, 2006, chap. 12.

Merton, Robert C. "The Theory of Rational Option Pricing." *The Bell Journal of Economics and Management Science* 4 (1973): 141–183.

Merton, Robert C., and Myron Scholes. "Fischer Black." *The Journal of Finance* 50 (1995): 1359–1370.

TEST YOUR KNOWLEDGE

1. Explain how a dynamic delta hedge is used to derive the option price in the BSM model.
2. What method did Black use to solve the partial differential equation that gave him the correct formula?
3. Was the model immediately recognized by academia as an important discovery?

Option Pricing:
The Binomial Model

In Essay 27 I presented a brief overview of the Black-Scholes-Merton (BSM) model for pricing European options. In this essay I shall discuss the binomial model, which is an alternative but consistent model for pricing options.

The origins of the binomial model are something of a mystery. The first appearance in print was in the textbook *Investments* by William F. Sharpe in 1978. Sharpe used the model to explain option pricing at a very elementary level, and in doing so, he established the pedagogical value of the model. He probably did not realize at the time that what he seemed to view largely as a teaching device would eventually become a major tool in the theory and practice of options. Formal derivations of the model appeared in Cox, Ross, and Rubinstein (1979) and Rendleman and Bartter (1979).

Let us begin by asking the question of why we need another model when we have BSM. Technically, we do not need another model for standard European options, but the binomial model serves several useful purposes. One is that the detailed mathematics involved in deriving the BSM model are quite difficult. This fact is unfortunate because the intuition is not all that difficult. You simply hold the underlying asset and sell a call in the appropriate proportions such that the call price change and the asset price change offset, leaving a riskless position that should grow in value at the risk-free rate. The position must be revised continuously because the appropriate number of units of the asset per option changes constantly.[1] The binomial model enables us to see how this happens without having to place ourselves in a theoretical world of continuous trading. Let me explain how that works and then I shall conclude with the other reason why we need the binomial model.

---

[1] You can also fix the number of units of the asset and let the number of options vary.

Suppose a stock is priced at $100. We propose that it can go up to $112 or down to $92, values that can be obtained by reference to the volatility of the stock. Consider a call on the stock with a strike of $100 that expires when the stock gets to either $112 or $92. What is a fair price for the call today? The answer is simple though it takes a few step to get it.

Suppose you purchase 60 shares of stock and sell calls on 100 shares of stock. How much will this combination cost? Sixty shares of stock will cost 60($100) = $6,000, but the 100 calls will pay for a portion of that cost depending on what price you can get for them. When the option expires, the stock will be at either $112 or $92, meaning that the call will expire worth either $12 or $0. So the value of your position will be either 60 shares worth $112 each minus 100 calls worth $12 each for a total of $5,520 or 60 shares worth $92 each for a total of $5,520. Note that in this case, your calls expire worthless. Thus, you are hedged and that $5,520 value should represent a return equal to the risk-free interest rate. Suppose the risk-free rate is 5%. That means your initial outlay should be $5,520/1.05 = $5,257. Since the 60 shares of stock cost $6,000, the 100 calls should cost $743, or $7.43 each. In other words, 60 shares of stock purchased at $100 each, less 100 calls sold at $7.43, would cost $5,257 and would return $5,520 one period later with no risk, a rate of 5%, the current rate on alternative risk-free investments.

If the call is not priced at $7.43, you could earn an arbitrage profit by either selling it if it is overpriced and buying the shares, or buying it if it is underpriced and selling short the shares. Thus, $7.43 is the only call price at which everyone would agree that nothing is to be gained by engaging in riskless arbitrage.

The actual manner in which the price is obtained does not technically require that you set up and work through a risk-free hedge. Rather, the option price can be shown to be a probability-weighted average of the possible future option prices discounted at the risk-free rate. These probabilities are not the actual probabilities of these stock prices, as we shall see in Essay 31.

If we added a period to the problem and let the stock go from 112 or 92 to some other values, we could maintain the hedge by adjusting the number of calls per share. We would ultimately earn the same risk-free return over each of the two periods if and only if the call is selling at its correct, arbitrage-free price. Each time we allow the stock to make one more move, we are adding what is called a time step.

We can continue to add time steps, letting an actual option's real life be represented by a large number of these time steps. This array of prices is often referred to as a *binomial tree* or sometimes a *binomial lattice*. Assuming we let the number of time steps become sufficiently large and the length of each time step become very small, our tree begins to approximate real-world short-term movements in the stock price, and we would find, by appropriately setting the percentages by which the stock can go up and down, that the binomial price will bounce around and converge to the BSM price. My experience has found that it usually takes a minimum of 50 time steps for standard European options. Obviously a computer is necessary for any calculations involving more than a few time steps, but programming the binomial model is simple and requires surprisingly few lines of code. What is happening is that the binomial model transparently solves a difference equation, which is similar to the differential equation that I mentioned in Essay 27 as being the key toward obtaining the BSM formula.

Thus, one advantage of the binomial model is that it does not require knowledge of continuous-time models, Brownian motion, stochastic differential equations, and the like. In fact, the basic binomial model requires no calculus at all. Yet it captures all of the essential principles involved in option pricing. Consequently, the binomial model has pedagogical value in learning option pricing. For example, the binomial model shows us that the price of an option can be stated as a discounted expected value of the option at expiration. The probabilities involved in computing the option's expected value are those that would exist if investors are risk neutral, meaning that they do not perceive any advantage or disadvantage to risk. This point sounds a bit paradoxical, and we shall take it up in a later essay. The BSM model leads to the same conclusion, but in the BSM model, the point is more obscure.

There is yet another major advantage of the binomial model. We hardly need it to verify the BSM price, but often we are interested in options that are not standard European. American options, for example, are sometimes exercised early and therefore should sell for higher prices than their European counterparts. The binomial model enables us to check at the various points in an option's life for the possibility of early exercise. If early exercise makes sense at any point in time, we assume the option holder would do so. Then the otherwise computed values of the option are replaced by the exercise values. Only one additional line of code is required in most programs. Other more complex options of the type often seen in over-the-counter markets today can also be priced by using the binomial model or a variation thereof, but the code does become quite detailed and the procedure slows down considerably. In many cases the trees become quite bushy.

The binomial framework is also useful in modeling movements in the term structure of interest rates, which allows us to obtain arbitrage-free prices of bonds and derivatives on bonds and interest rates. We shall cover this topic in Essays 60 to 64.

In summary, the binomial model offers the advantages of mathematical simplicity, pedagogical value, and the ability to adapt itself well to more complex problems that do not lend themselves to closed-form solutions as in the BSM case. These advantages of the binomial model are not meant to suggest that continuous-time closed-form models are deficient on these matters. Continuous-time closed-form models are usually faster, so they are generally preferred when they can be used.

FOR MORE READING

Chance, Don M., and Robert Brooks. *An Introduction to Derivatives and Risk Management*, 7th ed. Mason, OH: Thomson South-Western, 2007, chap. 4.

Chriss, Neil A. *Black-Scholes and Beyond: Option Pricing Models*. Chicago: Irwin Professional Publishing, 1997.

Cox, John C., and Mark Rubinstein. *Options Markets*. Englewood Cliffs, NJ: Prentice-Hall, 1985, chap. 5.

Cox, John C., Stephen A. Ross, and Mark Rubinstein. "Option Pricing: A Simplified Approach." *Journal of Financial Economics* (1970): 229–264.

Hsia, Chi-Cheng. "On Binomial Option Pricing." *The Journal of Financial Research* (1979): 41–46.

Hull, John C. *Options, Futures, and Other Derivatives*, 6th ed. Upper Saddle River, NJ: Prentice-Hall, 2006, chap. 11.

Jarrow, Robert A., and Andrew Rudd. *Option Pricing*. Homewood, IL: Irwin, 1983, chap. 13.

Jarrow, Robert A., and Stuart M. Turnbull. *Derivatives Securities*, 2nd ed. Mason, OH: Thomson South-Western, 2000, chap. 5.

McDonald, Robert L. *Derivative Markets*, 2nd ed. Boston: Addison Wesley, 2006, chaps. 10, 11.

Nelson, Daniel B., and Krishna Ramaswamy. "Simple Binomial Processes as Diffusion Approximations in Financial Models." *The Review of Financial Studies* (1990): 393–430.

Rendleman, Richard J., and Brit J. Bartter. "Two-State Option Pricing." *The Journal of Finance* (1979): 1093–1110.

Sharpe, William F. *Investments*. Englewood Cliffs, NJ: Prentice-Hall, 1978.

Stapleton, R. C., and M. G. Subrahmanyam. "The Valuation of Options When Asset Returns Are Generated by a Binomial Process." *The Journal of Finance* (1984): 1525–1539.

Van der Hoek, John, and Robert J. Elliott. *Binomial Models in Finance*. New York: Springer, 2006.

TEST YOUR KNOWLEDGE

1. Name the three principal advantages of the binomial model.
2. What is a binomial tree or lattice?

Option Pricing: Numerical Methods

This essay is the third in a series on the different methods for computing an option price. We previously covered the Black-Scholes-Merton and binomial models. Now we take a look at what are called *numerical methods* for pricing options.

First let us consider why we might need another method. As previously explained, the Black-Scholes-Merton model is the solution to a partial differential equation (PDE). In some cases, the type of option is so complex that a solution to the PDE is not possible or is very difficult to find. When that is the case, it is nearly always possible to obtain the option price by a numerical method. A numerical method either solves the differential equation at each point during the option's life or simulates the possible outcomes and determines the average option price that would lead to the outcomes observed. These techniques are called numerical methods, because they involve obtaining the solution by brute computational force, and they typically require a very large number of calculations. We shall see what this means in the next few paragraphs.

We have actually already covered one numerical method, the binomial model. Yes, the binomial model is a numerical method. It takes a set of possible final stock prices at the option's expiration and systematically determines the option price today that would lead to the various possible final option values at expiration. For more complicated options, it creates a set of possible paths that the stock might take and then values the option by weighting its outcomes by special probabilities of the paths it took to reach the respective outcomes. As noted in Essay 28, these probabilities are not the actual probabilities, which we shall get into in Essay 31.

The binomial model solves a difference equation, which is a variation of a differential equation that considers only discrete values and finite changes in the variables. It creates a tree of these paths, wherein at each point in the tree there are two branches to which the stock may move.

A similar method is the finite difference approach. In this procedure, the differential equation is solved by laying out a rectangle with rows representing a range of possible stock prices and columns representing the time to expiration. The rectangle, thus, looks like a grid representing various combinations of the stock price and time to expiration. The column at the far right contains the option prices at the expiration for the range of possible stock prices. The differential equation can then be converted into a series of easily solvable algebraic equations. The solution, however, can be done only for one column at a time. Thus, starting at the far right, you solve the equations, which then produces the option prices for the range of stock prices if the option has just a little time to go before expiration. Stepping back one column to the left, you proceed to solve the remaining equations until reaching the far-left column, which gives the option price today for a range of stock prices.

There are two general methods of solving the equations, the *explicit finite difference method*, which solves for an option price in terms of three possible prices at the next time step, and the *implicit finite difference method*, which solves for three option prices in relation to each other and one future option price. There are several other variations of these methods. The explicit method is equivalent to a trinomial method, which is just a variation of the binomial in which there are three possible outcomes instead of two.

Reading off the option price that corresponds to the actual current stock price gives us the actual current option price. The finite difference method, in effect, solves the differential equation for the option price at every point in time in the option's life for a range of reasonable stock prices. To obtain the current option price, however, you have to start at the end of the option's life and work successively back to the present, which is true also of the binomial method.

Admittedly in this nontechnical essay, I cannot do the finite difference method full justice. Suffice it to say, however, that the technique is not all that difficult if you are comfortable with algebra. Its advantage, however, over the binomial model is quite limited. It seems to be more efficient if it is necessary to compute the prices of numerous options, and it is probably faster for computing the partial derivatives of the option price with respect to the stock price, which is essential information for hedging the option, a topic we shall cover later. I suspect, however, that most financial institutions use the binomial model or a variation thereof and are quite satisfied with the results.

Another numerical method used to price complicated options is Monte Carlo simulation. In business applications, Monte Carlo simulation is a method of analyzing the effects of decisions under uncertainty. Random numbers are drawn from a probability distribution whose properties are comparable to those of the underlying variable of uncertainty, such as future sales, labor costs, and so on. In option pricing, you simply simulate the stock prices that might occur at the option's expiration.

For example, let the stock price today be 100 and the exercise price be 100. Suppose we draw a random number that produces a stock price at expiration of 105. Then a call option would have a value at expiration of 5. Suppose the next random stock price drawn is 98. Then the option expires worth zero. We proceed to draw many more of these random stock prices and then average the corresponding set of option prices at expiration. Then we discount the average back to the present to get the current option price.

How good is the answer? We can gauge its accuracy by comparing it against the Black-Scholes-Merton value for a standard European call. For this essay I ran a Monte Carlo simulation with only 1,000 random numbers of an option with a stock price of 72, an exercise price of 70, a risk-free rate of 6%, a time to expiration of 42 days, and a standard deviation of 0.32. I ran this 1,000-trial simulation three times and obtained prices of 4.46, 4.36, and 4.58 (remember that each price was obtained using 1,000 random stock prices). The correct answer using the Black-Scholes formula is 4.46, so the answer is pretty close, but obviously not exact. There are some methods for speeding up the process and increasing its accuracy, and a great deal of research is going on to improve the method.

Monte Carlo simulation is most valuable for more complicated options such as Asian options, where the payoff is based not on the price of the stock on the expiration day but on the average price of the stock over the life of the option. Unfortunately, upward of a million random numbers usually must be drawn. Again, research on speeding up the method is bringing considerable improvements.

Another method used in option pricing is the polynomial approximation. It is a well-known rule in mathematics that virtually any well-behaved function can be approximated with a polynomial. Most option prices are represented by well-behaved functions, however shy those functions might be in revealing themselves to us. Thus, researchers have developed a set of models that are approximations to the actual formulas. As approximations, they vary in their accuracy, in some cases being extremely accurate over a given range of parameters and in others showing severe biases. They do, however, reduce the time and computational complexity and enable us in some cases to obtain accurate answers to the prices of complicated options.

In general, numerical solutions are inferior to closed-form solutions that give us simple, easily computable formulas. Alas, real-world problems do not always lend themselves to such nice results, as scientists and mathematicians can attest. Fortunately, computers have made numerical solutions more easily attainable. Simulations that required mainframe computers years ago are now routinely performed on desktop computers.

FOR MORE READING

Boyle, Phelim. "Options: A Monte Carlo Approach." *Journal of Financial Economics* 4 (1977): 323–338.

Brennan, Michael J., and Eduardo S. Schwartz. "Finite Difference Methods and Jump Processes Arising in the Pricing of Contingent Claims: A Synthesis." *Journal of Financial and Quantitative Analysis* 13 (1978): 461–474.

Broadie, M., and J. Detemple. "Recent Advances in Numerical Methods for Pricing Derivative Securities." *In Numerical Methods in Finance*, ed. L. C. G. Rogers and D. Taley. Cambridge, UK: Cambridge University Press, 1997, 43–66.

Dupire, Bruno, ed. *Monte Carlo: Methodologies and Applications for Pricing and Risk Management*. London: Risk Books, 1998.

Geske, Robert, and Kuldeep Shastri. "Valuation by Approximation: A Comparison of Alternative Option Valuation Techniques." *Journal of Financial and Quantitative Analysis* 20 (1985): 44–72.

Hull, John, and Alan White. "Valuing Derivative Securities Using the Explicit Finite Difference Method." *Journal of Financial and Quantitative Analysis* 25 (1990): 87–100.

Kritzman, Mark. "What Practitioners Need to Know about Monte Carlo Simulation." *Financial Analysts Journal* 49 (November–December 1993): 17–20.

Lehoczky, John P. "Simulation Methods for Option Pricing." *Mathematics of Derivative Securities*, ed. Michael A. H. Dempster and Stanley R. Pliska. Cambridge, UK: Cambridge University Press, 1997, 528–544.

McDonald, Robert L. *Derivative Markets*, 2nd ed. Boston: Addison Wesley, 2006, chap. 19.

Wilmott, Paul. *Derivatives: The Theory and Practice of Financial Engineering*. Chichester, UK: John Wiley & Sons, 1998, chaps. 46–49.

TEST YOUR KNOWLEDGE

1. Why are numerical methods needed in option pricing?
2. How does the finite difference method work in solving for an option price?
3. How is Monte Carlo simulation used to obtain an option price?

Dynamic Option Replication

In this essay we take a look at the way in which options can replicate or be replicated by a class of strategies called *dynamic trading*. In general, there are many ways in which options, assets, and bonds can be combined so as to produce the same results. When that is the case, we remember that equivalent combinations must have the same price, which is a useful tool for pricing options and other derivatives.

A classic example comes from the relationship known as put-call parity, which we covered in Essay 22 for European options. In put-call parity, we found that the combination of one unit of an asset and a put on the asset is equivalent to one call on the asset and risk-free bonds that have a face value equal to the exercise price of the options. Or, in other words, the put price plus the asset price equals the call price plus the present value of the exercise price, which can be expressed mathematically as $p + S = c + PV(X)$, where p is the put price, c is the call price, S is the asset price, and $PV(X)$ is the present value of the exercise price. Put-call parity can be rearranged to show that $p = c + PV(X) - S$, meaning that a put is equivalent to a call, risk-free bonds, and shorting the asset. Obviously there are other ways of rearranging the equation. The key point is that the transaction implied by the left-hand side can be replicated by the transaction implied by the right-hand side.

This replication procedure is one strategy in a class of transactions called *static replication*. You can replicate a put by holding a call, buying a risk-free bond with face value equal to the exercise price, and selling short the asset. It is sufficient to buy the call and the bond and short the asset. No other transactions are necessary now, during the life of the options or at expiration. At expiration when the asset price is S^*, the call, bonds, and short asset will produce the same result as the put: The holder will have $X - S^*$ if S^* is less than X and zero otherwise. It is possible, however, to replicate positions in another manner: by continuously adjusting long and short positions so as to produce the same price movements in the replicating combination as in the instrument being replicated. The discovery of dynamic replication is one of the premier contributions of modern option pricing theory and has been used successfully in trading. In this essay I explain some of the more common forms of dynamic replication.

Perhaps the most basic example of dynamic trading is the transaction called *delta hedging*. Delta hedging involves taking a long position in an asset and a short position in calls on the same asset. If the number of units of the asset equals the number of calls, then the transaction is just a covered call, which we cover in Essay 40. While that strategy may be satisfactory for a given situation, the purpose of a delta hedge is to construct a risk-free position, perhaps to capitalize on the option being mispriced, or to hedge a dealer's position as it makes a market in options. A risk-free combination of long asset and short calls can be constructed by buying $N(d_1)$ units of the asset and selling one call. The term $N(d_1)$ is a number between zero and 1 and is obtained from the Black-Scholes-Merton model, covered in Essay 27. It is the delta of the option and represents the approximate change in the option price for a change in the asset price. If $N(d_1)$ is 0.5, then the sale of calls on 200 units of the asset would be hedged by the holding of 100 shares of units of the asset. If the asset falls by \$1, you lose \$100 on the asset but the 200 calls fall by \$0.50 each for a matching gain of \$100. This position is said to be *delta neutral*.[1]

The strategy of delta hedging works only over a brief instant of time. This statement is true because the delta is but a measure of the approximate change in the option price over the change in the asset price. The delta is technically correct only if the asset changes by a very small amount over a given but very short time interval. The delta will change constantly as the asset moves up and down and as time passes. An in-the-money call will have its delta move toward 1 and an out-of-the-money call will have its delta move toward zero. At expiration the delta is either 1 if in-the-money or zero if out-of-the-money. How fast the delta moves depends on the degree of uncertainty over whether the call will expire in- or out-of-the-money. The delta will move the fastest for options that are approximately at-the-money for that is where there is the most uncertainty over whether the call will expire in- or out-of-the-money. Also, this uncertainty will increase as the option moves closer to expiration if the asset price remains near the exercise price. The change in the delta relative to the change in the asset price is called the *gamma* and is used in making delta hedges more accurate. Any large moves in the asset price will result in the option price not changing

---

[1] In this example we fixed the number of calls and used $N(d_1)$ units of the asset. Alternatively we could fix the number of units of the asset and use $1/N(d_1)$ calls per unit. We can be long calls and short assets or long assets and short calls.

by the amount given by the delta. A trader can, however, add a position in another option and construct a gamma hedge, meaning that the overall position will have a delta of zero and a gamma of zero. This position is said to be delta neutral and *gamma neutral.*

If successfully executed, delta hedging will return the risk-free rate. If executed only approximately, there will be some risk, and the delta hedger can expect on average to slightly beat the risk-free rate. The risk is that associated with the gamma and derives from the position not being precisely gamma neutral.

Now suppose that you wished to replicate a call. Using the Black-Scholes-Merton formula, we know that $c = SN(d_1) - Xe^{-rT}N(d_2)$. This tells us that one long call is equivalent to $N(d_1)$ units of the asset and the borrowing of $N(d_2)$ units of debt with a face value of X and a present value of Xe^{-rT}. Thus, a call can be replicated by borrowing $N(d_2)$ units of debt with a face value of X and present value of Xe^{-rT} and holding $N(d_1)$ shares of stock. Naturally, the correct proportions of stock and debt, $N(d_1)$ and $N(d_2)$, are valid for small asset price movements only and will constantly change. The delta hedger would need to constantly change the mix of asset and debt. Of course, this cannot be done perfectly, giving rise to gamma risk.

Another popular form of dynamic replication is to synthetically create a put. Suppose you owned an asset and wanted to hedge it by holding a put. The asset and a put, otherwise known as a protective put, would have a delta equal to the delta of the asset, which is 1, plus the delta of the put, which is $N(d_1) - 1$ (Note: From put-call parity, the put delta equals the call delta minus the asset delta.) Thus, the protective put has a delta of $N(d_1)$, which is also the call delta. This statement should not be surprising because a protective put is a lot like a call.

One way in which a protective put can be replicated is by holding the asset and risk-free bonds so that the delta of the asset and bonds equals what would be the delta if the asset and the put were held. The asset delta is 1 and the delta of the risk-free bonds is zero. For example, if $N(d_1)$ were 0.5, then the delta of the combined position of asset and risk-free bonds could be set to 0.5 by having half of your money in the asset and half in risk-free bonds. As noted, however, the delta is valid only for a brief instant in time. Then it would need to be readjusted. How fast it would need to be readjusted depends on the gamma. How successful the trader is in keeping the position delta set to the desired delta will determine how well the replicating strategy works to reproduce the original desired transaction.

Several obvious questions should come to mind. How can you conceivably trade continuously, as is assumed in the dynamic trading strategies? The simple answer is certainly that you cannot. The more complex answer is that it does not necessarily require continuous trading to come fairly close to the target result, particularly if the gamma is small. Would transaction costs consume all of any gain? In theory, continuous trading would require an infinite number of transactions so any transaction cost at all would generate an infinite cost. Most institutions that engage in dynamic trading balance the transaction costs against the risk produced when trading is naturally less than continuous. In addition, there are ways to keep the transaction costs down. For example, futures can be used as a substitute for the asset and can result in significant savings.

Why would someone want to do dynamic replication? It might appear that the instrument being replicated could be obtained directly. That is sometimes the case. Because of mispricing, however, dynamic replication might offer a cheaper alternative or, in other words, allow you to exploit an arbitrage situation. In addition, it is sometimes the case that the desired instrument does not exist or does not have a sufficiently liquid market to justify direct purchase. Dynamic replication can provide a good substitute. If you were a dealer in options, you might wish to hedge a long (short) position in an option by dynamically replicating a short (long) position in the same option. By hedging the risk of buying or selling options, the dealer can make money off of its market-making activity without taking market risk.

The key point in distinguishing dynamic replication from static replication is that in the former, it is necessary to execute trades on an ongoing basis to generate the desired results. Static replication, however, requires only the initial trades. The ability to dynamically replicate financial instruments is one of the most powerful results in derivative pricing theory. It rests on the fact that two combinations of financial instruments that provide the same payoffs must have the same value.

FOR MORE READING

Jarrow, Robert A., and Stuart M. Turnbull. *Derivatives Securities*, 2nd ed. Mason, OH: Thomson South-Western, 2000, chap. 10.

McDonald, Robert L. *Derivative Markets*, 2nd ed. Boston: Addison Wesley, 2006, chap. 13.

Neftci, Salih N. *Principles of Financial Engineering*. San Diego: Elsevier Academic Press, 2004, chap. 7.

TEST YOUR KNOWLEDGE

1. What is the difference between static replication and dynamic replication?

2. Why might a delta hedge be constructed?
3. What happens if a large move in the asset occurs while a delta hedge is in place? What can be done to hedge against such a move?
4. Using the Black-Scholes-Merton formula, show what combination of the asset and a call option would replicate a zero-coupon risk-free bond that pays X dollars at maturity where X is the option exercise price. Is this replication static or dynamic?

Risk-Neutral Pricing of Derivatives: I

This essay on the topic of risk-neutral pricing is the first of two essays that address this important topic. It is undoubtedly one of the most critical, most misunderstood, and most misapplied concepts in finance. It turns out that derivatives can be priced by assuming investors are risk neutral, which sounds pretty radical given that no one is actually risk neutral. Yet how a person feels about risk is essentially irrelevant where derivatives are concerned.

We start by reviewing what we mean by risk preferences. Suppose you are offered an opportunity to engage in a coin-tossing game. If the coin turns up heads, you win $1. If it turns up tails, you win nothing and lose nothing. Would you play this game? The answer depends on whether it costs to play the game. Let us first say it costs nothing. Then of course you would play. You have nothing to lose. You have exhibited the first axiom of utility, which is *nonsatiation*. Given the opportunity to increase your wealth without regard to any risk, you would do so.

Suppose now that you are charged a fee to play the game. Let us say the fee is the expected outcome of $0.50. Do you play? You recognize that over the long run, you would win only what you paid, which would not be acceptable to a risk-averse investor. The feelings of disappointment, frustration, and fear of further losses would mean that an expected return equivalent to the expected payoff would not compensate you for the risk incurred. Suppose you played twice, losing first and then winning. While you would have broken even, you would prefer to have not played at all. Risk-averse people would, therefore, pay less than the expected outcome to play the game. The difference between what you pay and the expected outcome is the *risk premium*, the additional expected return that compensates you for the taking on the risk.

If you were risk neutral, however, you would willingly pay $0.50 to play the game. Your risk neutrality would mean that every loss you incurred would not bother you; you would see it as only a sidestep on the path to possible future gains.

We typically feel that most people are risk averse, but we do observe people who appear to be risk neutral and maybe even risk loving. The latter would pay more than $0.50 to play. They enjoy the risk and would willingly pay to assume more of it. Gamblers may appear to be anywhere from risk neutral to risk loving, but in fact they are probably as risk averse as anyone else. They receive a nonpecuniary reward in the form of the thrill of playing. After accounting for that reward, they are probably risk averse. Most of modern investment theory assumes that investors are risk averse. Hence, the price one pays for a security is set so that the investor expects a minimum return of the risk-free rate and a risk premium commensurate with the degree of risk, however measured. This statement does not, of course, mean that after the fact the investor would earn a risk premium. It means only that the risk premium is expected before the fact. In the long run, however, investors must receive risk premiums after the fact or they would stop investing in risky ventures.

Suppose an investor purchases an asset and holds it until a future date. Recognizing the risk, the investor decides to hedge the position with a forward (or futures) contract that calls for her to deliver the asset at the specific future date. What is an appropriate price for the asset and the futures? The asset will be priced, as described, such that the investor expects to earn a risk-free return and a risk premium. The existence and use of the derivative contract do not affect the underlying asset's price.[1]

The derivative price is found by invoking the no-arbitrage principle. If the investor buys the asset at S and immediately sells it with a forward contract, she guarantees receipt of a price known today, which we shall label as F. The investor might incur storage costs, but we will assume none here for simplicity. We shall assume the asset offers no yield like a dividend though this could be easily added. Let r be the risk-free rate. The transaction guarantees that the investor will have F dollars at the end of the holding period. She will, however, have paid S dollars at the start, which effectively becomes $S(1 + r)$ by the end of the transaction, reflecting the opportunity cost. The transaction is risk free and thus should not be expected to produce a risk premium. In addition, the transaction should generate no profit beyond the interest. Otherwise it would mean that a risk-free transaction would earn

---

[1] We could argue the point of the tail wagging the dog—meaning that maybe the derivative market is driving the underlying market instead of vice versa—but we shall not do so here.

more than the risk-free rate. Such a transaction would be very attractive, and everyone would want to do it. To rule out this opportunity for profitable arbitrage, the forward price F must equal the spot price grossed up by the factor $1 + r$.

Now, how does risk-neutral pricing come into play? Suppose I told you that the investor was not risk averse, but rather was risk neutral or even risk loving but I gave you the spot price S. Without knowing where that price came from, you would still arrive at the same forward price formula, $F = S(1 + r)$. The spot price S is determined independently of the forward price. It reflects the investor's risk preferences, the risk-free rate, and the expected future price of the underlying. So regardless of how the investor feels about risk, if given the spot price, the forward price is still the spot price—however obtained—factored up by the risk-free rate.[2]

This result suggests that the risk preferences of investors do not matter when arriving at the derivative price. That being the case, we could just as easily assume that investors are risk neutral. If that were true, then risk premiums do not exist so every asset has an expected return equal to the risk-free rate. We would be able to find the expected future spot price by grossing it up by the risk-free rate and that would equal the forward price.

Risk-neutral pricing is typically explained in the context of an option and often with the binomial model. I am taking a different and, I hope, simpler approach. Options are more complicated than forwards because it is necessary to look at two distinct states of nature at expiration, in-the-money and out-of-the-money. Forwards (and futures) can be evaluated by considering only one state or outcome: The spot price is at any given level, and the contract pays off the spot price minus the original forward price. That one outcome subsumes all possible outcomes.

Let us look at the problem another way. Suppose we find an identical planet to ours in which the populace is risk neutral. Let us call it Planet RN. Planet RN is as advanced as ours with similar financial markets and securities. We find an identical asset trading on Earth and Planet RN with the same probability distribution. That asset will trade at a lower price on Earth than on Planet RN because earthlings are not risk neutral.

Does everything I have said about risk neutrality imply that forwards will trade at the same price on both planets? Recall that I stated that investor risk preferences are irrelevant to the pricing of derivatives. That statement sounds like the forward price would be the same in both cases, but

---

[2] Of course, any cash flows, storage costs, or convenience yield would effect the forward price, as we have previously covered.

it is not. Investor risk preferences are not irrelevant to the *absolute* price of the derivative. They are irrelevant to the *relative* price of the derivative. By relative price, we mean the price of the derivative in relationship to the price of the underlying asset. In other words, the mathematical relationship between the derivative and its underlying asset is invariant to the risk preferences of investors who hold the asset. That means that the underlying asset price is taken as given, having been determined from the risk preferences of investors. Given that price, the derivative price is determined according to the cost-of-carry formula or whatever other formula is appropriate.

This little trick of using risk neutrality has made it possible to solve many complex derivative pricing problems, but it has been misinterpreted and misstated in many cases. Using risk neutrality is not the same as assuming that investors are risk neutral. Moreover, using risk neutrality to derive a pricing model does not mean that absolute derivative prices are invariant to risk preferences. In fact, absolute derivative prices are quite sensitive to risk preferences, but this sensitivity manifests in the form of the derivative's sensitivity to the price of the underlying asset, which is determined by risk preferences. Relative derivative prices are invariant to risk preferences. This distinction is rarely made but doing so helps clear up the confusion engendered when so many financial engineers imply that they are assuming risk neutrality to derive a pricing model. They are not really *assuming* risk neutrality. They are simply *using* risk neutrality.

FOR MORE READING

Baxter, Martin, and Andrew Rennie. *Financial Calculus*. Cambridge, UK: Cambridge University Press, 1996, chaps. 1–3.

Björk, Thomas. *Arbitrage Theory in Continuous Time*. Oxford, UK: Oxford University Press, 1998, chaps. 2, 6.

Hull, John C. *Options, Futures, and Other Derivatives*, 6th ed. Upper Saddle River, NJ: Prentice-Hall, 2006, chaps. 13, 25.

Jarrow, Robert A., and Stuart M. Turnbull. *Derivatives Securities*, 2nd ed. Mason, OH: Thomson South-Western, 2000, chap. 6.

McDonald, Robert L. *Derivative Markets*, 2nd ed. Boston: Addison Wesley, 2006, chaps. 20, 21.

Neftci, Salih N. *An Introduction to the Mathematics of Financial Derivative*, 2nd ed. Orlando, FL: Academic Press, 2000, chap. 2.

Neftci, Salih N. *Principles of Financial Engineering*. San Diego: Elsevier Academic Press, 2004, chap. 11.

TEST YOUR KNOWLEDGE

1. Explain the difference between a person who is risk averse and one who is risk neutral.
2. Why does the standard approach to derivative pricing result in the appearance of the expected return equaling the risk-free rate?
3. Explain why a risk-neutral investor and a risk-averse investor would arrive at the same derivative price.

Risk-Neutral Pricing of Derivatives: II

In this second essay on the topic of risk-neutral pricing of derivatives, I carry the issue a little further. It is a fact that if there are no arbitrage opportunities in the market, relative pricing can proceed as if investors are risk neutral. This condition implies the existence of a set of probabilities of the various possible outcomes that when applied to the prices of all assets and derivatives will produce the correct prices and reduce the expected returns to the risk-free rate. These probabilities are sometimes called *risk-neutral probabilities*. They are also called *equivalent martingale probabilities*.

A martingale is a stochastic process in which the underlying random variable on average does not change. With respect to assets in arbitrage-free markets, it implies that the price of the asset, scaled by the risk-free return, will on average not change. This statement is consistent with the risk premium having been eliminated. Remember, however, that I do not mean that there is no risk nor do I imply the absence of a risk premium. I mean only that the risk premium has been eliminated under the risk-neutral or equivalent martingale probabilities. A simple numerical example will be helpful.

Let us consider an asset priced at $100 and a call option with exercise price of $100 and one period to go before expiration. If the asset goes up, let us say it increases by 25% and if it goes down, it decreases by 20%. The risk-free rate is 7%. Let the probability of a price increase be 0.65 and the probability of a price decrease be 0.35. You should, of course, recognize this framework as that of the binomial model, which we covered in Essay 28. Note, however, that the probabilities stated here are the true probabilities, which are not required in binomial option pricing.

Let us first look at how the asset is priced. The expected price of the asset is $125(0.65) + 80(0.35) = 109.25$. The asset is priced at 100; thus, the appropriate discount rate on the asset must be 9.25%. In other words, $109.25/1.0925 = 100$. Investors price the asset independently of the option.

They take into account the risk-free rate and the risk premium they require. With the risk-free rate being 7%, the risk premium for this asset must be 2.25%.

If we used the binomial model to price the option, we would find that the option is worth 14.02. This result can be obtained, as we did in an earlier essay, by building a risk-free combination of the option and the asset, or more directly by the formula $c = [pc^+ + (1 - p)c^-]/r$ where c^+ is the option price if the asset moves up and c^- is the option price if the asset moves down, r is 1 plus the risk-free rate, and p is the risk-neutral/equivalent martingale probability, which is given by the formula $p = (r - d)/(u - d)$ with u being 1 plus the asset price change if it moves up and d being 1 plus the asset price change if it moves down. In this problem, $r = 1.07$, $u = 1.25$, $d = 0.80$, $c^+ = \text{Max}(0,125 - 100) = 25$, $c^- = \text{Max}(0,80 - 100) = 0$, and $p = (1.07 - 0.80)/(1.25 - 0.80) = 0.6$. Then the option price today is found to be $c = [0.6(25) + 0.4(0)]/1.07 = 14.02$.

Note what happens when we apply the risk-neutral probabilities to the asset and discount by the risk-free rate: $[0.6(125) + 0.4(80)]/1.07 = 100$. We obtain the correct asset price, in spite of the fact that investors are not risk neutral. We have changed the probabilities and still obtained the correct price for not only the option but also the asset. This procedure is what is called the *change of measure*, which is essentially a shift in the probabilities that preserves the essential properties of the probability distribution. Note that I said it preserves the *essential properties*. It preserves everything we need to properly price securities and derivatives, which is specifically the volatility. It does not, however, preserve the property of telling us the probability that any event or group of events will occur.

It is a simple matter to demonstrate in a market with nothing but one asset and a risk-free bond that no arbitrage implies the existence of risk-neutral probabilities. Suppose someone borrowed $100 at 7% and purchased the asset, believing that this transaction would guarantee a positive return. This would indeed be the case if the worst outcome, Sd, were greater than Sr or, in other words, $d > r$. The worst outcome would still allow the investor to pay back the interest on the borrowed funds from the proceeds from sale of the asset. Suppose someone else sold short the asset and invested the proceeds in the risk-free bond, believing that this strategy could guarantee a positive return. This would indeed be the case if the worst outcome, Su (remember, this is a short sale asset), were less than Sr (i.e., $u < r$). Then even the worst case would be that the interest earned would cover the cost of buying back the asset. Neither of these two situations could hold in a no-arbitrage world. So we must have $d < r$ and $u > r$, or simply $u > r > d$. In other words, the up return is better than the risk-free rate, which is better than the down return. This must hold to prevent arbitrage.

It is a mathematical fact that if $u > r > d$, we can find a number x such that $xu + (1 - x)d = r$. Solving for x gives us $x = (r - d)/(u - d)$. Thus, x has the same formula as the risk-neutral probability p and clearly *is* the risk-neutral probability p. We have just shown that if there are no arbitrage opportunities in a market with only an asset and a bond, then there exists a risk-neutral probability. It is also possible to show that if there is a risk-neutral probability, then there are no arbitrage opportunities. This proof is slightly more complex and we shall skip it here, because hopefully the main point has been established. Risk neutrality implies no arbitrage opportunities and vice versa.

Recall that we stated that risk neutrality implies that the asset follows a martingale. Upon clarification, we stated that this means that the asset price discounted at the risk-free rate is a martingale, meaning that its expected change is zero. This point is easy to see. We had $S = [pS^+ + (1 - p)S^-]/r$. The discounted asset price is either S^+/Sr or S^-/Sr the next period. Consequently, the discounted probability-weighted price, $pS^+/Sr + (1 - p)S^-/Sr$ is today's asset price, implying zero expected change.

Note that we did all of this without a derivative contract. Introducing a derivative such as an option changes nothing as long as we assume that there are no arbitrage opportunities involving the derivative. This assumption is reasonable as long as the derivative is correctly priced by a no-arbitrage procedure, such as the binomial model.

These arguments were all handled within the binomial framework. Were we to prove these arguments in the continuous time framework, involving the Brownian motion stochastic process followed by the asset, the proofs would become much more difficult. To change the probabilities in the continuous framework would require a rule called *Girsanov's theorem*, which is simply a proof that if certain other conditions are met, you can change a continuous probability measure by shifting its mean and preserve the essential properties that allow that probability measure to determine the prices of assets. The nonexistence of arbitrage opportunities assures us that these conditions are met.

The actual change of the probability measure is accomplished by application of a concept called the *Radon-Nikodym derivative* (referring now to a calculus "derivative"), which is, more or less, just the derivative of the new risk-neutral probability measure with respect to the original probability measure. We then say that the price of the asset or derivative is such that the expected return under the risk-neutral or equivalent martingale measure is the risk-free rate. Again, we have not changed how investors feel about risk. We have simply used a permissible adjustment to the probabilities and an offsetting adjustment to the discount rate, reducing it to the risk-free rate, that preserves the correct prices of assets and, of course, options and other derivatives. Again, this adjustment does *not* preserve the property that it can tell us the probabilities of events or groups of events. That is why option pricing models tell us a lot about options but do not tell us the expected returns on assets or options or the likelihood of an option expiring in-the-money.

Finally, let us add that the Black-Scholes-Merton option pricing model can be obtained directly by application of the risk-neutrality principle. We simply define that the option price today is the expected option price at expiration under the risk-neutral probability measure and then discount at the risk-free rate. Letting S^* be the asset price at expiration, we have $\{E[\text{Max}(0,S^* - X)]\}\exp[-rT]$, where we now define r as the continuously compounded risk-free rate. This expression is equal to $E[S^* - X]\exp[-rT]$ conditional on $S^* > X$, the in-the-money case. Then this expression can be further broken down into $E[S^*]-\exp[-rT]$ conditional on $S^* > X$ times $\exp[-rT]$ times the probability that $S^* > X$. The expected values are taken by assuming the asset price follows the lognormal Brownian motion process with an expected return of the risk-free rate. Although the math is a bit messy, the end result is the Black-Scholes-Merton formula.

The risk-neutrality/equivalent martingale/no-arbitrage rule is probably one of the most important in all of finance. It provides the appropriate relative prices of assets and derivatives. While it will not tell us how the assets obtain their prices from the expectations and risk preferences of investors, it will, given the asset price, the risk-free rate, and, in the case of options, the volatility, tell us the prices of options and other derivatives.

FOR MORE READING

Baxter, Martin, and Andrew Rennie. *Financial Calculus*. Cambridge, UK: Cambridge University Press, 1996, chaps. 13.

Björk, Thomas. *Arbitrage Theory in Continuous Time*. Oxford, UK: Oxford University Press, 1998, chaps. 2, 6.

Hull, John C. *Options, Futures, and Other Derivatives*, 6th ed. Upper Saddle River, NJ: Prentice-Hall, 2006, chaps. 13, 31.

Jarrow, Robert A., and Stuart M. Turnbull. *Derivatives Securities*, 2nd ed. Mason, OH: Thomson South-Western, 2000, chap. 6.

McDonald, Robert L. *Derivative Markets*, 2nd ed. Boston: Addison Wesley, 2006, chaps. 20, 21.

Neftci, Salih N. *An Introduction to the Mathematics of Financial Derivative*, 2nd ed. Orlando, FL: Academic Press, 2000, chap. 2.

Neftci, Salih N. *Principles of Financial Engineering*. San Diego: Elsevier Academic Press, 2004, chap. 11.

TEST YOUR KNOWLEDGE

1. What is a martingale, and what role does it play in derivative pricing?
2. What are risk-neutral probabilities?
3. In a binomial model, why does the risk-free rate have to fall between the return if the asset goes up and the return if the asset goes down?
4. What is Girsanov's theorem?

It's All Greek to Me

Not long after the Black-Scholes-Merton (BSM) option pricing model was developed, someone decided that a natural next step was to determine the amount by which an option price changes when one of the inputs changes. This operation, known in economics as *comparative statics*, involves taking the first derivative (i.e., the calculus derivative) with respect to the asset price, exercise price, risk-free rate, time to expiration, and standard deviation. You can then also move on to the second derivative and so on. Of course, the calculus derivatives tell us only what happens to the option price if the input variable changes by a very small amount.

What seemed primarily like an exercise in mathematics has now developed into an extremely important banking concept. Banks have become vendors of options, forwards, and swaps. When a bank sells an option, it takes a naked short position. It then typically buys an option or other derivative to offset the risk, attempting to earn the bid-ask spread off of buying at one price and selling at a higher price. The correct number of positions in this offsetting instrument is given by what is commonly called *the Greeks*.

For example, let us assume the underlying asset is a stock. When the stock price changes, by how much does the option price change? This amount is approximately given by the first derivative with respect to the stock price and is called the *delta*. Recall that we covered delta hedging in Essay 30. From the BSM model, it is the value $N(d_1)$. If you are short call options on 1,000 shares of stock with a delta of 0.5, you will need to hold 500 shares of the stock. If the stock goes down by $1, you will lose $500 on the stock and each option will fall by $0.50. With 1,000 options, you will gain $500 to offset. The delta is always nonnegative for a call option, because it should be apparent that stock price increases should lead to call price increases. The delta will range between 0 and 1 and will, at expiration, equal zero if the call option expires out-of-the-money and 1 if it expires in-the-money. The delta of a put is the delta of a call minus 1, meaning that the delta will always be between zero and -1.

The delta is correct, however, only for very small stock price changes. An actual option price increase will be more than 50% of the stock price increase. In fact, the larger the stock price increase, the more the call price change will deviate upward from 50%. On the downside, the call price change will be less than 50% and the difference will be greater the larger the stock price change. This is the second-order effect coming from the second calculus derivative, which is known as the *gamma* and results from the convex shape of the call price curve with respect to the stock price. The gamma is the change in the delta for a change in the stock price. It will always be positive for both a call and a put. Large gammas mean that the delta is very sensitive, and this means that delta hedging is much more difficult. The magnitude of the gamma is consistent with the uncertainty about whether the option will expire in- or out-of-the-money. For an expiring option either in- or out-of-the-money, the gamma will move toward zero. For an expiring option that is approximately at-the-money, the gamma will be very large. That is because at expiration the delta is going to jump to either 1 or zero. To protect against a large gamma, the bank can gamma hedge as well as delta hedge, though this requires a position in at least one additional instrument.

Another measure of the option's uncertainty is the *vega*, the first calculus derivative with respect to the volatility or standard deviation. Actually vega is not a Greek letter, and this term is occasionally referred to as *kappa* or *lambda*, but vega is the most commonly used term. The vegas of both a call and a put are equal and positive, reflecting the fact that an option price is directly related to the volatility. An option price is also very sensitive to the volatility, and this effect can induce substantial risk to an otherwise hedged position. We should note, however, that the BSM model is actually inconsistent with changing volatility. It assumes volatility is constant so taking the derivative really means nothing more than saying what the option price would be if you plugged a different volatility in the model. But the model presumes that the volatility will remain constant for the full life of the option. I like to compare this to what you get in Einstein's famous $E = mc^2$. You can take the derivative with respect to c, the speed of light, and you obtain $2mc$. Energy will change by two times the mass times the speed of light for a change in the speed of light. But the speed of light does not change! Now in this case, the model fits reality. In the BSM case, the model does not completely fit reality. It does not allow volatility to change, but in reality volatility does change. Other more sophisticated models can account for changing volatility, though the added complexity of the models is not always worth it.

Hedging the risk of a changing volatility can be quite difficult and requires adding a position in another option. You might wish to refer back to Essay 19 on volatility derivatives. Also, we shall cover volatility more in the next essay.

The time decay of the option is reflected in the *theta*. It is the first calculus derivative with respect to time. A negative theta, associated always with calls, indicates time value decay. For European puts, the theta is usually negative indicating time value decay, but for some deep in-the-money puts, the theta is positive, a result of the trade-off between the value of waiting longer and the cost of forgone interest on the exercise price that could be earned if the put could be exercised. If the put were American, however, its theta would always be negative. The time effect of theta, however, is not a source of risk since there is no question of how much time remains in an option's life and the rate at which time will elapse. Any position that has nonzero value will have a nonzero theta.

The effect of a change in the risk-free interest rate is called *rho*. It is the first calculus derivative with respect to the risk-free rate. Calls have positive rhos and puts have negative rhos. Standard options have very low rhos, meaning that interest rates do not impart much of an effect on their prices. As in the case of volatility, however the BSM model assumes away any interest rate changes. Other more sophisticated models do permit interest rate changes but still often fail to capture the complex interaction among interest rates, stock prices, and the volatility.

Finally, while there is a calculus derivative with respect to the exercise price, standard options do not have changing exercise prices so no one pays much attention to this concept, and it does not have its own Greek name. I should note that it is possible to construct options with changing exercise prices, which will be covered in Essay 49.

Hedging the risk of changes in the stock price, volatility, and interest rates is an important activity for options dealers. As they buy and sell options, meeting the needs of their clients, they create risks for themselves. By hedging away those risks, they put themselves in a position to be immune to changes in these variables and yet profit from any spread between the buying and selling prices of the options. Options dealers invest heavily in sophisticated software designed to give accurate estimates of these hedge parameters and tell them which offsetting transactions to execute.

FOR MORE READING

Chance, Don M. "Translating the Greeks: The Real Meaning of Call Option Derivatives." *Financial Analysts Journal* 50 (July–August, 1994), 43–49.

Hull, John C. *Options, Futures, and Other Derivatives*, 6th ed. Upper Saddle River, NJ: Prentice-Hall, 2006, chap. 15.

Jarrow, Robert A., and Stuart M. Turnbull. *Derivatives Securities*, 2nd ed. Mason, OH: Thomson South-Western, 2000, chaps. 9, 10.

McDonald, Robert L. *Derivative Markets*, 2nd ed. Boston: Addison Wesley, 2006, chap. 13.

Rendleman, Richard J. Jr. *Applied Derivatives: Options, Futures, and Swaps.* Malden, MA: Blackwell, 2002, chap. 6.

Wilmott, Paul. *Derivatives: The Theory and Practice of Financial Engineering.* Chichester, UK: John Wiley & Sons, 1998, chap. 7.

TEST YOUR KNOWLEDGE

1. Assume that a delta of an at-the-money call is 0.5. What happens to the delta as the underlying price increases and expiration approaches? What happens to the delta as the underlying price decreases and expiration approaches? How would your answer change if the option were a put?
2. A large gamma implies what about the probability of exercise of an option?
3. Why does the concept of theta pose no risk to an option?
4. How important is the rho in determining the risk of a standard European option on an asset?

Implied Volatility

One of the most fascinating and complex topics in option pricing is that of implied volatility. Implied volatility is the standard deviation, or variance if you prefer, that forces the value obtained from an option pricing model to equal the current market price of the option. The model is said to "imply" the level of volatility in the underlying asset and, thereby, reveal to the market what investors expect the volatility of the asset to be over the remaining life of the option. Implied volatility can be much more useful in quoting option prices, because regardless of the exercise price, expiration, or whether it is a put or a call, implied volatility is still supposed to be the volatility of the underlying asset. Thus, a three-month option worth $3.25 and a four-month option worth $5.14 are hard to compare. But if the three-month option has an implied volatility of 32% and the four-month option has an implied volatility of 29%, the former is priced high relative to the latter. Many markets have evolved to the point of actually quoting bid and offer prices in terms of implied volatility. The reliance on this concept necessitates that we look at some of the issues associated with implied volatility.

Let us begin with a technical matter. How do you are calculate the implied volatility? This is tantamount to having a formula that says that X is a function of Y and Z but where we know the value of X and Z and do not know Y. For simple functions, we can sometimes rearrange the equation to solve for Y in terms of X and Z. That rearrangement is virtually impossible for most option pricing models, because the function is complicated and the unknown variable, the volatility, appears several times. For the Black-Scholes-Merton (BSM), model, it appears twice in the formula for d_1, once as the standard deviation and once as the square of the standard deviation (i.e., the variance). It also appears again in d_2. The values of d_1 and d_2 are then transformed by the normal probability function into probabilities. Consequently, it is impossible to isolate the volatility.

The usual alternative is an iterative solution. You simply plug in values of the volatility until the price obtained from the model equals the market price of the option. This procedure can take a few steps or many, depending on the method used to reset the volatility for the next iteration. Standard equation-solving tricks can cut the time. These procedures include the secant method, the false position method, and bisection method. One of the more widely used is the Newton-Raphson method, which takes advantage of the fact that the first derivative of the option price with respect to the volatility, which we introduced as the vega in Essay 33, is known. This method gives a reasonable estimate of the amount by which the function will change if the volatility is changed by a small amount. Of course, the function must be well behaved, meaning that it cannot change too drastically over a short interval.

For the BSM formula, the option price is almost linear with respect to the volatility. That means that it is possible, with only a slight loss of accuracy, to express the volatility directly as a function of the option price. The solution is

$$\sigma = c\sqrt{2\pi}/S\sqrt{T}$$

where c = Option price, T = Time to expiration, S = Asset price, and π = Ratio of the circumference of a circle to its diameter.

This formula is valid only for at-the-money options. I published an extension of this formula that works reasonably well for options that are not at-the-money, and there have been several other methods of arriving at the implied volatility for options not at-the-money.

Assuming that you can then compute the implied volatility, another problem arises. The volatility is supposed to represent the volatility of the underlying asset over the life of the option. The existence of options with different times to expiration gives rise to different implied volatilities. This concept is called the *term structure of implied volatility*. While it would be nice if these volatilities were all the same, they simply are not. What is more disconcerting is the fact that options with the same expiration and different exercise prices also produce different implied volatilities. A plot of the implied volatility against the exercise price tends to show high implied volatilities for options with high and low exercise prices. This U-shaped curve has come to be known as the *volatility smile*. No one truly knows why the smile exists, but it is possible that the calculations for options away from the money are being distorted by the low liquidity. Others have proposed that skewness in the distribution of asset prices can lead to the smile.[1]

---

[1] The smile has been mostly observed on index options. Other types of options typically have failed to produce the U shape, but other patterns have been observed. These other patterns have often been described as a skew or smirk.

The existence of the smile is not only a curious phenomenon but also one that cannot be justified without invalidating itself. The smile is generated by initially assuming that the BSM model holds for at-the-money options. Then we calculate implied volatilities, which assumes that each of the options is on the same underlying asset. Consequently, the model does not permit different volatilities across the same asset. Thus, we produce the smile by assuming a model that does not permit it to exist. We strangle the BSM model until it coughs up something it has already rejected. Then we attempt to analyze the residue to see why the model is wrong and, in some cases, force the residue back into the model to see if we can get the model to use it properly. It seems likely that the model is simply not correct in the first place, perhaps even invalid for at-the-money options.

Another disconcerting result is that the implied volatility of a call is not usually the same as the implied volatility of the put with the same terms. How can that be? Again, these are options on the same underlying asset. We simply do not know why these results are found.

So why is all of this effort expended toward forcing the BSM model to produce a better fit of volatilities? It is because the BSM model is not only the most popular model, but it is also the simplest model. When fit to the volatilities of standard European options, it gives us these puzzling results. Yet we know of no other approach to pricing standard European options that is easier and more rational. We want it to work. We need it to work. So we do everything possible to force it to work.

Clearly the concept of implied volatility "implies" in itself a particular option pricing model. A given option pricing model would produce one implied volatility while another model would of necessity give another implied volatility. Unless all investors and traders were using the same model, it would be ludicrous to talk about a particular level of implied volatility as being the market's estimate of future volatility. Since much of the trading that goes on today is based on different opinions about volatility, it is apparent that much of the trading must be motivated by different opinions as to what is the correct option pricing model.

Some attempts to deal with these problems have taken the form of stochastic volatility models. These models assume that the volatility itself fluctuates in much the same way as does the asset price. Unfortunately, researchers have encountered many obstacles toward operationalizing these models, and we seem to be a long way from making them commonly used.

Ignoring all of the complexities of computing implied volatilities and worrying about the enigma of the smile, what do we do to consolidate the information on implied volatility into a single number? We can simply take an average of the implied volatilities of the various options used. The average can be unweighted or weighted by, say, the sensitivities of the option price to the volatility. This sensitivity measure, the vega, will be largest for at-the-money options, meaning that those options should have the largest weights. Another alternative is to find a set of weights that will produce a single implied volatility that minimizes the variation in the implied versus actual option prices. Finally, we can simply use the implied volatility of the option closest to at-the-money, in effect assuming that it contains the most information. Researchers have been somewhat divided on the best approach, but the findings tip slightly toward simply using the closest to at-the-money option.

The ultimate question on everyone's mind is whether implied volatility predicts the future volatility better than does historical volatility, the latter calculated by taking a sample of the asset's returns over a recent time period. This subject has been studied at great length, and the results are quite mixed. There is little question that on a comparative basis, implied volatility comes out ahead of historical volatility. Yet it has been shown in an empirical study that implied volatility predicts poorly for index options! And these have been on only exchange-listed options.

So what can we conclude about the usefulness of implied volatility? Option traders have two problems. One is that they do not know the true model that generates option prices. We are probably never going to find this answer. Have we ever found a true model for anything that is random? Even if we did find such a model, we have the second problem: Traders have different opinions of the expected future volatility. Whoever has the best opinion would make the most money. The implied volatility of that person's model would be the best estimate of the future volatility.

FOR MORE READING

Brenner, Menachem, and Marti G. Subrahmanyam. "A Simple Formula to Compute the Implied Standard Deviation." *Financial Analysts Journal* 44 (October–November 1988): 80–83.

Chance, Don M. "A Generalized Simple Formula to Compute the Implied Volatility," *The Financial Review* 31 (1996): 850–857.

Corrado, Charles J., and Thomas W. Miller Jr, "A Note on a Simple, Accurate Formula to Compute Implied Standard Deviation." *Journal of Banking and Finance* 20 (1996): 595–603.

Derman, Emanuel, and Iraj Kani. "Riding on a Smile." *Risk* 7 (February 1994): 18–20.

Derman, Emanuel, Iraj Kani, and Neil Chriss. "Implied Trinomial Trees of the Volatility Smile." *The Journal of Derivatives* 3 (Summer 1996): 7–22.

Dupire, Bruno. "Pricing with a Smile." *Risk* 7 (January 1994): 32–33, 35, 37–39.

Hull, John C. *Options, Futures, and Other Derivatives*, 6th ed. Upper Saddle River, NJ: Prentice-Hall, 2006, chaps. 13, 16.

Jarrow, Robert A., and Stuart M. Turnbull. *Derivatives Securities*, 2nd ed. Mason, OH: Thomson South-Western, 2000, chap. 8.

Mayhew, Stewart. "Implied Volatility." *Financial Analysts Journal* 51 (July–August 1995): 8–20.

McDonald, Robert L. *Derivative Markets*, 2nd ed. Boston: Addison Wesley, 2006, chap. 12.

Rubinstein, Mark. "As Simple as One, Two, Three." *Risk* 8 (January 1995): 44–47.

TEST YOUR KNOWLEDGE

1. What is the advantage of quoting an option price in terms of the implied volatility?
2. Explain how an iterative approach can be used to obtain the implied volatility.
3. In the Black-Scholes-Merton formula, the option price is nearly linear with respect to the volatility. What advantage does this characteristic offer?
4. What is the term structure of implied volatility?
5. What is the volatility smile?

American Call Option Pricing

In Essay 16 we looked at how American options differ from European options. In this essay we look at how those differences are manifested in different prices of American calls and European calls. Specifically we look at the ways in which early exercise is incorporated into option pricing models. First off, let us review how an American call differs from a European call. The former gives the right to exercise early while the latter permits exercise only on the expiration day. Early exercise of a call, however, is justified only if the asset makes a cash payment, such as a dividend on a stock. If there are no dividends during the life of the option, early exercise would be equivalent to buying something earlier than you need it and then giving up the right to decide later whether you really wanted it. If, however, it is possible to save a little money doing so, early purchase/exercise can sometimes be justified. Early exercise is not appropriate every time there is a dividend, but if early exercise is justified, it should occur just before the stock goes ex-dividend. Waiting until this point minimizes the amount of time value thrown away and still results in receiving the dividend.

In the early days of option pricing theory, the first crude approach to incorporating early exercise into the Black-Scholes-Merton (BSM) model was to use what was called the *pseudo-American call* method. If a stock paid a single dividend over the life of the option, you would simply calculate the BSM value under the assumption that you exercise just before the ex-dividend date and again under the assumption that you do not exercise until expiration. The correct option price was taken to be the larger value of the two. This approach, however, assumes that you know with certainty whether the option will be exercised early. It would make more sense to assume some probability of early exercise and then compute a probability-weighted average of the candidate values. That approach is exactly what is provided by the Roll-Geske-Whaley model.[1]

In 1977 Richard Roll discovered that the American call option price could be obtained by a simple arbitrage proof. His proof was made possible because his colleague at UCLA, Robert Geske, had developed a model for pricing compound options, which we cover in more detail in Essay 46. A compound option is an option on an option, that is, a call giving the right to buy a put, a call giving the right to buy a call, a put giving the right to sell a call, or a put giving the right to sell a put. Geske obtained an exact formula for the value of a compound option. For our purposes here it is sufficient to say that such an option can be constructed and its price could be obtained. Using a compound option and two standard European options, we can price the American call when there is one dividend during the life of the option. The model is called the Roll-Geske-Whaley model with the latter name added because Robert Whaley corrected a mistake in the original derivation.

Let us take a look at the Roll-Geske-Whaley model. Suppose we are just before the ex-dividend date. We know that as soon as the stock goes ex-dividend, there will be no dividends remaining. Because an American call with no dividends remaining during its life will not be exercised early, the BSM model for European options would then provide the correct ex-dividend price of the option. Given the stock price just before ex-dividend, and knowing that the stock will drop by the amount of the dividend, we know what the value of the option will be as soon as the stock goes ex-dividend. Naturally there is some noise in the stock price while it goes ex-dividend, meaning that the stock may not drop by the exact amount of the dividend, but the difference is not all that significant and could be built into the model if desired.

It is possible to solve by iteration for the critical stock price that will force the exercise value of the option on the ex-dividend date to equal the BSM value immediately after the stock goes ex-dividend. This point should be easy to see. We simply insert values of the stock price into the BSM formula until we find a value that forces the BSM price to equal the ex-dividend exercise value of the option, Let us call this critical stock price S'. This result is the ex-dividend stock price that would trigger early exercise on the ex-dividend day. Just before the stock goes ex-dividend, the trigger price would be $S' + D$ where D is the dividend.

With X representing the exercise price of the American option, we know that it will pay off $S' + D - X$ at the ex-dividend date if the actual stock

---

[1] As seen in Essays 31 and 32, the probabilities used in option pricing are not the true probabilities, but the risk-neutral probabilities.

price with the dividend is above $S' + D$. If the actual stock price with the dividend is below $S' + D$, then the call will not be exercised and the holder will simply be left holding a standard European call that will either end up in-the-money or out-of-the-money on the expiration day.

It is a simple matter to construct a portfolio of calls that will replicate these outcomes. First we buy a standard European call with an exercise price of X, expiring on the expiration day of the American call. Call this our option A. Then we sell a European compound call—a call option to buy an underlying call option—where the underlying call option is the standard European call we just bought, which we are calling A. The exercise price of this compound option is $S' + D - X$. Call this compound option our option B. Then we buy a standard European call expiring on the ex-dividend day of the American call we are trying to replicate. The exercise price of this call will be S'. Call this our option C.

Now suppose we have moved forward to just before the ex-dividend date, and the actual stock price is S. Suppose $S < S'$. Option A is simply a European option and cannot be exercised. Option B is an expiring compound option with exercise price of $S' + D - X$. Is option B in-the-money or, in other words, is option A worth more than $S' + D - X$? We know that a European call where the price of the underlying stock is S is worth less than one where the price of the underlying stock is S', since $S < S'$ in this case. We know, by the definition of S', that a European call where the price of the underlying stock is S' is worth exactly $S' + D - X$. It follows that option A is worth less than $S' + D - X$. Thus, our compound option, option B, expires out-of-the-money. Option C is an expiring European call that is clearly out-of-the-money since its exercise price is S' and $S < S'$. The combination of these three options in the case where $S < S'$ leaves us holding option A, a standard European call expiring at a later date.

When $S > S'$, we are still holding option A. Now, however, from reversing the preceding arguments, we find that option B, the compound option, is expiring in-the-money and would be exercised. Since we are short that option, we deliver option A and receive $S' + D - X$. Option C is in-the-money so we pay S' and receive the stock. We are left holding the stock, which is worth S, receiving its dividend, D, and having paid out X dollars.

The payoffs from these three options replicate the outcomes from an American call. The value of the American call must, therefore, equal the sum of the values of the three options, which can be obtained from the Black-Scholes model for options A and C and the Geske compound option model for option B.

The overall formula appears quite complex but is actually just a probability-weighted average of the payoffs at the ex-dividend date and at expiration. The actual computation requires the evaluation of a bivariate normal probability distribution that reflects the risk-neutral/equivalent martingale probability of the exercise of the option early and at expiration. For example, the payoff, of the option if it is in-the-money at expiration depends on the joint probability that the option is not exercised early and that it is exercised at expiration. The payoff if the option is exercised early depends only on the probability of early exercise. These are, of course, the risk-neutral probabilities.

The extension of the problem to a second dividend would require evaluation of a trivariate normal probability, which is still feasible but more complex and has appeared in the literature. Each additional dividend requires an additional variable in the multivariate normal probability distribution, which will then be of an order of one higher than the number of dividends. The computational problem quickly becomes difficult.

Recall, however, that we can obtain an American option price by using binomial or trinomial methods. As an example, consider a stock whose value minus the present value of the dividend is 100. We let it go up by 10% or down by 20% each of two binomial periods. The risk-free rate is 6%. Thus, at time 1, the stock can be worth 110 or 80, and at time 2, the stock can be worth 121, 88, or 64. Note, however, that this value excludes the value of the dividend. Suppose the stock will pay a dividend of $10 at time 1. Consider a two-period call option with an exercise price of 100.

At expiration, the option will be worth 21, 0, or 0 corresponding to stock prices of 121, 88, or 64. If the stock goes up to 110, the option will be worth $(0.867(21) + 0.133(0))/1.06 = 17.18$, where $0.867 = (1.06 - 0.8)/(1.1 - 0.8)$, 1.1 and 0.8 are the up and down factors for the stock and 1.06 is 1 plus the risk-free rate. Note, however, that at that point, immediately before the stock goes ex-dividend, its full price is $110 + 10 = 120$. Thus, if the option could be exercised early, it would be worth $120 - 100 = 20$. So it would be exercised early. At time 0, the option would be worth $(0.867(20) + 0.133(0))/1.06 = 16.36$. If it were European, it would be worth only $(0.867(17.18) + 0.133(0))/1.06 = 14.05$.

Other methods of pricing American calls include analytic approximations, which are formulas that estimate the value of the early exercise premium based on its known characteristics. Monte Carlo methods have not generally been viewed as good approaches to American option pricing. Monte Carlo simulation prices an option by simulating forward in time while valuation of an option generally starts at expiration and moves backward to the present.

Of course there are American options on assets other than stocks that could be exercised early. Bonds and currencies pay interest, and these interest payments could trigger early exercise. If there are multiple payment dates in the life of the option, binomial and finite difference methods are usually employed.

In the next essay we look at pricing American put options.

FOR MORE READING

Ait-Sahalia, F., and P. Carr. "American Options: A Comparison of Numerical Methods. In *Numerical Methods in Finance*, L. C. G. Rogers and D. Talay. Cambridge, UK: Cambridge University Press, 1997, 67–87.

Barone-Adesi, Giovanni and Robert E. Whaley. "Efficient Analytic Approximation of American Option Values." *The Journal of Finance* 42 (1987): 301–320.

Geske, Robert. "The Valuation of Compound Options." *Journal of Financial Economics* 7 (1979): 63–81.

Jarrow, Robert A., and Stuart M. Turnbull. *Derivatives Securities*, 2nd ed. Mason, OH: Thomson South-Western, 2000, chap. 9.

Jarrow, Robert A., and Andrew Rudd. *Option Pricing*. Homewood, IL: Irwin, 1983, chap. 13.

Roll, Richard. "An Analytic Valuation Formula for Unprotected American Call Options on Stocks with Known Dividends." *Journal of Financial Economics* 5 (1977): 251–258.

Welch, Robert N., and David L. Chen. "On the Properties of the Valuation Formula for an Unprotected American Call Option with Known Dividends and the Computation of Its Implied Standard Deviation." *Advances in Futures and Options Research* 3 (1988): 237–256.

Whaley, Robert E. "A Note on an Analytical Formula for Unprotected American Call Options on Stocks with Known Dividends." *Journal of Financial Economics* 7 (1979): 375–380.

Wilmott, Paul. *Derivatives: The Theory and Practice of Financial Engineering*. Chichester, UK: John Wiley & Sons, 1998, chap. 9.

TEST YOUR KNOWLEDGE

1. What types of options are used in the Roll-Geske-Whaley model to replicate an American call option on a stock with dividends?
2. Briefly explain how the binomial model is used to capture the value of early exercise in pricing American call options.
3. What types of assets other than stocks are likely to have American call options exercised early?

American Put Option Pricing

In the last essay we looked at pricing American calls. In this essay we look at pricing American puts. Let us begin by reviewing why the American put price will differ from the European put price. You may wish to review Essay 16 where we first introduced the differences between American and European options.

Suppose we had previously purchased a European put option. If the value of the underlying asset goes to zero, then the option has reached its maximum value. It allows us to sell a worthless asset for the exercise price. We would like to exercise it, but since the option is European, it cannot be exercised just yet. The option value will simply be the present value of the exercise price, and of course, this value will gradually rise by the time value of money until expiration, at which time the option will be exercised. Clearly this is a situation where we would have wished the option were American and if it were, it would be exercised if the asset value is zero.

This example clearly indicates that there would be a demand for a put option that allows early exercise. It is not necessary, however, that the asset price go all the way to zero. It is a simple matter to show that the European put price must be at least the present value of the exercise price minus the asset price. (To do this, you can simply show that a European put always performs at least as well as a bond with a face value equal to the exercise price, maturing at the option's expiration, and a short position in the asset.) The European put price will sell for nearly this value the lower is the asset price. Obviously the present value of the exercise price minus the asset price is less than the exercise price minus the asset price, which is the amount that could be claimed if the put could be exercised early. Consequently, the European put can sell for less than the exercise value.

This line of reasoning shows that there is a critical asset price at which a European put is worth the exercise value of its American counterpart. The latter, however, will sell for more than the former, so the critical asset price is not the one that would trigger early exercise. The reason the American put would not be exercised at that point is that the holder would be throwing away the right to exercise it later when there is at least some chance of it being even deeper in-the-money. There is a point where the right to exercise early is at its maximum value, and at that point the American put would be exercised. Finding that point is difficult but to do so is to unlock the mystery of pricing the American put. Consequently, a great deal of research has focused on finding that critical asset price.

The only surefire way to price the put correctly is to use a numerical procedure such as the binomial or finite difference methods as covered in Essay 29. This procedure is akin to partitioning a two-dimensional space of time and the asset price into finer points and solving either a difference or differential equation at each time point. The process starts at expiration, successively working its way back to the present by using the solution at the preceding step. Because of the importance of this procedure in pricing the American put, I will give an example here using a two-period binomial model.

Let the asset price be 100. It can go up by 10% each period or down by 20% each period. The risk-free rate is 6%. That means that one period later, the asset will be worth 110 if it goes up or 80 if it goes down. If the asset goes to 110, one period later it can go to 121 if it goes up again or 88 if it goes down. If the asset originally went to 80, one period later it can go to 88 if it goes up or 64 if it goes down again. Let the put have a strike of 100.

If the asset ends up at 88, the put ends up worth 12. If the asset ends up at 64, the put ends up worth 36. To have the possibility of reaching either 88 or 64, the asset would have to be at 80 after one period. The value of a European put after one period when the asset is worth 80 is found as $(0.867(12) + 0.133(36))/1.06 = 14.33$, where 0.867 and 0.133 are the risk-neutral/equivalent martingale probabilities of asset price moves, and 0.867 is found as $(1.06 - 0.8)/(1.1 - 0.8)$, where 1.1 and 0.8 are the up and down factors for the stock and 1.06 is 1 plus the risk-free rate.

Thus, if the option were European, when the asset is at 80 at time 1, it would be worth 14.33, The option is American, however, and is worth 20 if exercised, Thus, the holder of the American put would exercise it. If the asset goes up at time 1 to 110, the European put is worth $(0.867(0) + 0.133(12))/1.06 = 1.51$. At that point, the option is out-of-the-money so it would not be exercised if it were American.

Today, when the asset is worth 100, the European put is worth $(0.867(1.51) + 0.133(14.33))/1.06 = 3.03$ while the American put would be worth $(0.867(1.51) + 0.133(20))/1.06 = 3.74$, a result of it exercising early when the asset goes to 80.

Iterative search procedures using a large number of time steps could reveal the critical asset price. It will be below the exercise price but will rise to the exercise price as expiration approaches.

As noted, a binomial or finite difference computational procedure that uses enough time steps would give a fairly accurate answer for the put value. Yet since the beginning of the history of options research, financial economists have sought an exact closed-form solution for the American put price. There have been a couple of polynomial approximations, but these have some biases for certain ranges of input values.

It is correct to say, however, that a closed-form solution does exist. Geske and Johnson have shown, that the American put can be viewed as an infinite series of compound options, which are options on options and which we cover in a later essay. At each point in time, the holder of the put has the right to decide whether to exercise it or not. The decision not to exercise the put is tantamount to a decision to exercise the compound option and obtain a position in a new compound option, which can be exercised an instant later. This procedure continues on to the expiration day. This logic can lead to an intuitive, albeit complex, mathematical formula that contains an infinite number of terms. As unsatisfying as that may be, it is, nonetheless, a precise solution. The holder of an American put faces an infinite series of early exercise decisions.

These infinite-term models have achieved some level of practicality, however, as a result of simplifying them to allow the early exercise decision to be made at only a finite number of time points. The computations typically require the evaluation of multiple integrals so there are practical limits on the number of exercise points that can be accommodated. As noted in Essay 35, Monte Carlo simulation is typically used to price American options.

All in all, pricing American puts is difficult. Unlike American calls, which in some cases have no probability of carly exercise, American puts nearly always have some chance of early exercise. The only case where it would not pay to exercise the put early would be for the case of a nearly continuous stream of sufficiently large dividends, but even then, if there is any possibility that the dividends stream will stop, there is always a chance of early exercise. If we introduce dividends into the picture, we do two things. We reduce but do not eliminate the probability of early exercise. This is because the dividends hold the stock price down, which makes it more attractive to hold on to the put. Still, there is a chance of early exercise because the stock has a finite probability of going to zero. Another thing that happens if we introduce dividends is that it does simplify things somewhat. There is virtually no chance of exercising until just after the stock goes ex-dividend. We have reduced the number of points in time at which we must consider exercising early. With currency options, wherein the underlying pays interest frequently if not continuously, this problem is quite acute.

Thus, we are stuck with the difficulty of assessing the market value of either an infinite or fairly large series of early exercise decisions. We can pretty much give up on a tractable closed-form solution with a reasonable number of terms that permits efficient computation. But with the increasing speed of computers and shortcuts to numerical techniques, the binomial and finite difference methods are quite practical.

FOR MORE READING

Ait-Sahalia, F., and P. Carr. "American Options: A Comparison of Numerical Methods. *In Numerical Methods in Finance*, L. C. G. Rogers and D. Talay. Cambridge, UK: Cambridge University Press, 1997, 67–87.

Barone-Adesi, Giovanni, and Robert E. Whaley. "Efficient Analytic Approximation of American Option Values." *The Journal of Finance* 42 (1987): 301–320.

Geske, Robert, and H. E. Johnson. "The American Put Option Valued Analytically." *The Journal of Finance* 39 (1984): 1511–1524.

Jarrow, Robert A., and Stuart M. Turnbull. *Derivatives Securities*, 2nd ed. Mason, OH: Thomson South-Western, 2000, chap. 9.

Jarrow, Robert A., and Andrew Rudd. *Option Pricing*. Homewood, IL: Irwin, 1983, chap. 13.

Johnson, H. "An Analytic Approximation for the American Put Price." *Journal of Financial and Quantitative Analysis* 18 (1983): 141–148.

Wilmott, Paul. *Derivatives: The Theory and Practice of Financial Engineering*. Chichester, UK: John Wiley & Sons, 1998, chap. 9.

TEST YOUR KNOWLEDGE

1. Briefly explain how the binomial model is used to capture the value of early exercise in pricing American put options.
2. What is different about the potential frequency of exercising American put options in comparison to American call options?
3. What is meant by a "critical" asset price for early exercise of American puts? Where does this price lie in relation to the exercise price?

Swap Pricing

In Essays 9, 10, 13, and 15, we covered interest rate swaps, currency swaps, equity swaps, and commodity swaps, but we did not get into the details of pricing them. "Pricing a swap" means to determine the terms under which the two series of cash flows will be structured. For a plain vanilla swap, in which one party pays a fixed rate and the other pays a floating rate, "pricing" means to determine the fixed rate. For a currency swap, "pricing" means to determine the fixed rates, if applicable, and the two notional principals. For an equity swap, "pricing" means to determine the fixed or floating rate against which the equity return will be paid. For commodity swaps, "pricing" means to determine the fixed price that will be paid for the floating commodity price. In each case, however, the swap either involves no initial exchange of cash or, as in a currency swap, involves the exchange of an equivalent current amount of cash. Thus, the swap is a zero-value transaction at the start. Pricing a swap involves determining the terms that would make the current present values equal, thereby rendering the terms consistent with no initial value.

Let us begin with the plain vanilla interest rate swap and take a simple case in which payments will be made yearly at the quoted rate. Consider a term structure in which the one-year rate is 6% and the two-year rate is 8%. A two-year swap would involve the exchange of a pair of cash flows at the rate F for the one-year floating rate, which is currently 6%. Recall that the rate is set at the beginning of the year and payment is made at the end of the year. For a \$1 notional principal, equating the present value of the fixed payments to the present value of the floating payments, we have $0.06/1.06 + r^*/(1.08)^2 = F/1.06 + F/(1.08)^2$ where r^* is the one-year rate realized in one year. Unfortunately, this equation has two unknowns. To price the swap we must take a different approach.

Suppose we add to each side of the cash flows the repayment of the principal at time 2. This payment is not actually made in a swap, but by hypothetically adding it to both sides, we do not affect the cash flows or the value of the swap. Note that now the floating side has a present value of $0.06/1.06 + r^*/(1.08)^2 + 1/(1.08)^2$. We appear to have an unknown here, but in fact this expression is equivalent to the value of a newly issued floating rate bond. By definition, this value must equal par value, or 1. In the event you do not see this point, consider this. At time 1, the one-year rate will be r^* and its present value, from time 2 discounted to time 1, will be $r^*/(1 + r^*)$. Adding the principal payment at time 2, the value of the floating rate bond at time 1 will be $r^*/(1 + r^*) + 1/(1 + r^*) = (1 + r^*)/(1 + r^*) = 1$. Stepping back to time 0 and knowing that the floating rate bond will be worth 1 at time 1, the value of the floating rate bond at time 0 will be $0.06/1.06 + 1/(1.06) = 1.06/1.06 = 1$. Thus, the floating rate side, with principal included at time 2, is worth 1 at time 0.

The fixed rate side, with principal included, is worth $F/1.06 + F/(1.08)^2 + 1/(1.08)^2$. Equating this to the floating rate side, with principal included, gives us $F/1.06 + F/(1.08)^2 + 1/(1.08)^2 = 1$. Now we can easily solve this equation, and the answer is 7.92%. The swap fixed rate is, in fact, simply the coupon rate on a par-value fixed-rate bond. In practice, some adjustments must be made to reflect the way the interest is paid, such as using 360 or 365 or the exact day count between settlement periods. No adjustment is required for the principal payment, however. By adding it to both sides, we do nothing to the swap value, while facilitating the pricing process.

If the swap were a basis swap, meaning that both sides were floating, the procedure is only slightly more complex. Let us assume that in the example just given, the term structure given is the Treasury bill (T-bill) term structure. Let the LIBOR (London Interbank Offer Rate) term structure be 7% for one year and 8.7% for two years. Solving for the fixed rate using the LIBOR term structure would give 8.63%. A basis swap with one side paying T-bill and the other paying LIBOR would be quoted with one side paying T-bill plus 71 basis points (8.63 – 7.92) and the other side paying LIBOR. In other words, the side paying the lower rate, T-bill, must add on a spread.

In pricing currency swaps we must consider that there are four basic types:

1. Pay domestic currency fixed, receive foreign currency fixed.
2. Pay domestic currency fixed, receive foreign currency floating.
3. Pay domestic currency floating, receive foreign currency fixed.
4. Pay domestic currency floating, receive foreign currency floating.

Of course, you can do the opposite of any of these four positions. To price a currency swap is fairly simple, however, requiring only the term structures in the two countries and the spot exchange rate. Let us use the LIBOR structure just given for the domestic term structure and let the foreign term structure be 8.2% for one year and 9.4% for two years. In the foreign country, the fixed rate on a plain vanilla swap would be 9.35%. Let the current exchange rate be that 1.25 units of the domestic currency equals 1 unit of the foreign currency.

Now recall that a currency swap normally requires principal payments. Suppose domestic customers enter into a currency swap with both sides paying a fixed rate. They will pay fixed in their domestic currency and receive fixed in the foreign currency. We know that the domestic fixed rate of 8.63% will make the present value of the stream of domestic payments, principal included, equal par value of 1. Looking at the foreign country, we know that the rate of 9.35 will make the present value of the stream of foreign payments, principal included, equal par value of 1 unit of the foreign currency. One unit of the domestic currency will equal $1/1.25 = 0.8$ units of the foreign currency. When the domestic party entering the swap chooses the domestic notional principal as N, the foreign notional principal is automatically set at $0.8N$. This adjustment will make the current present value of the domestic payments equal the current present value of the foreign payments. These same notional principals will apply to any of the other three swaps, a result of the fact that the fixed rates in the respective countries equate, in their own currencies, the present values of the fixed payments to the present values of the floating payments.

Pricing an equity swap is slightly more difficult. Also, there are many variations of the equity swap, and here I shall cover only one basic form. Consider a two-period equity swap with one party paying the equity return over each period and the other paying a fixed rate, with the notional principal fixed over both periods. We omit any dividends on the stock. We let S_0, S_1, and S_2 be the stock prices at times 0, 1, and 2. We use the same LIBOR term structure in the previous problems. In this swap, one party makes fixed payments of F and the other makes payments based on the realized equity returns of $S_1/S_0 - 1$ and $S_2/S_1 - 1$.

For a \$1 notional principal and using the same LIBOR term structure as before, the present value of the equity payments will be $[(S_1/S_0) - 1]/(1 + E(R_1)) + [(S_2/S_1) - 1]/(1 + E(R_2))^2 = F/(1.07) + F/(1.087)^2$. The terms $E(R_2))$ and $E(R_1)$ are the expected returns on the stock over the first and second periods, respectively, both stated as annual returns. S_0 is known, but we still have five unknowns, F, S_1 and S_2, and $E(R_1)$ and $E(R_2)$, It turns out that we can simplify things by constructing another and simpler portfolio that will replicate the equity swap payments. We borrow $(1 + F)[1/1.07 + 1/(1.087)^2]$ dollars and invest \$1 in the stock and \$1/1.07 in the risk-free asset.

At time 1, we sell the stock, which will be worth S_1/S_0. The $1/1.07 invested in the risk-free asset will be worth $[\$1/1.07](1.07) = \$1$. We take this dollar and purchase new stock. We pay back a portion of our loan, which costs us $[(1 + F)/1.07]\,1.07 = 1 + F$. This gives us a total cash flow of $S_1/S_0 - (1 + F) = S_1/S_0 - 1 - F$, which is the same as the first swap cash flow. At time 2, we shall have the stock, which we sell for S_2/S_1, and we owe the remaining portion of our loan, which now costs us $[(1 + F)(1/1.087)^2]\,1.087^2 = 1 + F$. Thus, the total cash flow at time 2 is $S_2/S_1 - 1 - F$. This procedure replicates the second cash flow on the swap. Since this portfolio replicates the swap cash flows and the swap value at time 0 is zero, this portfolio must have an initial value of zero, giving us the equation $1 + 1/1.07 - (1 + F)[1/1.07 + 1/(1.087)^2] = 0$. We now have a single equation with one unknown and can easily solve it.

Want to venture a guess as to the answer? Roll back a few paragraphs to the interest rate swap problem using the LIBOR term structure. The solution is the same 8.63%, which is the fixed rate on a LIBOR-based plain vanilla swap. Interestingly, the stock price has no effect on the equity swap rate. Though we will not demonstrate this point here, the stock price, however, does affect the value of the swap between settlement dates.

In a commodity swap, one party pays a fixed price and the other pays the commodity price with the payments occurring at the settlement dates. Thus, the fixed payments will be F at times 1 and 2 and the floating payments will be P_1 at time 1 and P_2 at time 2 where P_1 and P_2 are the commodity's prices. Let us assume that the commodity storage cost per unit is c per period expressed in dollars. We could replicate the swap by doing this: At time 0, we buy two units of the commodity and borrow $(F - c)/1.07 + (F - 2c)/(1.087)^2$ dollars.

At time 1, we sell one unit of the commodity at the price P_1. Our net price, however, is only $P_1 - c$ because of the storage costs. We pay back a portion of our loan, the original amount $(F - c)/1.07$, for which we now owe $[(F - c)/1.07]1.07 = F - c$. Thus, our total cash flow is $P_1 - c - (F - c) = P_1 - F$. Then at time 2, we sell the commodity for a net value of $P_2 - 2c$. (Note the storage costs over two periods). We pay back the remaining portion of our loan, owing $[(F - 2c)/(1.087)^2](1.087)^2 = F - 2c$. Our total cash flow is $P_2 - 2c - (F - 2c) = P_2 - F$. We have, therefore, replicated the cash flows from the commodity swap. Since the swap has no initial cash flow, the current value of the replicating portfolio is zero. This action gives us the equation $2P_0 - (F - c)/1.07 - (F - 2c)/(1.087)^2 = 0$. We would know the current value of the commodity, P_0, and the storage costs c, so solving for F is easy.

In commodity swaps, it is more common to base the payoff on the average price of the commodity over the settlement period. This adjustment smooths out the payoffs so that they are not completely dependent on the price on a single day. This adjustment complicates the process a bit, however, but the basic principle is the same. We construct a replicating combination of the commodity and a loan. This combination must produce a value at each settlement date that reflects the average price of the commodity over the settlement period. This procedure would require a slight adjustment to the number of units of the commodity we buy and the amount we borrow at time 0.

FOR MORE READING

Brown, Keith C., and Donald J. Smith. *Interest Rate and Currency Swaps: A Tutorial*, Charlottesville, VA: Research Foundation of the Institute of Chartered Financial Analysts, 1995.

Buetow, Gerald W., and Frank J. Fabozzi. *Valuation of Interest Rate Swaps and Swaptions*. New Hope, PA: Frank J. Fabozzi Associates, 2001.

Chance, Don M., and Robert Brooks. *An Introduction to Derivatives and Risk Management*, 7th ed. Mason, OH: Thomson South-Western, 2007, chap. 12.

Chance, Don M., and Don R. Rich. "Asset Swaps with Asian-Style Payoffs." *The Journal of Derivatives* 3 (Summer 1996), 64–77.

Hull, John C. *Options, Futures, and Other Derivatives*, 6th ed. Upper Saddle River, NJ: Prentice-Hall, 2006, chap. 7.

McDonald, Robert L. *Derivative Markets*, 2nd ed. Boston: Addison Wesley 2006, chap. 8.

TEST YOUR KNOWLEDGE

1. The fixed rate on a plain vanilla swap is equivalent to what value?
2. In a currency swap involving fixed payments in one currency and fixed payments in the other currency, what are the two fixed rates equivalent to?
3. Briefly explain how equity swaps are constructed. Is the replicating portfolio static or dynamic?
4. How do storage costs factor into a commodity swap price?

Four

Derivative Strategies

In this section we take a look at some derivatives strategies. If someone buys a call, that person pays the option price and obtains the right to buy the underlying at a fixed price, the exercise price. At expiration, if the price of the underlying is above the exercise price, the option holder exercises the option and obtains a value equal to the value of the underlying minus the exercise price. If the price of the underlying is below the exercise price, the option holder does not exercise the option and walks away with nothing. The seller of the call has the opposite position. In return for receiving the option price up front, the seller will be forced to sell the underlying for the exercise price if the underlying value is above the exercise price at expiration. If the underlying value is below the exercise price at expiration, the call will not be exercised and the seller has no further obligation. Thus, call buyers have the potential for unlimited gains if the underlying value is above the exercise price at expiration and lose nothing but the price paid for the option if the underlying value is below the exercise price at expiration. So call buyers have unlimited gains on the upside and limited losses on the downside. Call sellers have the opposite position and have unlimited losses on the upside and limited gains on the downside.

If an investor buys a put, he pays the option price at the start and obtains the right to sell the underlying at the exercise price. At expiration, if the price of the underlying is below the exercise price, the option holder exercises and obtains a value equal to the exercise price minus the value of the underlying. If the price of the underlying is above the exercise price, the option holder does not exercise the option and walks away with nothing. The seller of the put has the opposite position. In return for receiving the option price up front, the seller will be forced to buy the underlying for the exercise price if the underlying value is below the exercise price at expiration. If the underlying value is above the exercise price at expiration, the put will not be exercised and the seller has no further obligation. Put buyers have the potential for rather large gains on the downside. These gains are not unlimited because the underlying can go no lower than zero, so the maximum gain is the exercise price. Put buyers lose nothing but the price paid for the option if the underlying value is above the exercise price at expiration. So put buyers have large gain potential on the downside and limited losses on the up side. Put sellers have the opposite position and have large potential losses on the downside and limited gains on the up side.

From these principles you can see why an investor might do each of the four basic strategies. You might buy a call if you want to benefit from a rising price of the underlying but want to limit losses if the underlying falls. You might be motivated to sell a call if you anticipate a flat or falling price of the underlying, but that position is highly vulnerable to a rising price. You might buy a put if you want to benefit from a falling price of the underlying but want to limit the loss from a rising price. You might sell a put if you want to benefit from a flat or rising price of the underlying, but that position is exposed to a falling price.

These strategies are quite simple. In this section, however, we want to go beyond the basics and see how derivatives are used by professional investors. In this section, there are six essays. We first look at how asset allocation is practiced using derivatives. Then we look at protective puts and portfolio insurance and then covered calls. We then examine hedge funds, which are heavy users of derivative strategies. We conclude with several derivative strategies that alter the payoffs from the basic ones just described. You will see that combining derivatives leads to a lot of interesting possibilities for structuring an investor's risk-return profile.

Asset Allocation with Derivatives

Asset allocation is one of the investment world's greatest inventions, not for what it is but for how it sounds. Mutual funds that call themselves "asset allocation funds" have sprung up in droves. Investment managers declare themselves to be asset allocators and extol the risk-reducing and return-enhancing features of the strategy. I am not here to praise asset allocation, or to bury it. My focus is on how derivatives can be used to execute asset allocation strategies.

Let us first describe what we mean by the term "asset allocation." In an asset allocation strategy, the universe of available investments is divided into general classes, such as domestic stocks, international stocks, domestic bonds, international bonds, cash, real estate, and so on. The number of classes is a function of how distinct you want the classes and, of course, whether you are permitted to invest in certain types of assets. Asset allocators do not select individual component investments within a given asset class. Rather they decide on an overall allocation across classes. In some sense asset allocation is an attempt to time the market by being in the best-performing classes and out of the worst at the right time. Taking the simple case of only two asset classes, stocks and cash, an asset allocation strategy would be a pure market timing strategy that asks "Will stocks beat cash over the upcoming period?" Of course, two asset allocators who answer "yes" to that question would not necessarily recommend the same percentage allocation to stocks and to cash, which leads to the second question how much to allocate to stocks versus cash, based on investors' perception of the expected differential between stock returns and the cash return and the risk they are willing to take.

The process of *strategic asset allocation* refers to the percentages that the allocators attempt to maintain over a longer period of time. *Tactical asset allocation* defines the short- and intermediate-term percentages, justifying them as deviations from the strategic targets on some basis. Asset allocators use a variety of macroeconomic/financial tools to provide signals and determine allocations.

Do asset allocators outperform a simple buy-and-hold strategy? Some may, but I am largely skeptical of asset allocators as a whole. I see no reason, however, why any investor should not reallocate a portfolio periodically. Increases in the market value of an asset class automatically change the effective allocation so there are nontiming reasons for looking for ways to easily and cheaply alter the percentages to a desired level.

Derivatives provide just such a way. Assume that an investor has a percentage invested in stock, roughly approximated by the Standard & Poor's (S&P) 500, and the remaining percentage invested in cash, as reflected in a typical money market fund. The investor would like to decrease the allocation to stock. This adjustment could be done by selling off some stock and putting the funds into cash. The sale of the stock, however, could result in significant transaction costs. Moreover, the investor might be considering the possibility of changing the allocation again in the near future. Derivatives can do the job quite easily and effectively.

First let us recall a basic derivatives principle: A long position in stock and a short position in futures = a long position in cash. Of course, we are assuming that the underlying index for the futures matches the stock. If that assumption is correct, then the investor can sell futures against a portion of the stock. For example, if the investor wanted to reduce the risk by about 10%, she could sell futures with a face value equal to 10% of the stock owned. Thus, 10% of the stock would be matched up, that is, hedged, with futures contracts. When teaching this subject in workshops to investment managers, I have noticed that some of them have a difficult time seeing why this strategy effectively generates cash, given that you still hold the stock. The reason is that the block of stock matched up with the futures is effectively presold by the futures position. The sale price of the stock is locked in. This strategy is, of course, just a form of hedging. If the futures are correctly priced in the market, the stock is hedged for a return of the risk-free rate, which should match pretty closely the money market return. If this block of stock pays dividends, the investor will collect the dividends, but the futures price will be lower by the effect of the dividends.

This procedure works in the other direction as well. An investor wanting to increase the allocation to stock can buy futures. This strategy replicates the process of borrowing at the risk-free rate to purchase additional stock, which is equivalent to trading on margin.

Of course, the principle also works for a portfolio of domestic securities that needs to be reallocated to include some international exposure. For example, suppose you hold only S&P 500 stocks and wanted some exposure to the Japanese market. You can sell S&P 500 futures and buy futures on the Nikkei. Depending on the number of contracts used, you can set the allocation to the equivalent of a specific percentage in the S&P 500 and the remaining percentage in the Nikkei. Alternatively you can adjust the exposure between stocks and bonds. Unfortunately, this strategy does not work quite as well for the bond market because there are no highly liquid futures contacts on a broad-based bond index. The Chicago Board of Trade's note and bond futures contracts, however, can be used together to span the range of maturities, though there is no exposure across credit classes.

Futures are not the only derivatives that can be used. Options will work in principle, but an option's risk changes constantly. Thus, it can be difficult to set and hold a portfolio to a desired risk level, which is precisely what asset allocation attempts to do. For portfolios large enough, swaps and other over the counter derivatives can be used and in fact are widely used today. They may even work better because they can be customized to eliminate the basis risk between the derivative and the actual assets in the portfolio.

This comment brings up an important point. No one would argue that a futures strategy would work perfectly to reset the effective allocation to the desired allocation. There is, of course, the aforementioned basis risk. Also, the futures will require daily settlements, which can produce losses that require cash deposits. Of course, the cash required is effectively offset from the gain on the assets themselves, but that does not mean that the assets can be liquidated to produce the cash. Moreover, the futures can be mispriced on occasion, necessitating the sale of underpriced contracts, which produces a return less than the risk-free rate.

But when all is said and done, asset allocators have generally agreed that derivatives can certainly make their job easier. Moreover, it is estimated that the transaction cost savings can approach 95%.

FOR MORE READING

Chance, Don M. *Analysis of Derivatives for the CFA Program.* Charlottesville, VA: Association for Investment Management and Research, 2003, chaps. 6–8.

TEST YOUR KNOWLEDGE

1. What is asset allocation? Explain the difference between strategic asset allocation and tactical asset allocation.
2. Explain how derivatives can be used to save costs if the asset allocation of a portfolio needs to be changed.
3. If a stock portfolio is completely hedged using futures, how is this transaction equivalent to converting the stocks to cash?
4. What cash flow problem might occur if a stock portfolio is hedged using futures?

Protective Puts and Portfolio Insurance

This essay deals with a popular option strategy called the protective put. Here the investor holding the underlying asset purchases a put. If at expiration the underlying asset price is below the exercise price, the asset is delivered and the exercise price is received. If the asset price is above the exercise price at expiration, the put expires worthless and the investor gains from the increase in the price of the asset. I have always felt that the protective put is one of the most useful strategies for instructional purposes. It brings to light much of the mystery of options. Yet ironically it may be one of the most useless strategies for most investors.

As I explained in Essay 24, options are often described as being a form of insurance. Nowhere is this more obvious than with the protective put. The put serves as an insurance policy on the underlying asset. The seller of the put is the insurer and receives a premium in return for promising to cover any losses below the exercise price. Let us compare the protective put to a common form of protection, the homeowner's insurance policy.

Consider the homeowner's deductible, which is the amount of the loss that the insured agrees to bear. The greater the deductible, the more risk assumed by the insured and the lower the premium charged by the insurer. For the protective put, you can effectively raise the deductible by selecting a put with a lower exercise price. This adjustment lowers the put/insurance premium and means that the insured will incur a larger loss on the downside.

An interesting point in regard to the protective put is that it is the only option strategy I can think of in which the investor buys a single option and hopes that it expires out-of-the-money. The best outcome is for the asset to go up and the put to expire worthless. Like homeowner's insurance, the insured should hope that the insurance is not used, though it is certainly good to know that it is there.

On a personal level, I have never found a need for a protective put. In my capacity as an advisor to a small fund, I have also never found a need for the fund to use puts. I doubt that this opinion will ever change. In spite of the apparent attractiveness of the transaction, I would be surprised if it benefits many individual investors and even many professional investors.

The protective put strategy enables you to achieve a minimum return at a target date. Unless you are investing a sum of money with the sole objective of having a certain amount of money available on a specific date, what do you gain by locking in that minimum? Suppose you owned a stock that had gone up substantially in a short period of time and you would like to hold the stock a while longer, but would experience great regret if the stock falls back down. In that situation a put might make sense from the standpoint of feeling less regret about not having sold. That reason strikes me as more of an emotional justification for a put, and investing on emotions is not sensible investing. If you are a long-run investor, then you should not need puts, which are typically short term, because there are no intermediate targets. Now, it is possible that long-term options such as Long-Term Equity Anticipation Securities (LEAPS) might be useful if you wanted to assure a minimum amount of funds available, say to fund a future college education. Even then, however, I would probably skip the insurance and buy a solid, well-diversified portfolio.

So who should buy protective puts? Professional investment managers, such as pension fund managers, who are required to generate a minimum amount of cash at a future date are big users of the strategy. In addition, investment managers who are evaluated over short periods at specific dates are likely to use puts. Unfortunately, this is not always the way things should be. For example, suppose a mutual fund manager has earned a high enough return for three quarters to be ranked among the year-to-date leaders. The manager remains bullish for the fourth quarter but knows that if the market turns down, he could fall out of the pack, lose some of a potentially high bonus, and otherwise miss out on the fame and fortune that accompanies such success. The manager can help assure his success by purchasing puts, but that would, in my opinion, be for the wrong reason. From the standpoint of sound investment management, locking in past profits is not a good reason for using puts. Unfortunately, the reward system often induces people to do so, so it is the reward system that is at fault.

Because protective puts are not always available with the expirations and exercise prices needed by investment managers, they sometimes turn to a dynamically adjusted version of the protective put. This strategy came to be known in the mid-1980s as portfolio insurance. It works like this. Remember the concept of a delta, which we covered in Essays 30 and 33? The delta of an any derivative, asset, or porttolio is the change in its value relative to the change in the value of an underlying variable. For example, the delta of an S&P 500 option might be 0.5, meaning that the option changes by 50% of the change in the S&P 500. Option pricing models provide the values—technically just approximations—of deltas.

If you actually owned a put with the desired expiration and exercise price, the combination of stock and put would have a delta that would, as all deltas do, change with the passage of time and changes in the underlying asset price. Due to the existence of option pricing models, you always know what the delta of a protective put position should be. For example, the delta of a portfolio identical to the S&P 500 plus a put on the S&P 500 would be 1.0 plus the put delta, the 1.0 coming from the fact that the delta of the S&P 500 is 1.0.

A portfolio that had the same value and delta as the protective put would produce the same results. Thus, instead of using puts, you could simply combine the stock with futures or Treasury bills in such a manner that the combination has the same delta as the desired combination of stock and put. Moving through time, the delta of the stock-put portfolio is recomputed and the combination of stock and futures or stock and Treasury bills (T-bills) is readjusted to have the right amount of each relative to the other so as to match the stock-put delta. The replicating combination would be long stock and short futures or long stock and long T-bills. As stock prices increase (decrease), the desired delta would increase (decrease), reflecting the fact that the portfolio is increasingly less (more) likely to fall below the minimum. To increase (decrease) the delta of the combination of stock-futures would require buying (selling) either stock or futures. For the strategy to be effective, the market must make only small moves. The estimated value of the delta is obtained from pricing models and is represented by the first (calculus) derivative, which assumes infinitesimal changes in the underlying stock. Thus, when markets move quickly, dynamic replication or protective puts may not work as effectively.

This strategy was widely offered by a group of firms calling themselves "portfolio insurers" during the 1980s. During the famous crash of 1987, portfolio insurers had to sell quickly, because the market moves were faster and larger than their models had assumed. This effect is the gamma factor in delta hedging, a topic covered in Essay 30. Massive selling by portfolio insurers got a very bad and undeserved name. On that day, while everyone else was panicking, portfolio insurers were rationally attempting to achieve the desired level of insurance. Unfortunately, the market was moving too fast for the insurance to work effectively. Exacerbating the problem was the fear that the markets might be closed, which eventually did happen. This action removed the opportunity to adjust the insurance. Despite the failure of portfolio insurance to achieve its targets, those who had portfolio insurance were still better off than those who did not.

FOR MORE READING

Abken, Peter A. "An Introduction to Portfolio Insurance." *Federal Reserve Bank of Atlanta Economic Review* 72 (1987): 2–25.

Chance, Don M., and Robert Brooks. *An Introduction to Derivatives and Risk Management*, 7th ed. Mason, OH: Thomson South-Western, 2007, chap. 6.

Figlewski, Stephen, N. K. Chidambara, and Scott Kaplan. "Evaluating the Performance of the Protective Put Strategy." *Financial Analysts Journal* 49 (July–August, 1993): 46–56.

Leland, Hayne E. "Who Should Buy Portfolio Insurance?" *The Journal of Finance* 35 (1980): 581–94.

McDonald, Robert L. *Derivative Markets*, 2nd ed. Boston: Addison Wesley, 2006, chap. 2.

O'Brien, Thomas J. "Portfolio Insurance Mechanics." *The Journal of Portfolio Management* 14 (Spring 1988): 40–47.

Rubinstein, Mark. "Alternative Paths to Portfolio Insurance." *Financial Analysts Journal* 41 (July–August, 1985): 42–52.

TEST YOUR KNOWLEDGE

1. How is a protective put like insurance? How does the exercise price relate to the deductible on an insurance policy?
2. Under what circumstances might an investor justifiably use a protective put?
3. How does portfolio insurance replicate a protective put?

Misconceptions about Covered Call Writing

Covered call writing appears to be one of the most popular strategies for serious option traders. Over the years I have noticed, however, that covered call writing is often presented to novices in a very misleading manner. Thus, I am going to use this essay to air my own personal grievance about the way in which so-called experts (meaning oftentimes consultants and more often than not brokers), describe this strategy.

Let us begin by giving a quick description of exactly what covered call writing is. For simplicity, let us consider a stock that pays no dividends and that the options are European style, meaning that they cannot be exercised until the expiration day.

If you buy a stock and it goes up, you make money. If it goes down, you lose money. If you sell a call, without owning the stock, and the stock goes up and ends up above the exercise price, the call is exercised. You have to buy the stock at whatever price it is selling for and deliver it to the call buyer, who pays you the exercise price. If the call expires out-of-the-money, you do nothing. In either case, you keep the premium.

If you combine owning the stock with selling the call, you end up either keeping the stock or selling your stock for, at most, the exercise price. On the downside, the loss on the stock is cushioned by the retention of the option premium. On the upside, your stock profit is the exercise price minus what you originally paid for the stock plus the call premium that you get to keep.

My complaint about this strategy, or rather with the way in which it is presented by many brokers and consultants, is that it is described as an *income-enhancement strategy*. The argument goes like this. You own a stock. You do not plan to sell it. The stock is not expected to go up by much if at all. Why not sell a call against it and pick up some income? This argument makes it sound like either there is money on the floor waiting to be picked up or that your stock is generating some income and you are not getting your share.

OK, go ahead and pick that money up. But you need to realize what you could be missing. You are giving up all of the capital gains beyond the exercise price. Those gains go to the buyer of the call. This idea may seem simple, but you would not believe how many people are duped by it.

I once had an investment manager tell me that her organization had taken the advice of a consultant about a year earlier and instituted a covered call writing program. The consultant had presented it as an income-enhancement strategy. The fund then missed out on a strong bull market. Of course, it is easy for us to criticize after the fact. Who are we to brag about market timing ability? But the simple fact was that the consultant had not made it clear what the organization would be missing if the market went up. Or at least no one asked the question "What's the catch?"[1]

Covered call writing is a risk-reducing strategy. It is designed to do precisely what investors do when they select stocks that pay high dividends over stocks that have greater growth prospects. Covered call writing converts the prospects for uncertain future capital gains into immediate cash flows that resemble dividends. There may be good reasons to do an occasional covered call, but a formal program of regular covered call writing might well be no better than simply buying high-dividend stocks instead. Of course, there *is* a big difference where the broker is concerned. A systematic program of covered call writing generates commissions, not only from the initial sale of the call but also from the occasional exercise of the call, resulting in the delivery of the stock, and from the rolling over into new calls as the old ones expire. The broker will be quite happy if the client does covered calls, and that should immediately make you suspicious.

The sad thing is that many retired people owning stocks are being misled. The notion that they should be willing to give up capital gains for current income may make sense, but they should not see covered call writing as the only way to achieve that goal.

Another misunderstanding about covered calls arises from the way in which the profit is calculated. First ignore the transaction costs. Let S be the stock price when the call is written, X be the exercise price, c be the call premium, and S^* be the stock price when the call expires. If the call expires out-of-the-money, the profit is $S^* - S + c$. If the call expires in-the-money, the profit is $X - S + c$. Many people have a hard time seeing why we subtract the stock price at the time the call is written. They argue that you might well

---

[1] This would have been a good time to have had the thought, "If it sounds too good to be true, it probably is."

have bought the stock prior to when you wrote the call. If that is the way you think, then you do not see the opportunity cost in holding a stock. When you attached the call to the stock, you made a conscious decision to hold on to the stock. You could have sold it, liberating the S dollars for use elsewhere. Thus, you have to account for the S dollars even though you may have bought the stock much earlier.

Having said all of that, we should be aware that covered call writing is a popular strategy and is the exclusive strategy of at least one very successful mutual fund. Moreover, the Chicago Board Options Exchange (CBOE) has created indices based on the performance of a covered call strategy where the underlying is an index like the Standard & Poor's 500 or Nasdaq. A number of financial institutions have created investment products based on the CBOE's covered call indices. Clearly the covered call is a legitimate investment strategy, but it is a risk-reducing strategy. *When risk is reduced, expected return is reduced as well.* This concept is one of the principles of finance. The investor who does not understand this point has the luckiest broker in the world.

FOR MORE READING

Chance, Don M., and Robert Brooks. *An Introduction to Derivatives and Risk Management*, 7th ed. Mason, OH: Thomson South-Western, 2007, chap. 6.
Yates, James W. Jr., and Robert W. Kopprasch Jr. "Writing Covered Call Options: Profits and Risks." *The Journal of Portfolio Management* 7 (1980): 74–79.

TEST YOUR KNOWLEDGE

1. How does a covered call result in the elimination of upside gains on a stock?
2. Why are covered calls referred to as income-enhancement strategies?
3. If a call is sold on a stock that was purchased at a prior date, why should the current price of the stock be used to determine the profit from the strategy?

Hedge Funds and Other Privately Managed Accounts

The first edition of this book contained an essay about a type of investment account called *managed futures*. It is worthwhile for us to review managed futures and related accounts. Since the first edition, these accounts have been largely supplanted by a somewhat new type of account called the *hedge fund*. It would not be an understatement to say that hedge funds are one of the most rapidly growing phenomena in the investment world. While the managed futures fund and its variants are largely focused on derivatives-related transactions, hedge funds are much more general. They use derivatives and potentially anything else. It is not surprising that they have grown so rapidly, because they are more flexible.

Prior to the era of the modern hedge fund was the era of the managed futures account, which itself had roots in an account called the *commodity fund*. Just as mutual funds began their explosive growth in the 1960s, so too did this family of investments that focused on commodity futures. While mutual funds are highly regulated and open to the general public, commodity funds are less unregulated and are open only to certain high-net-worth and sophisticated investors. Mutual funds are generally restricted to conventional investments, such as stocks and bonds. Commodity funds were created to offer investors opportunities to invest indirectly in futures contracts on commodities. Subsequent studies showed that investing in commodity futures offered opportunities to improve the diversification of a portfolio, that is, to get more expected return for the same risk or less risk for the same expected return. Of course, in the early 1970s, futures contracts on currencies began to trade, and interest rate futures were created in the mid-1970s. Given the addition of these types of opportunities, the funds soon began to be known as *futures funds* and ultimately to *managed futures*.

One of the important characteristics of these funds is that they enabled the investor to gain exposure to markets using futures contracts without the risk of losing more money than invested. Recall that in a long position in a futures contract, the mark-to-market losses can easily result in complete destruction of the account's margin balance. If investors maintain a position in the market, they must deposit additional funds. Ultimately, long futures investors can lose the full price of the futures contract, which is many times the initial margin. Of course, investors can pull out at any time and thereby stop the bleeding. A short position, however, can result in a loss of no limit. That is, the price of a futures contract can rise infinitely, thereby imposing a loss on investors that has no bound. Futures funds (and their predecessors) were structured so that investors could lose no more than the amount invested. The funds invested are mostly placed in safe, interest-bearing securities, and only a very small portion are used as margin deposits for futures transactions. The fund manager monitors the risk and engages in transactions to reduce the exposure if the risk increases to a level that threatens the fund's ability to maintain its promise that investors can lose no more than the amount invested.

Futures funds have now been largely supplanted by hedge funds, which have considerably more freedom to invest. Although some hedge funds specialize, many can invest in virtually any type of instrument in any market around the world. Thus they can buy stocks and bonds, using little or a lot of leverage. They can invest in real estate, small nonpublicly traded stocks, futures, options, forwards, swaps, and so on. You name it, they can generally do it. By giving the managers much more flexibility, the funds believe they can exploit opportunities wherever they exist.

In this regard, it is interesting to consider why these products are called hedge funds. The name was created by financial journalist Alfred Winslow Jones in the late 1940s to describe a type of fund he proposed in which the manager could go long and short, a process he viewed as a sort of hedge. Jones went on to create funds of this sort, which did extremely well for many years. Over the decades, more such funds began to be created. Many legendary names in investments, such as George Soros, Julian Robertson, T. Boone Pickens, and Paul Tudor Jones, are associated with hedge funds.

The modern hedge fund, however, should almost never be viewed as a hedge. In fact, this name is probably one of the most misleading in the entire financial world. Hedge funds may or may not engage in hedging. Many do engage in arbitrage, whereby they purchase one security and sell a comparable one with the idea that the prices of the two securities are misaligned and will converge. Obviously arbitrage is designed to have little or no risk and, thus, is a form of hedging. In reality, this type of arbitrage is rarely true arbitrage, because it involves the risk that convergence will occur on two *comparable but not identical* securities and usually will occur over the near horizon. Hedge funds do employ many extremely bright and technically knowledgeable personnel and have access to a considerable amount of data from which to analyze for opportunities and monitor the risk. Nonetheless, hedge fund investing can vary considerably from low risk to extremely high risk.

Further complicating matters is the fact that most hedge funds require investors to keep their money invested in the fund for several years. Moreover, most hedge funds do not reveal to their investors how they trade or what they hold. Thus, hedge fund investors are investing blindly, trusting the funds' management to take the right actions.

Hedge fund investing can also be quite expensive. Most funds charge a management fee of 1% to 3% and also take an incentive fee calculated as a percentage of the profits that can easily run 20% to 50%. Of course, they do not bear a percentage of the losses. Many funds do, however, use a *high-water mark* fee structure in which incentive fees are not paid until the fund reaches a previously established value. Thus, if the fund's performance falls relative to the previous "high-water mark," no further incentive fees can be earned until the fund reaches the high-water mark. If the fund performs well, takes a percentage of the profits, performs poorly, catches up, takes a percentage of the profits earned catching up, and so forth, it cannot continue to be rewarded for climbing the same mountain again and again.

Hedge funds escape regulation by restricting their investments to fewer than 100 investors, all of whom have to be considerably knowledgeable and aware of the risks. Otherwise, the fund falls under mutual fund regulations that are covered in the 1940 Investment Company Act. Restricting an account to fewer than 100 investors is one reason why there are so many hedge funds. The Lipper HedgeWorld database covers more than 4,000 funds, and that is certainly not all of them. By contrast, there are only about 3,300 companies on the New York Stock Exchange, about 3,100 on Nasdaq, and about 7,000 mutual funds. By comparison to mutual funds, however, the hedge fund industry is quite small. Many hedge funds are very small operations, often employing fewer than 10 people and managing less than $50 million.

Futures funds remain and are regulated by Commodity Futures Trading Corporation (CFTC). Hedge funds are mostly unregulated, and most are registered in certain well-known, highly business-friendly countries such as the Cayman Islands, the Bahamas, and Dubai. In 2004 the Securities and Exchange Commission attempted to impose a registration requirement on hedge funds, but this effort was rejected in a federal court ruling in 2006.

What lies ahead for hedge funds is difficult to forecast. Continued growth is likely because there is a great deal of wealth in the United States and other countries in desperate need of markets in which to invest that offer opportunities not found in conventional markets. Simply put, there is a lot of money chasing few opportunities. Because the size of hedge funds is greatly restricted, there are likely to be more and more of them.

Some worry that hedge funds are a ticking time bomb. Their large numbers, high leverage, and a perception that they engage in herd behavior do lend some reason to worry that mass panic among them could lead to a financial crisis. The fact that most of their investors cannot arbitrarily withdraw their money, however, lends some stability to the industry that is not present in mutual funds. Hedge funds did deliver a scare in the 1998 failure of one of the largest, Long-Term Capital Management, but many lessons were learned from that incident. It is my opinion that most hedge funds do a pretty good job of managing their risk, but certainly the possibility exists that a single fund will, either intentionally or unintentionally, allow its risk to exceed prudent levels and fail. The failure of any single highly leveraged entity does pose some systemic risk. It remains to be seen whether hedge funds will gain the kind of broad respect that mutual funds hold, or whether they will come cascading down like a house of cards.

FOR MORE READING

Lhabitant, François-Serge. *Handbook of Hedge Funds*. Hoboken, NJ: John Wiley & Sons, 2007.

Tran, Vinh Q., and Thomas Schneeweis. *Evaluating Hedge Fund Performance*. Hoboken, NJ: John Wiley & Sons, 2006.

TEST YOUR KNOWLEDGE

1. What is the main difference between managed futures and a hedge fund?
2. How are managed futures and futures funds distinguished from ordinary mutual funds?
3. How are hedge fund managers typically paid?

Spreads, Collars, and Prepaid Forwards

In this essay we take a brief look at a very popular type of option strategy involving a long position in an option with a given exercise price and a short position in another option differing only by the exercise price. This strategy is commonly known as a spread, but since there are spreads based on differences in time to expiration, it is more correctly labeled a *money spread, strike spread*, or *vertical spread*, the latter term arising out of the manner in which option price quotes were once presented in newspapers with exercise prices arrayed vertically.

Consider a call option with an exercise price of X_1 and another otherwise identical call option with an exercise price of X_2 where $X_2 > X_1$. Their prices are c_1 and c_2, and we know that the call with the lower exercise price will have the greater price, $c_1 > c_2$. Suppose we buy the call with the lower exercise price and sell the call with the higher exercise price. This strategy will require an outlay equal to the net of the price paid for the long call minus the price received for the short call. At expiration let the underlying asset price be S^*. Then if S^* is higher than X_2, both options expire in-the-money. The option we hold will allow us to buy the asset paying X_1, and the option we sold will require us to sell the asset receiving X_2. If the asset price ends up between X_1 and X_2, the option we hold will allow us to buy the asset paying X_1 whose value will not exceed X_2 in that range. If the asset price at expiration is below X_1, both options expire out-of-the-money.

Thus, in the worst case, we lose the net premium, which occurs when $S^* < X_1$. In the best case we earn $X_2 - X_1$ minus the net premium, which is a fixed amount and occurs for $S^* > X_2$. In between X_1 and X_2, we net $S^* - X_1$ minus the net premium. Both our gain and loss are capped. The advantage of the strategy is best seen by comparing it to the purchase of an ordinary call, which also has a limited loss but has an unlimited gain. By selling a call at a higher exercise price, we reduce the maximum loss by substituting a limited gain for an unlimited gain. In comparison to the sale of an ordinary call, which has a limited gain and unlimited loss, we place a limit on the loss by giving up some of the unlimited gain. The spread in comparison to the long or short call is thus a type of hedge wherein the opposite position in one call helps offset the risk of the other. This transaction is usually called a *bull spread*, because it profits in a rising market. If the opposite transaction is done, buying the call with the high exercise price and selling the call with the low exercise price, it is called a *bear spread*. When the transaction is done with puts, buying the put with the high (low) exercise price and selling (buying) the put with the low exercise price will profit in a falling (rising) market and is called a bear (bull) spread.

An investor already holding a position in the asset will often reduce the risk by buying a put. This is, of course, the protective put, which we covered in Essay 39. The position has a limited loss but unlimited gains and therefore can still participate with no limit in any upside potential. One way to reduce the cost of a protective put is to give up some of the upside movement. The investor can sell a call with a higher exercise price, collect the premium, which helps offset the premium on the put, and be subject to delivering the underlying asset if the asset price at expiration ends up above the upper exercise price. This strategy is sometimes called a *risk reversal*. Although it is not necessary, the exercise price on the short call is often set such that the call premium received offsets the put premium paid.

This structure places an upper and lower limit on the effective asset price. If the asset price ends up above X_2, the exercise price on the call, the investor delivers the stock and receives X_2. If the asset price is below X_1, the investor sells the stock using the put and receives X_1. If the asset price at expiration is between X_1 and X_2, the investor simply holds on to the asset and earns a value of S^*. These payoffs differ from those of the spread only in that the spread payoffs are each lower by X_1. Consequently, if we borrowed the present value of X_1 in conjunction with the risk reversal, we would pay back X_1 and the payoffs would match those of the spread. In other words, the value of the risk reversal at the start is $S + p_1 - c_2$. If we had taken out the loan, we would have $S + p_1 - c_2 - X_1(1 + r)^{-T}$ with the latter term representing the present value of the lower exercise price. Recall that the spread value would be $c_1 - c_2$. These two expressions are equated by invoking put-call parity. Taking the spread value $c_1 - c_2$ and substituting $p_1 + S - X_1(1 + r)^{-T}$ for c_1, we have $p_1 + S - X_1(1 + r)^{-T} - c_2$, which is the risk reversal plus the loan.

Naturally each of these transactions can be constructed by doing the opposite of what we did here. This causes the payoffs to be highest when the asset price is below the lower exercise price and lowest when the asset price is above the higher exercise price.

Some variations of risk reversals are more commonly referred to as *collars*. Recall that in a risk reversal, we own the asset and a put struck at X_1 and have sold a call struck at X_2. Let us back up and reconstruct this transaction from a common scenario. Consider an investor owning the asset and thus being exposed with a value of S. The investor wants downside protection, so the purchase of a put struck at X_1 is an appropriate course of action. Of course, we noted that this strategy is a protective put. Many investors, however, do not want to expend the cash required to pay for the put. As noted in the risk reversal, the call struck at X_2 is sometimes added to reduce the cost. Naturally this strategy sounds like a risk reversal, but a risk reversal can technically have X_1 greater than the current asset price, S. All we require is that X_2 be greater than X_1. If X_1 is set below S and X_2 is set above S, we refer to this strategy as a collar. The payoffs of the risk reversal and collar are the same: X_2 if $S^* < X_1$, S^* if $X_1 \leq S^* < X_2$, and X_1 if $S^* \geq X_2$. The difference in the collar and risk reversal lies only in the fact that the collar positions the strikes around the current asset price. The options are said to "collar" the current asset price. They effectively create a minimum price below the current price and maximum price above the current price at which the asset will be sold. A risk reversal is more general. The strikes can be set both above or both below the current asset price, and the collar is a special case in which the current asset price is between the two strikes.

In a collar, the strikes can be arbitrarily set, with X_1 set at any level below S and X_2 set at any level above S. It is, however, common to first choose the strike X_1 and then set X_2 such that the premium on the call sold at X_2 is equal to the premium on the put bought at X_1. In this manner, the call generates sufficient premium to offset the premium on the put. This special case is called a *zero-cost collar*, although this term is somewhat misleading. There is zero cash cost at the start, but the true cost is the fact that the investor gives up more of the upside gain with a zero-cost collar than with a collar that does have a positive cost. Of course, there is no reason why the call strike cannot be set arbitrarily high or low above S, but the zero-cost case is certainly the more common.

Collars are popular with investors wanting to protect gains in a stock but not wanting to pay cash to buy the put necessary to do it. Collars are widely used on portfolios and also for individuals who have heavy and possibly somewhat illiquid exposure to a given stock. For example, executives of companies have large investments in the company's stock that they feel they must retain. The shares can be retained while the exposure is reduced with a collar. The strategy is somewhat controversial, however, because the executive owns the shares, thereby maintaining significant voting rights and appearing to have exposure, but in reality has considerably reduced risk.

An extension of the collar strategy is the *prepaid forward*. In this strategy a collar is combined with a loan. Thus, investors effectively reduce their exposure to the stock and borrow money that can be used for whatever purpose but often is invested in a diversified portfolio, thereby reducing overall market risk. Recall that the prepaid forward has a minimum payoff of X_1. Consequently, a lender should be willing to lend up to the present value of X_1. Of course, this strategy now takes us full circle to the risk reversal combined with the loan, which we covered previously. We saw that this strategy can be shown, using put-call parity, to equal the bull spread. Thus, the prepaid forward is essentially equal to the bull spread, except that the prepaid forward is typically done for the purpose of investing the borrowed funds into a diversified portfolio of stock. This strategy is becoming very widely marketed to high-net-worth individuals with concentrated positions in a stock.

So in this essay we have seen how multiple options can reduce risk. We will look at some options in Essay 50 that serve similar purposes.

FOR MORE READING

Chance, Don M., and Robert Brooks. *An Introduction to Derivatives and Risk Management*, 7th ed. Mason, OH: Thomson South-Western, 2007, chap. 7.

Hull, John C. *Options, Futures, and Other Derivatives*, 6th ed. Upper Saddle River, New Jersy: Prentice-Hall, 2006, chap. 10.

McDonald, Robert L. *Derivative Markets*, 2nd ed. Boston: Addison Wesley, 2006, chap. 3.

TEST YOUR KNOWLEDGE

1. How would an investor construct a call option bull spread?
2. How does a risk reversal differ from a bull spread?
3. What type of risk reversal is referred to as a zero-cost collar?
4. How does a prepaid forward differ from a collar?

Box Spreads

This essay deals with a strategy that is altogether different from those you hear the most about. The box spread could be viewed as a rather dull strategy; its return is the risk-free rate. Yet it is one of the more fascinating of all option strategies, because it is a static risk-free strategy. That means it can be put into place and ignored and earn a risk-free return. No dynamic adjustments are required to maintain the risk-free position. If there is a mispriced option, you can capture an arbitrage profit without having to monitor or revise the position.

Recall that in Essay 42, we described the strategy called a money spread, which involved the purchase of a call priced at c_1 with an exercise price of X_1 and the sale of a call priced at c_2 with an exercise price of X_2. Remember that this strategy creates a limit on the value of the position on the downside of zero and a limit on the value of the position on the upside of $X_2 - X_1$. We can construct a similar transaction using puts. We buy the put worth p_2 with an exercise price of X_2 and sell the put worth p_1 with an exercise price of X_1. This strategy will create a limit on the value of the position on the upside of zero and a limit on the value of the position on the downside of $X_2 - X_1$. If the call transaction is combined with the put transaction, we have a box spread. The term arose because the way in which call and put options with different exercise prices were formerly arrayed in the newspapers gave the appearance of a box.[1]

Let us examine these results for the three possible ranges of the asset price at expiration of the options. Remember that we have a long call and short put with an exercise price of X_1 and a long put and short call with an exercise price of X_2. The asset price at expiration is S^*. It can be less than X_1, between (and inclusive of) X_1 and X_2, or greater than X_2. If $S^* < X_1$,

---

[1] *If* you use your imagination, with option prices no longer appearing in newspapers, you *really* have to use your imagination or be old enough to remember when they did.

both puts expire in-the-money and both calls expire out-of-the-money, so your total payoff is $X_2 - X_1$. In effect, you must buy the asset at X_1 using the short put and you will sell the asset at X_2 using the long put. If S^* is between X_1 and X_2, the long call and long put are in-the-money and the short call and short put are out-of-the-money. You buy the asset at X_1 using the long call and sell it at X_2 using the long put for a total payoff of $X_2 - X_1$. If the asset ends up at $S^* > X_2$, both calls are in-the-money and both puts are out-of-the-money. You buy the call at X_1 using the long call and are forced to sell it at X_2 using the short call for a total payoff of $X_2 - X_1$. So for every possible outcome, you will end up buying the asset at X_1 and immediately selling it for X_2.

To purchase the box spread, you pay the premiums c_1 and p_2 for the long call and put and receive the premiums c_2 and p_1 for the short call and put. The total is $c_1 - c_2 + p_2 - p_1$. The call with the lower exercise price costs more than the call with the higher exercise price, and the put with the higher exercise price costs more than the put with the lower exercise price. This statement means that the initial value of the box spread is positive, which is equivalent to saying that the net effect is that we will have to pay money and not receive money to set up the box spread in this manner.

So picture this. You invest a sum of money, $c_1 - c_2 + p_2 - p_1$, and are guaranteed that at a future date T periods later, you will have a positive value $X_2 - X_1$. This transaction is riskless and can be easily evaluated by discounting the sure payoff at the risk-free rate and comparing it to the initial value. If the present value of the payoff exceeds the initial value, the box spread is underpriced. This statement means that the long call and/or long put are underpriced and/or the short call and/or short put are overpriced. In other words, these four options are somehow mispriced in relation to each other. We cannot tell which options are mispriced relative to the underlying asset. There may be only one option mispriced, but it does not matter. If the overall spread is underpriced, then purchasing it will guarantee a positive inflow that exceeds the outflow and will have no risk. If the present value of the box spread is less than the initial value, the spread is overpriced. Then we should reverse each of the previous transactions. In that case we receive cash up front and have to pay out $X_2 - X_1$ at expiration.

Another way to look at the box spread is to view it as the difference between two put-call parities. Consider put-call parity for options with an exercise price of X_1: $c_1 = p_1 + S - X_1(1 + r)^{-T}$. For options with an exercise price of X_2: $c_2 = p_2 + S - X_2(1 + r)^{-T}$. Let us subtract the second equation from the first: $c_1 - c_2 = p_1 + S - X_1(1 + r)^{-T} - (p_2 + S - X_2(1 + r)^{-T}) = p_1 - p_2 + (X_2 - X_1)(1 + r)^{-T}$. Thus, $c_1 - c_2 + p_2 - p_1 = (X_2 - X_1)(1 + r)^{-T}$. This statement can be interpreted as saying that a long call with exercise price c_1, a short call with exercise price of X_2, a long put with exercise price of X_2, and a short put with exercise price of X_1 is equivalent to a risk-free bond with face value of $X_2 - X_1$ and a present value of $(X_2 - X_1)$ $(1 + r)^{-T}$. This is, of course, the box spread.

A box spread can also be examined by inferring the risk-free return implied by the current prices of the four options. Given the statement $c_1 - c_2 + p_2 - p_1 = (X_2 - X_1)(1 + r)^{-T}$, we can solve for the risk-free rate and obtain $r = [(X_2 - X_1)/(c_1 - c_2 + p_2 - p_1)]^{1/T} - 1$. This value is the implied rate of return and can be compared to the cost of obtaining financing or the lending rate to identify whether the box spread is worth doing.

These examples have each been constructed by assuming that the options are European. If the options are American, then some problems might result from early exercise. We are under no obligation to exercise any options we own, but the options we are short could be exercised on us.

For the case where we own the call with exercise price X_1 and the put with exercise price X_2, early exercise poses no problem. If the short call is exercised, the long call is even deeper in-the-money and can be exercised for a total payoff of $X_2 - X_1$. If the short put is exercised, the long put is even deeper in-the-money and can be exercised for a total payoff of $X_2 - X_1$. So in any case the payoff expected at expiration is simply received earlier. This result cannot hurt the holder of the box spread; it can only help by forcing convergence of the option price to its terminal value earlier than expected. If, however, you do the opposite box spread, where you hold the call with the higher exercise price and the put with the lower exercise price, early exercise can result in paying out the terminal value earlier than expected. This result is not good, because it is like a loan that is called in early. Thus, the box spread with American options can present some risk, depending on which variation you execute.

Probably the most attractive feature of the box spread is that it does not require any information about the volatility of the underlying asset. No formal valuation model such as Black-Scholes-Merton (BSM) is required, though the BSM model is not inconsistent with the valuation rule obtained from the box spread. In the box spread, however, the options are simply judged to be mispriced or not relative to each other. Even mistakes made in executing or pricing the box spread are low-cost mistakes. It is risk free or nearly risk free in the case of American options and cannot result in substantial losses due to mistakes. That it requires no adjustments to the combination of puts and calls makes it particularly attractive for arbitraging, relative to delta hedging. There are, however, four sets of transaction costs, so consideration must be given to determining whether any mispricing is worth exploiting.

FOR MORE READING

Chance, Don M., and Robert Brooks. *An Introduction to Derivatives and Risk Management*, 7th ed. Mason, OH: Thomson South-Western, 2007, chap. 7.

TEST YOUR KNOWLEDGE

1. What instruments does a long box spread consist of?
2. Why does a box spread produce a risk-free return? Assume European options.
3. If the options are American, what problems can this cause for someone using a box spread?

Five

Exotic Instruments

In this section we take you a little further than you might have expected. Consider this as the part of the thrill ride you didn't think was coming. Assuming you have gotten this far, you should realize that derivatives are extremely flexible. They provide all sorts of possibilities for structuring investment positions. The people who create derivatives have realized their potential for designing a lot of different sophisticated instruments. These instruments have come to be known as exotics. Although that word is probably a bit misleading, it has stuck and there is little we can do to rename things.

Exotic instruments, most of which are options, provide payoffs that potentially differ a lot from the standard instruments. For example, one instrument we cover is the barrier option. On one hand, it is a standard option, but on the other, it can terminate prematurely or even fail to officially activate, meaning that it could expire in-the-money and not be exercisable. Another type of exotic option is the digital option, which has a much simpler payoff than that of a standard option. Digital options are usually classified as exotics, but they are actually the easiest options to understand.

In this section there are nine essays on various exotic instruments. Some of them may challenge you. Do not worry. If you get stuck, keep reading. These essays are all pretty independent of each other. Unlike most books, the rest of this one does not require that you master everything before you go on to the next topic.

Barrier Options

This essay addresses a group of exotic derivatives called barrier options. These options have become popular, particularly in currency markets. *Barrier options* are options that contain a special provision that causes them to either expire prematurely or fail to come into existence even though the premium has been paid.

There are two general classes of barrier options: *in-options* and *out-options*. With an in-option, the buyer pays a premium up front and receives an option that will not start until the price of the underlying asset hits a certain level, which is called the *barrier*. If the asset price never touches the barrier, the option never comes into existence and would then expire with no value at expiration, even though it might otherwise appear to expire in-the-money. For example, consider one form of this type of option called a *down-and-in option*. Let it be a call. This call grants the right to buy the underlying asset at $40, the exercise price. The current asset price is $50. We arbitrarily set the barrier at $45. The buyer pays the premium up front, but the option will never actually start unless the asset price falls to $45. Once the asset hits $45, the option is activated and, from that point, it is an ordinary call option. When the barrier is hit and the option is activated, the option is in-the-money. If the barrier is set below the strike, the option will be out-of-the-money when it comes into existence. In-options are also known as *knock-in options*. In addition to down-and-in options, there are *up-and-in options*, which are barrier options that activate if and when the underlying asset price rises and hits the barrier.

Out-options, sometimes called *knock-out options*, are barrier options that terminate before expiration if the underlying asset price reaches the barrier. For example, consider a *down-and-out option*, which we shall make a call. Let the asset price be $50 and the exercise price be $40. Set the barrier at $35. If the asset price falls to $35 during the option's life, the option expires immediately with no value. Out- or knock-out options can be either down-and-out options, meaning that the barrier is below the current asset price or *up-and-out options*, meaning that the barrier is above the current asset price.

If we combine a down-and-out call with a down-and-in call, we obtain an interesting result. If the barriers and exercise prices are the same on the two options, the down-and-out call terminates when the barrier is hit, but the down-and-in call then immediately activates. Thus, the combination of these two options creates an ordinary European option. Naturally the sum of the formulas for pricing these two options equals the Black-Scholes-Merton formula.

Barriers are also sometimes attached to forward contracts and swaps, resulting in an alteration of the payoffs that depends on whether the barrier has been hit during the contract life.

Some barrier options have an additional feature called a "rebate." In such a case, if the asset price on an out-option hits the barrier and the option thus terminates, the holder is paid a sum of money as a form of a rebate. On an in-option, the rebate is paid at expiration if the asset price never reaches the barrier.

Pricing formulas for standard barrier options are well known and not particularly difficult to use. They are based on several somewhat complex principles associated with stochastic processes. For example, the formulas must take into account the risk-neutral probability of the barrier being hit, which utilizes the concept of the *first passage time* of the process, the probability associated with the time it takes the process to reach a certain level. Other than the chosen barrier, the formulas require no more information than is required to price an ordinary European option. One slightly complicating factor, however, is that the formulas are each based on the condition that breaching the barrier is defined as occurring whenever the asset price touches the barrier. Many barrier option contracts recognize the touching of a barrier only at the close of a trading day. In such cases, numerical methods such as the binomial model—with very careful calibration to ensure that the barrier is set at a node—can give reasonably accurate prices.

In the real world, barrier options trade in the over-the-counter market. There have been some experiments with barrier options on the exchange-listed market. The Chicago Board Option Exchange's Standard & Poor's (S&P) Caps were option contracts that were effectively bull and bear spreads that expired when they reached their maximum value at the close of any trading day. For whatever reason, these were not traded much and were eventually delisted.

The most important question about barrier options is probably why anyone would want one of these exotic creatures. The most obvious reason is that the options are cheaper. The condition that the option can terminate early or never come into existence creates outcomes that provide no payoff, except maybe a rebate, that are not present in ordinary options. For this reason, the cost of a barrier option is ordinarily cheaper than a standard option, again assuming no rebate on the former. Consequently some users find them more attractive. In effect, users are paying a lower price by not paying for outcomes they think are not very likely.

For example, suppose you held a portfolio that is roughly equivalent to the S&P Mid-Cap index. You would like to buy an ordinary put on this portfolio to protect an accumulated profit. An options dealer will gladly sell you this over-the-counter option. You feel, however, that it is more costly than you are willing to pay. The dealer suggests an up-and-out put. This option will terminate if the value of the Mid-Cap Index rises to a certain level. You find that condition to be acceptable, because if the index rises to that level, you will feel more confident that you do not need the protection; thus, you pay a lower premium. The risk you take is that the index hits the barrier and then falls below the strike by the expiration, but perhaps you deem this scenario to be highly unlikely. A barrier option would, therefore, be a much cheaper way to go. It is not hard to construct other scenarios in which a specific user's expectations could be best matched by using a barrier option.

FOR MORE READING

Boyle, Phelim P., and Sok Hoon Lau. "Bumping Up against the Barrier with the Binomial Method." *The Journal of Derivatives* 1 (Summer 1994): 6–14.

Hull, John C. *Options, Futures, and Other Derivatives*, 6th ed. Upper Saddle River, NJ: Prentice-Hall, 2006, chap. 22.

Jarrow, Robert A., and Stuart M. Turnbull. *Derivatives Securities*, 2nd ed. Mason, OH: Thomson South-Western, 2000, chap. 20.

McDonald, Robert L. *Derivative Markets*, 2nd ed. Boston: Addison Wesley, 2006, chaps. 14, 22.

Rubinstein, Mark, and Eric Reiner. "Breaking Down the Barriers." *Risk* 4 (August 1991): 31–35.

Wilmott, Paul. *Derivatives: The Theory and Practice of Financial Engineering*. Chichester, UK: John Wiley & Sons, 1998, chap. 14.

TEST YOUR KNOWLEDGE

1. Explain the difference between "in" barrier options and "out" barrier options.
2. Explain the difference between "up" barrier options and "down" barrier options.
3. What kind of option is obtained if an up-and-out put is combined with an up-and-in put?

Straddles and Chooser Options

Although this section deals with exotic options, we are going to take a side look at a popular option strategy called the *straddle*. There is nothing especially exotic about a straddle, but it is very similar to a particular type of exotic option called a *chooser option*. To understand the latter requires that we first look at the former.

It may well be the case that almost everyone who has done any reading on option strategies has encountered a discussion of the straddle. Beyond the simple strategies of buying or selling a single call or put, the straddle seems to be one of the more popular strategies for illustrative purposes. This is most unfortunate for I think the strategy is quite deceptive for the inexperienced person.

A straddle is certainly a simple strategy. You buy an equal number of calls and puts. Assuming you hold the position until expiration, either the call or the put will expire in-the-money, except in the unlikely case that the asset price ends up right on the exercise price.[1] Thus, the straddle's profit graphed against the asset price at expiration is shaped like a V. If the asset price ends up above or below the strike by at least the sum of the premiums on the call and the put, the strategy makes money. The upside gain is unlimited, and the downside gain, while limited by the fact that the asset can go no lower than zero, is still quite high. The maximum loss is the sum of the call and put premiums. This maximum loss occurs only when the asset price ends up at the exercise price. Any slight deviation from that point reduces a loss.

The straddle is typically portrayed as a strategy for those who feel the asset is going to be volatile. This view is a very misleading picture of a straddle. While any large move is certainly possible, even for an asset with low volatility, straddles will be successful over the long run only if the

---

[1] In that case both options are expiring at-the-money and are not worth exercising. In fact, you should always consider, "at-the-money" the same as "out-of-the-money."

investor feels that the market has underestimated the volatility. If everyone shares the opinion that the volatility should be higher, the option premiums will be higher to reflect that view.

As I have done many times, ask any group of individuals—even professional investment managers—when a straddle would be appropriate and they are likely to say "around something like an earnings announcement or a major news-producing event." This answer must, however, be qualified. If an event is coming and everyone knows it, the volatility of the asset will already be high and the option premiums will be high as well. For example, recall that in January of 1991, President Bush gave Saddam Hussein a deadline for pulling Iraqi troops out of Kuwait. Everyone knew the deadline, and oil straddles were a popular strategy since people thought that either war would follow with anything possible or Iraq would pull out and oil prices would fall. But the only way such logic would make sense is if the investor believed that everyone else, though fully aware of the critical date, had underestimated the true volatility.

The best way to analyze a straddle is a simple method that you rarely see explained in books. Consider the Dow Jones Industrial Average (DJIA) February 125 Straddle. On January 23, 2007, the average closed at 12,533.80. The options are scaled at $1/100$ the value of the average so the index is effectively 125.34. The February 125 call closed at 1.40 and the February 125 put closed at 0.90. Ignoring transaction costs, the DJIA would have to close above 12,730 or below 12,270 for the straddle to be profitable. These values were obtained by adding and subtracting both the put and call premiums to the exercise price, reflecting the $1/100$ adjustment of the quoted average to the average on which the options are based. An increase to 12,730 is a gain of 1.56%. A decrease to 12,270 is a loss of 2.11%. The options have a mere 24 days of life left. Thus, the purchaser of a straddle is betting that the Dow will charge ahead at an annual rate of $(365/24)(0.0156) = 23.78\%$ or fall at an annual rate of $(365/24)(0.0211) = 32.03\%$. I would be willing to bet that very few holders of that straddle, if asked the simple question. "Do you believe the Dow will move up at an annual rate of at least 23.78% or move down at an annual rate of at least 32.03% over the next 24 days?" would have replied "Yes." Now, certainly the market has moved at a phenomenal rate at times. Also, the market must move at that rate only over a short period of time, the options' remaining life. Thus, this straddle holder is really betting on a short burst of energy rather than a prolonged upward or downward surge, and short bursts, though they do occur, are very unpredictable.

The over-the-counter options market has created an interesting variation of the straddle called the *chooser option*, which is sometimes called an *as-you-like-it option*. With a chooser option, the buyer pays a premium, but at a specific date before expiration, the buyer designates whether the option will be a call or a put. Thus, the buyer gets to "choose" the type of option later during the option's life.

The standard chooser is a very simple option that can be replicated by ordinary European calls and puts. It can easily be shown that a chooser is equivalent to an ordinary call expiring at the chooser expiration, with an exercise price equal to the exercise price on the chooser option, plus a put expiring at the date on which the choice must be made. The put's exercise price is equal to the call's exercise price discounted from the expiration date to the choice date. For example, if the call expires in 100 days and the chooser option requires that the holder decide if it is a put or a call 30 days before expiration, then the put's exercise price is set as the present value of the call's exercise price found by discounting over 30 days. This lower exercise price means that this put will cost less than an ordinary put. Since the chooser is worth the value of a put with this discounted exercise price plus the value of an ordinary call, a chooser costs less than a straddle. Intuitively that is because the straddle will end up in-the-money unless the asset price ends up right on the exercise price. A chooser, however, can more easily end up out-of-the-money, because the holder could designate it as a call or put and then subsequently the asset price falls deeply or rises deeply by expiration.

Choosers can also be structured to permit the choice to be made at any time the holder desires. Also, the put and call implicitly contained in the chooser option can have different expirations and different exercise prices. These are called *complex choosers*.

Thus, while a straddle is a relatively expensive transaction, designed to satisfy the needs of investors who cannot decide if they are bullish or bearish, the chooser option is a cheaper alternative, permitting investors to decide if the option is a call or a put, but bearing the risk that the decision could turn out to be wrong. In both cases, a key ingredient of the process is how the investor feels about the market's volatility. If the investor feels that other investors have underestimated the market's volatility, either strategy makes sense. If the investor feels that the market is correctly assessing current volatility, it is probably the case that neither strategy makes much sense, since both strategies are equivalent to buying two options, thereby paying two premiums.

FOR MORE READING

Hull, John C. *Options, Futures, and Other Derivatives*, 6th ed. Upper Saddle River, NJ: Prentice-Hall, 2006, chap. 22.

Jarrow, Robert A., and Stuart M. Turnbull. *Derivatives Securities*, 2nd ed. Mason, OH: Thomson South-Western, 2000, chap. 19.
Rubinstein, Mark. "Options for the Undecided." *Risk* 4 (April 1991): 43.

TEST YOUR KNOWLEDGE

1. How far does the underlying need to move to make a straddle profitable?
2. Why is a straddle not a good strategy if it is based only on the expectation of high volatility? What would make it a good strategy?
3. How does a chooser option differ from a straddle?

Compound and Installment Options

This essay is about a type of option that we have previously discussed. In Essays 35 and 36, where we described how American calls and puts are priced, we mentioned the compound option. This instrument is, quite simply, an option on an option. You can buy a call that provides the right to buy another call or a call that provides the right to buy a put. You can buy a put that provides the right to sell a call or a put that provides the right to sell another put. Thus, there are four types of compound options: a call on a call, a call on a put, a put on a call, and a put on a put. On the expiration date of the compound option, the holder simply compares its exercise price to the price of the underlying option and decides whether to exercise and acquire the position in the underlying option.

The compound option was created and analyzed in 1977 by Robert Geske. Whereas a standard option is modeled by assuming that the underlying asset follows a particular stochastic process and then setting up a no-arbitrage strategy, the compound option is slightly more complex. Since a compound option has an option as its underlying asset, the pricing problem is complicated by the fact that the underlying asset now has nonconstant volatility. This point may not seem clear at first, but simply consider that an ordinary European option is an instrument representing a leveraged return on the underlying stock. We can express the degree of leverage in terms of the option's elasticity with respect to the underlying stock price, $\in = (\Delta c/c)/(\Delta S/S)$ where the deltas represent the change in c, the call price, or S, the stock price. This is the standard definition of elasticity: the percentage change in one variable divided by the percentage change in the other variable. Let us rewrite this statement as $\in = (\Delta c/\Delta S)(S/c)$, which can then be written as $\Delta_c(S/c)$ with Δ_c representing the delta of the call price with respect to the stock price. Recall that the delta is given by $N(d_1)$ in the Black-Scholes-Merton (BSM) formula. Thus, the leverage or elasticity is the option's delta times the ratio of the stock price to the call price. Since the delta constantly changes and S and c constantly change, the leverage is constantly changing. The stock's volatility over the next time increment, which we usually denote by $\sigma\sqrt{dt}$, is by definition $SD[\Delta S/S]$, which is the standard deviation of the stock return. It follows that, by definition, the option's volatility is $SD[\Delta c/c]$. Then the option's volatility over the next time increment is, therefore, $\in SD[\Delta S/S])$. Thus, we see that the option's volatility increases directly with the leverage and with the stock's volatility. It is far from constant. This characteristic makes valuing an option on an option a bit more problematic.

It can, however, be shown that a no-arbitrage strategy can be constructed involving a combination of the compound option and the asset on which the underlying option is written. This strategy will lead to a risk-free position, and the compound option can be priced in the style of BSM. The formula bears some resemblance to the BSM formula because it is basically an option on a BSM type option. While the BSM formula incorporates the univariate normal probability distribution, the compound option formula requires both the univariate and bivariate normal probability distributions. The bivariate probability reflects the joint probability that the underlying option will expire in-the-money and that the compound option would have been exercised, granting the holder a position in the underlying option. As we have noted previously, the probability is the risk-neutral/equivalent martingale probability and not the true probability, which is not needed at all.

One common application of the compound option is in modeling a stock as an option. Yes, a common stock is indeed an option. It is simply an option on the assets of the firm. Consider an all-equity firm with assets worth A. The firm then decides to issue a one-year zero-coupon bond with a face value of F. Now, at the end of the year, the bond matures. Let A^* be the value of the assets at that time. If $A > F$, the firm is able to pay off its debt. The bondholders receive F and the stockholders receive the rest, $A - F$. If $A \leq F$, the firm is in default. The bondholders receive A and the stockholders receive nothing. The payoff to the stockholders is exactly like a call option on the assets with an exercise price of F. The option is written by the bondholders. This point, which is one of the most powerful and enlightening results in all of finance, will be explored in more depth in Essay 67.

For now, however, suppose someone creates an ordinary call option on the stock. Then that call option is a compound option. The BSM formula is not correct for valuing that option. The assumption of constant volatility of the stock is not correct because the stock's volatility will be determined by the asset's volatility and the firm's leverage, which will be constantly changing as the market values of the equity and debt change.

Thus, a share of stock is indeed an option. For those who somehow believe that options are dangerous and ought to be outlawed or for those who believe in buying stocks but not buying options, this little demonstration pretty well shows the absurdity of that position. As long as the firm has debt, an ordinary option on the stock is really a compound option.

Compound options are not just academic creations. They are actually used. The kind described here is appropriate if a firm or investor is thinking that it might need an option someday but is not sure. It might be willing to pay a premium now for the right to acquire the option at the later date.

An interesting variation of the compound option is the *installment option*. An installment option is an option in which the premium is paid in installments over the life of the option. For example, consider a two-year European call on the Standard & Poor's 500. Suppose instead that we structure the call as an installment option, specifying that half of the premium is paid up front and half is paid one year later. At the end of the first year, the holder has the right to decide if he would like to pay the second half of the premium in order to continue with the option. This arrangement is of the same form as a compound option, though it is just a little more complex. Applying the compound option formula requires that one solve iteratively to force the exercise price on the compound option to equal the premium on the compound option. In other words, the buyer pays a premium today. Then one year later, the compound option holder decides whether to pay the same premium again in order to continue. Paying the second premium is really like paying the exercise price on the compound option, because if the holder exercises the compound option, he pays the exercise price and acquires the underlying option.

Of course, the option could be designed to have multiple premium dates, which would make it a multiple compound option. Calculating option prices is then normally done using numerical methods that iterate to force the exercise prices on each of the underlying options to equal the premium on the compound option. The premiums on the compound option will collectively add up to more than if the option had the same maturity but were a standard European option. Of course the premiums do not need to be equal, but while this feature complicates pricing, it simplifies explaining the instrument to a potential buyer. Also note that if the option holder chooses not to exercise the compound option, it is equivalent to not paying the installment, but not equivalent to a default, so it has no credit implications. For over-the-counter options, which typically have no organized secondary market, this can be particularly useful.

As mentioned in the first paragraph, an understanding of compound option theory has resulted in great progress in understanding American options, whose exercise features can be viewed as compound options. If compound options were never used in reality, this benefit would outweigh the cost of understanding them.

FOR MORE READING

Geske, Robert. "The Valuation of Compound Options." *Journal of Financial Economics* 7 (1979): 63–82.

Hull, John C. *Options, Futures, and Other Derivatives*, 6th ed. Upper Saddle River, NJ: Prentice-Hall, 2006, chap. 22.

Jarrow, Robert A., and Stuart M. Turnbull. *Derivatives Securities*, 2nd ed. Mason, OH: Thomson South-Western, 2000, chap. 19.

Karsenty, Franck, and Jacques Sikorav. "Installment Plan." *Risk* 10 (October 1993): 36–37, 40.

McDonald, Robert L. *Derivative Markets*, 2nd ed. Boston: Addison Wesley, 2006, chaps. 14, 22.

Rubinstein, Mark. "Double Trouble." *Risk* 5 (December 1991–January 1992): 73.

Wilmott, Paul. *Derivatives: The Theory and Practice of Financial Engineering.* Chichester, UK: John Wiley & Sons, 1998, chap. 16.

TEST YOUR KNOWLEDGE

1. Explain how a compound option differs from an ordinary option.
2. What does the bivariate normal probability reveal about a compound option?
3. How does an installment option relate to a compound option?
4. What is the most important contribution of compound option theory?

Digital Options

Rarely is anything as complex as it seems. Try to keep that point in mind as you study thermodynamics, zoology, the writings of Kierkegaard, or derivatives. This essay should make that point clear. *Digital options*, sometimes called *binary options*, appear on the surface to be just another exotic instrument. Upon slightly closer examination, however, we find that digital options are to ordinary options what atoms are to molecules. They are but simple building blocks.

There are two basic types of digital options: *cash-or-nothing options* and *asset-or-nothing options*. First consider the asset-or-nothing option. This option, like most other options, has an exercise price and a time to expiration. On the expiration day.

1. If the underlying asset price exceeds the exercise price, the holder receives the asset from the writer, or
2. If the underlying asset price is less than the exercise price, the holder receives nothing and the option expires with no value.

This structure takes the form of a call option, paying off the asset if the asset price exceeds the exercise price at expiration. An asset-or-nothing put would pay the asset if the underlying asset price at expiration is less than the exercise price and nothing otherwise. In either case, the holder receives the asset without paying the exercise price. This sounds like a great deal on the surface. But before we analyze the deal, let us look at the cash-or-nothing option.

A cash-or-nothing option also has an exercise price and expiration just like an ordinary option. For a cash-or-nothing call, on the expiration day,

1. If the underlying asset price exceeds the exercise price, the holder receives the exercise price from the writer, or
2. If the underlying asset price is less than the exercise price, the holder receives nothing and the option expires with no value.

If the cash-or-nothing option is specified as a put, it pays the exercise price if the underlying asset price is less than the exercise price and nothing otherwise. It is somewhat more common, however, to reduce the cash-or-nothing option to a more fundamental form in which the option pays one unit of currency if it expires in-the-money and zero otherwise. In this form, the option is more frequently referred to as a *binary option* or a *digital option*.

Let us examine what these options would be worth. The asset-or-nothing option has a payoff equal to the value of the asset, provided that the value of the asset is above the exercise price. The probability of this payoff is the probability of the asset price exceeding the exercise price at expiration. The present value of this payoff is the present value of the asset's value at expiration conditional on the asset value exceeding the exercise price at expiration times the probability of the asset value exceeding the exercise price at expiration.

The cash-or-nothing option has an expected payoff of one unit of currency times the probability that the asset price is greater than the exercise price at expiration. Let X be the exercise price. The current value of this payoff is found by discounting the payoff at the risk-free rate over the life of the option. Suppose you buy the asset-or-nothing option and sell X units of the cash-or-nothing option, both with the same expiration and exercise price. Then the payoff to your overall position will be

1. If the asset price exceeds the exercise price at expiration, you pay X units of currency, which is your obligation on the X units of the short cash-or-nothing option, and receive the asset, which is your entitlement on the asset-or-nothing option, or
2. If the asset price is less than the exercise price at expiration, you neither pay nor receive anything.

This combination of long the asset-or-nothing option and short X units of the cash-or-nothing option is precisely the payoff from an ordinary European call option. Therefore, the value of the combination of these two options must be the value of a standard European option, which we know is given by the Black-Scholes-Merton (BSM) formula.

Recall from Essay 27 that the BSM formula can be written as

$$C = S N(d_1) - Xe^{-rT} N(d_2)$$

where
$$Xe^{-rT} = \text{Present value of the exercise price}$$
$$N(d_1) \text{ and } N(d_2) = \text{Normal probabilities}$$

The first expression on the right-hand side is the value of the long position in the asset-or-nothing option. The second expression on the right-hand side is the value of X units of the cash-or-nothing option. Note the minus sign reflecting the short position in the cash-or-nothing option.

Some comments on the interpretation of $N(d_1)$ and $N(d_2)$ are in order. First let us look at $N(d_2)$, which is easier to interpret. $N(d_2)$ is the probability that the asset price will exceed the exercise price under the assumption that the expected return on the asset is the risk-free rate. This is, of course, not the expected return on the asset, so the true probability of the option expiring in-the-money is higher than given by $N(d_2)$. This probability is based on risk-neutral valuation, a topic covered in Essays 31 and 32. The interpretation of $N(d_1)$ is much more complicated. While it is indeed a probability, it is a much more complicated probability, and its interpretation cannot be divorced from the value S. In other words, you have to interpret $SN(d_1)$ jointly, not separately. $SN(d_1)$ is the present value of the expected value of the asset price at expiration, conditional on the asset price exceeding the exercise price at expiration, times the risk-neutral probability that the asset price will exceed the exercise price at expiration, discounted to the present at the risk-free rate. From earlier, that is simply the value of the asset-or-nothing option. Of course, $N(d_1)$ is also a standard European option's delta or hedge ratio, but that interpretation is for an entirely different purpose. For that matter, $N(d_2)$ is also a hedge ratio, meaning that it is the number of risk-free bonds to sell along with holding $N(d_1)$ shares of stock, to replicate one European call.

Digital or binary options are thus more fundamental securities than a standard European option. They are neither new nor exotic. To borrow an analogy coined by well-known consultant Charles Smithson, they are like the individual pieces of Legos that can be combined to make seemingly more complex creations. But often these complex instruments are quite simple when their components are examined separately.

FOR MORE READING

Hull, John C. *Options, Futures, and Other Derivatives*, 6th ed. Upper Saddle River, NJ: Prentice-Hall, 2006, chap. 22.

Jarrow, Robert A., and Stuart M. Turnbull. *Derivatives Securities*, 2nd ed. Mason, OH: Thomson South-Western, 2000, chap. 19.

McDonald, Robert L. *Derivative Markets*, 2nd ed. Boston: Addison Wesley, 2006, chaps. 14, 22.

Rubinstein, Mark. "Unscrambling the Binary Code." *Risk* 4 (October 1991): 75–83. Erratum, *Risk* 5 (January 1992): 73.

TEST YOUR KNOWLEDGE

1. How does an asset-or-nothing option differ from a cash-or-nothing option?
2. How can an ordinary European call option be combined with an asset-or-nothing call to replicate a cash-or-nothing call option?
3. How do digital puts differ from digital calls?

Geographic Options

This essay has an unusual title: geographic options, meaning options named after locations. We are all familiar with American options, which can be exercised early, and European options, which cannot be exercised early. Most options listed on options exchanges are American, though European options are widely used, especially in the over-the-counter options markets. We covered European and American options in Essays 16, 22, 23, 35, and 36.

While we are going from continent to continent, let us look at the *Asian option*. This instrument is an option in which the payoff is not based on the asset price at expiration but rather on the average price of the asset over the option's life. An Asian option is also called an *average price option*. No one really knows why these instruments were named Asian options, but it is believed that they originated in the foreign currency options markets, and with the terms "American" and "European" already taken, someone called them Asian options and it stuck.

Asian options are useful for hedging a stream of foreign cash flows when the hedger is more concerned about hedging the average exchange rate. Asian options are less expensive than European options. In addition, they are useful in markets that are highly concentrated and, therefore, susceptible to manipulation or temporarily distorted prices. In fact, Asian-style derivatives are very common in the oil markets, which are volatile and dominated by a small number of suppliers.

Ironically, in an attempt to keep the instrument as simple as possible, Asian options became among the most complex of all derivatives with regard to pricing. Consider the two different ways you can compute an average: arithmetic and geometric. An arithmetic average of the prices 100, 102 and 105 is $(100 + 102 + 105)/3 = 102.33$. A geometric average of these prices is $(100)(102)(105)^{1/3} = 102.31$. A geometric average is always lower than the corresponding arithmetic average, unless all of the values are the same. Because most people are generally familiar with arithmetic averages and not particularly familiar with geometric averages, the former are usually used in Asian options.

Unfortunately, arithmetic averaging makes pricing the option quite difficult. The problem stems from the fact that it is customary, for reasons we covered in Essays 25 and 26, to work under the assumption that the underlying asset price follows the geometric Brownian motion model. This formulation results in the probability distribution of the asset price at expiration being of the lognormal form. Recall that a lognormally distributed variable is a variable whose log is distributed normally. Pricing the option requires that you evaluate the probability distribution of the average asset price at expiration. A lognormally distributed variable changes proportionately to its previous value.

The probability distribution of the geometric average of a lognormally distributed variable can be fairly easily derived. The probability distribution of the arithmetic average of a lognormally distributed variable is a complex and unwieldy function. The probability distribution of the arithmetic average of a normally distributed variable is simple, but this result depends on assuming that the asset price follows the arithmetic Brownian motion process. This assumption is usually unpalatable, because it permits negative prices. The solution to pricing the arithmetic average Asian option is generally obtained via Monte Carlo simulation or by approximation methods.

A variation of the average price option is the *average strike option*, in which the final payoff is based on the difference between the asset price at expiration and the average price over the life of the option. The average serves as the exercise price. This feature does not, however, simplify the pricing problem mentioned in the last paragraph. Some Asian options are further complicated by being of the American style, meaning that they can be exercised early.

Another geographic option is the *Bermuda option*. Why Bermuda? It is between America and Europe. A Bermuda option is an option that lies somewhere between an American option and a European option, meaning that it has a limited early exercise feature. Typically, a Bermuda option can be exercised early, but only at specific times. Thus, the early exercise period might start somewhere during the life of the option. One unusual example was issued a few years back in Japan and was called a *Japanese option*. It allowed early exercise but—and do not ask me why—only on Thursdays. I do not think these instruments are still around.[1]

---

[1] Of course, in the over-the-counter market, anything can be created. So do not be surprised if a Wall Street firm creates an option exercisable only on days on which the New York Yankees beat the Boston Red Sox in baseball. Don't laugh, it *could* happen.

Several years ago some mathematicians invented a *Russian option*. I think one of the authors was Russian and, exercising the right of any inventor, chose to honor the motherland. A Russian option is a lookback option that can be exercised early. We will cover lookback options in Essay 51.

Finally, there is the *Canadian option*. Actually this is just a joke I once heard while in Canada and a bit corny, but I shall tell it nonetheless. A Canadian option is an option that can be exercised only after receiving approval by the Canadian government, an obvious reference to Canada's alleged reputation for extensive government intervention. Let me emphasize that it was a Canadian who told that joke.

FOR MORE READING

Hull, John C. *Options, Futures, and Other Derivatives*, 6th ed. Upper Saddle River, NJ: Prentice-Hall, 2006, chap. 22.

Jarrow, Robert A., and Stuart M. Turnbull. *Derivatives Securities*, 2nd ed. Mason, OH: Thomson South-Western, 2000, chap. 19.

Kemna, A. C. G., and A. C. F. Vorst. "A Pricing Method for Options Based on Average Asset Values." *Journal of Banking and Finance* 14 (1990): 113–120.

Levy, E., and S. M. Turnbull. "Average Intelligence." *Risk* 5 (February 1992): 53–59.

McDonald, Robert L. *Derivative Markets*, 2nd ed. Boston: Addison Wesley, 2006, chap. 14.

TEST YOUR KNOWLEDGE

1. What is the advantage of a geometric average price option over an arithmetic average price option, and what is the disadvantage?
2. In an Asian option, the average price of the underlying over the life of the option can serve as either of which two values in the option payoff formula?
3. What is a Bermuda option?

Multi-Asset Options

Most of the options encountered have one underlying asset. There are also options that have two or more underlying assets. For lack of a better name, these instruments are sometimes simply called *multi-asset options*. There are two general types of these options that I will cover here. The first type is the *exchange option*.

The exchange option, sometimes called the *Margrabe option* (named for its creator, William Margrabe) is an option in which the holder has the right to exchange one asset for another. In other words, the terms specify that upon exercise, the holder turns over one asset and receives another. Usually the asset given up is an asset similar to the one that is received. A typical example might be the right to surrender one asset, call it asset Y, and receive another asset, call it asset X. This instrument would be described as a call option to exchange asset Y for asset X. Asset Y then serves as the exercise price. In fact, this type of option can be viewed as an option with a stochastic exercise price.

A put option to exchange asset X for asset Y is the right to turn over asset X and receive asset Y. Consequently, a put option to exchange asset Y for asset X is an option to give up asset Y and receive asset X. Thus, it is identical to the call option to exchange asset Y for asset X, described in the previous paragraph.

It would appear that pricing an option with a stochastic exercise price would be quite difficult, but in fact it is fairly simple. We assume that both assets follow the same type of stochastic process but with different volatilities. We must also know the correlation between the returns of the two assets. The payoff of this option at expiration is $Max(0, X^* - Y^*)$ where X^* and Y^* are the values of the two assets at the option's expiration. There is a small mathematical trick that greatly reduces the dimension of the problem. A function is linearly homogeneous with respect to a given variable if you can multiply the variable by a factor c and the overall function changes by simply multiplying itself by c. For example, $z = q^2$ is a linearly homogeneous function because $cz = cq^2$. A linearly homogeneous function has a special relationship between the function and the partial derivatives of its component variables, which is known as Euler's rule.

The payoff of an exchange option is linearly homogeneous with respect to both asset prices. This result can be seen by multiplying both asset prices by $1/Y^*$. This gives us $\text{Max}(0,X^*/Y^* - 1)$ which is the same as $(1/Y^*)\text{Max}(0,X^* - Y^*)$. We can do the same with X^*. Margrabe used this method to express the option price in terms of its partial derivatives. Then by forming a risk-free hedge involving long one asset, short the other, and short the option, you can eliminate the risk. This technique leads to a non-stochastic partial differential equation, with a solution that looks a lot like the Black-Scholes-Merton (BSM) formula except that the volatility reflects the relative volatility of one of the assets to the other and also the correlation between the two assets.

Naturally in practice an exchange option on two assets whose values are on different orders of magnitude would not be very meaningful. For example, an option to swap a $150 asset for a $60 asset would not make much sense. Consequently in most cases the option is written so as to settle in cash at expiration based on which asset performed the better. For example, we calculate the return on asset X over the option's life. If it exceeds the return on asset Y over the option's life, the holder can receive the cash payoff of $\text{Max}(0, R_x - R_y)$. This adjustment effectively scales the payoff to assume a $1 investment rather than a one-unit investment in the underlying asset. This type of option is usually referred to as an *outperformance option*.

The exchange option gives many insights into the BSM option. By assuming that the asset given up is simply cash, which has a known risk-free return, the exchange option formula converts to the BSM formula. Thus, the exchange option formula is more general than the BSM formula. Though exchange options are not widely traded, the formula has proven to be applicable to pricing a number of other types of options, such as performance incentive fees, margin accounts, indexed bonds, and delivery options in futures contracts.

Another type of multi-asset option is the *min-max option*, which is sometimes called a *rainbow option*, an *alternative option*, an *either-or option*, or a *better-of-two option*. It is a call or put option whose payoff is determined by first identifying which of two assets performs the better (or the worse) relative to each other and then comparing the better (or the worse) performer to the exercise price. For example, a call on the better of two assets X or Y will have a payoff of $\text{Max}(0,\text{Max}(X^*,Y^*) - K)$, where K is the exercise price. So at expiration we observe the prices of the two assets, X^* and Y^*, and determine which of the two is greater. This is the inner expression Max(X^*,Y^*). Then we compare the greater asset value to the exercise price K as we would an ordinary call.

This option is often referred to as a *call on the max*. We could also have a *put on the max*, which would compare the better-performing asset to the exercise price as a put. Its payoff would be Max($0,K -$ Max(X^*,Y^*)). We could also have a *call on the min*, which would be Max(0,Min(X^*, Y^*) $-$ K), and a *put on the min*, whose payoff would be Max($0,K -$ Min(X^*, Y^*)). Options *on the min* would pay off based on the lower valued of the two assets. There are also min-max options with three or more assets.

As with exchange options, min-max options are often written with proportional payoffs, that is, where the returns on the two assets are compared with an exercise price, expressed in the form of a percentage.

The pricing of these options is fairly simple and relies on the construction of a riskless hedge involving the option and the two assets. The correlation among the assets is an important factor in pricing the options. The formulas require the evaluation of a bivariate normal probability distribution if there are two assets and higher-order multivariate normal probability distributions if there are more than two assets.

Min-max options can be particularly useful for portfolio managers who are considering investing in one of two (or more) sectors. Instead of investing in both sectors, the manager can purchase a call option that pays off based on the better performing of the two sectors. Protection can be acquired against a badly performing sector by purchasing a put on the worse performer of two assets. This alternative will be less expensive than a put on both sectors. In a world with a broad array of sectors in which to invest, the ability to use multi-asset options in order to capitalize on the better or worse performer greatly increases the flexibility that managers have to invest in and manage the risk of certain sectors.

FOR MORE READING

Hull, John C. *Options, Futures, and Other Derivatives*, 6th ed. Upper Saddle River, NJ: Prentice-Hall, 2006, chap. 22.

Margrabe, William. "The Value of an Option to Exchange One Asset for Another." *The Journal of Finance* 33 (1978): 177–186.

McDonald, Robert L. *Derivative Markets*, 2nd ed. Boston: Addison Wesley, 2006, chaps. 14, 22.

Rubinstein, Mark. "Somewhere Over the Rainbow." *Risk* 4 (October 1991): 63–66.

Rubinstein, Mark. "One for Another." *Risk* 4 (July–August 1991): 30–32.

Rubinstein, Mark. "Return to Oz." *Risk* 7 (November 1994): 67–71.

Stulz, René. "Options on the Minimum or Maximum of Two Risky Assets." *Journal of Financial Economics* 19 (1982): 161–186.

Stulz, René. *Risk Management and Derivatives*. Mason, OH: Thomson South-
Western, 2003, chap. 17.

Wilmott, Paul. *Derivatives: The Theory and Practice of Financial Engineering*.
Chichester, UK: John Wiley & Sons, 1998, chap. 11.

TEST YOUR KNOWLEDGE

1. Explain why an exchange option is really an option with a stochastic (random) exercise price.
2. Briefly explain how an option on the max works.
3. How would an outperformance option be structured if one asset starts off with considerably higher value than the other?

Range Forwards and Break Forwards

In this essay I discuss two types of instrument that, while considered exotic, are really quite simple. First we consider the range forward, which is a forward contract with limits on the amount that can be made or lost. It can easily be shown that a range forward is equivalent to a long position in a standard forward contract, a long position in a European put with an exercise price less than the forward price, and a short position in a call with an exercise price higher than the forward price. The exercise prices on the put and call are not arbitrary. They are, in fact, the exercise prices that would make the put and call have equivalent prices. Finding them, however, requires searching for the right combination of exercise prices. The range forward is comparable to the fairly basic and well-known option strategies called a *bull spread* and a *collar*, which we covered in Essay 42. The comparisons among the range forward, bull spread, and collar are an interesting and worthwhile exercise.

Consider an example. Let the underlying asset be a generic stock index and the maturity of the range forward contract be one year. Let the index be at 966.58. The one-year risk-free interest rate is about 5.4%, and we shall assume the dividend yield on the index is 1.8%. Both rates are discrete compounded rates. That means that the forward price is $966.58(1.054)/(1.018) = 1000.76$.

Now go long a forward contract on the index with a one-year maturity at a price of 1000.76. Then buy a put with an exercise price less than the forward price and sell a call with an exercise price more than the forward price. Set the two exercise prices such that the put and the call prices are equal. Finding these prices is not all that difficult. We can arbitrarily set either the put or call exercise price and then search for the other. Let us set the call strike to 1050, which gives a call value of 37.75. This figure was obtained using the Black-Scholes-Merton model based on a volatility of the index of

15% and converting the risk-free rate and dividend yield to continuously compounded equivalents. A put with an exercise price of 958.48 would have a price of 37.75. Thus, the call strike exceeds the forward price of 1000.76, the put strike is less than the forward price, and the put price and call prices are equal. We are long the put, long the forward contract, and short the call.

Now consider what happens at expiration. Suppose the index is at S^* at expiration. First let S^* be less than the put strike of 958.48. The forward contract always pays off $S^* - 1000.76$, which is a loss. The put pays off because its strike is 958.48 and its payoff is, therefore, $958.48 - S^*$. The call expires out-of-the-money. Thus, the total payoff is $958.48 - 1000.76 = -42.28$. This value is not dependent on the specific value of the index at expiration, except that its occurrence is restricted to cases where S^* is less than the put strike of 958.48. Thus, in the range of $S^* < 958.48$, the value of this combination, -42.28, is constant.

Now suppose S^* is greater than or equal to the put strike of 958.48 but less than the call strike of 1,050. Again, the forward contract always pays off $S^* - 1000.76$, which is still negative but increases with the level of S^*. Both the call and the put expire at or out-of-the-money.

Let S^* be greater than the call strike of 1050. The forward contract again pays off $S^* - 1000.76$, which is positive. The call now pays off $-(S^* - 1050)$ for a total payoff of $1050 - 1000.76 = 49.24$. This value is not dependent on the value of the index, except that it is restricted to values of at least 1050. Thus, the value of this combination, 49.24, is constant.

Now recall the option strategy called a bull spread. This transaction is executed by buying a call with one exercise price and selling an otherwise identical call with a higher exercise price. The payoff of the range forward is a lot like, though not identical to, that of a bull spread. It is also a lot like a collar. It is much closer to a collar except that normally a collar is considered to include a long position in the underlying asset. Let us see why these analogies hold.

Let X_1 be the lower exercise price and X_2 be the higher exercise price. A bull spread using calls is constructed by buying a call with an exercise price of X_1 and selling a call with an exercise price of X_2. Let us now decompose the bull spread by taking a closer look at the long call with an exercise price of X_1.

Using put-call parity, we can see that this option is equivalent to a long put with an exercise price of X_1, a long position in the underlying asset, and a loan with a face value equal to the present value of X_1. Note that we have implicitly borrowed money to finance the position of the asset. Owning the underlying asset financed with a loan is similar to being long a forward contract. Holding the asset and borrowing the present value of X_1 is not exactly a forward contract, though it will be close. To be equivalent to a forward contract would require that we borrow the present value of the forward price instead of the present value of X_1.

In a bull spread, the two exercise prices are set arbitrarily. In a range forward, they are not set arbitrarily. They must be set to specific values to make the transaction truly like a forward contract, meaning that it has zero value at the start. The lower strike X_1 must be set such that the long put with an exercise price of X_1 has the same price as the short call with an exercise price of X_2. X_1 is required to be less than the forward price and X_2 greater than the forward price. Thus, our long position in the underlying asset and our loan is not exactly a forward contract because the face value of the loan is not the forward price. This combination has a positive cash flow up front, which implies that it requires an initial outlay. How do we know this?

Once again, we appeal to put-call parity. Remember that we must have $p + S = c + X(1 + r)^{-T}$, with the latter term representing the present value of the exercise price. Using X_1 as the exercise price, this means that we could write it as $p_1 + S = c_1 + X_1(1 + r)^{-T}$. Then we must have $p_1 + S - X_1(1 + r)^{-T} = c_1$. Thus, a put with an exercise price of X_1 plus long the underlying asset and borrowing the present value of X_1 is worth the same as a call with the same exercise price. The combination we are working with here, however, has the call with an exercise price of X_2, which is higher than X_1. It is well known that the price of a call is lower the higher the exercise price. Thus, we can say for sure that $p_1 + S - X_1(1 + r)^{-T} > c_2$. Rearranging, we have $p_1 + S - X_1 (1 + r)^{-T} - c_2 > 0$. This statement implies that owning the put with an exercise price of X_1, owning the underlying asset, borrowing the present value of X_1, and being short the call with an exercise price of X_2 has a positive value. This makes it a net long position, requiring that we pay this positive initial value up front. This net positive outlay is obviously equal to the difference between a long call with an exercise price of X_1 and a short call with an exercise price of X_2, or precisely the bull spread.

Thus, a range forward is quite similar to but not exactly the same as a bull spread. Just remember that a range forward has no initial value as it costs nothing to establish up front. A bull spread has a definite cost up front.

In the example here, the bull spread value would be the value of the long call with an exercise price of 958.48, which is 77.91, less the value of the short call with an exercise price of 1050, which is 37.75, or 40.16. The maximum value of the bull spread at expiration is $1050 - 958.48 = 91.52$, and the minimum value of the bull spread at expiration is zero. Compare this to the maximum value of the range forward at expiration, which we found to be 49.24, and the minimum value, which we found to be -42.28. These values are not close, nor should they be, but the range is the same. For an initial outlay of zero, we obtain a range of -42.28 to 49.24, a range of 91.52. For an initial outlay of 40.16, we obtain a range of 0 to 91.52, obviously a range of 91.52.

In Essay 42 we showed how a collar is similar to a bull spread. Thus, we see that a range forward is also similar to a collar. Each of these three transactions creates an equivalent range. The range forward is simply a forward contract, which naturally has zero value up front, with a maximum and minimum terminal value. A bull spread is a combination of options with a maximum and minimum terminal value. A collar is a combination of options with zero initial value that is attached to a long position in the asset to assure a maximum and minimum terminal value.

Now we take a look at another exotic instrument and show how it, too, is similar to certain basic instruments. A break forward contract is equivalent to a combination of a call and a loan where the amount borrowed is the cost of the call. The interesting feature of a break forward is that its outcome looks like a call option, but it is structured so as to require no initial cash payment up front. A break forward can sound like a transaction with everything to gain and nothing to lose, but on closer inspection, we find that at expiration, it can have a negative payoff, unlike an ordinary call. This is not to suggest that this transaction is not a good one in some situations. Indeed, it offers a call-like payoff of limited downside loss and unlimited upside gain but requires no cash outlay up front. This characteristic occurs because you are effectively borrowing the call premium from the writer.

Let S be the price of the underlying, F be the forward price of the underlying, and S^* be the price of the underlying at expiration. Then, let S' be the price of the underlying after discounting by the dividend yield. The exercise price of the call is set at the forward price, F. Let the value K be the forward price plus the compound value of the call price with compounding at the risk-free rate. Using c as the current call price, we have that $K = F + c(1 + r)^T$ where T is the number of years of the call's life.

The break forward consists of a long call with exercise price F and a loan in which you borrow the present value of the difference between K and F. Thus, you are borrowing the price of the call.

Now suppose we are at expiration and $S^* > F$. Then the call is worth $S^* - F$, and we pay back the amount $K - F$ on the loan for a total cash flow of $S^* - K$. This amount can be negative, but if S^* is sufficiently large, meaning it exceeds K, the payoff is positive. Suppose at expiration, $S^* \leq F$. Then the call expires worthless, and we pay back the amount $K - F$ on the loan for a total cash flow of $F - K$, which is negative.

Thus, the break forward pays off either $F - K$, which is negative but fixed at this amount for any value of S^* less than F, or $S^* - K$, which can be negative but is positive for any value of $S^* > F$ and increases with S^*. If the payoff is graphed on a vertical axis against S^*, the graph will look like a call option. The important difference, however, is that while the payoff of a break forward can be negative, the payoff of a call option is never negative. Of course, the *profit* of a call option, obtained by subtracting the initial cost of the call from the payoff, can certainly be negative.

Consider an example using the generic index described earlier in this essay. The index is at 966.58, and the forward price is 1000.76. A call option with an exercise price of 1000.76 is worth 56.77. Thus, K is $(1000.76 + 56.77)(1.054) = 1060.60$.

At expiration the break forward will pay off $S^* - 1060.60$ if $S^* > 1000.76$ and $1000.76 - 1060.60 = -59.84$ if $S^* \leq 1000.76$. The payoff when $S^* > 1000.76$ can be negative, and the payoff when $S^* \leq 1000.76$ is strictly negative. The break forward costs nothing up front as it can be shown to be equal in value to a call with exercise price of 1000.76 and a loan with face value of the present value of 59.84, obtained as 1060.60 $- 1000.76$. The present value of 59.84 is $59.84 \ (1.054)^{-1} = 56.77$, which we said was the value of a call with an exercise price of 1000.76.

A break forward contract can also be constructed another way. Due to the parity relationship among puts, calls, the underlying asset, and the forward price, we can accomplish the same result by taking a long position in a forward contract, borrowing the present value of $K - F$, and buying a put with an exercise price of F. In other words, a long forward contract and a put is the same as a call, given that the put and call exercise prices are the forward price. This relationship is what is sometimes called *put-call-forward parity*.

Thus, the break forward contract is somewhat like a call in that it has a fixed minimum value and unlimited upside potential and somewhat like a forward contract in that it requires no initial outlay up front. This statement should not, however, be interpreted as being the best of both worlds. The "cost" of not having to pay cash up front is that when the contract expires, unlike a call option, we may have to pay out a certain amount. For whatever advantage a break forward offers, it also has a disadvantage. No instrument is clearly dominated by another instrument, for if that were so, there would be an obvious arbitrage opportunity, which we know cannot be the case.

Range forwards and break forwards and their equivalent replicating combinations can also be constructed in the reverse manner. Thus, these bullish strategies are then turned into bearish strategies.

FOR MORE READING

Hull, John C. *Options, Futures, and Other Derivatives*, 6th ed. Upper Saddle River, NJ: Prentice-Hall, 2006, chap. 22.

TEST YOUR KNOWLEDGE

1. Briefly explain what a range forward is.
2. What two other strategies that were covered earlier are very similar to the range forward with respect to their payoffs?
3. Briefly explain what a break forward is.

Lookback Options

A *lookback option* is an option that allows the holder to purchase or sell the underlying asset at the most attractive price that the buyer could possibly have obtained during the life of the option. In so doing, the lookback option permits optimal market timing. The holder of a lookback option will either get to buy the asset at its lowest price during the life of the option or sell the asset at its highest price during the life of the option. A lookback option is sometimes called a *no-regrets option*, because the holder of the option will never have any regrets about not selling it or exercising it at the wrong time. It has also been called a *hindsight option*.

There are two basic types of lookback options, *standard lookbacks and extremum lookbacks*. A standard lookback call permits the holder to buy the underlying asset at the expiration at the lowest price it was at during the life of the option. Letting S_{min} represent the lowest price reached by the asset during the life of the option, the expiration payoff is, therefore, $Max(0, S_T - S_{min})$ where S_T is the asset price at expiration. Thus, the exercise price is variable. A standard lookback call will always expire no worse than at-the-money.

A standard lookback put allows the holder to sell the underlying asset at expiration at the highest price achieved during the life of the option. Letting S_{max} be the highest price reached by the asset during the life of the option, the expiration payoff is therefore $Max(0, S_{max} - S_T)$. Again, the exercise price is variable. Like a standard lookback call, a standard lookback put will always expire no worse than at-the-money.

Pricing formulas exist for standard lookback options. Though the formulas are complex, they require no more information than that required for standard European options, other than the current maximum or minimum asset price, obviously an easily obtainable value. If the current time is during the life of the option, the current maximum or minimum can be observed over the history of the asset price since the option was first written. If the current time is at the beginning of the life of the option, the current asset

249

price is both the maximum and minimum. The formulas require computation of the standard normal probability, which is obviously not difficult. The formulas are based on the risk-neutral/equivalent martingale expectation of the payoff of the option at expiration and therefore take into account the probability distribution of the expected maximum and minimum values of the asset during the option's life. Standard lookback options are quite expensive relative to standard European options, because they are guaranteed to expire in-the-money.

While standard lookback options have a variable exercise price, extremum lookback options have a fixed exercise price. An extremum lookback call allows the holder to buy the asset for the fixed exercise price specified in the contract but permits the holder to sell the asset for the highest price the asset reached during the life of the option. An extremum lookback put allows the holder to sell the asset for the fixed exercise price but allows the holder to buy the asset at the minimum price it reached during the life of the option. Note that the asset price at expiration has no effect on the value of extremum lookback options, except to the extent that it might end up being the maximum or minimum asset price during the option's life. Pricing formulas for extremum lookback options differ according to whether the current asset price is greater or less than the exercise price.

For an extremum lookback call in which the current asset price is greater than the exercise price, it is apparent that the option will expire in-the-money. Of course, the amount by which the option will be in-the-money is unknown, but in such a case, the option is much more like the underlying asset and it is guaranteed to end up with positive value. For an extremum lookback put in which the current asset price is less than the exercise price, it is also apparent that the option will expire in-the-money. If these conditions are not yet met, extremum lookback options are not guaranteed to expire in-the-money. Consequently, they are not as expensive as standard lookback options. They are, however, more expensive than standard European options. This is due to the fact that their payoffs substitute the maximum price for calls and minimum price for puts for the asset price at expiration. Thus, only in the outcome that the asset price at expiration is the maximum or minimum price is the payoff identical to that of the standard European option. In all other outcomes the extremum lookback option beats the standard European option.

There are several variations of lookback options. A *lookforward option* provides the holder a payoff based on the difference between the price at the beginning of the option's life and the maximum or minimum price, depending on whether it is a call or a put, reached during the option's life. It is, however, easy to see that the lookforward option is just an extremum lookback option with the exercise price fixed at the asset price at the beginning of the option's life. There is also a lookback options with an early exercise feature, which has acquired the name *Russian option*.

Lookback options for portfolio managers have been described as a device for obtaining perfect market timing. A lookput call that allows purchase of the underlying at its lowest price and a lookback put that allows sale of the underlying at its highest price results in perfect market timing. But there is no guarantee that the difference between the purchase and sale prices of the asset will cover the cost of the options.

FOR MORE READING

Conze, Antoine, and R. Viswanathan. "Path-Dependent Options: The Case of Lookback Options." *The Journal of Finance* 46 (1991): 1893–1907.

Garman, Mark. "Recollection in Tranquillity." *Risk* 2 (March 1989): 16–18.

Goldman, M. Barry, Howard B. Sosin, and Mary Ann Gatto. "Path-Dependent Options: 'Buy at the Low, Sell at the High.'" *The Journal of Finance* 34 (1979): 1111–1127.

Hull, John C. *Options, Futures, and Other Derivatives*, 6th ed. Upper Saddle River, NJ: Prentice-Hall, 2006, chap. 22.

Jarrow, Robert A., and Stuart M. Turnbull. *Derivatives Securities*, 2nd ed. Mason, OH: Thomson South-Western, 2000, chap. 19.

Wilmott, Paul. *Derivatives: The Theory and Practice of Financial Engineering.* Chichester, UK: John Wiley & Sons, 1998, chap. 17.

TEST YOUR KNOWLEDGE

1. What is the difference between a standard lookback option and an extremum lookback option?
2. How can lookback options be used to assure that you "buy low, sell high"? Why is this not the perfect investment strategy?

Deferred Start and Contingent Premium Options

In this essay I look at a couple of options and their variations in which some aspect of the option's characteristics does not start or is not determined until a later date.

A *forward start option* is an option in which the premium is paid today, but the option does not start until a future date. At the time the premium is paid, the buyer specifies a relative degree of moneyness. For example, the buyer might pay the premium today and in three months be guaranteed to receive an at-the-money call option to expire six months later. Alternatively, the buyer can specify up front that the option be any percent in- or out-of-the-money. This kind of option is very similar to the arrangements in which employees and managers receive incentive options at various times in the future that when issued will be at-the-money. Pricing this option is quite simple and makes use of the principle of linear homogeneity, which we covered in Essay 49. Briefly, a function is linearly homogeneous with respect to a variable if you can multiply that variable by a constant and the value of the function can be written as the original value of the function times the constant. We used this result to price exchange options.

Let us define three time points: today when the premium is paid, time t when the option is issued, and time T when the option expires. At time t, the option price can be written as $c(S_t, \alpha S_t, T - t)$ where the arguments indicate that the asset price at t is S_t, the exercise price is αS_t, and the time to expiration is $T - t$. If the option buyer wants an at-the-money option, α is equal to 1. If, for example, $\alpha = 1.10$, then the exercise price is set 10% higher than the asset price at t. Since an option price is linearly homogeneous with respect to the asset price and exercise price, we can say that $c(S_t, \alpha S_t, T - t) = S_t c(1, \alpha, T - t)$. In other words, at t, the option we receive is worth the same as S_t options with moneyness α when the asset price is at \$1. The value $c(1, \alpha, T - t)$ is a known and constant value, obtainable from the Black-Scholes-Merton (BSM) model. Thus, if we purchased $c(1, \alpha, T - t)$ units of the asset today, at time t, we will have a position worth $c(1, \alpha, T - t)S_t$. So this static position of $c(1, \alpha, T - t)$ units of the asset purchased at t will replicate the position of receiving an option worth $c(S_t, \alpha S_t, T - t)$, Consequently, the premium that we must pay today is simply value $c(1, \alpha, T - t)$ times S_t where S_t is the asset price today.

The intuition behind why this incredibly simple replication strategy works is that the call has a fixed time to expiration at time t and is linearly homogeneous with respect to the asset price and exercise price, and today's asset price is the current value of the unknown future asset price at t.

A combination of an ordinary option plus a series of options expiring at various dates in the future is called a *tandem option*. It can be valued by pricing the first expiring option as an ordinary European option and the remaining sequence of options as a combination of forward start options with different start and expiration dates.

Forward start derivatives also exist in the form of swaps. Thus, a forward start swap is an agreement to enter into a swap at a later date. It is essentially a forward contract on a swap. A forward start option is essentially a forward contract on an option with the ability to fix the moneyness.

A *contingent premium option* is one in which the premium is paid at expiration and only if the option expires in-the-money. It does not matter whether the option expires sufficiently in-the-money to cover the premium; there is, of course, no guarantee of a profit. Such an option can be easily constructed with other options. Letting S^* be the asset price at expiration, X be the exercise price, and c_p be the premium of the contingent premium call, the payoff at expiration is $S^* - X - c_p$ if $S^* > X$ and zero if $S^* \leq X$.

Now recall that in Essay 47 we covered digital options, which include the cash-or-nothing option. This option pays \$1 if the asset price exceeds the exercise price at expiration. Recall that the value today of such an option is $(\$1)e^{-rT}N(d_2)$, where r is the risk-free rate, T is the time to expiration, and $N(d_2)$ is a cumulative normal probability from the BSM. Suppose we purchase an ordinary call and sell c_p cash-or-nothing calls. Then at expiration if $S^* > X$, the ordinary call pays $S^* - X$ and we have to pay c_p on the cash-or-nothing call for a total of $S^* - X - c_p$. If $S^* \leq X$, we have no cash flows on either option. This combination replicates the contingent premium option; therefore, its current value must equal the current value of the contingent premium option. Since we pay nothing today for the contingent premium option, we must have $c - c_p e^{-rT}N(d_2) = 0$. Substituting the BSM formula for c gives us a left-hand side of $SN(d_1) - Xe^{-rT}N(d_2) - c_p e^{-rT}N(d_2)$, which can be rewritten as $SN(d_1) - (X + c_p)e^{-rT}N(d_2)$, which must equal zero. We can then easily solve for c_p and obtain $c_p = SN(d_1)/N(d_2)e^{-rT} - X$.

It is important to note that c_p is greater than c, the price of an ordinary call. Recall that $c - c_p e^{-rT}N(d_2) = 0$. Since $e^{-rT}N(d_2) < 1$, we must have $c_p > c$ for the equality to hold. Intuitively, the contingent premium option must be more expensive than the standard option, because the option holder continues to earn interest on the money not paid up front with the contingent premium option and because of the possibility that the contingent premium option will never have to be paid for.

The contingent premium option is useful for situations in which the option buyer believes that the option is very likely to expire with significant value. In this case, the option premium can be reduced, effectively to zero today, by implicitly selling the cash-or-nothing option. As long as expectations are realized, the option holder more than covers the premium paid at expiration. If expectations are not realized, the option holder can incur a larger loss.

There is also an option in which the premium is paid at expiration, regardless of whether the option expires in- or out-of-the-money. With no premium paid up front, this instrument is essentially the same as a forward contract in which the expiration payoff has a lower limit on the downside and there is no limit on the upside. This instrument is the same as a *break forward*, which we covered in Essay 50.

Other variations of the contingent premium option include one in which the premium is paid only if during the life of the option the underlying asset touches a specific level, which could be higher or lower than the current level. This instrument is a variation of the barrier option, covered in Essay 44.

FOR MORE READING

Blazenko, G. W., P. P. Boyle, and K. E. Newport. "Valuation of Tandem Options." *Advances in Futures and Options Research* 4 (1990): 39–49.

Gastineau, Gary. "Roll Up Puts, Roll Down Calls, and Contingent Premium Options." *The Journal of Derivatives* 1 (Summer 1994): 40–43.

Hull, John C. *Options, Futures, and Other Derivatives*, 6th ed. Upper Saddle River, NJ: Prentice-Hall, 2006, Chap. 22.

Kat, Harry M. "Contingent Premium Options." *The Journal of Derivatives* 1 (Summer 1994): 44–54.

Rubinstein, Mark. "Pay Now, Choose Later." *Risk* 4 (February 1991): 44–47.

Turnbull, Stuart M. "The Price Is Right." *Risk* 5 (April 1992): 56–57.

TEST YOUR KNOWLEDGE

1. What is the static portfolio that replicates a forward start option?
2. A contingent premium option requires payment of the premium only if the option expires in-the-money. Explain why this instrument does not guarantee a profit.
3. Consider a variation of the contingent premium option not mentioned in this essay. With this option you pay the premium only if you exercise it, but you are not obligated to exercise it. Over what range of asset prices at expiration would you exercise it?

Six

Fixed Income Securities and Derivatives

We noted earlier that the underlying of a derivative is usually a stock price, interest rate, exchange rate, or commodity price. Stock prices, exchange rates, and commodity prices all have something in common. They are the prices of assets: stocks, currencies, and commodities. An interest rate, however, is not an asset. It is a type of return on an asset. It is possible to create a derivative on an interest rate, which is close to but not exactly like a derivative on an asset. This notion is somewhat more complex than just creating a derivative on a stock, currency, or commodity. For that reason, I am devoting an entire section of 12 essays to these instruments.

The section starts with some basic fixed-income concepts such as duration, convexity, and the term structure of interest rates. Then we move on to understanding how the term structure is modeled. We then illustrate how binomial trees are used to price interest rate derivatives. This group of essays might be the most numerical of the entire book. There are a lot of examples and calculations, but the math is simple.

Duration

For the first topic in this section we shall look at duration, one of the simplest and most practical methods for measuring the interest rate risk of a bond portfolio. Duration is what we might call a "traditional" measure of interest rate risk. It has fallen out of favor among those who advocate the more modern approaches to interest rate risk management, which we cover in later essays in this section. It is still useful, however, to look at what duration tells us, if for no other reason than to be aware of the limitations of this widely used measure. First let us be specific in referring to the particular type of bond we shall be using. This discussion applies only to the standard fixed-coupon, noncallable, default-free bond. The implications of other types of bond provisions on duration will be noted in Essay 54.

It is customary in the world of bonds to define the bond price in terms of its yield, which is the single discount rate that equates the present value of the bond's cash flows to the market price. With B defined as the bond price, y is the solution to the equation $B = c(1)(1 + y)^{-1} + c(2)(1 + y)^{-2} + \cdots + c(T)(1 + y)^{-T}$, where T is the years to maturity and $c(1), c(2), \ldots, c(T)$ are the cash flows, coupon, and/or principal on the bond. The use of the concept of a yield makes the heroic assumption that all of the information embedded in the term structure is captured by a single rate. As we show in later essays, the evolution of the term structure is much more complex than that. For now, however, let us examine the change in the bond price for a given basis point change in the yield. This is the concept of duration, which was discovered somewhat independently in the 1930s and 1940s by the economists Frederick Macaulay, John Hicks, and Paul Samuelson.

Using calculus, we can obtain the change in price divided by the basis point change in yield. Letting D be the duration and using deltas to represent changes, we have $\Delta B/\Delta y \approx -DB/(1 + y)$, though we must recognize that this result holds strictly only for infinitesimal yield changes, which pretty much rules out most actual interest rate changes. We can rewrite this expression as $\Delta B/B \approx -D\Delta y/(1 + y)$, which gives us the percentage change in bond price as minus the duration times the basis point change in yield over 1 plus the yield. In this form, duration appears to be a measure of bond price volatility. In other words, given a yield change, duration tells us how much the bond price should change. Subject to some conditions we shall see later, we can compare bonds with different durations and determine which is more volatile.

But how is duration actually calculated and what does it mean? Duration is traditionally described and calculated as a weighted average of the time it takes to reach each cash payment date. Consider a three-year bond with an annual coupon of c and a face value of F. Its cash flow stream is c at time 1, c at time 2, and $c + F$ at time 3. Its maturity in a traditional sense is clearly three years, but is it really? A bond is a series of promised payments. Part of the bond matures each time it makes a payment. Our coupon bond is equivalent to three zero-coupon bonds with maturities of 1, 2, and 3. The average maturity of these three zero-coupon bonds corresponds to the average maturity of our coupon bond. But that average maturity is not simply $(1 + 2 + 3)/3 = 2$. It is far better to determine a weighted average maturity, applying weights to each time (1, 2, 3) that correspond to the value of the cash flows paid at those times. Thus, the weights should be $w(1)$, $w(2)$, and $w(3)$, where $w(1) = c(1 + y)^{-1}/B$, $w(2) = c(1 + y)^{-2}/B$, and $w(3) = (c + F)(1 + y)^{-3}/B$. Here each weight is simply the present value of the corresponding cash flow divided by the overall price of the bond, which is the sum of the present values of all of the cash flows. This method is sometimes referred to as present value weighting. We see that duration is equivalent to a weighted average maturity of a bond, at least in the special case of a noncallable, default-free bond.

The duration measure will be a number with the dimension of time, which will range from the time to the first cash flow up to the maturity. So our three-year bond will have a duration between 1 and 3. Ten-years bonds typically have durations in the range of 6 to 8 years. A zero-coupon bond has a duration equal to its maturity. Rarely would you find a duration greater than 12 or 13 years.

With but one slight and rare exception, a bond is more volatile the lower the coupon and the longer the maturity. Thus, either coupon or maturity could be viewed in some sense as a measure of the bond's volatility. Duration consolidates the information about the volatility that is contained in the coupon and maturity into a single measure. The lower the coupon, the longer the duration and the longer the maturity, the longer the duration, with the aforementioned rare exception. Subject to its limitations, which we shall cover later, duration can be used as a one-dimensional measure of bond price volatility. We now see that in addition to being the weighted average maturity of a bond, duration is also a measure of its price volatility.

A final interpretation of duration is that it is the half-life of a bond. The concept of a half-life of an element is that it is the period of time over which half of its atoms decay. In the context of a bond, the half-life is the period over which the bond will have returned half of its value. For example, consider a 10-year bond with a duration of seven. When the seventh year is reached, the bond will have returned interest payments, which have been reinvested to earn additional interest, that equal in value the market value of the bond on that date. As we shall see, this condition, quite surprisingly, is independent of any yield changes during that period.

One of the primary uses of duration is in protecting a bond portfolio from interest rate changes. There is an interesting history of how this knowledge evolved. As noted earlier, economists discovered duration in the 1930s and 1940s as a measure of bond price risk, but it was not really used until the 1970s when financial economists begin studying its properties as a way to protect bond portfolios against interest rate risk.

During the period of 1940 to 1970, mathematicians who worked on problems in insurance established the theory of immunization. Insurance companies typically hold large portfolios of bonds and have specific obligations they have to meet. These obligations can often be met by staggering, sometimes called laddering, bonds across the maturity spectrum. Mathematicians discovered a more precise method of achieving this goal, which was by setting the duration equal to the length of the holding period. This method, which came to be known as immunization, worked in theory because of the half-life property of duration. The theory of immunization not only shows that a portfolio can be protected against interest rate risk by setting the holding period to the duration, but that the portfolio would actually be guaranteed *to achieve or surpass its target rate*. For example, a portfolio of bonds, which has a duration equal to the weighted average of the durations of its component bonds, with a duration of, say, five years will, after undergoing a given basis point change in yield, be worth at least as much as a zero-coupon bond with a five-year maturity. Thus, a five-year target return can be met and even exceeded by immunizing.

In the 1970s, immunization became a hot topic in bond portfolio management and formed the basis for many products, such as GICs (guaranteed investment contracts). By the early 1980s, however, the growth of bond derivatives led to other and often better ways to hedge bond price risk, such as by using delta and gamma.

Duration turns out to have some severe limitations. For one thing, it is effective only against small yield changes. There is, however, an extension of duration, called convexity, that can take care of this problem. Convexity measures the curvature of the line relating the bond price to the yield. We cover convexity in the next essay. For now, however, we should note that convexity, too, has severe limitations.

In addition, duration is applicable only for parallel shifts in the term structure and even then, only truly for bond yields and not the full term structure of spot rates, which is where the risk actually originates. In the next essay, we address the limitations of duration, to see which if any can be fixed and then draw some conclusions on its usefulness. This analysis will set the stage for more precise and accurate modeling of the term structure and better interest rate risk management.

FOR MORE READING

Bierwag, G. O., George M. Kaufman, and Cynthia M. Latta. "Duration Models: A Taxonomy." *The Journal of Portfolio Management* 15 (Fall 1988): 50–54.

Bierwag, G. O., George G. Kaufman, and Alden Toevs. "Duration: Its Development and Uses in Bond Portfolio Management." *Financial Analysis Journal* 39 (July–August 1983): 15–35.

Jarrow, Robert A. *Modeling Fixed-Income Securities and Interest Rate Options*, 2nd ed. Stanford, CA: Stanford University Press, 2002, chap. 2.

Jarrow, Robert A., and Stuart M. Turnbull. *Derivatives Securities*, 2nd ed. Mason, OH: Thomson South-Western, 2000, chap. 13.

Sundaresan, Suresh M. *Fixed Income Markets and Their Derivatives*, 2nd ed. Mason, OH: Thomson South-Western, 2002, chaps. 4–6.

Wilmott, Paul. *Derivatives: The Theory and Practice of Financial Engineering*. Chichester, UK: John Wiley & Sons, 1998, chap. 31.

TEST YOUR KNOWLEDGE

1. What two values are captured by duration?
2. How can duration be used in managing interest rate risk? What is this strategy called?

Limitations of Duration and the Concept of Convexity

In the last essay we introduced the concept of duration. We noted how, subject to some limitations, it can be used as a measure of bond price volatility and that holding a bond or portfolio for the period equal to its duration can immunize or protect a bond against interest rate changes. These results apply to non-callable default-free bonds.

Recall that we gave the formula $\Delta B/B \approx -D\Delta y/(1 + y)$, which is the function that expresses duration's characteristic as a measure of a bond's price volatility. The price volatility is on the left-hand side as the percentage change in price while the duration divided by $(1 + y)$, often called the *modified duration*, is multiplied by the basis point change in yield, Δy. The minus sign simply forces the bond price to move inversely to the yield change. As an example, a four-year bond with annual coupons of 8% and a 10% yield will have a duration of 3.56. If the yield immediately changes to 11%, the yield change is 0.01 and the formula says that its price will change by approximately $-3.56(0.01)/1.10 = -0.0324$ or -3.24%. If, however, we recalculated the bond price with an 11% yield, we would find that it actually falls by 3.17%.

This discrepancy is due to the fact that duration reflects only the change in price for a very small (infinitesimal) change in yield. Remember that when using the formula, we used the mathematical expression "$\approx$", which means approximately equal to. Duration is in fact obtained from the first derivative of the bond price with respect to the yield. The relationship between bond price and yield is not linear. Thus, the duration and slope of the line are not constant across yields, and this means that if the yield changes by more than an infinitesimal amount, the estimated new price change will contain error. The line expressing the relationship between a bond's price and its yield is in fact convex, meaning that the curve is shaped somewhat like a bowl tilted upward. Thus, duration will give estimates of bond price increases that are too low and estimates of bond price decreases that are too high.

The curvature of the price-yield relationship gives rise to the concept of *convexity*. It is possible to obtain a quantitative measure of the curvature, this measure being called convexity, and use it to add to the duration-estimated price so that a more accurate price measure is obtained. Convexity can be interpreted as a present value-weighted measure of the squared time to expiration. Unfortunately, this notion does not have a good interpretation, but suffice it to say that convexity measures the rate at which the duration changes. As such it is based on the second derivative of the bond price with respect to yield. You can then add the estimated convexity adjustment to the estimated price and obtain a new estimated price that is guaranteed to be at least a little closer to the actual price.

While duration captures what mathematicians would call a first-order effect, convexity captures the second-order effect. Higher-order effects could, of course, be added if they were felt to be necessary.

While convexity can be used to correct one major limitation of duration, there are other more subtle but more severe limitations of both duration and convexity.

Duration and convexity work well as interest rate sensitivity measures for single-bond portfolios, but most actual situations involve portfolios of multiple bonds. Consider a simple portfolio consisting of equal amounts invested in one bond with a duration of 5 and another with a duration of 10. The overall duration is 7.5. If the yields on both bonds change by an equal number of basis points and letting the yield change be small to ignore the convexity problem, duration can be used to immunize the portfolio against interest rate changes. But equal basis point changes in yields in bonds across the full spectrum of maturities, called a parallel shift, is a terribly restrictive condition. In practice, we often observe twists of the yield curve, which are certainly not parallel shifts. For all yields to change by the same number of basis points is highly unlikely.

In a world in which the yield curve undergoes nonparallel shifts, duration is not an effective measure of bond price volatility. Nonetheless, I do not mean to imply that duration provides no information. The original statement, $\Delta B/B \approx -D\Delta y/(1 + y)$, is still valid as a price volatility measure *for a given change in yield*. It is simply the case that the Δy will not be the same for different bonds, and we cannot, therefore, look at a single-dimensioned number like duration and conclude that one bond is more volatile than another. Similar statements hold for convexity, as it too assumes equivalent basis point changes in yields across the term structure.

As if that were not enough, there is a little-known theorem in finance that shows that such parallel yield curve shifts, if they occur, admit arbitrage.

The theorem goes like this. Take a zero-coupon bond of any maturity and duration, say T. Now take two zero-coupon bonds, one with a maturity greater than T, call it T_H, and one with a maturity less than T, call it T_L. Combine these two bonds in such a manner that they have the same value and duration as the first zero-coupon bond. It can be shown that as long as the interest rate shift is not infinitesimal, the combination of zero-coupon bonds with the same duration and value will outperform the zero-coupon bond. This means that you could short the zero-coupon bond, raising the cash to buy the combination. This situation would be a classic arbitrage opportunity that arises because the combination of zero-coupon bonds has greater convexity. Therefore, parallel shifts in the yield curve not only cannot be expected to happen by coincidence, they simply cannot happen at all in a well-functioning market. A formal proof of this result is in the paper by Ingersoll, Skelton, and Weil cited in the "For More Reading" section.

More realistic yield curve shifts would reflect the twists and turns of the yield curve observed in the market. Variations of how duration is calculated capture specific types of yield curve changes. But unless all possible yield curve changes can be captured in one class of movements and there is a single duration measure that captures the risk of those shifts, then duration becomes a very limited means of measuring bond price risk. On an individual bond basis, duration can be useful, but for purposes of comparing across bonds, it is quite limited.

So if duration and its sister convexity are so limited, what do we know about bond price risk? As we shall see in the upcoming series of essays on modeling the term structure and pricing bonds and interest rate derivatives, bond prices and interest rates evolve according to a stochastic process. This stochastic process must be realistic in terms of allowing bond prices to fluctuate and yet return to their principal values at maturity, and it must not admit arbitrage opportunities. On the latter point, bonds and their derivatives that are perfect substitutes for each other must be priced equivalently. The risk of bond price fluctuations is best captured by the concept of delta, which we know more familiarly as the change in an option price for a change in the rate or price of the underlying asset. While duration is related to a bond's delta, they are not the same measure. Second-order effects are captured by the bond's gamma, which is related but not equivalent to the convexity.

Both delta and gamma are functions of the stochastic process. You can, of course, argue that duration and convexity are also functions of the stochastic process. If you choose the wrong stochastic process, does it matter whether you use duration-convexity or delta-gamma? Probably not. The concepts of delta and gamma, however, are based on stochastic processes that are typically more flexible and admit the possibility of a variety of types of changes in interest rates across the full spectrum of bond maturities. While it is possible to derive a duration and convexity measure for a sophisticated stochastic process model, these measures have no advantages and some disadvantages over delta and gamma.

It is also important to note that duration-convexity and delta-gamma are measures based on instantaneous changes in interest rates. They do not reflect the change in time, which causes a bond to gravitate toward par. It is often the case that the pull toward par is far more important than the convexity or gamma. This phenomenon occurs because interest rate changes that can occur instantaneously are indeed small. Since bond price risk is typically measured over a finite holding period, however, it is important to capture the effect of time on the price change. This effect is similar to the theta effect in options.

For noncallable default-free bonds, we have seen that duration is the weighted-average time to maturity. This result holds because of the linearity of the relationship between the cash flows on a coupon bond and the cash flows of the component zero-coupon bonds that replicate it. A zero-coupon bond has a duration equal to its maturity. When aggregating a combination of zero-coupon bonds into a coupon bond, we simply add their prices and take a weighted average of their durations to obtain the price and duration of the coupon bond. You should never forget that other factors can affect a bond's duration, rendering the concept of a weighted average time to maturity almost meaningless.

For example, bond prices also change due to changes in their default risk. Another factor is that bonds usually contain option provisions, the most common one being the right for the issuer to call the bonds before maturity. The inclusion of a call feature has a significant effect on duration and convexity, but analyzing and understanding it is not easy. In addition, many complex instruments, such as mortgage-backed securities, which were covered in Essay 12, particularly certain trenches of a collateralized mortgage obligation, have extremely complicated durations that do not lend themselves to simple formulas based on weighted-average cash flow, and they often lock clear interpretations. More general methods for estimating duration usually take the approach of computing the average market value change for a basis point move upward and downward.

FOR MORE READING

Chance, Don M., and James V. Jordan. "Duration, Convexity and Time as Components of Bond Returns." *The Journal of Fixed Income* 6 (September 1996): 87–96.

Hull, John C. *Options, Futures, and Other Derivatives*, 6th ed. Upper Saddle River, NJ: Prentice-Hall, 2006, chap. 4.

Ingersoll, Jonathan E., Jeffrey Skelton, and Roman Weil. "Duration Forty Years Later." *Journal of Financial and Quantitative Analysis* 13 (1978): 627–650.

Jarrow, Robert A. *Modeling Fixed-Income Securities and Interest Rate Options*, 2nd ed. Stanford, CA: Stanford University Press, 2002, chap. 2.

Jarrow, Robert A., and Stuart M. Turnbull. *Derivatives Securities*, 2nd ed. Mason, OH: Thomson South-Western, 2000, chap. 13.

Sundaresan, Suresh M. *Fixed Income Markets and Their Derivatives*, 2nd ed. Mason, OO: Thomson South-Western, 2002, chaps. 4–6.

Wilmott, Paul. *Derivatives: The Theory and Practice of Financial Engineering.* Chichester, UK: John Wiley & Sons, 1998, chap. 31.

Winkleman, Kurt. "Uses and Abuses of Duration and Convexity." *Financial Analysts Journal* 45 (September–October 1989): 72–75.

TEST YOUR KNOWLEDGE

1. What does convexity measure for a bond?
2. What assumption about the manner in which interest rates are assumed to change is considered a weakness of duration and convexity?
3. What two option risk measures correspond closely but not identically to duration and convexity?

The Term Structure of Interest Rates

The term structure of interest rates is one of the most important and central topics in all of economics and finance. It has been of primary interest to economists for much of the 20th century. While most of the research on the term structure has yielded considerable insights, there has unfortunately been a lot of misunderstanding. Finance researchers have not helped much by simply rehashing what the economists had written. That is, until the advent of the era of option pricing theory.

We begin with a general and informal definition of the term structure of interest rates. The term structure of interest rates, sometimes just called the term structure, is the relationship between the interest rates and the maturities of debt instruments. We'll just use the term "bonds" in this essay instead of "debt instruments." This is the standard definition but one that requires some qualification. Strictly speaking, the concept of the term structure should apply only to zero-coupon bonds. That is not always the case in practice; we often see graphs of the yields on coupon bonds against their maturities. At the very least, all of the bonds should have the same coupon, but usually they do not, in which case we might as well mix apples with oranges. Even when they all have the same coupon, however, most of the principles that apply to the term structure do not apply in the same manner to coupon bonds. Personally, I use the expression "term structure" to refer to the relationship between the yields on zero-coupon bonds and their maturities. When I use the expression "yield curve," I am referring to the relationship between the yields on coupon bonds and their maturities.

Perhaps the reason why the term structure and yield curve are often confused is that until 1982, zero-coupon U.S. government bonds of maturities greater than one year were not available. Thus, it was not possible to construct more than a one-year term structure, except by using analytical or statistical methods. Consequently, a yield curve was often used as a proxy.

In addition, most of the theories of the term structure should apply only to default-free bonds. There is, of course, a term structure of default risky bonds, but any comprehensive attempt to explain the relationship among the interest rates on such bonds of different maturities must take into account default risk. It can confuse matters to incorporate both default risk and term structure effects in one model, so typically we handle them separately. The relationship between default risk and interest rates is called the *risk structure of interest rates* and can be modeled by using an option pricing approach that handles default risk, which is covered in Essay 67.

Now we provide a more formal definition of the term structure. The term structure of interest rates is the set of interest rates that define the present values of one dollar paid at times $1, 2, \ldots, n$. We shall write these rates as $r(0, 1), r(0, 2), \ldots, r(0, n)$. These are sometimes known as *spot rates*, and we sometimes use the expression *the term structure of spot rates*. The present values of a dollar at times $1, 2, \ldots, n$ are written as $P(0, 1)$, $P(0, 2), \ldots, P(0, n)$. These can be thought of as the prices of one-dollar face value zero-coupon bonds maturing at times $1, 2, \ldots, n$. We sometimes call each of these bonds a *unit discount bond*. Their prices are given by the expressions $P(0, 1) = 1/(1 + r(0, 1))$, $P(0, 2) = 1/(1 + r(0, 2))^2, \ldots, P = 1/(1 + r(0, n))^n$.

A coupon bond is a stream of payments $c(1), c(2), \ldots, c(T), T \leq n$ that define the interest and principal on a bond, typically called a coupon bond. The bond's price, B, is the present value of these cash flows, that is, $c(1) P(0, 1) + c(2) P(0, 2) + \cdots + c(T) P(0, T)$.

Consider a market in which you can contract today, at time 0, to borrow or lend at a future date at a rate agreed on today. That rate is what we mean by a *forward rate*. Let $f(0, 1, 2)$ be the rate that can be locked in today for a zero-coupon bond that would be issued in one year and matures one year later, or two years from now. This bond would have a one-year maturity, and its price is specified as $F(0, 1, 2)$. Now consider these transactions: Purchase a one-year bond at the price $P(0, 1)$, and enter into a forward contract to buy a one-year bond in one year at the price $F(0, 1, 2)$. At the end of two years you will have $[1/P(0, 1)] [1/F(0, 1, 2)]$ for every dollar invested. This amount must equal the return per dollar from buying a two-year bond today and holding it two years, which is $1/P(0, 2)$; otherwise, one transaction would be more profitable than the other, and, therefore, the less profitable transaction could be used to finance the more profitable transaction. An arbitrage profit would be possible unless $F(0, 1, 2) = P(0, 2)/P(0, 1)$. All we would require is the ability to issue or sell short any bonds as easily as we could buy or go long any others.

In addition to the forward price $F(0, 1, 2)$, there are other forward prices, such as $F(0, 1, 3)$, which is the forward price implied by the term structure today for a bond issued at time 1 and paid back at time 3; thus, it is a two-year bond. Likewise, we could have other forward prices like $F(0, 1, 4), \ldots, F(0, 1, T)$. In addition, we have forward prices like $F(0, 2, 3)$, which is the forward price implied by the term structure today for a bond issued at time 2 and paid back at time 3. We also have prices like $F(0, 2, 4)$, $F(0, 3, 5)$, etc. A special case of the set of forward prices is the set of prices $F(0, 0, 1)$, $F(0, 0, 2)$, and so on, which is nothing more than the set of spot prices. In other words, the forward prices for transactions to begin today are simply the spot prices. Using the same arbitrage arguments as we used previously, any forward price $F(0, i, j)$ is given as $P(0, j)/P(0, i)$.

It is important to recognize that this specification of the term structure, which defines the entire term structure in terms of forward prices, holds by definition. It does not require any assumptions about how investors feel about risk. It is not conditional on investors being risk neutral, and by no means does it make any statement about what investors expect in the future. Two investors with wildly divergent expectations would agree on the relationship between spot rates and forward rates. It is also important to note that specifying the spot rates or prices completely defines the structure of forward rates or prices, but not vice versa. In other words, with $F(0, 1, 2) = P(0, 2)/P(0, 1)$ there are many combinations of $P(0, 2)$ and $P(0, 1)$ that could lead to a given forward rate.

It is important to note that the product of successive forward prices is a spot price. For example, consider the product $F(0, 1, 2)\, F(0, 2, 3)$. We know from our arbitrage examples above that $F(0, 1, 2) = P(0, 2)/P(0, 1)$ and also that $F(0, 2, 3) = P(0, 3)/P(0, 2)$. Using these two relationships, we have $F(0, 2, 3) = P(0, 3)/[P(0, 1)\, F(0, 1, 2)]$, which can be written as $P(0, 1)\, F(0, 1, 2)\, F(0, 2, 3) = P(0, 3)$. Thus, the price today of a three-period bond is the product of the price today of a one-period bond and the forward prices, as implied by the term structure today, of a one-period bond starting at time 1 and another one-period bond starting at time 2.

Again, I emphasize that these relationships have nothing to do with expectations about future rates or prices. This point cannot be stressed enough. Too many people believe that the term structure implies something about future prices or rates, a result of an all-too-unfortunate obsession with the expectations theory, a topic we shall get to in the next essay. One by-product of this belief is a tendency to let the forward rates stand for the expected future spot rates on floating-rate loans or the floating payments on swaps. Forward rates or prices are equal to expectations of future spot rates or prices only when we give investors certain characteristics. And as we shall see, the characteristics we usually associate with rational investors result in forward rates or prices not equaling expected future spot rates or prices except over the very short term and in a risk-neutral sense, a result known as the *local expectations hypothesis.*

You undoubtedly noticed that I mention forward and spot prices as well as rates. If you have had garden-variety courses in finance and economics, you are more used to talking about forward and spot rates and not forward and spot prices. In many modern models of the term structure, it is more common to talk about forward and spot prices and let rates follow by implication, which is probably because with prices the use of exponents can be avoided. For example, the forward rate today for a two-year bond issued at time 1 is $[(1 + r(0, 3))^3) (1 + r(0, 1))]^{1/2} - 1$, whereas the forward price is simply $P(0, 3)/P(0, 1)$, which is slightly neater though no more informative. Of course, in many other models, rates are used. For the most part, it makes little difference.

In the next essay we continue looking at the term structure with an examination of the theories that attempt to explain its shape.

FOR MORE READING

Hull, John C. *Options, Futures, and Other Derivatives*, 6th ed. Upper Saddle River, NJ: Prentice-Hall, 2006, chap. 4.
Jarrow, Robert A. *Modeling Fixed-Income Securities and Interest Rate Options*, 2nd ed. Stanford, CA: Stanford University Press, 2002, chap. 3.
Sundaresan, Suresh M. *Fixed Income Markets and Their Derivatives*, 2nd ed. Mason, OH: Thomson South-Western, 2002, chaps. 5–6.

TEST YOUR KNOWLEDGE

1. What instrument is the basic building block for the term structure?
2. Distinguish between spot and forward rates with respect to the term structure.

Theories of the
Term Structure: I

As described in Essay 55, the term structure of interest rates is the relationship between the interest rates on zero-coupon bonds and the maturities of those bonds. The term structure is a topic of much interest to investors in fixed-income securities. It is also a topic of much interest to economics and finance professors. As a fellow finance professor once remarked, "When in doubt, teach the term structure." In other words, if you ever go to class unprepared or your well-prepared lecture just isn't working, try your term structure lecture. It fits just about anywhere. This is a compliment to the topic of term structure. It plays an important role in nearly all areas of finance.

Unfortunately, other finance professors and I have been guilty of perpetuating the celebrated but misleading theories that purport to explain the shape of the term structure. These theories, called the expectations, liquidity preference, and market segmentation theories, have been around for a long time but have not stood the test of time. That does not mean it is not important to teach them; it is important not only to understand them but also to be aware of their limitations. So here we go, *mea culpa*.

We begin with the *expectations theory*, which is sometimes called the *pure expectations theory* or the *unbiased expectations theory*. It simply states that a forward rate is the market's expectation or prediction of the corresponding future spot rate. For example, suppose today we observe the prices of one- and two-year zero-coupon bonds. Recall that $P(0,1)$ and $P(0,2)$ are the prices today of the one- and two-year zero-coupon bonds and that they can give us the forward price by the relationship $F(0,1,2) = P(0,2)/P(0,1)$. The forward price is the price that could be contracted today for a bond to be issued in the future. Implicit in the forward price is a rate of return, the forward rate, given as $1/(1+F(0,1,2))$. Without assuming the expectations theory, there is no presumption that the forward rate reflects anything other than the rate that can be locked in today for the future. It does not necessarily refer to anyone's expectation of a future rate.

In a world of interest rate certainty, however, forward prices/rates will equal future spot prices/rates. In other words, $P(0,2)/P(0,1)$, the forward price, would equal the known future spot price of a one-year zero-coupon bond issued at time 1, which is $P(1,2)$. No one would contract for a future transaction at a rate that did not equal the known future interest rate. Once we impose uncertainty, however, things change a little. If borrowers and lenders were risk neutral, forward rates and prices would equal expected future spot rates and prices because people who are risk neutral do not worry about the fact that they had contracted at a fixed price based on their expectation when there is uncertainty around that expectation. In other words, a lender might expect the one-year interest rate to be 10% in one year. If that lender is risk neutral, she would be willing to commit today to lend money in one year at 10%. Those who are risk averse would demand more than 10% to compensate for the losses expected when rates rise.

The expectations theory holds only in a world of certainty or risk-neutral borrowers and lenders. You will recall that we have previously discussed at great length the principle of risk-neutral or equivalent martingale pricing of derivatives. In that context, investors are not assumed to be risk neutral; rather, when hedging a derivative with the underlying asset, all investors can and will exploit arbitrage possibilities regardless of which direction prices or rates go. Hence, variance (i.e., risk) is not important. We are not assuming that people are risk neutral, We simply know that they price derivatives the same way, whether they are risk neutral or not. Except in the unusual case of a world of certainty, the expectations theory requires a much stronger statement: People *are* risk neutral. There is no hedging and no arbitrage basis associated with the expectations hypothesis. It is simply a statement about the pricing of zero-coupon bonds across time. Thus, consistent with the fact that we do not assume that people price stocks and other assets without regard to their feelings about risk, so too do we not make such an assumption about bond pricing.

Let us, however, briefly pretend to be wrong and assume that the expectations theory is correct. In so doing I believe we shall be able to see why the theory is so universally, but mistakenly, accepted.

If the expectations theory were correct, then the shape of the term structure provides a prediction of the direction of future interest rates. Specifically, forward rates become unbiased predictors of future spot rates. An unbiased predictor is, however, not necessarily an accurate predictor. It simply means that over the long run, the prediction is correct on average.

It may well be too high one time and too low another, but on average it is correct.

The implication is that an upward-sloping term structure will exist if longer-term rates are higher than shorter-term rates. This point is simple to see. Consider any forward rate $f(0,a,b) = [(1+r(0,b))^b/ (1+r(0,a))^a]^{1/(b-a)}$ -1. To simplify things, let the length of the period from time 0 to time a equal the length of the period from time a to time b. If the term structure is upward sloping, the $r(0,b)$ will exceed $r(0,a)$. This will mathematically imply that $f(0,a,b)$ will exceed $r(0,a)$. With the forward rate for the period (a,b) exceeding the spot rate $r(0,a)$, we can say that the expectation of the spot rate for (a,b) exceeds the current spot rate for $(0,a)$. This implies that the spot rate for a period of length a, which is the same length as $b-a$, is expected to rise. Thus, an upward- (downward-) sloping term structure suggests that investors expect spot rates to increase (decrease).

This feature of the expectations theory is probably the source of its widespread appeal. We could simply observe the shape of the term structure and discern what investors presumably felt about the direction of future interest rates. So we can easily determine the consensus forecast of future interest rates. But how good is that forecast? One way to test the expectations theory is to compare expected spot rates with forward rates. Yet we cannot observe expectations. It is reasonable to assume, however, that observed spot rates are measures of the realization of expected spot rates and are unbiased. If they were not, people would surely adjust their expectations so as not to systematically over- or underestimate. Thus, realized spot rates serve as proxies for expectations. Tests have then been constructed by comparing realized spot rates with forward rates that presumably equaled expected future spot rates.

Most of the studies show that the forecasts are not very good. Of course, the expectations theory does not argue that the forecasts are good but only that they are unbiased. Many studies show, however, that they are not unbiased either, though some studies have supported the unbiasedness. We do not know what the truth really is, but we do know this: Investors are not risk neutral, interest rates are volatile, and any presumption of the truth of the expectations theory requires a rejection of these fundamental truths. Yet the expectations theory continues to dominate textbooks and is central to most lectures on the term structure. Perhaps the reason is its simplicity and the hope that somehow it would be nice if expectations could be revealed by simply observing the shape of the term structure.

The other two theories are the *liquidity premium theory*, sometimes called the *liquidity preference theory*, and the *market segmentation theory*, sometimes called the *preferred habitat theory*. The liquidity preference theory says that lenders prefer to remain liquid and, therefore, to make short-term loans. To induce them to make long-term loans, they must receive an incentive in the form of a higher return. Closely related to this is the idea that longer-term bonds are more risky, either from the possibility of default or price volatility. In any case, these factors pull up long-term rates such that the forward rate, extracted from the long-term and short-term rates or prices, is biased on the high side as a prediction of the future spot rate. There are many who believe in the liquidity preference theory, but how can someone argue that investors always demand higher returns on longer-term bonds? We do not always see an upward-sloping term structure. We sometimes see downward sloping term structures and even nearly flat or humped term structures.

Finally, there is the market segmentation theory, which argues that some investors prefer to lend or borrow long term and some prefer to lend or borrow short term. Investors are presumed not to cross into other maturity ranges outside of their preferred ones, hence the name "preferred habitat." Consequently, separate supply and demand conditions in the different maturity ranges determine the shape of the term structure. This explanation, however, ignores arbitrageurs who trade across the term structure with ease. It also seems to chop up markets into "segments," hence the name market segmentation, which implies discontinuities. Yet it is not true that a bond of a given maturity is distinct from a bond of a slightly longer maturity, in terms of who buys and sells it. Proponents of the market segmentation theory cite such observations as the presence of insurance companies primarily in long-term bond markets and banks in short-term bond markets. Interestingly, these arguments were probably quite true at one time. In the modern era with thousands of arbitrageurs and numerous derivative contracts available, however, traders commonly cross maturity ranges.

I do not completely reject the liquidity preference and market segmentation theories, but I do not believe they play much of a role in the determination of the term structure. Most important, I do not believe that the expectations theory determines the shape of the term structure. I do not argue that these explanations perhaps make a small contribution to our understanding of the term structure. Investors' expectations always play a role in the pricing of securities. How investors feel about liquidity and risk also plays a role. If some borrowers and lenders stay strictly in certain segments of the market, it would surely have some effect.

Frankly, we do not know how the term structure is set. Perhaps we can make some general statements that simply have to be true. We do that in the next essay and then turn to an alternative way to look at the term structure.

FOR MORE READING

Jarrow, Robert A. *Modeling Fixed-Income Securities and Interest Rate Options*, 2nd ed. Stanford, CA: Stanford University Press, 2002, chaps. 4–5.

Ritchken, Peter. *Derivative Markets: Theory, Strategy, and Applications*. New York: HarperCollins, 1996, chap. 22.

TEST YOUR KNOWLEDGE

1. If forward rates are in fact expectations of future spot rates, what forecast is implied about the direction of future spot rates from current spot rates?
2. Under what characteristic about people would forward prices equal expected spot prices?
3. Under what market condition would forward prices equal expected spot prices?
4. Besides the expectations theory, what other two theories have been offered to explain the shape of the term structure? Which of the two is clearly inconsistent with the existence of arbitrageurs?

Theories of the Term Structure: II

In Essay 56 I discussed the traditional approach to understanding the term structure, which consists of the three famous theories of the term structure: expectations theory, liquidity preference theory, and market segmentation theory. I noted that each of those theories is deficient.

To understand how interest rates are really determined, we must begin by recalling how any asset is priced. An investor, whether it is the lender on a loan or bond or the purchaser of a share of stock or a unit of a commodity, formulates an expectation of the future price or payoff. That investor recognizes that if he ties up funds in the purchase of that investment, he will forgo interest and possibly incur costs of storing the asset. Consequently he will demand up-front compensation in the form of a lower price for the risk assumed. Although these are very general statements about how assets are priced, they must surely be true or people would simply not be rational.

Now suppose the investment is a default-free zero-coupon bond with a face value of one unit of currency. The expected future price of the bond is simply one unit of currency. There is no doubt that at the maturity date, the borrower will pay back one unit of currency. There is no cost of storing the bond. Consequently, the only compensation is for the opportunity cost or time value of money and risk. If the bond is a short-term bond, the risk compensation is essentially zero. In fact, it would be zero if the shortest holding period possible corresponded to the bond's maturity. The compensation for the time value of money reflects the so-called risk-free rate. This is determined by what is called the *marginal rate of substitution* of current for future consumption. If I lend a dollar today, how much will I expect back at the maturity of the loan to compensate me for the loss of current consumption? In other words, what is the trade-off between current and future consumption? There is no simple answer here. Economists generally believe that this rate, also called the *real rate of interest*, reflects the availability of productive economic activities. In a healthy economy, investors will have a high opportunity cost because there are numerous other activities competing for their investment funds. In a weak economy, the opportunity cost is low, as observed during the 1930s. Some economists believe the real rate of interest is constant across time and constant across countries, but that argument is hard to accept, because economies vary across time and countries.

Whenever investors move out to longer maturities, however, some compensation must be paid for the risk associated with holding bonds over periods in which interest rates are changing. If a bond is sold before maturity, there is possibly substantial price risk. Determining what this compensation should be is quite difficult. Numerous models of the economy and the term structure have been developed. Generally speaking, the compensation should reflect a return based on the covariance of the interest rate with the values of consumption goods and other assets in the economy. The well-known capital asset pricing model (CAPM) is one such model, and it captures this effect in the market portfolio, which reflects the market values of all risky assets in the economy.

We shall in the next essay look at two models that tell us how bonds are priced, given a correct specification of the evolution of the term structure. These are the Vasicek and Cox-Ingersoll-Ross models. We shall see, however, that in their original forms, the models if used in practice could result in investors executing arbitrage opportunities against the model user.

As much as we would like to know how long-term interest rates are determined relative to short-term rates, the need to know may be based more on a desire to find predictability in those rates. Such a goal is likely to be a waste of time. Interest rates and bond prices are as unpredictable as are stock prices. Recall that the purpose of these essays is to learn about how derivatives are priced. In keeping with the fundamental principle that arbitrage opportunities cannot exist, we drop any concern about how the term structure obtains its shape and focus on how derivatives based on bonds and the term structure are priced. In the equity markets, this approach is analogous to having no concern about how stock prices are derived, whether it is by the CAPM or whatever, and focusing on how options on stocks and stock indices are priced. As long as the spot market has revealed its prices, we can complete our task.

Recall from Essays 31 and 32 that in pricing stock options, we were able to agree that, given the price of the stock, the absence of arbitrage opportunities implies the existence of a new set of probabilities of future stock prices, which we called risk-neutral or equivalent martingale probabilities. These probabilities are not the actual probabilities of future stock prices, as they reflect a shifting of the expected future stock price so as to set the expected return to the risk-free rate. If arbitrage opportunities are nonexistent, such a set of probabilities also exists. This rule implies that we can price derivatives as if investors are risk neutral, though in fact they are not. Translating these principles into the bond market, the assumption of no arbitrage opportunities will also imply the existence of risk-neutral/equivalent martingale probabilities that set the expected return on a bond investment to the risk-free rate. But what particular bond investment and what risk-free rate do we use? Do we in fact even have a risk-free rate? We are, after all, trying to model interest rate risk. The answers to these questions require some sophisticated theorems, but the basic ideas are simple and easy to follow. They are captured by a principle called the *local expectations theory*.

Suppose we make a simple assumption that there is but one source of risk in the market. We call this a *one-factor model*. It means that movements in a given price or rate on any one zero-coupon bond at any time point are sufficient to determine movements in the price or rate on all other zero-coupon bonds in the market at that time. In such a world all zero-coupon bonds are perfectly correlated. The implication is that all bonds are perfect substitutes for each other. For example, you could hold a bond of maturity T or a combination of two or more other bonds and obtain the same result, meaning the same payoff at a future date. This result implies a no-arbitrage relationship. A combination of bonds that has an equivalent payoff to any other bond or combination of bonds must have the same value at all times.

Suppose we finance the purchase of a bond of a given maturity by selling short an equivalent combination of other bonds. Such a portfolio must have zero initial value and zero expected return over a given period. What does this result imply about the rate of return on this bond alone? We might say that it is the risk-free rate, but the concept of a risk-free rate is a problematic one in this world of changing interest rates. A position in a zero-coupon bond held to maturity provides a risk-free return, but not over the interim holding periods. The local expectations theory, however, says that the expected return over the shortest possible holding period is risk free and corresponds to the rate on the zero-coupon bond with the shortest holding period. This expected return, however, is based on the risk-neutral probabilities, not the actual probabilities. This means that the risk-neutral expected returns on bonds of all maturities are equivalent and equal the rate on the bond with the shortest holding period. This rate is the only true risk-free rate that exists in the market. All other rates are the returns on bonds held to maturity, but which are risky if liquidated before maturity. The bond with the shortest holding period, however, cannot be liquidated before maturity.

An interesting implication of this result is that forward prices will equal risk-neutral expectations of future spot prices for all bonds with holding periods equal to the shortest future point in time. As an example, let the shortest holding period, meaning the shortest maturity bond, be $(0,1)$. That is, a given forward price, $F(0,1,b)$, will equal investors' risk-neutral expectation of the future spot price, $P(1,b)$. This will be true regardless of when b is or, in other words, for any holding period starting at time 1. A forward price like $F(0,2,b)$, however, will not be the expectation of the future spot price $P(2,b)$.

Naturally, the local expectations hypothesis is dependent on whatever assumption the user makes about the shortest holding period. When modeling bonds in continuous time, the shortest holding period is the next instant. There are no hard-and-fast rules about an appropriate holding period for discrete time models, but a minimum of one month is probably reasonable.

The local expectations hypothesis, as it turns out, is a very powerful statement. Without showing the mathematical proof, if the local expectations hypothesis is true, then it is impossible to form a portfolio of bonds that will earn an arbitrage profit. Such a statement permits the pricing of bonds under similar conditions as the pricing of options. This statement is much more powerful than anything we can typically state about stocks. Stocks are not perfectly correlated so they do not perfectly hedge one another.[1]

The term structure of zero-coupon bonds is a common source of variation in all bonds. Of course, there can be multiple factors causing bond prices to change, but shifts in the term structure are common to all such bonds. This common source of variation, when coupled with the local expectations hypothesis, permits bonds to be priced relative to each other by arbitrage arguments.

Does this point enable us to forecast interest rates with sufficient accuracy to earn abnormal profits? No. We still do not have a forecasting model, But it does allow us to determine if bonds are mispriced relative to each other and to determine the prices of derivatives on bonds and interest rates. To that end we focus our attention in the next several essays.

FOR MORE READING

Campbell, John Y., "A Defense of Traditional Hypotheses about the Term Structure of Interest Rates," *The Journal of Finance* 41 (1986): 183–194.

---

[1] There is one theory of stocks that does claim a hedging relationship exists. This is the arbitrage pricing theory (APT). But this theory depends on accurate knowledge of the stochastic process that generates stock returns and the ability to fully diversity all sources of risk. Many long discussions about the validity of the APT have taken place, and I do not plan to get into this controversy here just to support a single minor comment.

Cox, John C., Jonathan E. Ingersoll Jr., and Stephen A. Ross. "A Re-Examination of Traditional Hypotheses about the Term Structure of Interest Rates." *The Journal of Finance* 36 (1981): 769–799.

Jarrow, Robert, "Liquidity Premiums and the Expectations Hypothesis," *Journal of Banking and Finance* 5 (1981): 539–546.

Jarrow, Robert A. *Modeling Fixed-Income Securities and Interest Rate Options*, 2nd ed. Stanford, CA: Stanford University Press, 2002, chaps. 4–5.

Ritchken, Peter. *Derivative Markets: Theory, Strategy, and Applications*. New York: HarperCollins, 1996, chap. 22.

TEST YOUR KNOWLEDGE

1. What is a one-factor model of the term structure?
2. In the term structure world, what instrument represents the notion of a risk-free bond?
3. What is the local expectations hypothesis?

Simple Models of the Term Structure: Vasicek and Cox-Ingersoll-Ross

In the last two essays we discussed the problem of explaining how the term structure works. We concluded that for our ultimate objective, the pricing of derivatives on bonds and interest rates, we do not need to know the exact manner in which interest rates are determined. We can accept the term structure as given, assume the no-arbitrage process, and proceed. In this essay, we take the next step by examining two models that capture the evolution of the term structure and provide formulas for the pricing of bonds and derivatives.

First let us distinguish between discrete and continuous models. Recall that when pricing options on stocks, we used a discrete model, the binomial (Essay 28), and a continuous model, the Black-Scholes-Merton (Essay 27). We can take similar approaches when modeling the term structure. In this context, discrete models specify that a bond price, interest rate, or the term structure evolves in discrete jumps. In addition to binomials, some models are based on a trinomial evolution of the term structure. Continuous models have the interest rate, bond price, or entire term structure follow a variation of an Itô process, changing in small instantaneous movements.

Likewise, term structure models can be classified into two groups, which I shall call "simple models" and "no-arbitrage models." The simple models are not really all that simple; in fact, some are quite complex. Calling the second group "no-arbitrage models" does not mean that the first group necessarily admits arbitrage opportunities, but such a possibility cannot be ruled out. In fact, even the no-arbitrage models can admit arbitrage because some of them do not constrain the interest rate to positive values.[1] The main difference between the two models, however, is the fact that the first group produces the term structure as an output, while the second group takes the term structure as an input. The so-called simple models are equilibrium models in the sense that they tell us what the zero-coupon bond prices should be and they are internally arbitrage free, but they are not externally arbitrage free. Thus, the simple models do not guarantee that the prices of zero-coupon bonds produced by the model will match the prices observed in the market. This point suggests the possibility of an arbitrage opportunity, provided that the parameters used to build the model are correct. The second group, no-arbitrage models, takes the current price of the asset, option, or bond as given and derives a model that specifies the evolution of the term structure from there. In this sense, they "fit" the current term structure.

If the first approach is taken—that is, the term structure is an output—then it is possible for a trader/dealer to offer investors an arbitrage opportunity against it. The market prices are the prices at which you can trade. If the dealer uses a simple model to generate prices to quote to counterparties, it is possible that counterparties can execute trades with the dealer and with other parties in the market that produce an arbitrage. Unless the dealer's quoted prices match the market's prices, there will be at least one security with two different prices, the classic definition of an arbitrage opportunity. This is not a problem when trading stocks because you cannot combine two stocks to produce a perfect substitute for a third stock. It is possible, however, to combine two bonds and form a perfect substitute for another, at least in a world in which bond price uncertainty is determined by a single factor. When there is more than one factor, more than two bonds will be required to form a perfect substitute.

In this essay we look at two models of the term structure that fall into the first group. These are the Vasicek and Cox-Ingersoll-Ross models. They were originally developed in the continuous time version but can be approximated with discrete time variations.

The Vasicek model begins by assuming that all zero coupon bonds are driven by a single source of uncertainty, a so-called "spot rate," which is the interest rate on a loan of instantaneous maturity. Let us call that rate r. The model specifies that the spot rate evolves according to the following

---

[1] A negative interest rate, if it could exist, would admit arbitrage. That is, if you could borrow money and pay back less than the amount borrowed, you could easily accumulate an infinite amount of wealth by simply borrowing, without regard to what you do with the borrowed funds.

process: $dr = a(b - r)dt + \sigma dz$. The first term, dr, is simply the change in the rate r. Thus, if r moves from 0.05 to 0.055, then $dr = 0.005$. On the right-hand side, the first term, $a(b - r)dt$, is the expected or average change in the rate and is consistent with the phenomenon of *mean reversion*. Interest rates do not typically drift upward or downward without encountering some resistance and a reversal of direction. For example, if interest rates have a positive expected change, over time we would find rates increasing with no upper limit. Though an unlimited upward drift makes sense for stocks, it does not for interest rates. Introducing a downward shift would drive rates far lower than we generally observe. In fact, negative rates would be a possibility. Thus, a good model will often incorporate a tendency for higher-than-average rates to be pulled down toward the average and lower-than-average rates to be pulled up toward the average.

In this model, the long-run average interest rate is b. The rate at which the interest rate is pulled is a, which is a positive number. If the current rate, r, is higher (lower) than the long-run average—that is, $r > (<) b$—the factor $a(b - r)dt$ induces a negative (positive) expected change, which pulls the rate down (up) toward the average at a rate proportional to the factor dt, the length of time over which the change is observed. The term σ is the volatility of the change in the spot rate, and dz is a Brownian motion, which is a standard normal variable times the square root of the time increment, as covered in Essays 25 and 26.

Vasicek then proceeds to build a combination of zero-coupon bonds and shows that by forbidding any arbitrage opportunities, a price can be found for any zero-coupon bond. By comparison, pricing an option on a stock is done by combining the option with the stock such that there are no arbitrage opportunities. By combining one bond with another, the price of a third bond can be inferred. The end result is a formula for the price of any zero-coupon bond. Again, note that although the absence of arbitrage is guaranteed here, that restriction applies only to the prices produced by the model. The model does not fit the current term structure, which implies that a dealer using the model could be offering arbitrage opportunities.

In Vasicek's model, interest rates are normally distributed and, as noted, mean reverting. Unfortunately, interest rates can become negative, though that is not necessarily a sufficiently frequent occurrence in the model to cause problems. In a subsequent model, Jamshidian derived a formula that prices options on zero-coupon and coupon bonds. That formula, as it turns out, is quite general and shows up in a slightly different form in many other term structure models.

There is no known solution for the prices of American options in the Vasicek model so the model must be captured using a binomial or trinomial tree, which, as we saw in Essays 28 and 29, can capture the value of exercising early.

The problem of fitting the current term structure to the model has been solved by Hull and White, who show that all that is needed is to allow some flexibility in certain parameters of the model. Cox, Ingersoll, and Ross, in an elegant and sophisticated model of a full economy, produce a term structure model that looks similar to Vasicek's but overcomes the problem of negative interest rates. The stochastic process of that model is of the form $dr = a(b - r)dt + \sigma r^{1/2} dt$. In other words, the volatility term contains the square root of the current interest rate. When the current rate moves to zero, the square root of zero causes the volatility to go to zero and the rate will be pulled up by its drift.

The model implies that interest rates follow the chi-square distribution, which is a skewed probability distribution. Cox, Ingersoll, and Ross provide formulas for the prices of bonds and European options. American options must be approximated with a binomial or trinomial tree. In the aforementioned Hull and White article, they show that one can also fit the Cox-Ingersoll-Ross model to the current term structure.

Though, as noted, there are ways of improving the model to incorporate the current term structure, models that begin by using the term structure as an input are perceived by some as having an advantage from the start. In the next essay we look at the two best known of those models, the Ho-Lee and Heath-Jarrow-Morton models.

FOR MORE READING

Cox, John C., Jonathan E. Ingersoll Jr., and Stephen A. Ross. "A Theory of the Term Structure of Interest Rates." *Econometrica* 53 (1985): 385–408.

Hull, John C. *Options, Futures, and Other Derivatives*, 6th ed. Upper Saddle River, NJ: Prentice-Hall, 2006, chap. 28.

Hull, John, and Alan White. "Pricing Interest Rate Derivative Securities." *The Review of Financial Studies* 3 (1990): 573–592.

Hull, John, and Alan White. "Using Hull-White Interest Rate Trees." *The Journal of Derivatives* 3 (Spring 1996): 26–36.

Jamshidian, Farshid. "An Exact Bond Option Formula." *The Journal of Finance* 44 (1989), 205–210.

McDonald, Robert L. *Derivative Markets*, 2nd ed. Boston: Addison Wesley, 2006, chaps. 14, 24.

Ritchken, Peter. *Derivative Markets: Theory, Strategy, and Applications*. New York: HarperCollins, 1996, chap. 23.

Vasicek, O, "An Equilibrium Characterization of the Term Structure." *Journal of Financial Economics* 5 (1977): 177–188.

TEST YOUR KNOWLEDGE

1. What is the difference between a simple model and a no-arbitrage model of the term structure?
2. Explain the concept of mean reversion, as used in the Vasicek model.
3. What is one of the deficiencies of the Vasicek model that is rectified by the Cox-Ingersoll-Ross model?

No-Arbitrage Models of the Term Structure: Ho-Lee and Heath-Jarrow-Morton

In Essay 58 we described two models in which the term structure is an output of the model. As we noted, this type of model can permit arbitrage if used by a dealer because traders can execute transactions at market prices, which can differ from the dealer's prices. The second class of models, called the no-arbitrage models, uses the term structure as an input. In other words, in these models, you start with the prices of zero-coupon bonds of various maturities and proceed to build a model that admits no arbitrage possibilities as bond prices and interest rates evolve through time.

These models can be broken down into two classes: one-factor and multifactor models. A one-factor model assumes that all bonds are influenced by the same source of uncertainty. This characteristic would make all bonds be perfectly correlated so that a combination of two bonds can serve as a perfect substitute for any other bond. If that is not the case, the term structure is being driven by something other than a single common source of variation in all bonds. By incorporating multiple factors, different types of shifts in the shape and location of the term structure can be captured. Unfortunately, the use of multiple factors greatly complicates the models and makes computation much more difficult. We shall focus on the one-factor models.

We start with the simplest model, the basic model of Ho and Lee. The Ho-Lee model begins with the current prices of zero-coupon bonds of various maturities, $P(0,1)$, $P(0,2)$, ... , $P(0,T)$. Recall from Essay 55 that we defined the forward price for a one-period bond one period from now to be $F(0,1,2)$. In other words, this is the price agreed on today for a bond that will be issued in one period and matures one period after that.

Ho and Lee then start with the obvious point that if there is no uncertainty in the market, the forward price will evolve into the spot price. In other words, $F(0,1,2)$ will become $P(1,2)$ when time 1 arrives. To introduce uncertainty, Ho and Lee assume that the term structure can undergo a shift either upward or downward. This shift is induced by multiplying the forward rate by a factor reflecting an upshift and a different factor reflecting a downshift. These factors are generally slightly more or less than 1.0. For a maturing bond, the factor is 1.0 reflecting the fact that there is no uncertainty in a maturing bond as its price converges to its face value. By the way, it should be noted that if interest rates shift up, bond prices will not necessarily shift down. The pull toward par will result in some short-term bonds increasing in price regardless of the direction of rates. This result is clearly the case with one period to go before maturity as any zero-coupon bond will increase in price to a terminal value of 1, but a bond's price can even increase prior to maturity when the interest rate shifts upward.

The Ho-Lee model will thus provide the prices of zero-coupon bonds as they evolve in a binomial tree. At time 2, there will be two possible sets of prices, (i.e., two possible term structures), reflecting an up move in rates and a down move in rates. Ho and Lee force the binomial tree to recombine, meaning that at time 3, there will be three possible term structures, reflecting an up move in rates followed by another up move, an up move in rates followed by a down move, which is equivalent to a down move in rates followed by an up move in rates, and a down move in rates followed by another down move. Without recombining, the tree would have the up-followed-by-down move not equal to the down-followed-by-up move. For a large number of time periods, this characteristic makes the tree explode very quickly and become unwieldy and slow to evaluate.

Using arbitrage arguments, it can be shown that the movements in the term structure can be described according to their risk-neutral/equivalent martingale probabilities. As we discussed many times before in option pricing theory, these probabilities do not represent the actual probabilities of movements nor do they assume that people are risk neutral. Rather they reflect the rule that if there are no arbitrage possibilities, then prices can be formulated by using risk-neutral probabilities. The prices we obtain are the same ones that would be obtained in an economy of risk-neutral investors. Again, this does not mean that investors are risk neutral, but it does mean that the local expectations hypothesis of the term structure, a topic covered in Essay 57, will hold.

An important implication of the Ho and Lee model is that it assumes that interest rates are normally distributed. The original version of the model does not incorporate mean reversion, though mean reversion can be built into the model. As a result of the assumption of a normal distribution, the model admits the possibility of negative interest rates, though the likelihood can be minimized.

A variation of the original Ho and Lee model allows the user to specify not only the original term structure but also the volatility of interest rates through time. The basic Ho-Lee model, keeps the volatility constant. This variation of the Ho-Lee model, however, is a much more complex model and requires solving some fairly complicated equations to specify the term structure tree. Yet this version of the Ho-Lee model is a definite improvement over the basic model because interest rates do exhibit changing volatility over time. The late Fischer Black along with Emanuel Derman and William Toy developed a variation of the Ho-Lee model in which interest rates are lognormally distributed.

Once the full binomial term structure is laid out, the computation of the prices of bonds and derivatives follows by standard procedures. I cover these computations in Essays 60 to 64. Suffice it to say at this point that the Ho-Lee model and its variations constituted a tremendous step forward in modeling interest rates. It was the first model to incorporate the current term structure, and it has considerable intuitive appeal, owing most of its tractability to the simplicity of the binomial option pricing framework.

In continuous time, the basic Ho-Lee model is written as $dr = adt + \sigma dz$, where adt is the expected change in the interest rate over the next time increment, dt. The second term σdz is the volatility of the interest rate times a standard Brownian motion, which is a standard normal random variable times the square root of the time increment.

As noted, however, the Ho-Lee model is a one-factor model. Heath, Jarrow, and Morton have extended and generalized the Ho-Lee model in such a manner that it has become one of the premier pricing models used in practice. Unfortunately, it is one of the most complex and computationally intensive. Because the objective of these essays is to provide only nontechnical discussions, it is impossible to do full justice to the Heath-Jarrow-Morton (HJM) model. The model has much intuition, however, and lends itself to a reasonably informative overview.

Recall that the Ho-Lee model uses a volatility factor to adjust the evolution of the forward rate into the spot rate. With no risk, the forward rate would turn into the spot rate. The HJM model starts with the same framework. The HJM model, however, permits more than one factor to influence the forward rates. In other words, HJM can have more than one source of volatility.

An important feature of the HJM model is that it permits interest rate volatility to change across time. This feature requires that the user specify how volatility changes. Though doing so is difficult, it gives the model flexibility. Moreover, it gives the model characteristics similar to the

Black-Scholes-Merton model. The model takes the price of the underlying asset, (the term structure), as given, requires knowledge of the volatility of the underlying asset, and proceeds to derive the model in an arbitrage-free framework. Heath, Jarrow, and Morton suggest several functional forms for the volatility of the term structure, such as letting volatility exponentially dampen, meaning that it decreases proportionally across time.

A two-factor HJM model can be developed in a discrete time framework by introducing a third interest rate change, thereby turning the process into a trinomial. This feature makes the tree expand quite rapidly and become what is known as bushy. In addition, the HJM model typically does not recombine, meaning that an up move followed by a down move does not leave you in the same position as a down move followed by an up move. This feature adds to the bushiness of the tree. Hence, computationally, the HJM model can be quite intense as there can be numerous paths that the rate can follow. While there are some computational shortcuts, overall the calculation of prices for bonds and derivatives can be quite time consuming.

In order to ensure that bond prices are arbitrage free, there are some restrictions on the values of the input parameters, specifically the drift in the interest rates. Some interesting research by Dwight Grant and Gautam Vora provides a clever way of deriving the drift. Also, Heath, Jarrow, and Morton show that for certain volatility structures, the model has closed-form solutions for the prices of all financial instruments.

The HJM model has proven to be one of the most popular models for describing the term structure. That does not mean it is the best model in all circumstances. For a comparison of HJM against some of the alternatives, I highly recommend the article by Leong. The mathematics of the HJM model are quite demanding, but the essential structure of the model can be grasped by reading Jarrow's book on fixed-income securities. This 250-page masterpiece provides an excellent grasp of the model and even comes with some sample software. One downside, however, is that the book is supposed to cover "modeling fixed income securities," but alternative models do not receive much attention. Still the reading is well worth it.

FOR MORE READING

Black, Fischer, Emanuel Derman, and William Toy. "A One-Factor Model of Interest Rates and its Application to Treasury Bond Options." *Financial Analysts Journal* 46 (January–February 1990): 33–39.

Grant, Dwight and Gautam Vora. "Implementing No-Arbitrage Models of the Term Structure in Discrete Time when Interest Rates are Normally Distributed." *The Journal of Fixed Income* 8 (May 1999): 85–98.

Heath, David, Robert Jarrow, and Andrew Morton. "Bond Pricing and the Term Structure of Interest Rates: A Discrete Time Approximation." *Journal of Financial Quantitative Analysis* 25 (December 1990): 419–440.

Heath, David, Robert Jarrow, and Andrew Morton. "Bond Pricing and the Term Structure of Interest Rates: A New Methodology." *Econometrica* 60 (January 1992): 77–105.

Heath, David, Robert Jarrow, and Andrew Morton "Contingent Claim Valuation with a Random Evolution of Interest Rates." *The Review of Futures Markets* 9 (1990): 54–76.

Heath, David, Robert Jarrow, Andrew Morton, and Mark Spindel. "Easier Done than Said." *Risk* 5 (October 1992): 77–80.

Ho, Thomas S. Y., and Sang-Bin Lee. "Term Structure Movements and Pricing Interest Rate Contingent Claims," *The Journal of Finance* 41 (1986): 1011–1030.

Hull, John C. *Options, Futures, and Other Derivatives*, 6th ed. Upper Saddle River, NJ: Prentice-Hall, 2006, chap. 29.

Jarrow, Robert. "The HJM Model: Its Past, Present, and Future." *The Journal of Financial Engineering* 6 (December 1997): 269–279.

Leong, Kenneth. "Model Choice." *Risk* 5 (December 1992): 60–61, 63–66.

Ritchken, Peter. *Derivative Markets: Theory, Strategy, and Applications*. New York: HarperCollins, 1996, chap. 24.

TEST YOUR KNOWLEDGE

1. What was the primary contribution of the Ho-Lee model?
2. What is a recombining tree? What is its advantage?
3. What is the difference in a one-factor and a multifactor term structure model?
4. What is the underlying variable that evolves in the Heath-Jarrow-Morton model?
5. What variable must be constrained in the Heath-Jarrow-Morton model to prevent arbitrage?

Tree Pricing of Bonds and Interest Rate Derivatives: I

This essay begins a series on the use of binomial trees to price interest rate derivatives. A binomial tree is a model of the sequence of possible movements in a stochastic variable, such as an interest rate or stock price, that is designed to capture the essential properties of real-world movements that are necessary to avoid arbitrage and price derivatives. It captures in a limited number of movements the essential elements of the process by which the underlying moves. In this essay I lay out the foundations of tree pricing when the underlying is an interest rate. In subsequent essays I use the tree developed in this essay to price specific types of bonds and interest rate derivatives.

Before beginning the process of modeling any type of interest rate, it is necessary to select a model. What I wish to accomplish here is to demonstrate how, given the tree of interest rate movements, bonds and interest rate derivatives are priced. It does not really matter what model is used, but I shall use the simple Ho-Lee version, which is more or less a one-factor Heath-Jorrow-Morton (HJM) model.

Let us do a brief review of the notation. Let $P(0,1)$, $P(0,2)$, etc. be the prices today of one dollar zero-coupon bonds maturing at periods 1, 2, and so on, Let $F(0,1,2)$ be the forward price today of a one dollar zero-coupon bond starting at time 1 and maturing at time 2. By definition, $F(0,1,2) = P(0,2)/P(0,1)$, which is necessary to prevent profitable arbitrage, Let $E[0,P(1,2)]$ be the expectation at time 0 of the price of a one-period zero-coupon bond starting at time 1 and maturing at time 2.

Because the Ho-Lee model is a model in which the term structure is taken as an input, we must take the prices of zero-coupon bonds maturing in one period, two periods, and so on from the market. Assume this information is: $P(0,1) = 0.905$, $P(0,2) = 0.820$, $P(0,3) = 0.743$, $P(0,4) = 0.676$, and $P(0,5) = 0.615$. We can use bonds of as long a maturity as we want, but the maximum maturity will limit the term structure model to one less period. So in other words, we model up to only period 4 and use five zero-coupon bonds. We actually carry the model to period 5 in a limited sense, but in period 5 we have only a single bond with a value equal to its face value of 1.0, so there is no uncertainty in that period.

The Ho-Lee model specifies that the entire term structure undergoes a multiplicative shift upward or downward. To accomplish this result, we begin by assuming that there is no uncertainty, in which case the forward price will evolve into the spot price the next period. For example, $F(0,1,2) = P(0,2)/P(0,1) = P(1,2)$. The forward price at time 0 for a one-period bond starting at time 1 will become the actual one-period price at time 1. To induce uncertainty, we disturb this relationship by applying a multiplicative factor λ^+ or λ^-. Let λ^+ induce an upward shift so that $[P(0,2)/P(0,1)]\lambda^+ = P(1,2)$ and with $\lambda^+ > 1$, $P(1,2) > F(0,1,2)$. Likewise, $[P(0,2)/P(0,1)]\lambda^- = P(1,2)$ and with $\lambda^- < 1$, $P(1,2) < F(0,1,2)$. Note that λ^+ (λ^-) is an upward (downward) shift in the forward price so it represents a downward (upward) shift in interest rates.

What is this λ^+/λ^- factor? It captures the volatility of interest rates, Ho-Lee give formulas for λ^+/λ^-, which vary by the bond's maturity. Letting n be the maturity, $\lambda(n)^+ = d^n/[p + (1-p)d^n]$ and $\lambda(n)^- = 1/[p + (1-p)d^n]$, where the d term is a type of volatility factor. This means that $\lambda(0)^+ = \lambda(0)^- = 1.0$ or, in other words, a maturing bond will have its spot price converge to its forward price, which will end up being its par value. Otherwise arbitrage would occur. The value p is the risk-neutral/equivalent martingale probability of an up or down movement. With some variations of the model, this number can be arbitrarily set to 0.5, though I do not do so in this specific example.

In our example using $d = 1.03$ and $p = 0.52$, the values of $\lambda(n)^+$ and $\lambda(n)^-$ are

Maturity	$\lambda(n)^+$	$\lambda(n)^-$
1	1.0000	1.0000
2	1.0154	0.9858
3	1.0308	0.9716
4	1.0462	0.9574
5	1.0616	0.9432

Now let us begin inserting interest rates into the tree. At time 0, we have the five bond prices. Consider an upward shift at time 1 of the price of a one-period bond. This will be $[P(0,2)/P(0,1)]\lambda(1)^+ = [0.820/0.905]$ 1.0154 = 0.920. A downward shift would be $[P(0,2)/P(0,1)]\lambda(1)^- = [0.820/0.905]0.9858 = 0.893$. Thus, at time 1, a one-period bond price could be either $P(1,2)^+ = 0.920$ or $P(1,2)^- = 0.893$. Similar calculations would have to be done to obtain the two possible prices of the other bonds at time 1, which would be bonds with maturities of 2, 3, and 4 periods. To obtain these, one would determine the forward prices at time 0 and disturb those prices by the factors for the appropriate maturity. This process would be repeated each successive period, at which one less bond would exist due to the maturity of each one-period bond the next period. The resulting tree would look as shown in Table 60.1.

Recall that in discussing the local expectations theory in Essay 57, we noted that the forward price is the expected future spot price, using the risk-neutral probabilities, for one period ahead only. For example, consider $F(0,1,2) = P(0,2)/P(0,1) = 0.820/0.905 = 0.906$. The expected future spot price at time 0 can be found by probability-weighting the next two possible spot prices. This procedure gives $E[0,1,2)] = 0.52(0.893) + 0.48(0.920) = 0.906$. The forward price several periods ahead, however,

TABLE 60.1 Binomial Zero-Coupon Bond Price Evolution

Time 0	Time 1	Time 2	Time 3	Time 4
				$P(4,5) = 0.859$
			$P(3,4) = 0.870$	
			$P(3,5) = 0.758$	
		$P(2,3) = 0.881$		
		$P(2,4) = 0.778$		$P(4,5) = 0.885$
		$P(2,5) = 0.687$		
	$P(1,2) = 0.893$			
	$P(1,3) = 0.798$		$P(3,4) = 0.896$	
	$P(1,4) = 0.715$		$P(3,5) = 0.804$	
	$P(1,5) = 0.641$			
$P(0,1) = 0.905$				
$P(0,2) = 0.820$		$P(2,3) = 0.908$		
$P(0,3) = 0.743$		$P(2,4) = 0.825$		$P(4,5) = 0.911$
$P(0,4) = 0.676$		$P(2,5) = 0.751$		
$P(0,5) = 0.615$				
	$P(1,2) = 0.920$			
	$P(1,3) = 0.847$		$P(3,4) = 0.923$	
	$P(1,4) = 0.781$		$P(3,4) = 0.853$	
	$P(1,5) = 0.722$			
		$P(2,3) = 0.935$		
		$P(2,4) = 0.875$		$P(4,5) = 0.938$
		$P(2,5) = 0.821$		
			$P(3,4) = 0.951$	
			$P(3,5) = 0.905$	
				$P(4,5) = 0.967$

is not the expected future spot price. For example, $F(0,3,5) = P(0,5)/P(0,3) = 0.615/0.743 = 0.828$. The expected future price of a bond beginning at time 3 and maturing at time 5 is the probability-weighted average of 0.758, 0.804, 0.853, and 0.905, the four possible prices of a two-period bond at time 3. The risk-neutral probabilities of these four prices are the binomial probabilities p^2, $3p^2(1-p)$, $3p(1-p)^2$, and $(1-p)^3$. Doing these calculations gives an expected future spot price of 0.826. Though these two values seem close, the difference is not a round-off error.

It is important to remember that this tree does not reflect the actual predicted evolution of the term structure, modeled here in the form of zero-coupon bond prices. It captures only the essential properties of the evolution of the term structure, and those properties are the set of risk-neutral probabilities and the set of possible future prices that rule out arbitrage possibilities.

This concludes this essay on setting up the interest rate tree. In essays that follow, we use this tree to price bonds and various derivatives.

FOR MORE READING

Hull, John C. *Options, Futures, and Other Derivatives*, 6th ed. Upper Saddle River, NJ: Prentice-Hall, 2006, chap. 28.

Jarrow, Robert A. *Modeling Fixed-Income Securities and Interest Rate Options*, 2nd ed. Stanford, CA: Stanford University Press, 2002, chaps. 6–8.

Jarrow, Robert A., and Stuart M. Turnbull. *Derivatives Securities*, 2nd ed. Mason, OH: Thomson South-Western, 2000, chap. 15.

Rendleman, Richard J. Jr. *Applied Derivatives: Options, Futures, and Swaps*. Malden, MA: Blackwell, 2002, chap. 11.

Ritchken, Peter. *Derivative Markets: Theory, Strategy, and Applications*. New York: HarperCollins, 1996, chap. 24.

TEST YOUR KNOWLEDGE

1. Explain why in a binomial term structure model, the number of bonds used to construct the binomial tree is one more than the number of periods in the model. That is, if n bonds are available, why is it not possible to construct a tree of n periods?

2. Ignoring the fact that an interest rate can change to more than two possible values, does a binomial term structure capture actual movements in interest rates?

Tree Pricing of Bonds and Interest Rate Derivatives: II

This second essay in the series on how binomial trees can be used to price bonds and interest rate derivatives uses the tree developed in Essay 60. For convenience, the tree is reproduced here in Table 61.1. In this essay I use the information in the tree to price coupon bonds, options on both zero-coupon bonds and coupon bonds, and futures on both coupon bonds and zero-coupon bonds.

It may be beneficial to review the material on binomial pricing of stocks from Essay 28. The general procedure is to start at the expiration of the derivative or the maturity of the bond and insert the payoff values. Then step back one node at a time and take a probability-weighted average of the next two possible payoffs. This value is then discounted at the appropriate one-period interest rate. In this case that means to multiply this probability-weighted average by the one-period discount bond price. Recall that the probabilities are the risk-neutral or equivalent martingale probabilities.[1]

As we have previously covered, a coupon bond can be modeled as a portfolio of zero-coupon bonds. For example, a two-period coupon bond with a face value of 1.0000 has the same cash flows as a combination of a zero-coupon bond maturing in one period and another zero-coupon bond maturing in two periods. The first bond has a face value of the coupon on the coupon bond and the second bond has a face value of 1.0000 plus the coupon on the coupon bond.

Using our zero-coupon bond tree at time 0, let us price a two-period 10.25% coupon bond with face value of 1.0000. Its price will be given as

---

[1] From time to time I may remind the reader that the word "probability" or its variants as used here is the risk-neutral probability. Most of the time I will not insert this reminder. If you cannot remember this point, go no further. The time you have spent reading this book has been wasted.

TABLE 61.1 Binomial Zero-Coupon Bond Price Evolution

Time 0	Time 1	Time 2	Time 3	Time 4
				$P(4,5) = 0.859$
			$P(3,4) = 0.870$	
			$P(3,5) = 0.758$	
		$P(2,3) = 0.881$		
		$P(2,4) = 0.778$		$P(4,5) = 0.885$
		$P(2,5) = 0.687$		
	$P(1,2) = 0.893$			
	$P(1,3) = 0.798$		$P(3,4) = 0.896$	
	$P(1,4) = 0.715$		$P(3,5) = 0.804$	
	$P(1,5) = 0.641$			
$P(0,1) = 0.905$				
$P(0,2) = 0.820$		$P(2,3) = 0.908$		
$P(0,3) = 0.743$		$P(2,4) = 0.825$		$P(4,5) = 0.911$
$P(0,4) = 0.676$		$P(2,5) = 0.751$		
$P(0,5) = 0.615$				
	$P(1,2) = 0.920$			
	$P(1,3) = 0.847$		$P(3,4) = 0.923$	
	$P(1,4) = 0.781$		$P(3,4) = 0.853$	
	$P(1,5) = 0.722$			
		$P(2,3) = 0.935$		
		$P(2,4) = 0.875$		$P(4,5) = 0.938$
		$P(2,5) = 0.821$		
			$P(3,4) = 0.951$	
			$P(3,5) = 0.905$	
				$P(4,5) = 0.967$

$cP(0,1) + (c + F)P(0,2)$ where c is the coupon rate and F is the face value. The answer will be $(0.1025)0.905 + (0.1025 + 1.0000)0.820 = 0.997$. This price can also be found as the present value over one period of the expected bond price plus the next interest payment. To demonstrate this point, we need to price the bond at time 1 in both the up and down states.

Suppose we are at time 1 in the up state (this is the state where $P(1,2) = 0.893$). At time 2, our bond will be worth its face value of 1.0000 plus it will pay interest of 0.1025. Technically its price in the time 1 up state will be a probability-weighted average of its price plus interest in each of the time 2 states it can move to, but those two states are at its maturity, so there is no need to weight the final interest and principal payment by the probability. Thus, its price in the time 1 up state is $1.1025P(1,2) = 1.1025(0.893) = 0.985$. In the time 1 down state its price will be $1.1025(0.920) = 1.0143$. Thus, at time 0 its value can be obtained as the discounted probability-weighted average of 0.985 and 1.1043 with each value supplemented with the coupon to be paid at that period. The value at time 0 is then obtained as $[0.52(0.985 + 0.1025) + 0.48(1.0143 + 0.1025)]0.905 = 0.997$, reflecting the fact that 0.52 is the risk-neutral probability of an up move in this example and 0.905 is the price of a one-period zero-coupon bond at time 0, which is the appropriate one-period discount factor.

Now let us turn to options. Consider a two-period call option on a three-period zero-coupon bond. Let its exercise price be 0.910. Looking at the zero-coupon bond price tree, we see that at time 2, at which time the option will have one period to go, this bond will be worth 0.881, 0.908, or 0.935, meaning that a European call option will be worth $\text{Max}(0, 0.881 - 0.910) = 0$, $\text{Max}(0, 0.908 - 0.910) = 0$ or $\text{Max}(0, 0.935 - 0.910) = 0.025$ at expiration. In the time 1 up state, this call has no chance of expiring in-the-money at time 2 so its value there will be zero. In the time 1 down state, its value is a discounted probability-weighted average of its two possible values in the next period. Thus, its value in the time 1 down state is $[0.52(0) + 0.48(0.025)]0.920 = 0.011$, where 0.920 is the one-period bond price in that state. Stepping back to time 0, we then find that the option price is $[0.52(0) + 0.48(0.011)]0.905 = 0.0048$.

Following this procedure, we can find the prices of any puts or calls on any zero-coupon bonds. Naturally the options must expire before the bonds mature. We can price options on coupon bonds the same way, but we would have to develop and use a full tree of coupon bond prices. This would be but a simple extension of the example we did earlier where we priced a two-period coupon bond at time 0. We would simply need to price the bond at all nodes in the tree.

If the options were American, it would then be necessary at each node to consider the possibility that the option would be worth more exercised. That will not be the case for an American call on a zero-coupon bond because, remembering a rule from elementary option pricing theory—that we covered in Essays 16 and 35—an American call will not be exercised early unless the underlying asset makes a dividend or interest payment or pays some other kind of cash flow. American puts on zero-coupon bonds might be exercised early, however, and both American calls and puts on coupon bonds might be exercised early.

As an example, I have calculated the price at time 0 of a four-period option on a five-period bond with a coupon of 10.25%. Note that we have only a four-period tree, but a five-period bond can be priced because it matures to a value of 1.0000 at time 5 With a strike of 0.975, the European call is worth 0.021, the American call is worth 0.043, the European put is worth 0.001, and the American put is worth 0.01. Similarly, four-period options with a strike of 0.910 on a five-period zero-coupon bond have these values: European and American call $= 0.007$, European put $= 0.007$, American put $= 0.295$. These values were all calculated on a spreadsheet so they could differ slightly from values calculated by hand, given the way round-off errors can accumulate in a binomial tree.

Now let us look at pricing a callable bond. A callable bond is equivalent to an ordinary bond with a call option held by the issuer. Consider a five-period 10.25% coupon bond with a par value of 1.0000, callable in three periods at 1.025. At time 5 there would be six possible final states, and in each state the bond value is par plus the final coupon. At time 4 there are five possible states. To price the bond in each of those states, we simply discount the face value plus the coupon by the one-period discount factor appropriate for that state.

Looking at the zero-coupon bond price tree, we see that those factors are 0.859, 0.885, 0.911, 0.938, and 0.967. Doing the calculations reveals that in the top two states, we would obtain prices of 0.947 and 0.975; in the middle state, we would obtain 1.004; and in the bottom two states, we would obtain 1.035 and 1.066. But at time 4 the bond is callable at a price of 1.025. Assuming the issuer acted rationally, it would call the bond in the bottom two states, paying 1.025, so the bond prices of 1.035 and 1.066 in the bottom two states are each replaced with 1.025. In this example, the coupon is not paid if the bond is called, although this condition can be inserted if appropriate.

Proceeding leftward in the tree reveals that the bond would be called in the bottom two states of time 3 as well. Substituting the call values in the appropriate nodes and working back to time 0 by successive discounting of the two probability-weighted next-period values gives a price of 0.992. By comparison, a five-period noncallable bond is worth almost precisely par value so the option reduces the price by about 0.008.

Now let us price futures contracts on bonds. A futures price is the probability-weighted expectation of the next-period futures price. At expiration, the futures and spot prices will converge. Because there is no outlay of funds for a futures, there is no opportunity cost. Thus, there is no necessity to discount from a future period back to a current period. Suppose we are at time 3 in the uppermost state. This is where $P(3,4) = 0.870$ and $P(3,5) = 0.758$. We wish to price a futures expiring the next period on the five-period zero-coupon bond. In other words, the futures is on the zero-coupon bond maturing at time 5 and the futures expires at time 4. One period later the futures will converge to the spot price, which will be 0.859 with probability 0.52 or 0.885 with probability 0.48. Thus, the time 3 futures price in the top node will be $0.52(0.859) + 0.48(0.885) = 0.872$. In the second node from the top, the futures price will be $0.52(0.885) + 0.48(0.911) = 0.898$. To find the futures price today, we simply roll back through the tree, at each node finding the probability-weighted average of the next two possible futures prices. At time 0, we would find the futures price to be 0.909.

An identical procedure is followed to find the price of a futures on a coupon bond. Keep in mind, however, that the futures contract does not pay or receive the interest on the coupon bond. Thus, when the futures price converges to the spot price, there is no claim on the interest. In our example, the price at time 0 of a futures expiring at time 4 on a bond maturing at time 5 with coupon of 10.25% would be 1.003.

Finally, it is possible to price options on futures using the same procedure. You would simply find the exercise value of the option at the appropriate expiration nodes and successively discount the probability-weighted average of the next two option prices. In our example, options with a strike of 0.995 expiring at time 3 on a futures expiring at time 4 on a coupon bond maturing at time 5 would have values of: European call = 0.011, American call = 0.012, European put = 0.005, American put = 0.006.

In the next essay, we introduce the notion of a short-term interest rate on which we shall price options and forward contracts.

FOR MORE READING

Jarrow, Robert A. *Modeling Fixed-Income Securities and Interest Rate Options*, 2nd. ed. Stanford, CA: Stanford University Press, 2002, chaps. 10–12.

Jarrow, Robert A., and Stuart M. Turnbull. *Derivatives Securities*, 2nd ed. Mason, OH: Thomson South-Western, 2000, chaps. 15–17.

McDonald, Robert L. *Derivative Markets*, 2nd ed. Boston: Addison Wesley, 2006, chaps. 14, 24.

TEST YOUR KNOWLEDGE

1. In a binomial interest rate, how does one find the price of a coupon bond, given the next two possible prices of the bond?
2. Briefly explain how a callable bond is priced using a binomial tree.
3. In pricing a futures contract using a binomial tree, why is the expected future value of the contract not discounted?

Tree Pricing of Bonds and Interest Rate Derivatives: III

This essay is the third in a series on the pricing of bonds and interest rate derivatives using binomial trees. In Essay 61, we priced bonds and derivatives directly on the bonds. In this essay we price derivatives directly on the one-period interest rate implied by the tree we developed in Essay 60 For convenience, the tree is reproduced here (Table 62.1).

An interest rate derivative is one in which the payoff is based on an interest rate. Swaps, options, and forward rate agreements (FRAs) the most common examples. In the real world, the interest rate might be 90-day London Interbank Offer Rate (LIBOR), but that is by no means the only rate used in such contracts. In this essay we simply use the one-period rate as the underlying, and we do only FRAs and interest rate caps and floors. We cover swaps and swaptions in the next two essays.

In pricing interest rate derivatives, we must first use the tree of zero-coupon bond prices to develop a tree of the evolution of one-period rates. These will be found by inferring the interest rate from the price of the various one-dollar discount bonds whose prices are given in the tree and are denoted, as $P(0,1)$, $P(1,2)$, $P(2,3)$, $P(3,4)$, and $P(4,5)$. Note that this is not the price of a single instrument as it evolves through time but rather the price of a zero coupon that matures one period later. This will always be a two-period bond the previous period, which then evolves into a one-period bond. In our example, $P(0,1) = 0.905$, so the one-period rate is $1/P(0,1) - 1 = 1/0.905 - 1 = 0.105$ or 10.5%. We call this $r(0,1)$. The next period, the one-period bond price can be $P(1,2) = 0.893$ or 0.920. This means that the one-period rate will be either 12% or 8.74%. (Note that the bond prices are rounded off; greater precision is in the interest rates.) At period 2 there are three possible one-period rates; 13.47%, 10.17%, or 6.96%. Summarizing the entire process, we obtain the tree of one-period rates as shown in Table 62.2.

TABLE 62.1 Binomial Zero-Coupon Bond Price Evolution

Time 0	Time 1	Time 2	Time 3	Time 4
				$P(4,5) = 8.859$
			$P(3,4) = 0.870$	
			$P(3,5) = 0.758$	
		$P(2,3) = 0.881$		
		$P(2,4) = 0.778$		$P(4,5) = 0.885$
		$P(2,5) = 0.687$		
	$P(1,2) = 0.893$			
	$P(1,3) = 0.798$		$P(3,4) = 0.896$	
	$P(1,4) = 0.715$		$P(3,5) = 0.804$	
	$P(1,5) = 0.641$			
$P(0,1) = 0.905$				
$P(0,2) = 0.820$		$P(2,3) = 0.908$		
$P(0,3) = 0.743$		$P(2,4) = 0.825$		$P(4,5) = 0.911$
$P(0,4) = 0.676$		$P(2,5) = 0.751$		
$P(0,5) = 0.615$				
	$P(1,2) = 0.920$			
	$P(1,3) = 0.847$		$P(3,4) = 0.923$	
	$P(1,4) = 0.781$		$P(3,4) = 0.853$	
	$P(1,5) = 0.722$			
		$P(2,3) = 0.935$		
		$P(2,4) = 0.875$		$P(4,5) = 0.938$
		$P(2,5) = 0.821$		
			$P(3,4) = 0.951$	
			$P(3,5) = 0.905$	
				$P(4,5) = 0.967$

Of course, there is no reason why we must focus solely on the one-period rate, but the tree for any other rate would be obtained in a similar manner, and the derivative pricing procedure to follow would be the same.

Let us first price the FRA, which we introduced in Essay 8. Standard FRAs mature at a given point in time and pay off at that point. They call for one party to make a discounted interest payment at the rate at that time. In the tree shown in Table 62.2, consider an FRA expiring at time 2. In the real world, this transaction might correspond to entering into a six-month FRA on 90 day LIBOR. Since the value of an FRA at time 0 is zero, the fixed rate, set at time 0, is the rate such that the risk-neutral expected payoff is zero. The three possible one-period rates at time 2 are 13.47, 10.17, and 6.96. The risk-neutral probabilities of these rates occurring are given by the binomial probabilities $(0.52)^2 = 0.2704$, $2(0.52)(0.48) = 0.4992$, and $(0.48)^2 = 0.2304$. Thus the rate on a two-period FRA, which

TABLE 62.2   Binomial Evolution of the One-Period Rate

Time 0	Time 1	Time 2	Time 3	Time 4
				$r(4,5) = 16.45$
			$r(3,4) = 14.95$	
		$r(2,3) = 13.47$		$r(4,5) = 13.66$
	$r(1,2) = 12.00$		$r(3,4) = 11.60$	
$r(0,1) = 10.50$		$r(2,3) = 10.17$		$r(4,5) = 9.76$
	$r(1,2) = 8.74$		$r(3,4) = 8.35$	
		$r(2,3) = 6.96$		$r(4,5) = 6.57$
			$r(3,4) = 5.20$	
				$r(4,5) = 3.46$

Note: These rates may not exactly equal those that you would obtain manually. They were obtained using a spreadsheet, which uses more exact values of the spot and forward prices.

we denote as FRA(0,2), is such that $0.2704(0.1347 - \text{FRA}(0,2))/1.1347 + 0.4992(0.1017 - \text{FRA}(0,2))/1.1017 + 0.2304(0.0696 - \text{FRA}(0,2)/1.0696$. Then FRA(0,2) = 10.27%. Thus, if a firm entered into a two-period FRA on the one-period rate, it would agree to make an interest payment at time 2 of 10.32% and agree to receive an interest payment at that date of whatever the one-period rate is. Other rates for various FRAs are FRA(0,1) = 10.41, FRA(0,3) = 10.12, and FRA(0,4) = 9.97. Of course, the actual payoffs would be determined by applying these rates to a notional principal and prorating over the appropriate number of days that the rate corresponds to. We will not concern ourselves here with these matters as they are straightforward. We quote all results in terms of a rate only.

Now let us turn to interest rate caps and floors, which are options on interest rates and were introduced in Essay 8. A cap (floor) is like a call (put) and pays off if the interest rate is greater (less) than the strike rate at expiration or earlier if American style and exercised early. The typical arrangement is that the actual payment occurs one period after the expiration. This corresponds to the convention found on floating-rate loans, where the rate is set at the beginning of the period and the actual interest payment occurs at the end of the period. Caps and floors are actually a series of independent options called *caplets* and *floorlets*. The expiration of each caplet or floorlet is usually set to correspond to the reset dates on floating-rate securities held or issued by the purchaser. The decision to exercise a caplet or floorlet is independent of the decision to exercise any other caplet or floorlet. That is, exercising one caplet or floorlet does not preclude or require exercise of any other.

The value of a cap or floor is the sum of the values of each component caplet or floorlet. Thus, we price the cap or floor as a portfolio of options.

Consider a four-period cap on the one-period rate. The cap consists of four component caplets, one expiring at time 1, another at time 2, another at time 3, and another at time 4. On each caplet expiration date, one caplet expires and is in-the-money (out-of-the-money) if the one-period rate is higher (lower) than the strike rate chosen by the buyer. The actual payoff is made one period later, so its value must be discounted back at the appropriate one-period rate.

Let our cap have a strike of 9%. The five possible one-period rates at time 4 are 16.45%, 13.06%, 9.76%, 6.57%, and 3.46%. In the uppermost state, the rate of 16.45% means that the final caplet expires in-the-money for a payoff of 16.45% − 9% = 7.45%. This payment will be made one period later, so we discount it using the one-period discount factor at that node in the tree, which is 0.859. Thus, the value of the option at expiration when the one-period rate is 16.45% is 0.0745(0.859) = 0.0640, which is interpreted as 6.40%. Moving down the tree at time 4 to the next four nodes would produce caplet values of 0.0359, 0.0070, 0.0000, and 0.0000, reflecting the rates of 13.06%, 9.76%, 6.57%, and 3.46% and one-period discount factors of 0.885, 0.911, 0.938, and 0.967.

Remember that we are still just finding the price of a single caplet, the interest rate call option that expires at time 4. We have five possible values, as noted. At each node, we step back one unit of time and find the probability-weighted discounted value. For example, in the time 3 topmost node, the caplet would be worth 6.40% if the rate goes up at time 4 or 3.59% if the rate goes down at time 4. Using our probabilities of 0.52 and 0.48, we have an expected rate of 0.52(6.40) + 0.48(3.59) = 5.05. This value is then discounted by the one-period factor at the topmost node of time 3 of 0.870 to give a value of 4.39 in that node.

As usual, we proceed backward through the tree, successively discounting the probability-weighted average of the next two possible values. At time 0 we have the value of the caplet that expires at time 4. But this value is just the value of one of four caplets that make up this cap. We also have caplets expiring at times 1, 2, and 3. Repeating this procedure to value those options, we obtain the full value of the cap (i.e., the sum of the values of the four caplets) as 4.93%. To value a floor, we follow the same procedure but have the floor pay off like an interest put (i.e., have a positive value at expiration if the one-period rate is below the strike rate).

Because they are so often used to manage the risk of resetting the interest rate on a floating-rate loan or security, which is done on a specific date, caps and floors are typically structured as European-style, but they can be and occasionally are done as American-style. If so, the exercise value of each option at each node prior to expiration would replace the computed value if the former were higher.

In the next essay, the fourth in this series on pricing interest rate derivatives, we address the pricing of swaps and swaptions.

FOR MORE READING

Jarrow, Robert A. *Modeling Fixed-Income Securities and Interest Rate Options*, 2nd. ed. Stanford, CA: Stanford University Press, 2002, chaps. 13–14.

Jarrow, Robert A., and Stuart M. Turnbull. *Derivatives Securities*, 2nd ed. Mason, OH: Thomson South-Western, 2000, chap. 17.

McDonald, Robert L. *Derivative Markets*, 2nd ed. Boston: Addison Wesley, 2006, chaps. 14, 24.

TEST YOUR KNOWLEDGE

1. Explain how a one-period zero-coupon bond can reveal the evolution of the one-period rate.
2. How is an FRA priced using a binomial tree?
3. Explain why a caplet or floorlet must be discounted to obtain the payoff at expiration at any given node.

Tree Pricing of Bonds and Interest Rate Derivatives: IV

This essay is the fourth in a series on pricing bonds and interest rate derivatives using binomial trees. In the last essay we priced options and forward rate agreements (FRAs) on the one-period interest rate. In this essay we price interest rate swaps. You may wish to review Essays 60, 61, and 62. The trees developed in Essays 60 and 62 will be used and are reproduced here as Tables 63.1 and 63.2.

You may recall that we covered swaps and interest rate swap pricing in Essays 6, 9, and 37. A plain vanilla interest rate swap consists of a series of interest payments between two parties, with one party paying at a fixed rate and the other paying at a floating rate. Pricing a swap means determining the fixed rate that equates the present value of the fixed payments to the present value of the floating payments. Although the floating payments are not known, they have a known present value at the start, because the rate will be reset to the current market rate each period. This is what happens with a floating rate security. Its rate is reset each period to the current one-period rate, and this adjustment results in its price coming back to par, a point we demonstrated in Essay 37. This result is useful in swap pricing.

The actual swap payment at a given time point is determined by the net of the fixed rate and the floating rate that was set as of the previous time point. The value of a swap is zero at the start, because the fixed and floating payments have the same present value by design, but during the life of the swap, the present value of one series of payments should exceed the present value of the other due to changing interest rates.

As noted, we previously demonstrated the very simple procedure of pricing a swap. Recall that we needed only the term structure. We did not need a full model of the evolution of the term structure. Now that we have such a model, however, it is worthwhile to price the swap, if for no other

TABLE 63.1 Binomial Zero-Coupon Bond Price Evolution

Time 0	Time 1	Time 2	Time 3	Time 4
				$P(4,5) = 0.859$
			$P(3,4) = 0.870$ $P(3,5) = 0.758$	
		$P(2,3) = 0.881$ $P(2,4) = 0.778$ $P(2,5) = 0.687$		$P(4,5) = 0.885$
	$P(1,2) = 0.893$ $P(1,3) = 0.798$ $P(1,4) = 0.715$ $P(1,5) = 0.641$		$P(3,4) = 0.896$ $P(3,5) = 0.804$	
$P(0,1) = 0.905$ $P(0,2) = 0.820$ $P(0,3) = 0.743$ $P(0,4) = 0.676$ $P(0,5) = 0.615$		$P(2,3) = 0.908$ $P(2,4) = 0.825$ $P(2,5) = 0.751$		$P(4,5) = 0.911$
	$P(1,2) = 0.920$ $P(1,3) = 0.847$ $P(1,4) = 0.781$ $P(1,5) = 0.722$		$P(3,4) = 0.923$ $P(3,4) = 0.853$	
		$P(2,3) = 0.935$ $P(2,4) = 0.875$ $P(2,5) = 0.821$		$P(4,5) = 0.938$
			$P(3,4) = 0.951$ $P(3,5) = 0.905$	
				$P(4,5) = 0.967$

TABLE 63.2 Binomial Evolution of the One-Period Rate

Time 0	Time 1	Time 2	Time 3	Time 4
				$r(4,5) = 16.45$
			$r(3,4) = 14.95$	
		$r(2,3) = 13.47$		$r(4,5) = 13.66$
	$r(1,2) = 12.00$		$r(3,4) = 11.60$	
$r(0,1) = 10.50$		$r(2,3) = 10.17$		$r(4,5) = 9.76$
	$r(1,2) = 8.74$		$r(3,4) = 8.35$	
		$r(2,3) = 6.96$		$r(4,5) = 6.57$
			$r(3,4) = 5.20$	
				$r(4,5) = 3.46$

Note: These rates may not exactly equal those that you would obtain manually. They were obtained using a spreadsheet, which uses more exact values of the spot and forward prices.

reason than to be sure that our swap price is consistent, meaning arbitrage free, with the prices of the other securities and derivatives we have been using. In addition, however, we shall look at how the value of the swap changes from zero to a positive or negative value as the term structure evolves.

Consider a three-period swap on the one-period rate. It will consist of payments at times 1, 2, and 3 based on the one-period rate at times 0, 1, and 2. Recall that in Essay 37 on swap pricing we showed that a trick to pricing an interest rate swap is to add a notional principal payment at the end of the life of the swap to both the fixed and floating sides. This device has no effect on the overall cash flows, but allows us to treat the fixed payments as a fixed-rate bond and the floating payments as a floating-rate bond. As noted, the value of the latter is always par at a coupon setting date, which includes time 0. Thus, pricing the swap comes down to finding the coupon on a fixed-rate bond.

Let the notional principal here be 1.0000. Then the swap price is the solution to the equation $cP(0,1) + cP(0,2) + (c + 1.0000)P(0,3) = 1.0000$. In our example, $P(0,1) = 0.905$, $P(0.2) = 0.820$, and $P(0,3) = 0.743$. The solution is 10.39% (Note that this result was obtained using a spreadsheet by directly inputting the term structure; solving by hand would give 10.41%.) Using 10.39% as the rate and noting that 10.50% is the one-period rate at time 0, the payment at time 1 on a receive-fixed, pay-floating swap, regardless of whether the one-period rate goes up to 12% or down to 8.74%, is 0.11% (10.50% − 10.39%).

Now consider the uppermost state at time 1 where the one-period rate is 12%. From that state the one-period rate can move up to 13.47% or down to 10.17%. In either case, the next swap payment will be 12.00% − 10.39% = 1.61%. Let us determine the value of the swap at that uppermost state at time 1. Viewed from the perspective of the floating-rate payer, intuition tells us that the swap value should be negative, because it was zero in the previous state and the one-period rate went up. The fixed receipts have a lower present value, while the floating payments will be higher, though this will be offset by the higher discount rate. The swap value can be found as the present value of the remaining fixed payments and subtracting the present value of the remaining floating payments. Consistent with our previous approach, we can use the fact that the present value of the floating payments automatically goes to par at the next payment date.

The fixed payments consist of a payment of 0.1039 at time 2 and 0.1039 at time 3. Adding the principal at time 3, we obtain a present value of $0.1039(0.893) + 1.1039(0.798) = 0.9737$. The next floating payment will be 12%, so we discount 1.12 for one period and obtain $(1.12)(0.893) = 1.0002$. Thus, the fixed receipts plus the notional principal have a present value of 0.9737 and the floating payments plus the notional principal have a value of 1.0002 for a total swap value of -0.0265.

An alternative and to some a more intuitive approach would be to price the floating payments as a series of FRAs. At the time 1 uppermost state, the next floating payment is 12%. The remaining floating payment, which is at time 3, is obtained as the forward rate, $F(1,2,3)$. This result can be derived by first obtaining the forward price as $P(1,3)/P(1,2) = 0.798/0.893 = 0.8936$. The one-period rate implied by this price is $1/0.8936 - 1 = 0.1190$. The next floating payment as implied by the forward rate is 11.90%. So we simply discount these two payments back by the one- and two-period discount factors in that state. Therefore, the value of the floating payments at the time 1 uppermost state is $(0.893)0.12 + (0.798)0.1190 = 0.2021$. The value of the remaining fixed payments is $(0.893)0.1039 + (0.798)0.1039 = 0.1757$. The value of the swap is then $0.1757 - 0.2021 = -0.0264$, a discrepancy from our previously obtained value of only 0.0001, which is a round-off error. This approach treats the swap as a series of forward contracts or FRAs but with the payments occurring at the end of the period rather than at the beginning, which is standard in practice. The other approach treats the swap as a combination of a fixed-rate bond and a floating-rate bond.

If we determined the value of the swap in the time 1 down state, we would obtain a positive value of 0.03. At the time 0 state, the value of the swap can be obtained by taking a probability-weighted average of the next two values, $0.52(-0.0265) + 0.48(0.030)$. No discounting back is required since there is no initial outlay and, therefore, no opportunity cost. The overall value is then zero, subject to a small round-off error, accurately reflecting the fact that the value of a swap at the start is, by definition, zero.

In practice, pricing an interest rate swap is a little more involved than what we have done here. Adjustments must be made for the length of the payment period and the manner in which the payments will be calculated (days/360, 30/360, or 365 days, etc.) But these are minor adjustments. The approach used here captures the essential principles.

In the final essay in this series, we look at the pricing of interest rate swaptions and forward swaps.

FOR MORE READING

Jarrow, Robert A. *Modeling Fixed-Income Securities and Interest Rate Options*, 2nd ed. Stanford, CA: Stanford University Press, 2002, chap. 13.

TEST YOUR KNOWLEDGE

1. Explain why it is not necessary to have a binomial tree model of the evolution of the term structure to be able to price a swap. What added benefit does the binomial model provide?
2. Instead of pricing a swap as a combination of a fixed- and floating-rate bond, what alternative approach can be used?

Tree Pricing of Bonds and Interest Rate Derivatives: V

This is the final essay in a series on the use of binomial trees to price bonds and interest rate derivatives. In the last essay we priced interest rate swaps. In this essay we price options on interest rate swaps, or swaptions, as well as forward swaps, which are forward contracts on swaps. You may wish to review Essay 17 on swaptions. We will use the binomial trees previously developed, which are reproduced here as Tables 64.1 and 64.2.

First let us do a very quick review. A swaption is an option on a swap. It can be set up as an option to pay fixed and receive floating, called a *payer swaption*, or an option to pay floating and receive fixed, called a *receiver swaption*. A payer swaption is somewhat similar to an interest rate call in that it increases in value in a market in which rates are rising. A receiver swaption is somewhat similar to an interest rate put in that it increases in value in a market in which rates are falling. A swaption specifies an exercise rate, which is the fixed rate at which the holder can enter into the swap.

Consider a payer swaption with an exercise rate of 10.50% where the underlying swap is a three-period swap on the one-period rate. At expiration, if the rate on new three-period swaps on the one-period rate is more than 10.50%, the holder will exercise. The holder then enters into a three-period swap to pay 10.50%. It can hold that position, knowing it has a positive value swap (because the rate on new three-period swaps is more than 10.50%) or enter into an offsetting three-period swap, agreeing to pay 10.50% and receive the floating one-period rate while receiving more than 10.50% and paying the floating one-period rate. The floating inflows and outflows are equivalent, and the net result is the establishment of an annuity equal to the difference in the market fixed rate and the exercise rate.

Pricing a swaption in the binomial tree framework is but a matter of observing the payoff at expiration and finding the discounted probability-weighted present value. The payoff at expiration, however, is structured

TABLE 64.1   Binomial Zero-Coupon Bond Price Evolution

Time 0	Time 1	Time 2	Time 3	Time 4
				$P(4,5) = 8.859$
			$P(3,4) = 0.870$	
			$P(3,5) = 0.758$	
		$P(2,3) = 0.881$		
		$P(2,4) = 0.778$		$P(4,5) = 0.885$
		$P(2,5) = 0.687$		
	$P(1,2) = 0.893$			
	$P(1,3) = 0.798$		$P(3,4) = 0.896$	
	$P(1,4) = 0.715$		$P(3,5) = 0.804$	
	$P(1,5) = 0.641$			
$P(0,1) = 0.905$				
$P(0,2) = 0.820$		$P(2,3) = 0.908$		
$P(0,3) = 0.743$		$P(2,4) = 0.825$		$P(4,5) = 0.911$
$P(0,4) = 0.676$		$P(2,5) = 0.751$		
$P(0,5) = 0.615$				
	$P(1,2) = 0.920$			
	$P(1,3) = 0.847$		$P(3,4) = 0.923$	
	$P(1,4) = 0.781$		$P(3,4) = 0.853$	
	$P(1,5) = 0.722$			
		$P(2,3) = 0.935$		
		$P(2,4) = 0.875$		$P(4,5) = 0.938$
		$P(2,5) = 0.821$		
			$P(3,4) = 0.951$	
			$P(3,5) = 0.905$	
				$P(4,5) = 0.967$

TABLE 64.2   Binomial Evolution of the One-Period Rate

Time 0	Time 1	Time 2	Time 3	Time 4
				$r(4,5) = 16.45$
			$r(3,4) = 14.95$	
		$r(2,3) = 13.47$		$r(4,5) = 13.66$
	$r(1,2) = 12.00$		$r(3,4) = 11.60$	
$r(0,1) = 10.50$		$r(2,3) = 10.17$		$r(4,5) = 9.76$
	$r(1,2) = 8.74$		$r(3,4) = 8.35$	
		$r(2,3) = 6.96$		$r(4,5) = 6.57$
			$r(3,4) = 5.20$	
				$r(4,5) = 3.46$

Note: These rates may not exactly equal those that you would obtain manually. They were obtained using a spreadsheet, which uses more exact values of the spot and forward prices.

a little differently from that of an ordinary option. Consider our payer swaption on the one-period rate and let it expire at time 2. Looking at the uppermost state at time 2, we need to find the rate on new three-period swaps. Recall from Essay 63 that this rate is obtained by solving this equation for c: $cP(2,3) + cP(2,4) + (c + 1.0000)P(2,5) = 1.0000$. With $P(2,3) = 0.881$, $P(2,4) = 0.778$, and $P(2,5) = 0.687$, the solution is $c = 13.32\%$ (Note that a manual calculation would likely obtain a value of 13.34, but using a spreadsheet to minimize rounding errors gives 13.32.)

A payer swaption with a strike of 10.50% would be expiring in-the-money by 2.82%. This value, however, is not the payoff value. It simply means that the holder has the right to receive the floating rate and pay the fixed rate of 10.50%. The holder can then enter a new swap to receive the market fixed rate of 13.32% and pay the floating rate. The 2.82% differential then represents a series of fixed interest payments representing an annuity over the next three periods. Note that the floating payments cancel. Thus, the value of the swaption at expiration is the present value of an annuity of three interest payments of 2.82% each over the next three periods. This value would then be $0.0282(0.881 + 0.778 + 0.687) = 0.0662$.

In the middle state at time 2, the new swap rate would be 10.02%. The payer swaption would be expiring out-of-the-money, as it would in the bottom state. The value in the top state at time 1 would then reflect the possibility that the swaption will move to a value of 0.0662 with probability 0.52 or to 0 with probability of 0.48. Taking the probability-weighted discounted value gives $[0.52(0.0662) + 0.48(0)]0.893 = 0.0308$. The value in the bottom state would be zero, as there is no possibility of the swaption moving to a state at time 2 with a positive value. The value of the swaption today would be $[0.52(0.0308) + 0.48(0)]0.905 = 0.0145$.

If the swaption were American style, it could be exercised early. In the uppermost state at time 1, the swaption had a value of 0.0308, as noted in the last paragraph. But in that state, the rate on a new three-period swap would be 11.86%. At a strike rate of 10.50%, this swaption is in-the-money by 1.36% and has a value of $0.0136(0.893 + 0.798 + 0.715) = 0.0327$. Thus, the value of the American payer swaption in the uppermost state at time 1 would be 0.0327, and this value would replace the computed value of 0.0308. The value today of the American swaption would then be $[0.52(0.0327) + 0.48(0)]0.905 = 0.0154$ if it is not exercised immediately. We must, however, still check for immediate exercise, but we would find that the current rate on a three-period swap is 10.39%, which makes the swaption be out-of-the-money. So the American swap value is 0.0154.

Receiver swaptions can be valued following the same procedure, but the expiration payoffs are valued such that the swaption expires in-the-money if the rate on the underlying swap is less than the strike rate.

Since there are options on swaps, it is natural for us to consider forward contracts on swaps. These are called forward swaps. Pricing means to solve for the fixed rate that will be on the swap that you are contracting to enter into at the forward contract delivery date.

One way to look at a forward swap is to treat it as a longer-term swap offset with a shorter-term swap. Consider a forward swap in which the parties are obligated in one period to enter into a two-period swap. The party from whose perspective we take will pay floating and receive fixed.

There are two ways in which we can price this kind of transaction. We can identify the floating payments at times 2 and 3 using the forward rates at time 0, $F(0,1,2)$ and $F(0,2,3)$. We find their present value and then find the fixed payment that has the same present value if paid at times 2 and 3. An equivalent approach is to assume that the swap can be replicated by issuing a two-period floating-rate bond at par at time 1 and use the proceeds to buy a two-period fixed-rate bond. I prefer the latter approach because it does not give the false impression that the forward rates equal the actual or expected future spot rates.

We must find the coupon on the fixed-rate bond that would allow it to be issued at par. The discount factors on the fixed-rate bond would be $F(0,1,2)$ and $F(0,1,3)$. Thus, we set up the equation $cF(0,1,2) + (c + 1.0000)$ $F(0,1,3) = 1.0000$. Note that we are not discounting back to time 0 but rather we are discounting back to time 1 using the forward rates in place at time 0. The two forward discount factors are $F(0,1,2) = P(0,2)/P(0,1) = 0.820/0.905 = 0.906$ and $F(0,1,3) = P(0,3)/P(0,1) = 0.743/0.905 = 0.821$. Thus, our equation becomes $c(0.906) + (c + 1.0000)0.821 = 1.0000$. Solving for c gives 10.36%. Thus, if two parties entered into a forward contract calling for them to enter into a two-period swap one period later, they would agree on a swap rate of 10.36%.

This completes the series of essays on tree pricing of bonds and interest rate derivatives. This section contains the greatest number of computations in this book. To understand this material well and be able to move on to more challenging material in the literature, it would probably be useful to go back and work through these examples, paying close attention to the particular states to which I refer at various times, and verifying each computation. As previously noted, each of these calculations was done on a spreadsheet with no rounding, so your answers obtained by hand may differ. Programming tree models on spreadsheets is itself an excellent learning process that I highly recommend.

FOR MORE READING

Jarrow, Robert A. *Modeling Fixed-Income Securities and Interest Rate Options*, 2nd ed. Stanford, CA: Stanford University Press, 2002, chap. 13.

Jarrow, Robert A., and Stuart M. Turnbull. *Derivatives Securities*, 2nd ed. Mason, OH: Thomson South-Western, 2000, chap. 17.

TEST YOUR KNOWLEDGE

1. Briefly explain how the value of a swaption is determined in a binomial tree.
2. How would swaption valuation differ if the swaption were American?

Seven

Other Topics and Issues

The final section of the book is like your attic or basement. It's where you store a lot of things that do not fit nicely elsewhere. These nine essays comprise a handful of topics that need some attention but do not fall into any of the other categories, and some rightly must occur at the end of the book. In this section we discuss stock options, those highly publicized instruments that companies award their employees and executives. We next cover Value at Risk. We also cover how stock itself can be viewed as an option, a notion that creates the possibility of modeling credit risk as an option. We then discuss the credit risk of derivatives, operating risk, how risk is managed in an organization, and how accounting and disclosure of derivatives positions are done. We then look at how some organizations have done a poor if not deadly job of using derivatives. After seeing the bad, we then look at the good: how derivatives should be properly used.

I hope this book has taken you on an interesting journey. Even if it has not, your time has not been wasted. Maybe you just learned that derivatives is not a subject for you. If the journey has been interesting, you will want to learn more. There are many excellent books and articles listed in the references. Remember that learning should never stop.

Stock Options

This book is filled with material on options, among other types of derivatives. The kinds of options we have covered until now, however, are those that are publicly traded either on an options exchange or on the over-the-counter market. In this essay I cover another type of option, which is often rather loosely referred to as a *stock option*. This terminology can be quite confusing, because publicly traded options on stocks could easily be (and sometimes are) called stock options.[1] But the kinds of options I cover here are the ones that are awarded by companies to employees and executives and permit purchase of the stock of the granting employer. When the options are granted to senior officers and board members, they are often called *executive stock options*. When they are granted to any other employees of the company, they are often called *employee stock options*. Technically, there is little difference. The term "employee stock options" would probably be the more general one, so it could encompass "executive stock options," but it is rarely used in this way. Usually when the options are awarded to executives, they are called "executive stock options."[2] To avoid confusion I will use the term "stock options."

Because the idea behind stock options is to enable their holders to benefit if the shareholders benefit from stock price increases, these options are always understood to be call options. Thus, we will not even use the term "call" in conjunction with these options. Most of these options provide for

---

[1] To avoid confusion, the term "equity options" is often (but not always) used to refer to publicly traded options on stocks.

[2] OK, I have to admit that I believe there is some prejudice on the part of the media. To many journalists, options awarded to executives are, by definition, bad, while options awarded to employees are, by definition, good. The only real difference is that executives have more control over the overall performance of the company, while nonexecutives, that is, employees, have control only over the small little piece of the company in which they do their jobs.

the actual purchase of the stock, but some are cash settled in the same way in which exchange-traded index options are cash-settled, thereby resulting in the holder receiving cash for the difference between the stock price and that exercise price.[3]

These instruments are widely used to compensate and incentivize executives and employees.[4] Let us take a look at how they work, and then we shall look at some of the issues and controversies.

Companies typically grant these options to executives and employees for two purposes. One is that the options can serve as compensation. A person granted options worth $1,000 should be willing to accept the options in lieu of some amount of cash. The amount of cash the person would forgo would not likely be $1,000, because $1,000 in cash has more flexibility than $1,000 of options, as the options cannot be liquidated so easily. We will discuss this point later. The second purpose in granting the options is to induce the recipient to work harder in the future, with the desired result being that the stock price increases, the options subsequently become quite valuable, and the company and the executive or employee both benefit. Of course, this is the incentive nature of the option. So on one hand, with options you are paying an employee for past work, and on the other, you are giving the employee a reason to work hard in the future.

Stock options are typically granted with the stock price equal to the exercise price, which is called at-the-money, as we explained earlier in this book. Stock options are usually illiquid, which arises from two constraints. One is that there is no market for these options, and the other is that most of these options have a vesting period during which they cannot be exercised. Although some companies have instituted a means of adding some liquidity, we must recognize that it is the illiquidity of the options that presumably induces the employee to remain with the company and be motivated to work hard. Hence, it would make no sense to give these options the same liquidity as traded options. The vesting period is a term of usually a few years, at the end of which the employee can exercise the option. Recall that in earlier essays we learned that traded call options should never be exercised early other than for the purpose of capturing a dividend. Stock options, however, do not conform to this rule. Let us consider why that is true.

---

[3] Cash-settled options are sometimes called *share appreciation rights* or *SARs*, but do not let this acronym make you picture employees wearing masks.

[4] With apologies to all of my former English teachers, I know that "incentivize" is not a word. It has, however, become widely used in the trade as a compact way of saying "provide incentives for." Therefore, the profession and yours truly have become inured to its usage, and frankly, it doesn't sound bad at all.

Assume that you own an exchange-listed call option that you purchased in a transaction that was executed on the Chicago Board Options Exchange. The price of the option has fluctuated, and there is still a month to go before expiration. The option has a current value of $10 per contract, so it is worth $1,000 in all. Suppose you wreck your car and need $900 for repairs. You can get the money by selling your option.[5] Suppose that instead of holding an exchange-listed option, you have stock options that were granted by your employer. If the options are not vested, you have no way to get cash from them to pay your repair bill. If the options are vested, however, you can exercise them. Suppose they are in-the-money by $900, the amount you need to fix your car. You can then exercise the options and sell the stock. Ignoring some small costs and taxes you might owe, you will have your cash. Recall, however, that we learned that a call option has intrinsic value and time value. By exercising now, you throw away the value of waiting to exercise later when the stock price could be higher. With traded options, the ability to liquidate the option and obtain option fair market value always dominates exercise, except in the case of an option on a stock about to go ex-dividend, and even then, only if the dividend is large enough. For stock options, throwing away the time value can be quite worthwhile, indeed necessary, if that is what it takes to get cash out of the option. Thus, stock options can and frequently are exercised early.

Stock options have typically been awarded with 10-year maturities and vesting periods that run at least 2 years and seldom more than 5. The average option is exercised after about 5 years. Of course, when exercise occurs, the holder is no longer incentivized from that group of options, though additional options that have not yet vested could well have been awarded.[6]

Stock options were tremendously popular during the 1980s and 1990s. Undocumented stories of low-level employees of technology firms getting rich from stock options are probably more common than actual cases, but there is no doubt that stock options helped fuel the technology boom. One reason for their success has almost surely been due to accounting. Until 2006

---

[5] Over-the-counter options work essentially the same way, but individuals generally do not own them, so my car wreck example might have to be modified if we need a story. Suffice it to say that organizations that need to liquidate their options can, however, go back to the dealer counterparty and sell an identical option, for which the dealer would typically give cash and cancel the original options, as they have been offset by the new options.

[6] This point explains why options are so commonly awarded on a periodic basis, usually annually. Holders get rid of them pretty quickly, so employers need to keep a fresh supply in the hands of their employees.

in the United States, accounting rules permitted companies to treat stock options as if they had no cost, as long as the options were not in-the-money when issued. This point partially explains why the options were usually issued at-the-money, though some have argued that at-the-money options provide the most incentives for the cost. This issue, whether to expense stock options or not, was extremely controversial and was heavily debated for more than 10 years. In the United States, the Financial Accounting Standards Board in 2004 issued Financial Accounting Standard (FAS) 123R (a revision of its ruling FAS 123 of 1995, which had permitted but only encouraged expensing). FAS 123 did require that the cost of the options be revealed in footnotes, but this meant that options awarded would not affect a company's reported earnings or cash flow. As you can probably tell, a small growing company could conserve cash and potentially mislead investors by using stock options in lieu of cash compensation. Certainly many did. FAS 123R now mandates expensing.

The debate about expensing stock options was intense. Opponents of expensing swore that American industry would all but die if the charade of treating stock options as free were not continued. They also argued that it was far better to ignore the cost because accurate valuation of stock options could not be guaranteed. They argued, correctly, that the Black-Scholes-Merton (BSM) model does not give the value of a stock option. As we know, the BSM model assumes the ability to trade the option, and as reasoned earlier, the inability to trade the option would make it less desirable to the holder and, therefore, worth less. Stock options are thus said to have a liquidity discount that, if not properly reflected, could result in overstatement of the cost of the options. The effects of vesting and early exercise, however, offset some of the liquidity discount. There has been much research on this subject, and the issues are far too complex to cover in this essay. Let us just say, however, that the argument that assuming no cost is better than doing one's best to estimate the cost of the option is a poor one. Depreciation and pension expenses are excellent examples of cases in which accounting estimates are routinely accepted as the basis for charging an expense, and no one really believes that these estimates accurately reflect true value.

The proponents of expensing have won the argument, but it is not safe to say that the issue is settled. U.S. companies are now required to expense their stock options, but they continue to complain loudly and have active and sympathetic voices in the Congress. It remains to be seen whether the accounting rules will be changed again to accommodate those in favor of pretending that stock options are free to companies.

One immediate response to mandatory expensing, however, has been that many companies have reduced their use of stock options. Some have begun to use a variation of stock options called *restricted stock*. Restricted stock is simply stock that cannot be sold until the end of the vesting period. It has always been mandatory to expense restricted stock, and some consider its value easier to estimate, but that is not necessarily true. Restricted stock is really the same as stock options with a zero exercise price. Its value ought to be lower than that of ordinary stock, but many do not see it that way. Restricted stock has one very important feature: As stock, its downside risk is greater than that of options. Thus, employees holding restricted stock (or ordinary stock) lose more the more the stock price falls. With options, the losses are limited on the downside.

Two of the many highly publicized controversies over the use of options are *repricing* and *backdating*. The repricing controversy began in the late 1990s when many companies saw their options fall deep out-of-the-money.[7] The holders of these options felt unmotivated, because they believed that the options were so deeply out-of-the-money (referred to as *underwater*) that nothing they could do would ever bring the options back in-the-money by expiration. Some companies began resetting the exercise prices of their options, a practice that came to be known as repricing. One variation of repricing was to cancel the outstanding underwater options and issue new at-the-money options. In either case, it appeared that the shareholders were getting the shaft. Options had been granted, the stock had performed poorly, and the option holders were then forgiven for their poor performance as employees and executives and given a second chance. If the poor performance was market or industry driven, it might make sense to cut the employees and executives a break. One study, however, coauthored by yours truly, showed that the poor performance was specific to the company and not driven by factors outside of it. Thus, it is tough to argue that employees and executives should be given a break. In spite of this fact, however, the actual cost of repricing is fairly small. Lowering the exercise price certainly increases the value of the option, but our study found that the overall effect on shareholders is small.

Nonetheless, my intuition tells me that while the cost of repricing is low, it just looks bad. If every time I buy groceries, the grocery store charges me an extra penny for no reason, it will not cost much, but if I find out about it, I will consider changing stores. Now, I am not going to say that the final word on repricing is that it is a bad thing. Much has been written and discussed over the years. There are other aspects to the problem and other points of view. Just don't say I didn't tell you about it.

---

[7] The technology bust was a major reason for the large number of out-of-the-money stock options.

But if repricing has stirred controversy, it has been nothing compared to the backdating issue. Some academics discovered that the issue dates of options were remarkably correlated to the dates on which stocks were at their lowest. Such perfect market timing could not have come at random. Further investigation showed that, indeed, many companies engage in a routine practice of awarding options on one date but setting their award dates to other dates. These other dates might be the date in the last 30, 60, or 90 days on which the stock was the lowest. A few other variations exist. In all cases, however, the options are effectively awarded in-the-money. Now, no one should be bothered by that fact, provided the full information is disclosed and properly accounted for. Needless to say, that wasn't the case. Some bizarre stories associated with backdating have emerged, including one where the chief executive fled the country to avoid prosecution. The government does appear intent on coming down hard on companies and individuals found guilty of backdating. This story is evolving so I cannot put anything resembling a finishing touch on it.

There is no way that I can do full justice to any of these topics in a short essay. I hope that this essay has familiarized you with the general issues and concepts associated with stock options. I also hope you have not come to approve or disapprove of them but will keep an open mind. My own opinion is that restricted stock is a much better device from the shareholders' perspective, but clearly an equilibrium has to be reached in which employees and executives receive something they value sufficiently high to make the proper effort that will benefit themselves and the shareholders. It may well be that they prefer stock options over restricted stock, because the avoidance of downside risk is the reward they receive for tying their careers and much of their investment portfolios to a single company.

FOR MORE READING

Carpenter, Jennifer N. "The Exercise and Valuation of Executive Stock Options." *Journal of Financial Economics* 48 (1998): 127–158.

Core, John, and Wayne Guay. "Stock Option Plans for Non-Executive Employees." *Journal of Financial Economics* 61 (2001): 253–287.

Hall, Brian J., and Kevin J. Murphy. "Stock Options for Undiversified Executives." *Journal of Accounting and Economics* 33 (2002): 3–42.

Huddart, Steven. "Employee Stock Options." *Journal of Accounting and Economics* 18 (1994): 207–231.

Kulatilaka, Nalin, and Alan J. Marcus. "Valuing Employee Stock Options." *Financial Analysts Journal* 50 (November/December 1994), 46–56.

Lang, Mark. *Employee Stock Options and Equity Valuation.* Charlottesville, VA: Research Foundation of the CFA Institute, 2004.

TEST YOUR KNOWLEDGE

1. What are the similarities and differences in *employee* stock options and *executive* stock options?
2. Why are stock options worth less than comparable options that trade on an options exchange or the over-the-counter market? What advantage to the issuing company does this feature provide?
3. What is the primary reason stock options have been issued at-the-money?
4. Identify and briefly describe two recent controversies in the use of stock options.

Value at Risk

Value at Risk, sometimes known as VaR, is surely one of the most widely discussed concepts in the field of risk management today. It is defined as the minimum amount of money that one could expect to lose in a portfolio with a given probability over a specific period of time. VaR is commonly used as a technique to facilitate the management of the position of a derivatives dealer or end user. Not too surprisingly, the incredible attention it has commanded has generated a great deal of criticism, suspicion, doubt, and outright rejection. Probably no other topic in derivatives has had so much written about it in such a short period of time. So why should I add something to that body of literature? Well, why not? Any book professing to cover derivatives would be remiss without it.

While VaR seems to be a recent development, its origins go back a lot further than one would probably think. It is based on the Markowitz portfolio theory, which lays out the principles involved in managing multiple assets and was first published in 1952. Yet VaR seems to have been first discovered and used in the 1990s.

The J. P. Morgan Company was (and still is under the name JP Morgan Chase) one of Wall Street's oldest and best financial institutions. In the early 1990s, the firm was led by an innovative chief executive named Dennis Weatherstone and was developing its derivatives business at a rapid pace. The firm was an active market maker, buying and selling derivatives and hedging its position with other derivative or spot transactions. Weatherstone, a former trader, was aware of the potential that, if not managed properly, these transactions could endanger the firm. It was said that he requested that a report appear on his desk at 4:15 p.m. every day that would give some indication of the amount of money the firm could lose in its derivative trading. Realizing that Weatherstone would not want to see rows and columns of statistics, the traders looked for a simple way of conveying information about the risk in the firm's positions. Knowing something about modern portfolio theory, they proposed to identify a point representing the left tail of the distribution. This information was allegedly called the firm's "value at risk," though no one knows for sure exactly when that name was given. In any case, the 4:15 report began to appear on Weatherstone's desk every day and indicated the minimum amount of money the bank could lose with a given probability. The idea caught on, and other firms began using this measure. In the meantime, JP Morgan created its own subsidiary, which it named RiskMetrics, that would market and provide data to be used by others to calculate VaR and other risk measures. The RiskMetrics subsidiary later expanded into the area of credit, forming a group called CreditMetrics, and eventually the subsidiary was spun off the firm. It was, to say the least, extremely successful.

Thus, from the simple request of a concerned chief executive, a risk measure was created that began to be very widely used. While not without controversy, it is accurate to say that probably no other single risk measure had as much impact as Value at Risk. Let us see what it means.

The definition of VaR has three elements:

1. A *time horizon*. A derivatives user might be concerned about possible losses over one day, one week, one month, and so on. Users must define the specific time horizon.
2. A *tolerance level* or probability, stated as a percentage. Users must identify what percentage of the time they are willing to bear a loss beyond a certain amount. Common percentages are 5% and 1%.
3. A *unit of currency*. Users must define the unit of currency in which they will state the exposure as indicated by the VaR.

Consider, for example, a dealer with a $20 million portfolio. She might find that her VaR for a one-day period, with a 1% tolerance level, is $200,000. This means that the dealer can expect to lose at least $200,000 on any given day about 1% of the time or, in other words, 2.5 times in a year (assuming 250 trading days). Of course, the user can specify any tolerance level or holding period.

The concept of VaR is a very appealing one. It can be developed for any kind of portfolio and can be aggregated across portfolios of different kinds of instruments. For example, a bank might have a portfolio of interest rate swaps, a portfolio of currency swaps, and a portfolio of equity swaps, as well as its regular loan and bond portfolios. The VaR for each separate portfolio can be calculated and aggregated across all portfolios. I do not mean to imply that estimating VaR or aggregating across portfolios is a simple process; the correlations across portfolios should be accounted for, a point I cover later. VaR does, however, provide a consistent measure across portfolios. Assuming away those problems for now, VaR can provide users with an overall measure of exposure. VaR is also an easily monitored and easily interpretable concept. Senior management and anyone without much technical knowledge of derivatives can still understand the basic idea.

I think VaR is a particularly appealing concept because it is consistent with the objective of shareholder wealth maximization, the central paradigm of business and finance. VaR represents the minimum potential loss in share-holder wealth with a given probability over a specific period of time. Any Chief Executive Officer (CEO) or board member can relate to this idea.

There are three primary methods of computing a VaR, the *historical method*, the *analytical method* and the *Monte Carlo method*. In other articles you may see these referred to with different names. For example, the analytical method is often called the *variance-covariance method* and sometimes the *delta-normal method*.

The historical method calls for obtaining a data set of the returns on the portfolio over a recent history. The returns are then assembled into a histogram. The user then simply observes the value in the tail beyond which the desired percentage of observations lies. For example, consider this frequency table based on 100 days of historical returns on a portfolio.

Return	# of days
Less than −6%	5
−6% to −3%	12
−3% to 0%	16
0% to 3%	32
3% to 6%	22
Greater than 6%	13

If we are interested in a 5% VaR, we would conclude that a loss of 6% or more would be experienced 5 days out of 100. If the portfolio had a value of $50 million, then we would report the VaR as ($50 million)(0.06) = $3 million. Note that if we wanted a 1% VaR, we would group the data into smaller ranges so as to isolate the lowest single return.

For the historical method to be accurate, we must feel confident that the probability distribution of the portfolio currently in place is accurately captured by the historical data. This could be quite a problem for a portfolio in which the composition is changing rapidly.

The analytical method requires information on the expected value and variance of the portfolio of interest. This information is often obtained by collecting historical data. For some portfolios, however, there is sufficient information in current market prices. For example, option prices imply a volatility. The expected return is more difficult to obtain, but for daily VaR, it is quite common to use an expected return of zero. Thus, given the knowledge that the expected return is zero and that the volatility is a certain amount, we can, using normal probability theory, infer the value of the underlying asset beyond which a desired percentage of the observations falls. For example, given a portfolio of a single option on the Standard & Poor's (S&P) 500, we might assume normality for the S&P 500. Given its volatility, we could find the return that defines the 5% left tail. The value of the S&P 500 at that point could be inserted into an appropriate option pricing model to infer an option price that could be compared to a current option price to determine the loss.

A variation of the analytical method is the *delta-normal method*. It uses the option's delta and sometimes its gamma to linearly estimate the sensitivity of the option to a movement in the underlying. Linearizing the option results in a slight loss of accuracy but gains the advantage of retaining the normality characteristic.

Another method involves using the parameters from the analytical method to generate random observations that can then be used to construct a frequency distribution from which the VaR can be taken. This is, of course, the *Monte Carlo simulation method*, which we covered in Essay 29. The Monte Carlo method may well be the most widely used method for estimating VaR, because it is so flexible. Most large financial institutions hold thousands of positions that are driven by numerous risky variables. It is virtually impossible to capture the interactions among the variables using the historical or analytic methods. With Monte Carlo simulation and a sufficiently fast computer, it is not difficult to randomly generate outcomes, even when the variables are not independent of each other, that represent the market prices and rates. These outcomes can fairly easily be assembled into a distribution that reveals the critical left tail value.

These are the basic approaches to estimation of VaR. A number of further problems are encountered in practice. For one thing, the different methods are known to give quite diverse results. Decisions such as the length of the time interval over which you measure the returns when using the historical method can lead to quite different VaRs. Nearly every portfolio is a combination of securities and derivatives. The computation of the portfolio's volatility must take into account not only the variances of the individual instruments but also their covariances with each other. This can lead to very complex large-scale problems. Keep in mind that we are talking about the possibility of having stocks, bonds, currencies, commodities, and derivatives of all types. There can be huge problems in collecting and analyzing the data so as to arrive at a probability distribution or parameter values. In addition, the analytical method assumes normality, but returns are almost surely not normal. How far must departures from normality be before we should become concerned? Another problem is that VaR is nearly always quoted in currency units, but the level of currency units at risk will change partially with growth or contraction of the portfolio's value. For example, a $1 million VaR for a $50 million portfolio is quite different from a $1 million VaR for a $100 million portfolio.

In spite of these problems, VaR is well suited for handling market risk. Yet market risk is definitely the easiest risk to model and to control. What about credit risk? VaR can, in theory, handle credit risk. You would simply need to be able to model how credit risk affects returns. While this is not simple, there is definitely some theory to guide you here. What about model risk, operational risk, and legal risk? Can VaR provide information on the possibility that a model will fail, or you will find a rogue trader, or a counterparty will sue? In theory, yes. In practice, no one has really been able to quantify these kinds of risks, primarily because the events, fortunately, occur so infrequently.

Critics contend that users of VaR do not appear to be aware of these types of problems. They blindly go about calculating VaR and verifying that the level of VaR is not beyond a preestablished limit. The dangers of overreliance on VaR can certainly be quite severe. Moreover, VaR focuses only on the negative tail of the distribution so it disregards the positive benefits that a portfolio can have.

In spite of its critics, VaR has been widely accepted. For example, U.S. banking regulators require that banks report their two-week VaR for a 0.01 risk level. Also, the U.S. Securities and Exchange Commission requires that publicly traded companies state in the annual reports how much risk they have in their derivatives positions. VaR is one of three acceptable methods of conveying this information. As long as users do not employ VaR to the exclusion of other measures of market return and volatility and as long as judgment and experience can override, then VaR is a useful technique for managing risk. In fact, therein lies its greatest benefit, which is that it forces firms to focus on the measurement of risk. Prior to the creation of VaR, firms often expressed their views on risk with more qualitative characteristics. If nothing else, VaR has brought most firms up to a higher level of quantitative sophistication.

To supplement VaR, good risk managers will often subject their portfolios to stress tests and propose certain hypothetical scenarios to see how the portfolios perform. These techniques provide additional information beyond that provided by VaR.

FOR MORE READING

Beder, Tanya S. "VAR: Seductive but Dangerous." *Financial Analysis Review* 51 (September–October 1995): 12–24.

Chance, Don M., and Robert Brooks. *An Introduction to Derivatives and Risk Management*, 7th ed. Mason, OH: Thomson South-Western, 2007, chap. 15.

Duffie, Darrell, and Jun Pan. "An Overview of Value at Risk." *The Journal of Derivatives* 4 (Spring 1997): 7–49.

Hendricks, Darryll. "Evaluation of Value-at-Risk Models Using Historical Data." *Federal Reserve Bank of New York Economic Review* 2 (April 1996): 39–69.

Hull, John C. *Options, Futures, and Other Derivatives*, 6th ed. Upper Saddle River, NJ: Prentice-Hall, 2006, chap. 18.

Jorion, Philippe, "Risk 2: Measuring the Risk in Value-at-Risk." *Financial Analysts Journal* 52 (November–December, 1996): 47–56.

Jorion, Philippe. *Value at Risk: The New Benchmark for Managing Financial Risk*. New York: McGraw-Hill, 2001.

Marshall, Chris, and Michael Siegel. "Value at Risk: Implementing a New Risk Measurement Standard." *The Journal of Derivatives* 4 (Spring 1997): 91–111.

McDonald, Robert L. *Derivative Markets*, 2nd ed. Boston: Addison Wesley, 2006, chaps. 14, 25.

Simons, Katerina. "Value at Risk—New Approaches to Risk Management." *Federal Reserve Bank New England Economic Review* 6 (September–October 1996): 3–13.

Smithson, Charles, with Lyle Minton. "Value-at-Risk (1)." *Risk* 9 (January 1996): 25–27.

Smithson, Charles, with Lyle Minton. "Value-at-Risk (2)." *Risk* 9 (February 1996): 38–39.

www.gloriamundi.org

TEST YOUR KNOWLEDGE

1. What does Value at Risk measure?
2. Identify the three methods of measuring Value at Risk.
3. Which of the three methods of measuring Value at Risk require the assumption of a specific probability distribution?
4. What other techniques are used to supplement Value at Risk?

Stock as an Option

In this essay I address the subject of how stock is really an option itself. Consider this, example. Say a company has a book value of its assets of $1.5 million, a book value of its debt of $0.5 million, and, therefore, a book value of its equity of $1 million. Now suppose the market value of its assets is $300,000. The market value of its debt is $250,000 and the market value of its equity is $50,000. If the debt were due now, the company would be in default and the equity would have essentially a market value of zero. Yet the equity is worth $50,000. Clearly this company is deeply in debt with over 80% of the market value of its assets claimed by the bondholders, but it is not yet in default.

Realizing the gravity of the situation, however, management, acting on behalf of the owners, invests the assets in a highly speculative venture with an 80% chance of failure that would leave the firm with assets worth only $200,000 and consequently equity of −$300,000. The creditors would end up with $200,000 in assets, which by law would fully discharge their claim of $500,000. If the venture is successful, the assets would have a market value of $600,000, leaving the owners with a value of $100,000, given the creditors claim of $500,000. The owners have everything to gain and essentially nothing to lose.

The right that stockholders have to walk away from their obligations with no claims levied against their personal assets is generally referred to as *limited liability*. Once you understand options, however, it is easy to see that the stockholders really have a call option that was written by the creditors. The stockholders have everything to gain on the upside and little to lose on the downside.

Recall that the value of a standard European call option on an asset with no underlying dividends or other payments is a function of five variables: the price of the underlying asset (S), the exercise price (X), the risk-free rate (r), the time to expiration (T), and the volatility of the underlying asset (σ). We know that at expiration with the price of the underlying asset at S^*, the call will have a value of $S^* - X$ if S^* is greater than X and 0 otherwise.

Now let us develop the analogy to the case of the stockholders of a firm with debt. Let the firm have a single issue of zero-coupon debt with face value of F. Let the assets currently be worth A. When the debt matures, if the value of the assets, A^*, exceeds the face value of the debt, the stockholders will pay off the debt and be left as the sole claimants on the remaining assets worth $A^* - F$. In other words, their investment, the value of the equity, E, would end up worth $A^* - F$. If the value of the assets is less than F, the stockholders would default on the debt, turning the assets over to the bondholders, and would end up with an investment worth zero. The stock is, therefore, identical to a call option on the assets.

The use of put-call parity further clarifies the important relationships here. Recall that for ordinary European options, put-call parity states that $c = p + S - PV(X)$, where c is the call price, p is the put price, S is the underlying asset price, and $PV(X)$ is the present value of the exercise price and represents the market value of a risk-free bond worth X at maturity. In other words, a long call is equivalent to a long put, a long position in the underlying asset, and a short position in a risk-free bond with a face value of X. Using the appropriate notation as presented in the last paragraph and substituting the analogous terms converts put-call parity to $E = p + A - PV(F)$. In other words, equity is equivalent to a put plus a long position in the assets and a short position in the bonds. Let us explore this interpretation of the stock a little further.

The short bond position should be clear. The stockholders have issued debt and owe F dollars at a future date, but the debt in the put-call parity equation is default free, which is not the case with the actual debt, a point we clarify in the next few paragraphs. The stockholders also have a claim on the assets so we see an A, the market value of the assets, on the right-hand side. Thus far we have $E = A - PV(F)$ or, alternatively, $A = PV(F) + E$, which looks like a balance sheet identity.

Recall, however, that in put-call parity we have the p term, which is the value of a European put. Remember that a put is an option to sell an asset at a fixed price. If the value of the asset falls below the exercise price at expiration, the holder of a put delivers the asset to the writer and receives the exercise price. From the perspective of the stockholders, the put is an option granted by the bondholders as permitted, indeed required, by the legal system. If the value of the assets falls below the face value of the debt at its maturity, the stockholders have the right to discharge the full amount of their obligation by simply turning over the assets to the bondholders. The legal system, by defining a corporation as a legal entity with limited liability, truncates the loss on the lower end. Firms with no debt do not have this right because no one else shares a claim on the assets. The stock of an all-equity firm is thus not a call option but rather just a full and direct claim on the assets. This point does not mean that an all-equity firm will always be profitable. Someone might invest personal funds in a business venture and end up with less value than originally invested, but the owner is not in default and, therefore, there is no analogy to an option.

By definition, the market value of the debt (B) is equal to the market value of the assets (A) minus the market value of the equity (E), that is, $B = A - E$. Substituting the right-hand side of the put-call parity relationship for E, we have $B = A - [p + A - PV(F)]$, which reduces to $PV(F) - p$. The interpretation of this is simple. $PV(F)$ is the market value of a risk-free claim on a future value of F. The term $-p$ is the value of a short position in a put. Thus, the bondholders have in effect purchased a risk-free bond and sold a put to the stockholders. This point should make sense. By lending the stockholders money, they have purchased a risk-free bond, but they have altered the bond from risk free to default risky by granting the stockholders the right to pay off the bonds by simply turning over the market value of the assets. The creditors' position is now certainly not risk free. In other words, they are telling the stockholders "You owe us F dollars but we will accept the market value of the assets in lieu of full payment if that is the best you can do." While this offer might make the bondholders sound not too smart, keep in mind that their claims are fairly priced and bondholders clearly pay a lot of attention to the credit risk when deciding what rate to charge on a loan.

This analogy was first proposed by the late Fischer Black and Myron Scholes in the classic article where they developed their option pricing model. It was further developed by Robert C. Merton and others. The analogy extends to cases where the firm has coupon debt and multiple debt issues with certain issues subordinated to other issues. The Black-Scholes-Merton model and appropriate variations thereof can be used to price the equity and the debt. In practice, however, most corporate capital structures are too complex to permit direct application of the model.[1] Its usefulness is in providing intuition that helps explain many important questions in finance. Capital structure, protective covenants on debt, mergers, conflicts between owners and managers, and yield premiums on debt with different default risk levels are just some of the many issues in which this model provides insights. Most importantly, this concept of default as an option has

---

[1] By making some pretty heroic assumptions and by using proxies because of less-than-perfect data, some companies such as Moody's KMV have been able to operationalize the model with great success if judged by their large clientele base.

played a critical role in recent advancements in modeling credit risk and, in particular, in developing instruments such as credit derivatives.

So let us remember that the model tells us that equity reflects the behavior of an underlying asset, namely the assets of the firm, in the same way that an option reflects the value of the asset that it is written on.

FOR MORE READING

Black, Fischer, and John C. Cox. "Valuing Corporate Securities: Some Effects of Bond Indenture Provisions." *The Journal of Finance* 31 (1976): 351–367.

Black, Fischer, and Myron Scholes. "The Pricing of Options and Corporate Liabilities." *The Journal of Political Economy* 81 (1973): 637–654.

Galai, Dan, and Ronald W. Masulis. "The Option Pricing Model and the Risk Factor of Stock." *Journal of Financial Economics* 3 (1976): 53–81.

Geske, Robert. "The Valuation of Corporate Liabilities as Compound Options." *Journal of Financial and Quantitative Analysis* 12 (1977): 541–552.

McDonald, Robert L. *Derivative Markets*, 2nd ed. Boston: Addison Wesley, 2006, chaps. 16, 26.

Merton, Robert C. "On the Pricing of Corporate Debt: The Risk Structure of Interest Rates." *The Journal of Finance* 29 (1974): 449–470.

TEST YOUR KNOWLEDGE

1. What financial instrument captures the feature of limited liability of equity?
2. Consider each term in put-call parity for conventional options and identify the corresponding term in put-call parity when the equity is considered a call option.
3. Use options to explain how a bond subject to default differs from a default-free bond.

The Credit Risk of Derivatives

In the last essay we discussed how options can be used to value stock and, in so doing, they reflect the risk that the stockholders will default to the bondholders. Continuing with the theme of default, in this essay we look at the default or credit risk of derivatives. For many years derivatives users have proceeded with little attention to the possibility that the counterparty would default. The exchange clearinghouses provided an assurance that they would step in when one side defaulted. That has indeed been the case in several episodes. Even the interbank currency market, which is the over-the-counter (OTC) market for forward contracts on currency, has had a remarkable record for credit performance. With the growth of over-the-counter derivatives, however, concerns have increased that more defaults will occur. These concerns could be justified. The growing use and increasing complexity of derivatives combined with the lack of knowledge of both the instruments and the appropriate way to measure and manage credit risk give everyone reason to need a better understanding of the credit risk problem.

The credit risk of an OTC derivative is a function of several factors. The most basic factor is the nature of the instrument. Credit is a considerably different concern in options than in forwards or swaps. Also, an option's credit risk is one-sided: The buyer is not obligated to do anything so it cannot default. Another important factor is the value of the derivative, which indicates the amount of money at risk. Another is the credit quality of the counterparties. Finally, market conditions are important to consider. An economic environment in which many firms are at risk of defaulting is quite different from one in which most firms are doing well.

Consider an option. The buyer does not have to do anything so the writer is not subject to any risk from the actions of the buyer. The buyer, however, assumes the risk that the writer will default. Prior to expiration, an option nearly always has value, so the buyer virtually never avoids some default risk. A forward contract, however, can have positive value to one but not both parties. At the time a forward contract is created, it has zero value. As the price of the underlying changes, one party gains and the other loses. The party to which the contract has positive value is therefore holding an asset and is subject to the risk that the other party will default. Of course, it might not take much of a change in rates or prices for this counterparty to find itself holding a liability. In that case, the other party would assume the risk of default.

Because a forward contract is similar to a swap, the general considerations in analyzing credit risk are similar. A swap, however, is a series of future payments whereas a forward contract is but one future payment. Thus, there is usually more at stake in a swap. For a swap, the risk of default can take on two forms. One is the *current risk*, which is the risk that any payments due immediately cannot be made. The other is the *potential risk*, which is the risk that future payments cannot be made. Potential risk is much harder to gauge and is typically done by simulating future market conditions combined with best estimates of the counterparty's ability to pay under those conditions. The amount of current risk is reflected in the market value, sometimes called *replacement value*, of the swap.

Keep in mind, however, that a swap involves a series of payments from each side to the other. There is a quid pro quo relationship between the two parties. Because each party bears risk from the other party, the risks serve to partially offset. Thus, a plain vanilla swap between two parties of high credit quality would entail extremely low credit risk. Only the net amount owed would be at risk, and each party would accept the other's credit risk in return for a bilateral acceptance of its own credit risk. Moreover, for interest rate swaps, there is no payment of the notional principal, so the amount at risk is much lower than it might appear, particularly if you measure the size of the contract by the notional principal.

For that reason, the credit risk of interest rate swaps is remarkably small relative to the credit risk assumed in a bond, note, or commercial loan. In a typical arrangement, the lender remits say $10 million, perhaps unsecured, to a corporation and expects to receive a stream of interest payments of say 8% a year for three years after which it expects to get back the $10 million. This kind of transaction happens every day. In an interest rate swap, however, the principal is not at risk because it is never paid, and only the net interest payment is made. On some payment dates, one party makes the payment; on others, the other party makes the payment. So the stream of interest payments at risk has a very good chance of being only about one-half of what it would be under a loan. A common rule of thumb is that the actual risk is estimated to be only 1% to 2% of the notional principal.

Of course, I am not implying that there is no credit risk. Indeed, there are reasons to be concerned. An individual transaction may appear to have little credit risk, but if a party is engaged in numerous transactions and does a poor job of managing the risk, the likelihood of a default is much higher.

There are several ways in which firms manage credit risk. Probably the most common is based on the principle of diversification, which in this context means to limit the amount of business done with a given party. Another method is the use of collateral. The parties to a typical transaction may or may not specify a collateral requirement up front, and/or they may specify that as the underlying prices or rates move, collateral must be posted. If the counterparty is a bank, then it might require that the end user maintain a line of credit at the bank. Swap subsidiaries have been created by many swap dealers to separate the swap business from the banking or investment business. This can permit the subsidiary to acquire a higher rating than its parent company. These subsidiaries are often called *special-purpose derivatives vehicles, special-purpose entities,* or *enhanced derivatives products companies.*

Some swap contracts require marking-to-market, just as in the futures market. Though not done daily, the process works in much the same way. Any net gain or loss is distributed, and the swap is rewritten at the current market rate for a swap with that remaining term.

As discussed in Essays 6 and 9, most of the time the parties to a plain vanilla swap agree to net any individual payments, which greatly reduces the credit risk. In addition, if the two parties have done many transactions with each other, then close-out netting is usually arranged to further reduce the risk. For example, suppose XYZ does numerous swaps and perhaps other derivatives with a particular dealer. Some of those transactions have positive value to XYZ and some have negative value. Suppose XYZ defaults. Then without netting, XYZ might find that it could default on all contracts in which it owes the dealer more than the dealer owes it and demand payment on the contracts in which the dealer owes it more than it owes the dealer. This practice, called *cherrypicking*, is considered unhealthy and exacerbates the credit risk. Nor should the nondefaulting party be able to walk away from amounts that it owes to the defaulting counterparty. A close-out netting arrangement provides that only the net amount of all of the derivative transactions between the two parties is owed. There are several different forms of netting, including those that incorporate net values owed under all business transactions, such as general purpose loans, and all have the power to reduce the credit risk.

The credit risk issue is a complex one, but when all is said and done, the markets have done a remarkable job of managing this risk. Actual credit losses have been quite small. Interestingly, one of the largest defaults was induced by the U.K. legal system. During the 1980s the London borough of Hammersmith and Fulham had entered into a number of swaps that had negative market value, A U.K. court invoked the doctrine of *ultra vires*, declaring that the municipality had no authority to enter into the swaps in the first place. This ruling was upheld by the House of Lords in 1991. The resulting defaults accounted for about one-half of all swap defaults recorded up to that time. So government and the legal system can be a source of risk as well. It is important to verify that the courts will enforce the contracts, especially such provisions as close-out netting. This will generally be the case in countries with more advanced markets and legal systems, but it is not necessarily clear in some of the countries of the so-called emerging markets.

As you should recall, we covered credit derivatives in Essay 18. They are derivative instruments that can be used to transfer credit risk from one party to another. Credit derivatives generally are used to transfer the credit risk of loans or bonds and should not be confused with the topic of this essay, the credit risk of derivatives. That said, there is no reason why the credit risk of derivatives could not be managed using credit derivatives. As it turns out, however, the credit risk of derivatives is, as noted, relatively low and manageable by less complex measures.

FOR MORE READING

Hendricks, Darryll. "Netting Agreements and the Credit Exposure of OTC Derivatives Portfolios." *Federal Reserve Bank of New York Quarterly Review* 19 (Spring 1994): 7–18.

Smithson, Charles W. *Managing Financial Risk: A Guide to Derivative Products, Financial Engineering, and Value Maximization*, 3rd ed. New York: McGraw-Hill, 1998, chap. 17.

Smithson, Charles, with Greg Hayt. "Exposure Measures." *Risk* 9 (October 1996): 70–71, 73.

TEST YOUR KNOWLEDGE

1. Why is the credit risk of an option one-directional?
2. Why is the credit risk of interest rate swaps overstated when considering notional principal?
3. What are the two primary means by which the credit risk of derivatives is managed?
4. What type of problem does close-out netting avoid?

Operational Risk

The derivatives revolution has led to enormous advances in the measurement and management of market and credit risk. As we know, taking market risk leads to taking credit risk. But taking any position creates another type of risk called *operational risk*, which is occasionally referred to as *operations risk* and sometimes even *operating risk*.

It is difficult to give a precise definition of operational risk. The Bank for International Settlements defines it as "the risk of loss resulting from inadequate or failed internal processes, people and systems or from external events." Basically, operational risk encompasses the threat of financial loss resulting from failures in an organization's operations, which can arise internally or from external forces. Operational risk is, therefore, the risk arising from people, processes, technology, and events.

Operational risk was made vividly clear through the events of September 11, 2001. The operations of all financial institutions were affected by the shutdown of the U.S. financial markets. Some institutions were directly affected by the attack. One firm, Cantor Fitzgerald, had its main offices on the 101st to 103rd floors of One World Trade Center destroyed and lost over 600 employees. Many firms that were not directly affected were able to restore operations quickly as a result of maintaining off-site backup systems, and Cantor Fitzgerald itself was trading within a week. Some of the lessons learned in the 1993 bombing of the World Trade Center had made many financial firms realize how vulnerable they were to a complete loss of operations and their financial records. Other lessons were learned simply through common sense. Business operations can be affected at any time, and it does not require an act of terrorism. A flood that went through the underground tunnels of the Chicago financial district on April 13, 1992, shut down operations of the Chicago Board of Trade and the Chicago Mercantile Exchange, resulting in a significant loss of transaction volume as traders took their transactions to foreign futures exchanges.

Hurricane Katrina hit New Orleans and the Gulf Coast in August 2005 and gave a particularly strong lesson in operational risk management. One small New Orleans business named Intercosmos provided data backup systems to other companies. Obviously a faraway company could be using Intercosmos's services and thereby be exposed itself to operational risk. Fortunately, Intercosmos had its own excellent operational risk plan. It was positioned on the tenth floor of a building and stocked with generators, fuel, and large supplies of food and water. Intercosmos successfully maintained operations throughout Hurricane Katrina and its aftermath. In contrast, vacuum cleaner manufacturer Oreck had its only factory in Long Beach, Mississippi, and its headquarters 75 miles away in New Orleans. Its emergency plans were to move its operations from Long Beach to New Orleans or its headquarters from New Orleans to Long Beach. It did not figure on both facilities being hit simultaneously. Nonetheless, quick thinking and an aggressive response plan enabled Oreck to reopen the Long Beach factory and conduct its administrative work from Houston only 11 days after the storm made landfall.[1]

Another principal source of operational risk is computers. So much of what we do to function in life is dependent on computers that operational risk of enormous magnitude can result from hackers, viruses, spyware, and events such as the mere turning of the calendar to a new century. On top of that, dishonest employees with access to highly secure information add another layer of threat. So many companies have information on individuals' social security numbers, credit card numbers, e-mail passwords, and the like that vulnerability is at an all-time high.

For firms that trade, the threat of a single trader jeopardizing the viability of an organization is a very real possibility. Ever since Nick Leeson, a 28-year-old clerk in the Singapore office of Baring's Bank, single-handedly brought down a conservative 200-year-old institution, this new type of risk emerged. Leeson was responsible for introducing the world to *rogue trader risk*, the threat of a single isolated person destroying an organization through speculative trading.[2]

Of course, organizations are also exposed to operational risk even from honest mistakes. An employee who unknowingly enters wrong information into a system can subject the firm to an obligation that can be quite costly.

Operational risk is a risk to virtually any company, but it can be particularly acute for financial institutions because they engage in so many

[1] Unfortunately Oreck has since moved its operations from the Gulf Coast to Tennessee, citing the increased cost of insurance.

[2] It is unclear whether the term "rogue trader" originated with Leeson, but he used the term as the name of his book on how he destroyed Barings.

transactions. Every deposit, every withdrawal, every loan or loan payment, and every securities purchase or sale is a transaction. Each transaction represents the potential for something to go wrong. The wrong number encoded on a deposit can result in an individual checking account customer receiving credit for an incorrect amount of money. Some individuals have used a mistake like that to steal from the bank.

But in spite of, or perhaps because of, its extreme exposure, banks have also been in the forefront of advancements in understanding, measuring, and managing operational risk. One of the reasons why operational risk is so difficult to manage is that it is so difficult to measure. Operational risk events do not occur often, which is certainly a good thing. When they do occur, the focus is on responding to the event by correcting the problem, attempting to minimize the loss, and in many cases deciding what to say to a customer, regulator, or reporter. There is little documentation of such events and hence very little recorded history of operational risk events. While there have been some efforts for firms to share information so as to build a large database, most firms are reluctant to provide this kind of information to competitors. The Bank for International Settlements in 2002 conducted a survey of 89 banks and found about 47,000 operational risk events. The majority of events occurred in retail banking, suggesting that errors related to personal deposits and check clearing were the most frequent. Of far less frequency, however, but similar in loss magnitude, were events in commercial banking, meaning losses associated with ordinary business transactions with corporate customers. High-frequency events included external fraud and execution, delivery, and process management. High-loss events included execution, delivery, and process management and also damage to physical assets.

This kind of information is extremely useful because it shows organizations where the greatest risk potential lies. A bank might never suffer a substantial loss in damage to physical assets. Indeed, only about 1.4% of the events reported were of this type. But financial losses from physical damage accounted for almost a fourth of all reported losses. Thus, a bank should focus considerable effort on protecting its physical assets.

Three principal methods of managing operational risk are insurance, outsourcing, and setting aside additional capital. Although insurance companies usually do take on some of the responsibility for reducing the risk of the insured client, insurance is primarily designed to compensate for the loss, not to prevent it. Outsourcing is becoming increasingly popular, but in a sense, it only passes the risk off to another party. If that other party does not engage in sufficient operational risk management, the risk still remains. Setting aside additional capital is much like insurance. In fact, it is a form of self-insurance. It does not reduce the likelihood of the event. It should be noted, however, that the new Basel II Bank Capital Regulations now require that about 8% of the capital set aside to meet regulatory requirements must be allocated to operational risk. Thus, like it or not, banks are required to use this form of operational risk management.

Of course, nonbank companies are generally not obliged to engage in any form of operational risk management, but most firms do. Airlines, for example, have action plans for such costly contingencies as power outages, extreme weather, terrorist attacks, strikes, and the like, but as we know, when such events occur, the actions taken by the airlines do not necessarily solve or even ease the problem. Nonetheless, we should not always blame the airlines or the government when these events occur. Operational risk is not the same as the ordinary day-to-day price fluctuations that traders face in the financial markets. Each risk event is different from the last. A plan that once worked may not work today. New risks arise constantly, and often the event must be experienced before anyone appreciates its frequency and magnitude.

I must share this story from my distant past that tells us from where we have come in the area of operational risk management. Several decades ago and fresh out of school, I began to work in the operational division of a large bank. We provided a variety of services to companies that helped these firms accelerate their cash flow. After a couple of years of employment, I was put in charge of this area. We had a rather informal system of operational risk management, which was my boss telling me "Chance, don't let anything bad happen today." Operational risk events were at that time viewed as preventable if the people in charge monitored the activities and took actions before the events occurred. As a result, if such events occurred, those of us in charge felt personally responsible. To manage that risk, I needed to be able to predict such events as when the computers would go down or when the weather would delay a critical shipment. Needless to say, the job was very stressful, and I soon learned that a career change was advisable. The rest is history.[3]

Fortunately, the banking business has learned that operational risk events come with the territory of providing financial services. They represent

---

[3] On at least two occasions, however, our operational risk management strategy presented me with a most unusual experience. I was instructed to personally take an approximately $100 million check to the Federal Reserve Bank, which was one block away, for deposit so that anything that delayed the processing of that check through the normal check-clearing system would not result in the bank paying a day's interest to a corporate customer without collecting the funds from the Federal Reserve. It was certainly the most important one-block walk of my life. I concluded that walking down the street with a $100 million check and a Federal Reserve deposit form was probably going to be the closest I would ever get to being in control of that much money; hence, another reason to change careers.

random events that are largely unpredictable. Rarely is anyone personally responsible, which is a fresh and much-needed change in this day and age in which almost every physical or financial loss to anyone is followed by litigation blaming someone or some organization. As more data become available on operational risk events, organizations can obtain better quantitative measures of operational risk. Such analysis nearly always provides improvements in how a firm prepares for such events and how it responds to them. And that is what operational risk management is all about.

FOR MORE READING

Basel Committee on Banking Supervision. "Sound Practices for the Management and Supervision of Operational Risk." (February 2003). www.bis.org.

Chernobai, Anna, Svetlozar T. Rachev, and Frank J. Fabozzi. *Operational Risk: A Guide to Basel II Capital Requirements, Models, and Analysis*. Hoboken, NJ: John Wiley & Sons, 2007.

Smithson, Charles, and Paul Song. "Quantifying Operational Risk." *Risk* 17 (July 2004): 57–59.

TEST YOUR KNOWLEDGE

1. Why is operational risk so difficult to manage?
2. What is rogue trader risk?
3. What are the principal means of managing operational risk?

Risk Management in an Organization

The use of derivatives has led to many concerns about the risk that an organization takes on. These essays and the plethora of writings by others on derivatives and risk management reflect a great deal of knowledge that has been acquired through experience and creativity. But most of this knowledge focuses on markets, instruments, and quantitative techniques. It is easy to forget that there are many organizational and human elements that confound even the best efforts to use derivatives wisely and manage risk effectively. In this essay I want to cover some of these "other" points that so often get ignored.

The term "risk management" has become an important buzzword in business circles. Most every company now likes to state that it is practicing some form of risk management. In reality, managing risk is the central focus of the entire discipline of finance. I have attended conferences on risk management that spend excessive amounts of time having speakers illustrate their latest successful investment strategies. What some people view as risk management, however, is not what risk management really entails.

When I think of risk management, I think of a practice that focuses on defining the risk that an organization wants, identifying the risk that the organization has, and aligning the latter to equal the former. Risk management is an organized, concerted, well-documented effort, and not just a group of people saying they are watching their risk as if it were some kind of corporate waistline that goes on an occasional diet. Saying you are practicing risk management sounds good, especially to senior management, but it can give a false and dangerous sense of security.

Let us take a look at the different ways in which an organization can practice risk management. Consider first an organization that practices risk management in a decentralized manner. Each division or group within the organization is responsible for taking the appropriate level of risk. As a result, we might find one division hedging and another speculating. At the overall firm level, however, there may be no one getting the big picture of the organization's risk. This structure is highly inefficient and potentially quite dangerous. The inefficiency arises from the fact that some efforts are duplicated. For example, suppose one division is a net buyer of Canadian dollars and the other is a net seller.[1] The first division hedges by buying forwards on Canadian dollars, and the second hedges by selling forwards on Canadian dollars. Looking at the big picture, there is likely to be no need to hedge as the two positions are somewhat offsetting.[2] Each division, however, is concerned with and responsible for its own performance, so each would be reluctant to cede over risk management to a higher level. But turning over risk management to a higher level is what should be done.

Indeed, some companies organize their risk management in a centralized manner. In the previous example, each division would be prohibited from hedging. At or near the top of the firm would be a group assigned to monitor the overall risk and engage in risk-reducing or risk-increasing transactions. Such an organization would be more efficient but would be subject to the concern expressed in the previous paragraph that division managers would have little control over their own risk. Nonetheless, a centralized risk management structure is almost surely better and offers other advantages. In particular, it leads to improvements in the allocation of capital to divisions and in performance measurement. Each division is likely to have different degrees of risk. Consequently, the firm must have sufficient capital to support the risk taken in the overall firm. The total capital required can be broken down into the capital required for each division. Divisions that take more risk should be assigned more capital. Extending this notion, we obtain a basis for performance measurement. The performance of each division should be evaluated by taking into account the cost of the capital required to support the risk taken by the division. In this manner, riskier divisions will have a higher hurdle to clear in order to show superior performance.

Centralized risk management also tends to lead to improvements in pricing the firm's products and services and allows a firm to identify pockets of exposure it might not otherwise know it had. Centralized risk management also typically leads to better collection and management of risk data.

---

[1] A net buyer of Canadian dollars might be a division that purchases raw materials from Canada and pays in Canadian dollars. A net seller of Canadian dollars might be a division that sells finished products or services in Canada and is paid in Canadian dollars.
[2] Whether they would truly offset depends on the size and timing of the cash flows of the two divisions. But if one buys the currency and one sells, there is at least some offsetting of positions and a reduced need for hedging.

Centralized risk management, however, is not the ultimate stage in risk management. That term has been reserved for *enterprise risk management*, which encompasses a centralized risk management system that includes *all* of the risks of a company. By "all" of the risks, we are typically adding in risks that are usually managed by insurance. Thus, the insurance policies that a firm might purchase to protect it against lawsuits and casualty losses would be managed in the same group that manages the firm's market and credit risk.[3]

The principal advantage of enterprise risk management is that by bringing all risks under the same umbrella, the firm has a better overall picture of its risk. There is little fundamental difference in a loss arising from a casualty event and a loss arising from a market movement or a default. A loss is a loss. Enterprise risk management can focus solely on managing all kinds of risks that can lead to loss as well as create possibilities for gains.

Another advantage of enterprise risk management is that it allows the firm to look for opportunities to manage both risks simultaneously. For example, if a firm is exposed to risk that one of its factories will be damaged due to a hurricane, that risk has no reason to be correlated with the risk that exchange rates will result in a loss in value of its foreign receivables. Because of this fact, some large financial institutions have found a way to package coverage of both risks into the same product, resulting in lower overall costs.

Enterprise risk management is only a slight step further from centralized risk management, but its emphasis on all risks concentrates the process in the hands of a specialized group within the firm that can focus on risk, while other groups can focus on what they do well, such as provide products and services, without worrying so much about risk.

Firms that use centralized risk management typically have a person called a *chief risk officer* or a slight variation of that title. This person should have direct authority over all of the firm's risks and should be reportable to the chief executive officer (CEO).

Of course, large banks typically have advanced risk management systems. Unfortunately, they are not found often enough in other organizations. Some organizations have virtually no risk management, as we shall see in Essay 72. In all too many others, the company adopts a program that it

---

[3] Many organizations have departments called "risk management." These departments have existed for many years and typically deal with insurance and not market and credit risks. In fact, the term "risk management" has existed as a synonym for insurance for many years. There is also a branch of engineering called "risk management."

calls risk management or sometimes enterprise risk management, but, in fact, it does very little to measure and monitor risk. Yet it pats itself on the back and feels good, because it believes it is practicing enterprise risk management.

Realistically, many companies are far too small to have risk management groups and chief risk officers. So what does such a company do? Is practicing risk management only for the big boys? Not at all.

Even a small company can consolidate its risk management into a single small group within the finance area. The important point is that there should be a group of financial experts who have access to accurate and current information on a firm's risks. At any randomly chosen time, the CEO should be able to call the person in charge of risk management and receive a briefing on all of the firm's risks, complete with quantitative assessments. If the risks are too much or too little, the firm should have a system in place in which the risk can be altered quickly. To make such a system work, the firm must have a risk management policy that defines its risk tolerance by identifying the risks it is willing to take and those it does not want to take and establishes policies and procedures for monitoring risk and adjusting the level of risk. These requirements are not too great for even a small organization.

But nothing, absolutely nothing, is more important than the necessity for separating those who manage the risk from those who take the risk. As we shall see in Essay 72, those who take the risk cannot be ones to decide if the amount of risk they are taking is consistent with the firm's overall policies. If it seems that risk management personnel are the policemen of the organization, that is simply not true. Risk management personnel should be viewed as facilitators. As one risk manager was quoted as saying:

> *Risk managers are often portrayed as the folks who make a living by saying "no." "No, you can't do that trade" or "No, you can't launch that product." But the best risk managers contend that they actually make their living by finding the right way to say "yes."*[4]

Risk managers should focus on making sure the risk being taken is consistent with the risk that the organization wants to take. If that means occasionally saying no, then so be it. But more often than not, it should involve saying "Yes. The risk is within our accepted parameters. We can do that."

---

[4] Yasuko Okamoto of JP Morgan, quoted in *AsiaRisk* (November 2000): 23.

FOR MORE READING

Allen, Steven. *Financial Risk Management: A Practitioner's Guide to Managing Market and Credit Risk*. Hoboken, NJ: John Wiley & Sons, 2003.

Chance, Don M., and Robert Brooks. *An Introduction to Derivatives and Risk Management*, 7th ed. Mason, OH: Thomson South-Western, 2007, chap. 16.

Lam, James. *Enterprise Risk Management: From Incentives to Controls*. Hoboken, NJ: John Wiley & Sons, 2003.

Shimpi, Prakash. *Integrating Corporate Risk Management*. New York: Texere, 2001.

Smithson, Charles W. *Managing Financial Risk: A Guide to Derivative Products, Financial Engineering, and Value Maximization*, 3rd ed. New York: McGraw-Hill, 1998, chaps. 19, 22.

TEST YOUR KNOWLEDGE

1. Identify the three forms in which risk management might be practiced within an organization.
2. Explain the difference between the most concentrated form of risk management and the second most concentrated form of risk management. (These are two of the three answers given in question 1.)
3. What is the most important organizational consideration in designing a risk management system with respect to lines of authority?

Accounting and Disclosure of Derivatives

Financial innovation, for all of its benefits in making financial markets better, has led to many complex questions about how to account for, tax, and regulate derivatives transactions. In this essay I take a look at the accounting and disclosure issues. Let me first note that I am not an accountant and I do not intend to get too far into the details of derivatives accounting and disclosure, but I will give you an overview.[1]

The practice of accounting is based on the principle of recording historical business transactions and reporting them in such a manner that a fair and honest picture of the past performance and current financial status of a business is given. Accounting does not pretend to measure the risks taken in the past, reflect differences in the timing of cash flows, or provide estimates of the future values of transactions. It also does not attempt to assess the reason why management made a company enter into a transaction.[2]

Accounting systems produce financial information, much of which is used to do the above-mentioned things. Thus, it is important that accounting do a good job of what it is supposed to do, but no more. Financial information is useful and important, but accounting is not finance. It is not valuation or risk management. It should go only as far and no further than dictated by the principles on which it is based.

---

[1] The usual disclosure that professional advice should be sought on accounting matters certainly applies here. My own opinions are nothing more than opinions, and they may be worth little.

[2] That said, there are surely many accountants who would disagree. Judging from the activities of professional accounting firms and the extension of their work into the consulting arena, the practice of accounting has overlapped with these other practices. This is probably not a good thing. Just remember Arthur Anderson and Enron.

The problems of accounting for derivatives are numerous. In fact, it took the accounting profession, as represented in the United States by the Financial Accounting Standards Board (FASB), 10 years to "resolve" the issue of how to account for derivatives.[3] Of course, the issue is hardly resolved, but at least some clarity has been added by its statement FAS (Financial Accounting Standard) 133, which went into effect in 2000. Similar rules were put into place for foreign firms under IAS (International Accounting Standard) 39, which went into effect in 2005.[4] Let us take a look at why FAS 133 was so necessary and such a long time coming.

Prior to FAS 133, most firms tried to use a practice called *hedge accounting*. Basically the idea behind hedge accounting is that if derivatives are used in a hedge, the hedger need not report the use of the derivative until the hedge has been terminated. Consider a company that owns a bond and hedges it by selling a futures contract. When the bond is sold, the gain or loss on the futures is added to the sale price of the bond to determine an effective selling price for the bond. No harm, no foul.[5]

The problem comes from the abuse of hedge accounting. A simple example will suffice. Consider a firm planning to issue a bond at a later date. It sells a bond futures contract today. When the time arrives to issue the bond, let us assume that interest rates have risen. The futures price will be lower, and the futures contract will show a profit. Suppose then that the firm

---

[3] In the United States accounting standards are set by the FASB. This was an independent trade association of professional accountants. Its standards were not obligatory, but auditors would be unable to completely certify financial statements if these standards were not adhered to. Following the passage of the Sarbanes-Oxley Act of 2002, the FASB became a de facto arm of a new oversight organization, the Public Company Accounting Oversight Board, whose budget must be approved by the United States Securities and Exchange Commission (SEC). Thus, the FASB is effectively no longer an independent trade association but the fingertip of the long arm of the U.S. government. In addition, the SEC requires publicly traded companies to comply with FASB standards. In short, accounting is not law, but it is pretty close.

[4] IAS 39 is slightly more stringent, calling for much more use of marking-to-market (essentially current value accounting) of assets and liabilities in general. By the way, we ought to comment that the United States has its own accounting standards, while pretty much the rest of the world adheres to a common but slightly different set of standards. There is much talk about merging these standards. Whether this will occur before the United States goes metric is hard to say.

[5] OK, this is a basketball analogy. For you nonathletes, it means that one basketball player commits a foul against the other but the foul had no impact on what was happening in the game. "No harm, no foul" means that the foul is not called. The team being fouled is unhappy, but the game is not delayed.

decides not to issue the bond. The hedge is therefore never undertaken. The profit from the futures is then used to augment the current-period profit. If the firm had gone ahead and issued the bond, the futures profit would have effectively raised the amount of the proceeds from the sale of the bond, implicitly lowering the interest rate on the debt. But the gain is spread out and fairly hidden over the life of the debt. By not issuing the debt and realizing the futures profit as a current-period profit, the firm can pump up current earnings. Given the obsession with short-term earnings in most companies, the incentives to annul the hedge are quite large. If the hedge had resulted in a loss, the firm could have effectively buried the loss in the bond issue. It is conceivable that many firms engaged in hedges of future actions that were not firm commitments, thereby allowing them some of this type of flexibility. Thus, abuses of hedge accounting appeared to be common.[6]

Critics of hedge accounting argued that the period-to-period fluctuations in the values of derivatives used in hedges resulted in gains and losses that were not showing up until the hedges were concluded. Thus, a quarterly, or potentially even annual, report would not reveal gains and losses on derivatives currently in place. Opponents argued that to reflect these gains and losses while a hedge is in place would result in more income volatility. Since hedges are designed to reduce risk, greater income volatility would give the exact opposite impression.

After years of study, the FASB took action by introducing FAS 133, which started off by establishing the principle that derivatives should be reflected on financial statements in any period in which they are used. The notion of not showing a derivative used in a hedge until the hedge is over simply makes little sense. If a firm is engaged in a financial transaction, it is important that this information be revealed. Thus, derivatives were required to be *marked-to-market*, meaning that the gains and losses in their values would have to be reflected in current income accounts. To avoid the problem of making income more volatile, a new classification system for hedges was designed.

FAS 133 defines four types of transactions involving derivatives: fair value hedges, cash flow hedges, hedges of net investment in foreign operations, and speculation. A *fair value hedge* is a transaction that uses a derivative to hedge the market value of an asset. Such a transaction is typically a hedge in which one owns an asset, expects to sell the asset at a later date, is concerned that the price could fall by that later date, and uses a

---

[6] It is unclear whether there was as much abuse as everyone feared. I have no knowledge that anyone really studied the matter to obtain a tally. Nonetheless, the potential for abuse was quite large.

derivative to hedge the future price of the asset. Gains and losses on the hedge are recorded in current income along with gains and losses in the value of the underlying asset. Thus, if the hedge works as it should, current income is unaffected.

This is the type of transaction that hedge accounting before FAS 133 would handle properly. A few other stipulations have been added, however, one being that the hedge must be firm and well documented. Thus, if a company planned to sell an asset at a future date, it would need documentation in advance that indicated a desire to do so. Then the sale would be expected to go through as planned. Little, if any, flexibility is afforded. In addition, the firm must have a means of assessing the effectiveness of the hedge. If the gains and losses on the derivative do not match the gains and losses in the value of the underlying, the hedge will be deemed ineffective. Then hedge accounting will not be permitted and this would make income more volatile because gains and losses on the underlying will occur in different periods than gains and losses on the hedge. We will talk more about this point later.

A *cash flow hedge* is the type that would have been subject to abuse under the old hedge accounting standards. A cash flow hedge is a hedge of an anticipated future cash flow. A common example would be a firm planning to take out a loan at a future date. The derivative is put into place for the purpose of monetizing movements in interest rates that occur between the date on which the hedge is established and the date on which the hedge is terminated, which is the date on which the loan is taken out. Naturally, marking derivatives to market will generate gains and losses, and there is no underlying to offset, as in a fair value hedge, because a position in the underlying has not yet been taken. To solve this problem, the rule stipulates that gains and losses on the derivative flow through to a temporary holding account called *other comprehensive income* (OCI). OCI is a balance sheet account that appears between debt and equity. As noted, it is a temporary account. When the hedge is terminated, its balance is transferred to the asset or liability account that is used to record the hedged transaction. By putting the derivative gains and losses in OCI, the figure is publicly reported, but OCI is not a current income account, so current income is not made more volatile by hedging. OCI is simply a place to put the figure until the hedge is over.

Of course, all of this presumes that the hedge is "effective." Both fair value hedges and cash flow hedges must be deemed effective. Unfortunately, FAS 133 does not define what is meant by "effective" or how to test hedge effectiveness. The industry has adopted an informal standard whereby effectiveness is defined as the derivative gain or loss being equal to 80% to 125% of the gain or loss on the underlying. FAS 133 requires firms to establish a standard of effectiveness, to periodically test effectiveness, and to put the portion of derivative gains and losses that is outside of the range of effectiveness into income. Cash flow hedges must also be well documented and must be considered highly likely to occur.

The third type of derivatives transaction is the *foreign currency hedge*. Perhaps because foreign currency futures existed before interest rate futures, the accounting profession has treated foreign currency hedges with separate standards. Although FAS 133 stipulates that foreign currency hedges must be classified as such, ultimately these hedges are treated as either fair value or cash flow hedges.

The final type of derivative transaction is *speculation*. Of course, firms and individuals that take risky positions are trading to make income. As such, derivatives gains and losses from speculation are, as they always have been, marked-to-market in the current period, and gains and losses flow directly to income.

FAS 133 does not solve all of the problems of accounting for derivatives, and it actually creates a few more. It does make progress, however, and we can always be thankful for a little clarity. Accounting, like regulation, is a work in progress. The fact that it must be fine-tuned is not a reflection of any weakness in accounting but of the complexity and dynamic nature of the derivatives world.

Now let us talk a little about disclosure. Concerned about the potentially large risks of firms that use derivatives, in 1997 the SEC issued Release No. 33-7386, which required that companies that use derivatives disclose this usage. Companies have to identify their exposures, describe how these exposures are managed, and reveal quantitative information on their derivatives usage. To do this, companies are permitted to use tables with summary figures, sensitivity analysis showing how cash flows would vary with certain changes in underlying risk factors, or quantitative measures such as value at risk, which we covered in Essay 66. Thus, annual reports started containing this type of information.

This requirement stirred quite a controversy when it was first proposed. Yours truly was a very vocal opponent, and I still have problems with the disclosure requirement. The principal concern is that it effectively forces a company to tell how it engages in risk management. This strikes me as private information that a company should not have to reveal to its competitors. In addition, the use of derivatives is singled out as a source of risk when, in fact, numerous other risks are not singled out. Now, I am not arguing for more disclosure of these other sources of risks, but think about it. Most airlines anticipate a crash on a rare occasion. They are quite aware of how many people are likely to die and how much the company is likely to suffer in financial loss and possible loss of confidence if a crash occurs. Airlines certainly must have an emergency plan that goes into place when a crash occurs. We do not require airlines to tell us how they plan for a crash and how they manage this risk. Frankly, I do not think we want to know how many people an airline thinks will die if one of its planes crashes. But not disclosing how the airline manages this risk does not mean it is not doing a good job of managing the risk. In fact, it has an enormous incentive in the form of the marketplace to do a good job of managing this risk.

Singling out derivatives for disclosure is simply inconsistent. There are many other operating and financial risks that are much more severe. In fact, virtually no risk is any greater than the risk of loss of customer confidence in the company. How companies measure and manage this risk ought to be confidential. Fortunately it still is, though perhaps the SEC will someday pull that plug too.

In summary, you can see that I am all for accounting for derivatives but somewhat against disclosure. Having said that, I must add that I do find reading the disclosure information in annual reports interesting. It may well be helpful to financial analysts and investors. I would not even be surprised if companies would continue to report this information even if the SEC relaxed the rule. But there is something about Big Brother making companies do this that makes me uneasy. I am willing to trust that companies will manage risk.

FOR MORE READING

Chance, Don M., and Robert Brooks. *An Introduction to Derivatives and Risk Management*, 7th ed. Mason, OH: Thomson South-Western, 2007, chap. 16.

Gastineau, Gary L., Donald J. Smith, and Rebecca Todd. *Risk Management, Derivatives, and Financial Analysis under SFAS No. 133*. Charlottesville, VA: Research Foundation of AIMR and Blackwell Series in Finance, 2001.

Kawaller, Ira G. "What Analysts Need to Know About Accounting for Derivatives." *Financial Analysts Journal* 60 (March–April 2004): 24–30.

TEST YOUR KNOWLEDGE

1. How is a fair value hedge accounted for under FAS 133?
2. How is a cash flow hedge accounted for under FAS 133?
3. How is hedging effectiveness usually gauged?
4. Under SEC regulations, how can derivatives activities be disclosed?

Worst Practices in Derivatives

As covered many times in other essays, derivatives are instruments for transferring risk. They have been correctly compared to insurance, because they permit one party to pay, either directly or indirectly, a premium to engage another party to take on a particular risk. Like insurance, derivatives must have a cost that is relatively low compared to the magnitude of the risk being transferred. That is, they must be efficient. No one would be willing to transfer a risk if the cost of doing so is excessive in relation to the risk.[1] Because the payment made to induce someone to take a risk is ordinarily small in relation to the potential loss, derivatives (and insurance) have a significant degree of leverage. Therein lies the potential danger.

A party can engage in a seemingly small derivatives transaction and end up destroying an organization. Unfortunately, this lesson has been learned in several very painful ways by some well-known organizations. These stories are quite interesting, and even entertaining in a slightly perverse way.[2] Most important, they teach us lessons. The first person to discover that certain mushrooms were poisonous paid a heavy price, but the human race benefited greatly. It is tempting for us to heavily criticize those who carelessly used derivatives as a form of financial poison, but we must keep things in perspective. What we know now is not what others knew in years past. Nonetheless, it is virtually impossible not to see how lack of common sense and out-of-control egos made some of these disasters happen. In this essay we take a look at a few stories of how organizations mishandled derivatives. In the next essay we look at how derivatives should be handled.

---

[1] For example, you would not insure a $30,000 automobile by paying $10,000 a year to an insurance company. Insurance efficiency lies in providing a cost sufficiently low relative to the value of the insured asset to justify the transfer of risk.

[2] At least one was entertaining enough to make into a movie. See *Rogue Trader* in "For More Reading."

Probably the three most widely cited stories of derivatives disasters were Orange County, Barings, and Procter & Gamble. Orange County, California, is one of the wealthiest counties in the United States. In the period leading up to fall 1994, its publicly elected treasurer Robert Citron, a 69-year old veteran of 24 years in the office, was riding on a wave of seemingly outstanding performance in the county's investment fund. This fund managed the excess cash of the county and also accepted deposits from various other California governmental agencies. It pooled the funds and operated what should have been a low-risk, short-term money market account. The fund was performing quite well, beating other funds by an impressive margin. In an upcoming election, however, Citron's opponent examined the strategy used by Citron and found that it was a time bomb waiting to explode. Nonetheless, the voters of Orange County, impressed with the fund's returns and Citron's explanation, reelected him.

It turns out that Citron was using reverse repurchase agreements to leverage the county's investments to a multiple of approximately 3. For example, the fund would hold, say, $100 million of Treasury notes and borrow another $100 million, pledging the notes as collateral. Then it would buy another $100 million of notes. It would then pledge those notes as collateral for another $100 million loan to be used to buy more notes. As a result, the approximately $7.5 billion fund controlled about $20 billion of Treasury notes. To the financially naive, the portfolio of $20 billion of U.S. government securities appeared safe. In terms of credit risk, it certainly was. And as long as interest rates remained stable or fell, the portfolio would perform quite acceptably if not quite well. The earnings from $20 billion were more than enough to pay the interest on the loans and leave a large return relative to the $7.5 billion original investment.

In late 1994, however, interest rates took a sharp turn upward. Rising interest rates, of course, mean falling prices of notes, and the fund began hemorrhaging, generating a market value loss of about $2 billion. The story hit the news, and the Orange County governing body, its board of supervisors, declared bankruptcy. Shock waves rippled across America. One of its wealthiest counties was bankrupt. Although it was unclear whether the county actually was bankrupt, there was no question that extreme leverage combined with sharp interest rate increases had combined to impose a massive loss on the county and its citizens.

Orange County then engaged in a period of budget tightness, layoffs, a reduction of services, and a series of lawsuits against the banks and brokers who had advised it on these transactions. Some settlements were reached, and a few years later, it emerged from bankruptcy. Mr. Citron was arrested but served no time. Prior to the problems he had argued that he knew what he was doing. After his arrest he was portrayed by his attorneys as virtually senile and having little real knowledge of finance.[3]

The Orange County story is not one of derivatives misuse, but therein lies one of the important lessons. The use of high leverage combined with seemingly low-risk securities can destroy an organization by itself. Derivatives are not required. Another lesson is that when performance is out of line with that of peers, one should look further into what is driving the performance. In this case, Citron's political opponent had seen the danger, but the voters of Orange County did not buy that story when they went to the polls. High returns are a strong selling point, and Citron had argued that he knew what he was doing.

Today Orange County is once again one of America's wealthiest counties. Let us move on. Barings Bank was a 200-year-old British institution that had financed the Napoleonic wars and held the accounts of Queen Elizabeth II. In 1994 it was destroyed by the trading of a 28-year-old clerk in its Singapore office. Nick Leeson had only a secondary school education but a talent for office management and organization. He had joined Barings in London and excelled in the back office. He was sent to the Barings Singapore office to improve its operations, not to trade. Leeson did an excellent job in Singapore but also found a way to start trading.

He began engaging in arbitrage by trading long and short positions on the Singapore Exchange and in Japan. Being long a contract in one market and short the same contract in the other, he was trying to take advantage of any pricing discrepancy. In such transactions, a gain is recorded on one contract and a loss is recorded on the other. Such profit opportunities are rare, however, because there are so many other traders processing the same information. Leeson manufactured his own profits by hiding his losses in a "special" account. By being the office manager, he controlled the "special" account and was able to keep it hidden from auditors. Consequently, the bank's top management in London began to notice Leeson's performance and rewarded him well. They even encouraged others in the bank to attempt to emulate Leeson.[4]

Leeson continued to hide losses, and his "special" account grew dangerously deep in the hole. Like so many others in similar situations, Leeson attempted to trade his way out of the problem. He began selling straddles, which means to sell a call and a put. This transaction generates cash that he used to meet margin calls and would be a profitable strategy if

---

[3] This strategy was evidently Citron's only one to clearly succeed.

[4] Fortunately no one did.

the market did not make a large move. But in February 1995 an earthquake in Kobe, Japan, sent the Japanese stock market reeling and Leeson's straddles deep underwater. Leeson had managed to erode the bank's $500 million of capital, thereby sending it into bankruptcy.

Leeson and his wife fled Singapore and ended up in Germany, where he was arrested by the German police. His attorneys wanted him extradited to England where it was felt he would be treated more fairly, but the British government was unable to come up with charges against him. Thus, Germany extradited him to Singapore, where he pled guilty to fraud and forgery and was sentenced to six and a half years in prison. During that time his wife filed for divorce and he contracted colon cancer. He was in excruciating pain and pled with the Singaporean authorities to treat him. He did receive surgery during that time and was released for good behavior after serving four and a half years.[5] Barings was eventually sold for £1 to the Dutch bank ING.

The lesson from the Leeson story is that a single person, given sufficient authority or lack of oversight, can destroy an organization. The term "rogue trader" began to be used in conjunction with Leeson and some others who have acted similarly.[6] But another lesson is identical to the one learned in Orange County. The performance Leeson had reported impressed senior management, but no one ever asked questions about Leeson. It would seem that management might want to know how a young man without a college education whose job was to organize the bookkeeping was able to contribute a huge percentage of the bank's profit. The bank's auditors had been unable to find anything wrong but had advised senior management that the potential for wrongdoing was great. Leeson was, after all, not only trading when he was not authorized but also in control of the risk management and the paperwork. The proverbial adage about not letting the fox guard the chicken coop was certainly the case here.

One of America's oldest and best-known companies is Procter & Gamble (P&G), manufacturer of thousands of consumer products and operating in dozens of countries around the world. Like most multinational firms, P&G faces a tremendous amount of exchange rate risk. It receives revenues in foreign currencies and eventually converts those revenues back into U.S. dollars. If the dollar increases in value, P&G receives fewer dollars

---

[5] Since that time, Leeson has completely recovered from the cancer, remarried, fathered a child, earned a college degree, written another book, and managed a soccer team. Living in Ireland, he offers his services as a public speaker and operates a website, www.nickleeson.com.

[6] See Leeson's own book *Rogue Trader* and the movie of the same name.

for a given amount of foreign currency. As such, P&G had for many years been a very active user of derivatives to hedge exchange rate risk. In late 1993, however, it began to engage in some complex swaps that involved pure speculation on foreign interest rates and exchange rates. If its guess turned out to be correct, P&G would find itself borrowing money at a very attractive rate. If not, it would end up borrowing money at an extremely unattractive rate. As can be expected, P&G guessed wrong. In April 1994 it announced that it had taken a $157 million loss, reflecting an effective borrowing rate of over 1,400 basis points over the commercial paper rate. Subsequent losses were uncovered that ran the tab up to about $200 million.

P&G sued its dealer, Bankers Trust (BT), in federal court in its home city of Cincinnati. P&G argued that the transaction should be declared null and void, because over-the-counter derivatives should have been viewed as securities and regulated by the Securities and Exchange Commission. P&G also claimed that BT had violated federal racketeering statutes and had engaged in fraud and breach of fiduciary duty. It argued that because it had maintained a long-standing relationship with BT, the latter had an obligation to advise it not to undertake such a transaction. It claimed that BT had misled it and had engaged in fraudulent sales tactics.

On the surface, P&G's case looked strong. BT's defense was that P&G had a very sophisticated treasury department that had operated as a profit center, meaning that the trading P&G did was for the purpose of taking risk and making a profit. P&G's treasury department did indeed have considerable experience in using derivatives. Unfortunately for BT, P&G was able to obtain copies of audiotapes of BT traders making fun of P&G for engaging in these transactions and implying that P&G was indeed being exploited.

P&G and BT settled out of court with P&G paying only about $35 million of the loss and assigning to BT some derivative transactions that had positive value. In spite of the out-of-court settlement, the judge made a ruling that over-the-counter derivatives were not securities, that there was no attempt to misrepresent, and that BT owed no fiduciary duty to P&G. The judge did, however, note that a dealer, being in possession of superior knowledge, had an obligation to disclose anything important.

From the P&G case, we learned a few more lessons. First, it seems safe to say that companies that specialize in nonfinancial products and services should not be speculating in financial markets. In particular, firms should not operate their treasury departments as profit centers. To believe that a team of corporate treasury specialists have the ability to forecast interest and exchange rates better than the rest of the financial world is pushing the limits of reasonableness. Also, it was clear that no one at P&G was watching what the treasury department was doing.

The P&G case in no way threatened the survival of one of America's best-known companies. Even the full loss of $200 million was only a tiny fraction of the company's net worth. But the ramifications of the P&G case had important implications well beyond the immediate participants. The case established standards that would be followed in future transactions. From that point forward, most dealers began to include language that made it clear that the dealer is a counterparty and not an advisor to the transaction.

The case also established that no federal agency should monitor over-the-counter derivatives transactions. Let the buyer and seller beware. But that is as it should be. Otherwise, the government will be telling participants they cannot engage in a mutually desirable transaction.

The stories covered here are the three highest-profile ones. Many of the losses were concentrated in the 1993 to 1994 period in which interest rates rose sharply. Quite a few involved Bankers Trust as a counterparty, which contributed greatly to that bank's decision to be acquired by Deutsche Bank. Although there are at least 70 stories of organizations announcing unexpected derivatives losses, most have not had the notoriety and impact of these three.[7] Virtually every year, however, there are a few more organizations to add to the growing list of those stung by the misuse of derivatives. In the next essay we look at how to avoid misusing derivatives and keep an organization off a list no one wants to be on.

FOR MORE READING

Boyle, Phelim, and Feidhlim Boyle. *Derivatives: The Tools That Changed Finance.* London: Risk Books, 2001, chap. 8.

Chance, Don M., and Robert Brooks. *An Introduction to Derivatives and Risk Management*, 7th ed. Mason, OH: Thomson South-Western, 2007, chap. 16.

Hull, John C. *Options, Futures, and Other Derivatives*, 6th ed. Upper Saddle River, NJ: Prentice-Hall, 2006, chap. 32.

Jorion, Philippe. *Big Bets Gone Bad: Derivatives and Bankruptcy in Orange County.* San Diego: Academic Press, 1995.

Leeson, Nick. *Rogue Trader: How I Brought Down Barings Bank and Shook the Financial World.* Boston: Little, Brown, 1996.

Marthinsen, John. *Risk Takers: Uses and Abuses of Financial Derivatives.* Boston: Addison Wesley, 2005.

Rogue Trader. Granada Film Productions and Newmark Capital Group. Directed and cowritten by James Dearden, 1999.

---

[7] A list through 2005 appears in Chance and Brooks, p. 572. Also, shortly before this book went to press, Société Générale, a $53 billion French bank, announced that a "rogue trader" named Jérôme Keruiel had amassed trading losses of $7.2 billion. Keep an eye on this story as it unfolds.

TEST YOUR KNOWLEDGE

1. How was Orange County's leveraging strategy successful for a period of time, and why did it eventually fail?
2. What important principle of risk management was violated by Barings Bank in allowing Nick Leeson to trade?
3. What important principle of risk management was violated by Procter & Gamble?

Best Practices in Derivatives

As seen in Essay 72, derivatives are high-powered instruments that, if misused, can get an organization into a great deal of trouble, if not completely destroy it. From the stories of Orange County, Barings, and Procter & Gamble, we have learned some important pieces of advice. Let us review them here.

If performance is exceptional, do not assume that it is not accompanied by excessive risk. Egos get in the way, and far too many people think that high returns are a result of skill and low returns are a result of bad luck. Consistent outstanding performance should *always* be questioned. High returns go with high risk. It is one of the most important rules in finance.

Make sure the people entering into derivatives transactions are sufficiently knowledgeable.[1] When the Orange County portfolio imploded, it was learned that Robert Citron had no qualifications for the job other than having already performed it for 24 years. Experience is usually given a nod over formal training, but clearly that was much of the problem here. Just as formal training is not a substitute for experience, neither is experience a substitute for formal training.

The front office, middle, and back offices must be separated. The front office, those who engage in derivatives transactions, simply cannot be the same people who process the transactions, the back office, and those who monitor the risk, the middle office. This is almost surely the most important requirement for effective risk management.

The counterparty dealer is not your advisor. Although in today's world, the language of these contracts makes that point quite explicit, it cannot be emphasized enough.

These points just represent some good common sense. Fortunately, there are several sets of formal prescriptions for the best practices to employ when

---

[1] A copy of this book would be a great way to put them on the right track, wouldn't it?

using derivatives. In 1993 the Group of Thirty (G-30), a global think tank of financial experts, published a report that established what it considered the best practices for derivatives use. Although focused on dealers, these practices also included some mention of end users. For a complete list of the G-30 standards, see http://riskinstitute.ch/138250.htm.

The report emphasizes the role of senior management and how risk management must start at the top of an organization. It goes on to note the importance that derivatives positions be valued on a regular basis, that the risk be quantified, that stress tests be performed , and that risk management be separated from trading. The report distinguishes market and credit risk, but the recommendations are similar for the two. It recommends that organizations have adequate professional expertise, reliable systems, and clear chains of authority. It promotes improvements in accounting, disclosure, legal complexities, and tax treatment. Although parts of the G-30 report have become somewhat outdated, most of it remains clearly relevant and is well worth detailed study. Any financial institution and most nonfinancial institutions that use derivatives should make the report an integral part of their risk management system.[2]

Institutional investors, meaning pension funds and mutual funds, have their own set of similar standards that were written by a group called the Risk Standards Working Group. You can read over these standards on the website of Capital Market Risk Advisors (www.cmra.com).

To use derivatives properly, you can go a long way by just answering a few simple questions:

- Do we have a formal policy that defines:
  - The risks we are exposed to?
  - The risks we are willing to take and the ones we are unwilling to take?
  - Which derivatives we can use?
  - Under what circumstances we can use them?
  - The chain of command for their usage?
- Are our personnel who are involved with derivatives sufficiently knowledgeable?
- Do we know what derivative positions we have in place right now?
- Can we measure our risk?
- Do we have controls in place so that the risk can be quickly adjusted?

---

[2] Unfortunately, I suspect that far too many firms view the G-30 report as a form of due diligence and more style than substance. A copy on the desk of the chief financial officer looks good but may not be worth much if the recommendations are not actually implemented.

- Are the personnel who engage in derivatives transactions different from and not supervisory to those who monitor our usage?
- Are senior managers and the board kept apprised of our derivatives activities?

These questions do not cover every detail, but they do encapsulate the principle areas of concern.

Derivatives have been compared to fire, chemicals, and pharmaceuticals. Used properly, they are extremely helpful. If misused or put in the hands of the untrained, they are extremely dangerous. Human societies have judged that fire, chemicals, and pharmaceuticals have benefits that outweigh the risks. It is unclear yet whether society believes that the benefits of derivatives outweigh the risks. Derivatives have not been outlawed, but they continue to take criticism, and there are frequent calls for greater regulation. But so far, derivatives seem to be winning the battle.

Let's hope it stays that way.

FOR MORE READING

Chance, Don M., and Robert Brooks. *An Introduction to Derivatives and Risk Management*, 7th ed. Mason, OH: Thomson South-Western, 2007, chap. 16.

Group of Thirty. *Derivatives: Principles and Practices*. Washington, DC: Author, 1993.

Lam, James. *Enterprise Risk Management: From Incentives to Controls*. Hoboken, NJ: John Wiley & Sons, 2003.

TEST YOUR KNOWLEDGE

1. Identify the four most important principles for good risk management.
2. What is the G-30 Report?

Recommended Reading

In the first edition of this book, I provided a recommended reading list at the back. This was done at a time when the Internet was just getting into full swing. Little did I realize that printed reading lists would get quite outdated in relation to those that could be managed dynamically on the Internet. While everything on that original reading list is still highly recommended, so much more has been added since that time. I maintain numerous web sites with much reference material that I keep fairly updated. So in this edition, I am simply going to give you links to my web sites.

READING LIST

This is the primary site I maintain with derivatives books:

```
http://www.bus.lsu.edu/academics/finance/faculty/dchance/
    Research/ReadingList.htm
```

Note that the site does not generally contain articles. There are literally thousands, but you will find them cited in these books. Also note that the essays of this book contain numerous article references.

DERIVATIVES SITES ON THE WEB

This is a site of sites:

```
http://www.bus.lsu.edu/academics/finance/faculty/dchance/
    Research/DerivativesSites.htm
```

Let me know if any links are out of date.

TERM STRUCTURE AND INTEREST RATE DERIVATIVES LITERATURE

This web site is a collection of every article I am aware of that deals with term structure modeling and interest rate derivative pricing:

```
http://www.bus.lsu.edu/academics/finance/faculty/dchance/
    Research/TermStructureLit.htm
```

Anyone doing research in this subject should find this an invaluable resource.

MISCELLANEOUS AND FUN STUFF

The next link is to DerivaQuote, a site of quotes about derivatives (and a few general quotes about finance). I have been collecting these quotes for about 20 years.:

```
http://www.bus.lsu.edu/academics/finance/faculty/dchance/
    MiscProf/DerivaQuote/DRVQ.htm
```

My hearty thanks go to those pithy geniuses who have unknowingly contributed to this interesting site.

This link is to a web site of references to somewhat strange and offbeat articles on derivatives:

```
http://www.bus.lsu.edu/academics/finance/faculty/dchance/
    Research/AlternativeLit.htm
```

I'm not ridiculing any of these articles. They are all excellent articles. They just present a different view. I think you will enjoy them. And if you don't, relax. Don't take derivatives too seriously.

AND IF ALL THAT IS NOT ENOUGH ...

Here is a collection of my "Teaching Notes," which are short technical essays on various topics. Be forewarned: These are technical.

```
http://www.bus.lsu.edu/academics/finance/faculty/dchance/
    Instructional/Instr.html
```

Answers to End-of-Essay Questions

ESSAY 1

1. A dealer is a financial institution that stands ready to buy and sell a security or derivative. It quotes a bid and an ask price, with the latter being higher than the former. It hedges the risk it takes on and earns a profit based on the prices at which it buys, sells, and hedges.
2. Most investment funds have a fiduciary duty that often prohibits them from using derivatives, even if those derivatives might help them reduce risk. Corporations have fewer restrictions, so many use derivatives to alter the risk and return patterns of their cash flows.
3. Unlike many state, local, and foreign governments, the U.S. government does not generally use derivatives. The Postal Service has used them and the U.S. government has in the past issued callable bonds, which are derivatives. But generally the U.S. government does not engage directly in derivative transactions. It is not clear why.

ESSAY 2

1. Futures contracts began at the Chicago Board of Trade in 1848. Originally called "to-arrive" contracts, they permitted farmers to lock in the price of their grain and make delivery at a later date. This feature alleviated a storage problem in Chicago whereby most grains would arrive in the city at the same time of the year, depressing prices and putting pressure on limited storage facilities.
2. In 1973 the Chicago Board of Trade created the Chicago Board Options Exchange, which was the first organized market for options trading. In addition, Fischer Black, Myron Scholes, and Robert Merton published articles that showed how option prices should be obtained. The model became a guide for traders at the new options exchange on how to price and hedge their positions.

3. The first noncommodity futures were the foreign currency futures contracts of the Chicago Mercantile Exchange.
4. The Kansas City Board of Trade created the Value Line Index futures in 1982.
5. The company had created its RiskMetrics system that pioneered the use of Value at Risk. It made the decision to post on its website, free of charge, the data that it had collected for calculating Value at Risk and other risk measures.

ESSAY 3

1. The primary reason for using derivatives is to provide an efficient means of transferring risk.
2. There are some periods in which a company feels uncomfortable about the high degree of risk. Thus, the hedge might be temporary. Also, the hedged asset is not necessarily the core asset of the business. The company might feel it needs to hedge a raw material in order to control costs and be able to provide the product or service in which it specializes. Other forms of hedging could occur in asset overlays in investment portfolios where the asset allocation is altered at the top of the organization, but the individual asset managers can maintain their positions without needing to cut back or increase their exposures.
3. If a hedger is attempting to get rid of risk, then there must be someone who is willing to take it. Speculators take the opposite side of derivatives transactions from hedgers.
4. Risk management means to align the risk being taken with the risk that you want to take. Risk can drift below the target amount of risk, so occasionally it will need to be increased. This is common in investment portfolios when higher-risk assets underperform lower-risk assets, resulting in a reduction of risk.
5. The personal wealth of managers is heavily exposed to the performance of the company. That is, managers have highly undiversified portfolios. Thus, they have an incentive to get the company to hedge to reduce the risk of their personal portfolios.

ESSAY 4

1. Customized contracts (forwards) have all of the terms agreed on by the two participants. Standardized contracts (futures) have all of the terms except the price set by the futures exchange. Customized contracts have

more flexibility. Each party can clearly negotiate for the terms it needs to fit its objectives. Standardization, however, creates a well-defined group of contracts that becomes more widely accepted by the broader marketplace and is generally more amenable to trading in a secondary market.

2. When created, a forward contract requires no cash payment. It is merely an agreement. It cannot appear on a balance sheet, because there is no defined possession or obligation with a market value. During the life of the contract, however, as the price of the underlying changes, the contract acquires either a positive value, making it an asset, or a negative value, making it a liability. A long forward contract becomes an asset when the underlying asset rises sufficiently and a liability when the underlying asset falls sufficiently.

3. The daily settlement feature enables the futures clearinghouse to control the credit risk. Since the clearinghouse guarantees to each party that it will pay if the other does not, the clearinghouse has a strong interest in the financial position of each party. By allocating gains and losses on a daily basis, it minimizes the possibility that one party will lose enough money in a short period of time to be unable to meet obligations.

ESSAY 5

1. A European option can be exercised only at expiration. An American option can be exercised at expiration and, in addition, at any other time prior to expiration.

2. In an option, the liability is only from the seller to the buyer. The buyer pays full cash at the start and has no further obligation. Therefore, the clearinghouse has to worry only about whether the seller will perform and then only if the option is exercised. It does this by requiring that the seller post margin money.

3. With a customized option, the party wanting to terminate the position early reenters the market and attempts to do a new transaction that matches the one it is trying to offset. The new transaction should have the same underlying, strike price, expiration, and exercise style (European or American). If the investor was long (short) on the original transaction, it should be short (long) on the new transaction. If the counterparty of the new transaction is the same counterparty of the old transaction, the two parties can exchange cash and remove both contracts from their records. If the counterparty of the new transaction is a different counterparty from the old transaction, both contracts remain outstanding, but the market risk is eliminated because gains on one

contract exactly match losses on the other. Credit risk remains, however, because a short counterparty could default.

ESSAY 6

1. In a plain vanilla swap, one party pays a fixed interest rate and the other pays a floating interest rate. In a basis swap, both parties pay a floating interest rate.
2. In a currency swap, the notional principals are in different currencies. In many currency swaps, the notional principals are exchanged. When they are exchanged at the start, they have equivalent value. When the reverse exchange is done at expiration, the values are not equivalent. Thus, it is economically meaningful to exchange notional principals in a currency swap. In an interest rate swap, the currencies are the same. Therefore, it is not economically meaningful to exchange the same amount of money in a given currency at the start and at the end.
3. Commodity swaps commonly pay off based on an average commodity price over a period of time rather than the specific price at a date in time. This feature removes the effect caused by an unusual and large price change at expiration that might not be reflective of prices near expiration.

ESSAY 7

1. Market risk, credit risk, operational risk, and other risks.
2. If a company's competitors include foreign companies, changes in exchange rates can change customers' perceptions of the company's products and services in relation to its foreign competitors. With different exchange rates, a foreign company's products can be less expensive.
3. With the exception of most companies' pension funds, few assets of typical companies are invested in the stock market. The stock market is a reflector of expectations of general business activity, but it is not the activity itself.

ESSAY 8

1. The primary rate used is LIBOR, which stands for London Interbank Offer Rate, which is the rate at which London banks borrow and lend dollars (and other currencies) to each other.

2. An FRA is like a typical forward contract in that it is a commitment to a future transaction. The long commits to make a fixed interest payment, and the short commits to make a floating interest payment. The interest rate is the underlying and therein lies the difference. In this case, the underlying is not an asset that you can purchase and hold though it does represent the payment on an asset, the fixed income security on which the rate is based.

3. When an interest rate option expires, the payoff is determined but payment is not made until later. If the underlying is a 90-day rate, payment occurs 90 days later. This feature corresponds to the common feature in floating-rate loans in which the rate is determined on one day but interest is paid at a later date.

4. Interest rate caps and floors consist of a package of interest rate calls and puts, respectively. Caps and floors are used to hedge floating-rate loan against rising interest rates and falling interest rates respectively.

ESSAY 9

1. If a borrower pays a floating rate of LIBOR plus a spread, the addition of a swap to pay a fixed rate and receive LIBOR will effectively convert the position into paying the swap fixed rate plus the spread on the loan.

2. If the borrower takes out a floating-rate loan and adds a swap (as explained in the answer to question 1), it takes on the credit risk that the dealer will default. If the borrower merely takes out a fixed-rate loan, it takes on no credit risk. The credit risk of the floating-rate loan plus swap should result in a lower overall rate. If the borrower is willing to bear the credit risk, the savings can be significant.

3. The present value of the fixed payments equals the present value of the floating payments.

4. When dealers quote rates on swaps, they are vulnerable to large and sudden interest rate movements that might occur right after they made a quote but before the potential counterparty has decided to enter into the transaction. If such an interest rate movement occurs, the Treasury rate will also move, thereby making the quote move in the same direction and affording some protection to the dealer.

ESSAY 10

1. A company borrows fixed (or floating) in its domestic currency, call it currency A. It then enters into a currency swap to receive fixed (or floating) in currency A and pay fixed (or floating) in currency B. The

payments received on the swap offset the payments made on the company's domestic currency loan. Thus, the combination of loan and swap results in borrowing fixed (or floating) in currency B.

2. When a company does this type of transaction, it takes advantage of its familiarity to a domestic lender. Thus, it might get a better rate than if it borrowed from the foreign lender directly. It might also get a better rate because it is taking on some credit risk from the swap dealer. When risk is taken on, there is the expectation of a reward, which comes from getting a slightly better rate.

3. A firm could enter into a swap to pay dollars fixed and receive yen fixed. It could also enter into a swap to pay yen fixed and receive dollars floating. The fixed yen payments offset, leaving the firm paying dollars fixed and receiving dollars floating.

ESSAY 11

1. Assume the issuer of a note promises to pay LIBOR with a minimum rate of 5%. The issuer can purchase a standard note paying LIBOR and buy an interest rate floor struck at 5%. It then issues the note promising to pay LIBOR and a minimum of 5%. When LIBOR is above 5%, it receives LIBOR from the note it holds and can therefore easily pay LIBOR. When LIBOR is below 5%, it receives LIBOR from the note it holds and its option pays 5% minus LIBOR. Thus, it nets 5% and can therefore pay 5% on the note it issued.

2. The most obvious way is that the inverse floater has its rate increase (decrease) as interest rates decrease (increase). Second, because the interest rate can go down, it has a possibility of becoming negative. A floor can be placed using an interest rate cap to prevent the rate from falling below zero. Third, an inverse floater often contains a leverage factor, meaning that the rate changes by a multiple of LIBOR.

3. Structured notes are typically constructed to meet the needs of a buyer who wants a particular type of payoff pattern. Structured notes allow investors to speculate on the direction of interest rates, volatility, range, and the shape of the term structure. In some cases, they may have been eligible for favorable tax and accounting treatment, and in some cases, they could serve as a hedge for some of the investor's other activities.

ESSAY 12

1. An ABS is a device that holds a portfolio of debt securities and issues securities that have a claim against the portfolio. It passes through

payments from the debt holdings to the holders of the ABS securities. The ABS securities are usually structured in tranches based on an order of priority in which prepayments and defaults are allocated to certain tranches before being allocated to other tranches.

2. Prepayment risk is the risk that a debt instrument (usually a mortgage) will be paid off prior to maturity. Often prepayment occurs because the borrower wishes to refinance the mortgage at a lower rate. When prepayments are made, the lender loses because it receives its money back in a lower interest rate environment. Thus, it cannot continue to earn the higher rate in effect when the mortgage was issued. The tranches in a CMO are arranged in order of priority in terms of prepayments. Thus, when mortgages are paid off early, these prepayments are paid to certain tranches first and others later.

3. CDOs have tranches that are defined by their order of priority of defaults. Thus, if a security held by the CDO defaults, the default is absorbed by the lowest-priority tranche. If defaults are sufficiently large, other tranches can also be required to bear some of the defaults. Thus, in general, defaults are allocated from lowest priority to highest.

4. ABS offer opportunities for investors to indirectly lend money in markets in which they would not otherwise be able to do so. For example, investors cannot make mortgage loans directly but can do so through holding MBS. They also cannot lend money to corporations and many other borrowers directly but can do so through CLOs and CDOs.

ESSAY 13

1. The other payment can be the return on another stock or index or a fixed or floating rate from a bond.

2. If the payments are on a foreign index, they can be structured so as to pay off in the domestic currency based on the rate earned on the foreign index. Alternatively, they can be structured to pay off in the foreign currency. Some people invest in foreign markets for the purpose of earning the foreign return as well as the currency risk, which can serve as a form of diversification. If that is desired, they would structure the swap to pay the foreign return in the foreign currency. Otherwise, the swap can be structured to pay the foreign return in the domestic currency.

3. A variable notional principal is like a portfolio that is periodically rebalanced to maintain the same dollar allocation to an asset class. A fixed notional principal is like a portfolio with no rebalancing.

ESSAY 14

1. By offering a return of principal and a fixed but low rate of interest, equity-linked debt is clearly a form of debt. The equity feature reflects a bonus return based on the upside or downside performance of a stock of index.
2. As noted in the answer to question 1, equity-linked debt is clearly a form of debt. The equity return is a one-sided return, meaning that you receive either any increases in the equity market or any decreases. This component of the return is equivalent to an option.
3. If a dealer issues an equity-linked note that pays a fixed rate plus any decrease in a market index, it can hedge it by purchasing a zero-coupon bond to guarantee payment of the fixed rate and a put option that pays off if the index goes down.

ESSAY 15

1. The oil market is quite volatile. Given the small number of producers and the explosive politics of oil, it is possible that the price of oil on the payoff day of a swap will be significantly out of line with the price on previous or subsequent days. In addition, many companies spread their purchases of oil out over a period of time and are interested in hedging the average price they pay. Average price swaps help address these two concerns.
2. Asian options are over-the-counter options that have an average price payoff. Also, the Chicago Board of Trade's Federal Funds futures contract has a payoff based on the average federal funds rate.

ESSAY 16

1. The option is worth more to sell it to someone else. In spite of your beliefs, the market never believes a stock cannot go any higher. Hence, there is upside potential, and the call will sell for more than its value as exercised. In addition, if you do believe the stock can go no higher, why would you want to convert the call to the stock? You forgo the interest on the exercise price just to acquire a stock that you believe is going no higher.
2. A dividend injects an automatic drop in the stock price at the ex-dividend instant. The holder of a call could find that the value gained by avoiding

this drop exceeds the cost, which is the interest on the exercise price and the give-up of the time value.

3. A call on a non-dividend-paying stock has no upper limit in value because the stock has no upper limit in value. A put has a lower limit, however, because the stock can go no lower than zero. This lower limit of the put's value is the exercise price. It can be advantageous to exercise the put if the interest on it is worth more than the potential for further gains in value if the stock falls further.

4. Dividends cause the stock price to fall on the ex-dividend day, which makes it more attractive to hold the put rather than exercise it. If exercise is worthwhile, it is better to do it immediately after the stock goes ex-dividend.

ESSAY 17

1. A payer swaption is the right to enter into a swap to pay a fixed rate and receive a floating rate. If the rate on the underlying swap in the market is above the strike rate on the swaptions, it is worthwhile to exercise the swaption. In doing so, the investor enters into a swap to pay the strike rate and receive the floating rate. It can leave the position as is or offset by entering into the market and doing the opposite swap, paying the floating rate and receive the swap rate in the market. This leaves a net position equivalent to an annuity that pays the difference in the swap rate in the market and the strike rate.

2. Interest rate caps and payer swaptions gain value when interest rates increase, and interest rate floors and receiver swaptions gain value when interest rates decrease. But caps and floors are combinations of *independent* options. The exercise of one option is independent of whether another one is exercised. There is only one exercise of a swaption.

3. The most obvious reasons are to enable it to enter into or exit a swap at a later date. Swaptions can also be used to hedge or replicate a callable bond.

ESSAY 18

1. Credit derivatives exist for the purpose of removing credit risk from a loan, bond, or derivative and enabling a party to trade it apart from the interest rate risk.

2. The most widely used credit derivative is the credit default swap. The party purchasing protection pays an annual premium to the party selling

protection. If the reference asset (bond, loan, or derivative of a third party) has a credit event, then the credit protection seller compensates the credit protection buyer either by accepting the underlying security and paying face value or by an equivalent cash settlement.

3. Pricing credit derivatives is difficult because normal probability theory does not apply to credit losses and because of the difficulty of collecting an adequate amount of data on credit losses, which are relatively rare events compared to movements in factors such as interest rates and exchange rates.

ESSAY 19

1. The "volatility of volatility" refers to the risk that volatility will change in an unpredictable manner. Volatility is a quantifiable measure of the variation in prices or interest rates. If the market has a certain degree of volatility, we can use that information in models to price and hedge securities and derivatives. But if the volatility can change to a higher or lower level in an unpredictable manner, we have a more difficult time using volatility correctly in models.

2. Because volatility is measurable, a derivative of virtually any type can be created in which the underlying is an agreed-on measure of volatility. The realized measure of volatility at expiration is inserted into the derivative's payoff formula to obtain the payoff. Hence, volatility in a volatility derivative works just like a stock price in an option on a stock.

3. It is an index of the implied volatility of options on the S&P 500 that trade on the Chicago Board Options Exchange.

ESSAY 20

1. Weather affects many businesses. In addition, there is an extensive amount of quantitative information on the weather. People in general are also fairly knowledgeable about it.

2. It is difficult to price and hedge weather derivatives, because it is not possible to hold the underlying and therefore to create a risk-free hedge that forms the basis for many pricing models. In the absence of risk-free hedging, you would need to estimate a risk premium or assume a zero risk premium, which is likely to be incorrect.

3. A cooling-degree day is defined as the difference between the average temperature in a day and 65 degrees Fahrenheit, while a heating-degree day is defined as the difference between 65 degrees Fahrenheit and the

average temperature. Thus, a day with an average temperature of 70 has five cooling-degree days. A day with an average temperature of 58 has seven heating-degree days. Derivatives can be structured to pay off based on the number of heating- or cooling-degree days over a period of time.

4. Companies possess rights to emit a certain amount of pollution in an area. Some companies have more rights than needed; others have less. Total pollution in an area is thus controlled, but each individual firm can pollute the amount it feels is necessary to maintain its operations at the right level. A market has developed for these rights. Derivatives are simply based on the spot prices of these rights.

ESSAY 21

1. The forward price should equal the spot price, compounded at the risk-free rate, plus the costs of storage, minus any cash payments, and minus the convenience yield.

2. If the forward price is too high, an arbitrageur could buy the underlying asset and sell a forward contract. While holding the asset, the arbitrageur incurs storage costs, but the forward price is sufficiently high to cover the storage costs and the risk-free rate. If the forward price is even higher, as noted in the question, then the arbitrageur earns the risk-free rate, an amount sufficient to cover the storage costs, and an additional return that reflects the mispricing. Thus, the arbitrageur does better than the risk-free rate at no risk.

3. If futures prices move directly with interest rates, profits will be earned on long futures positions when interest rates are increasing. These profits can then be invested at rising interest rates. If losses are earned, interest rates will be decreasing so the losses are incurred when interest rates are falling. Thus, it is advantageous to use futures instead of forwards when futures prices and interest rates are increasing. If the relationship between futures prices and interest rates is negative, the opposite arguments prevail and forwards are preferred. The type of contract that is preferred will have the higher price.

ESSAY 22

1. A fiduciary call is a call and a risk-free zero-coupon bond. A protective put is a position in the underlying asset and a long put on the asset.

2. The fiduciary call is underpriced and the protective put is overpriced. So the arbitrageur would buy the fiduciary call by purchasing the call and the risk-free bond and sell the protective put by selling short the asset and selling a put. The long call and risk-free bond and short asset and put would completely offset so that the position would neither pay nor receive anything at expiration. But the purchase of the underpriced fiduciary call and sale of the overpriced protective put would generate a positive cash inflow at the start. Thus, money comes in at the start and never goes out.

3. Put-call parity is $p + S = c + PV(X)$. Rearrange so that $S = c + PV(X) - p$. The left-hand side is a long position in the asset. Change the signs to make it $-S = -c - PV(X) + p$. Thus, the left-hand side is now a short position in the asset, and the right-hand side is a short call, short risk-free bond, and long put.

4. Buying a call and selling a put is equivalent to buying a forward contract and lending the present value of $F - X$. Therefore, buying a call, selling a put, and borrowing the present value of $F - X$ is equivalent to a forward contract. Note that if X is greater than F, you will be lending the present value of $X - F$ because $-PV(F - X) = +PV(X - F)$.

ESSAY 23

1. If $C + X < P + S$, the call and risk-free bond are underpriced and put and asset are overpriced. Note that the risk-free bond has a current value of X so its future value is X plus the interest on it. So you would buy a call and bond that has current value of X and future value of $FV(X)$. You would sell the put and asset.

2. If $P + S < C + PV(X)$, you would buy the put and asset and sell the call and a bond with current value of $PV(X)$ and future value of X.

3. Arbitrage earns the difference in value of the overpriced and underpriced portfolios. Given that $C + PV(X)$ will always be less than $C + X$, it would be better to do the transaction involving $C + PV(X)$. For example, if $C + X$ is 10, $C + PV(X)$ is 9, and $P + S$ is 11, it would be better to capture the difference between 11 and 9 than 11 and 10. So you would sell the put and asset and buy the call and bond with current value of $PV(X)$.

4. Dividends force an additional term into the equation, $PV(D)$, representing the present value of the dividends. If the dividends are known, this term can be accommodated by letting $PV(D)$ represent a risk-free bond with present value of $PV(D)$ and face value of D.

ESSAY 24

1. Using put-call parity, $c = S - PV(X) + p$. The left-hand side represents a call. The right-hand side consists of the asset and a loan, plus a put. The asset and loan are like a margin transaction. The put is a form of insurance, protecting the asset against downside loss.

2. Margin requirements dictate the maximum amount an investor can borrow to purchase stock. Hence, $PV(X)$ cannot exceed a certain maximum ratio to S. But by using options, you could technically even have $PV(X)$ exceed S. By purchasing an out-of-the-money call, $PV(X)$ will be high relative to S. Thus, $S - PV(X)$ will be low if not negative. An out-of-the-money call, however, will result in an in-the-money put, which will make p somewhat higher than otherwise, and this will offset the low or negative $S - PV(X)$ to produce the appropriate value of c.

3. As noted, a call option consists of a margin transaction plus insurance. There is no effect of volatility on a margin transaction (holding the asset price constant). Volatility increases the value of insurance. Thus, the positive effect of volatility on a call option comes from its insurance value.

ESSAY 25

1. Scottish scientist Robert Brown observed random movements of pollen particles suspended in water.

2. The time increment is an infinitesimal value, dt. The standard deviation is a measure of the volatility of the process. To obtain the standard deviation requires squaring dt. Under the rules of calculus, the square of a fixed infinitesimal value is zero, thereby making the volatility zero. Therefore, such a process could not be used to model a random variable like price or interest rate. By making the randomness proportional to the square root of dt, the squaring process does not eliminate the randomness.

3. If the Brownian motion stochastic process itself is squared, it becomes a new process with zero variance. In effect, what is happening is that the very small random changes are even smaller when squared. It can be shown that when squared, they reach a statistical limit that is fixed at dt. Therefore, there is no randomness. This phenomenon occurs only in continuous time. In discrete time, as might be observed in the market or in a simulation, squaring does not remove the randomness.

ESSAY 26

1. Stock prices should drift upward to reflect a positive return to bearing risk; stock prices are random; it should be more difficult to predict stock prices further into the future than over a shorter period of time; and stock prices should never be allowed to be negative. A good model should have these properties.
2. The Brownian motion term, $e(h)^{1/2}$, is multiplied by the stock's volatility.
3. Changes in the random variable in a Brownian motion are so small that they cannot go barreling through zero to a negative level. If the value is slightly above zero, any change can bring it only to zero, not below.
4. In the normal distribution, the probability distribution of the variable behaves according to the normal distribution. In the lognormal distribution, the logarithm of the variable behaves according to the normal distribution.

ESSAY 27

1. You can construct a hedge consisting of a long position of a certain number of shares of stock and a short position in call options, such that the risk of the stock is offset by the risk of the options. The position is dynamic, meaning that it must be constantly adjusted so that the number of shares reflects the option's delta or sensitivity to the stock price. If the hedge is maintained at no risk, it should earn the risk-free rate. The correct call price is the one that guarantees a risk-free return on this riskless transaction.
2. Black was unable to solve the differential equation necessary to obtain the model so he resorted to using the Capital Asset Pricing Model.
3. No. The model was initially rejected for publication in *The Journal of Political Economy* and then rejected by another top journal. Merton Miller, who later won a Nobel Prize, recommended that *The Journal of Political Economy* reconsider it, which it did and eventually published the article. Merton's work on the model was published in *The Bell Journal of Economics and Management Science*.

ESSAY 28

1. It is much easier to see how dynamic hedging leads to an option price in the binomial framework than in the continuous-time framework of

Black-Scholes-Merton. A second advantage is that it can accommodate the early exercise of American options and can model complex options. A third advantage is that it is useful in modeling the term structure.
2. A binomial tree or lattice is a diagram that illustrates the different prices the underlying can move to over time.

ESSAY 29

1. Option prices are solutions to partial differential equations. Some types of options are complex, and the partial differential equations cannot be solved by conventional methods. Numerical solutions allow us to solve the equation by laying out possible values of the underlying asset and the corresponding option prices.
2. The finite difference method is a rectangular grid in which the underlying price over a range is specified in the rows and time over the remaining life of the option is specified in columns. The option payoffs at expiration appear at the extreme right. Starting at that point and working backward, you can obtain the current option price by solving various equations.
3. In Monte Carlo simulation, random outcomes corresponding to the price of the underlying are created. The corresponding option values at expiration can then be determined by the various outcomes. A simple average of these outcomes is obtained and then discounted at the risk-free rate to obtain the current option price.

ESSAY 30

1. In static replication, you purchase and/or sell certain securities and options to replicate another security or option. You hold the replicating securities and options to the end of the investment horizon. In dynamic replication, you hold certain securities and options to replicate another security or option, but you must adjust the numbers of the replicating instruments to be able to produce the same result at the end of the investment horizon as the instrument being replicated.
2. A delta hedge might be constructed to take advantage of mispricing of an option or for a dealer to hedge a position it takes in order to service a client.
3. Delta hedging works only for small moves in the asset. For large moves, the hedge will be imbalanced. The effect is called the gamma. It can

be controlled by executing a gamma hedge, whereby the gamma of the position as well as the delta are set to zero.

4. Recall that the Black-Scholes-Merton formula is $c = SN(d_1) - Xe^{-rT}N(d_2)$. Rearrange to obtain $Xe^{-rT}N(d_2) = SN(d_1) - c$. Divide by $N(d_2)$: $Xe^{-rT} = SN(d_1)/N(d_2) - c/N(d_2)$. The left-hand side is the present value of X. Thus, it represents the present value of a zero-coupon risk-free bond paying X dollars at time T. The right-hand side is $N(d_1)/N(d_2)$ units of the asset and $1/N(d_2)$ short calls. This replication would be dynamic because $N(d_1)$ and $N(d_2)$ change so the units of the asset and calls would need to be changed as you move through time and the asset price changes.

ESSAY 31

1. A risk-averse person dislikes risk and demands a higher expected return to bear risk. A risk-neutral person does not demand a higher expected return to bear risk.

2. Derivatives are typically priced by constructed a risk-free hedge. The correct price of the derivative is the one that assures that a risk-free hedge will return the risk-free rate. As a result, the expected return on all assets and derivatives will appear equal to risk-free rate. That does not mean that in reality the derivative is expected to earn the risk-free rate. It simply means that risk-neutral pricing gives the correct derivative price, and risk-neutral pricing treats investors as if they are risk neutral, which is what produces an expected return of the risk-free rate. Risk-neutral pricing does not, however, assume people are risk neutral.

3. Each investor would observe the same price of the underlying and use it, through the principle that no arbitrage profits can be earned, to arrive at the price of the derivative. That there should be no arbitrage returns is agreed on by both types of investors. Hence, if both use it to price derivatives, they will both arrive at the same derivative price.

ESSAY 32

1. A martingale is a stochastic process in which the expected return is zero. In derivative pricing, the stochastic process of the underlying asset is converted to a martingale by scaling by the risk-free rate return.

2. Risk-neutral probabilities are probabilities assigned to the possible future prices of the underlying asset. These probabilities are not the real

probabilities, but they convert the stochastic process of the underlying to a martingale and permit pricing of the derivative by risk neutrality.

3. Otherwise, an arbitrage opportunity would exist. You could either borrow money and buy the asset such that the worst outcome would exceed the cost of borrowing the money or short sell the asset and lend money such that the worst outcome would be less than the cost of lending.

4. Girsanov's theorem is the continuous-time procedure that converts the true probability distribution to the risk-neutral probability distribution. It results in a shifting of the mean so that the expected return is converted to the risk-free rate.

ESSAY 33

1. As the underlying price increases and expiration approaches, the delta approaches 1. As the underlying price decreases and expiration approaches, the delta approaches zero. For puts, as the underlying price increases and expiration approaches, the delta approaches zero. As the underlying price decreases and expiration approaches, the delta approaches −1.

2. The magnitude of the gamma varies directly with the likelihood that the option will be exercised.

3. Theta reflects the change in option price as it moves through time, or the time value decay. Time is not a random variable. For example, if we have a 30-day option today, there is no possibility that tomorrow its time to expiration will be anything other than 29 days. While time value decay reduces the value of the option, this reduction is not a source of risk.

4. Rho, which is the change in the option price for a change in the risk-free interest rate, is not particularly important, because standard European options on assets are not very sensitive to interest rates.

ESSAY 34

1. Options on the same stock differ in price according to time to expiration and moneyness. Thus, it can be hard to compare two options on the same stock. By quoting the price in terms of implied volatility, you can determine that one option is priced higher than the other, after taking into account the obvious factors of time to expiration and moneyness on which the two options differ.

2. Because you cannot rearrange the option pricing formula so that the volatility is isolated on one side of the equation, an iterative approach can lead to a solution. This procedure is done by inserting values on the right-hand side for the volatility, obtaining an estimated value of the option, and comparing it to the market value of the option. Then you try new values of the volatility until it makes the market price equal the model price.

3. Near linearity of the volatility with respect to the option price means that it is possible to obtain a closed-form approximation formula for the implied volatility.

4. The term structure of volatility is the relationship between the implied volatilities of options on a stock with a specific exercise price and time to expiration of the option.

5. The volatility smile is the observed relationship be the implied volatilities of options on a stock with a specific time to expiration and different exercise prices. The curve is predominately U-shaped.

ESSAY 35

1. Two standard European calls and a compound call in which the underlying option is one of the two standard European calls are used in the Roll-Geske-Whaley model.

2. In the binomial model, the value of the option when the stock goes ex-dividend is compared to the value captured by early exercise. If the latter is greater, then the exercise value is designated as the value of the option, and the remaining tree calculations follow in the normal manner.

3. Bonds and currencies pay interest, so these payments can trigger early exercise.

ESSAY 36

1. At each point in the binomial tree in which the option is in-the-money, the value of the option if it is not exercised early is compared to the exercise value. If the latter is greater, then the exercise value is designated as the value of the option, and the remaining tree calculations follow in the normal manner.

2. In Essay 35 we learned that American call options are exercised only an instant before the stock goes ex-dividend. American put options might

be exercised at any time during the option's life, provided the option is in-the-money.

3. The critical asset price is the asset price at which the option is worth the same not exercised as its value if exercised. This price will lie below the exercise price but will be higher the closer it is to expiration and will equal the exercise price at expiration.

ESSAY 37

1. It is the rate on a par bond with payment dates that match those of the swap.
2. Each is the fixed rate on a plain vanilla swap in their respective currencies.
3. An equity swap is constructed by creating a portfolio that replicates the payments on the swap. The portfolio will consist of a certain number of shares of stock and a certain amount invested in risk-free bonds. The replicating portfolio is dynamic, because at each payment date other transactions must be done to maintain the replication.
4. Storage costs help determine the amount of money borrowed in the replicating portfolio that will consist of units of the commodity and a loan.

ESSAY 38

1. Asset allocation refers to the percentages of a portfolio that are allotted to different asset classes, such as stocks, bonds, money market funds, and so on. Strategic asset allocation refers to the long-run desired percentages. Tactical asset allocation refers to short-run deviations in the strategic asset allocation that might be undertaken for a variety of reasons that are temporary.
2. If an asset class needs its exposure reduced, you can engage in a derivative that hedges the asset class. If an asset class needs its exposure increased, you can engage in a derivative that speculates on the asset class. For the former case, you might sell futures, forwards, swaps, or calls or buy puts. For the latter case, you might buy futures, forwards, swaps, or calls or sell puts.
3. If the stocks are completely hedged with a derivative, then they should earn the risk-free rate. Thus, the stocks effectively earn the return that would be earned on cash.

4. Losses on the futures will require cash to fund the margin account on a day-to-day basis. The stocks will be generating gains but unless the stock is liquidated, the gains are only on paper.

ESSAY 39

1. A protective put is a strategy that consists of an asset and a put on the asset that allows the holder to sell the asset at a fixed price. Thus, if the asset incurs a loss, the put serves as a form of insurance. On an insurance policy, the deductible serves to allocate a portion of the risk to the insured. A higher deductible allocates more risk to the insured but lowers the premium. With a protective put, a lower exercise price allocates more risk to the insured and lowers the premium.
2. Any investor who needs to achieve a target value at a certain future date could reasonably use a protective put to ensure that the target is met.
3. Portfolio insurance is a strategy consisting of the underlying and a second instrument, the risk-free asset or futures. The asset and the second instrument are combined in such a way that the delta of that instrument is matched to the delta of the asset and a hypothetical put that would serve to make the strategy a protective put. Because deltas change, however, the portfolio insurance strategy requires adjustment of the number of units of the underlying to the second instrument.

ESSAY 40

1. If the option expires with the stock price above the exercise price, the option will be exercised. The covered call writer will then have to sell the stock for the exercise price, which is lower than the stock price at expiration. Thus, upside gains are forgone.
2. Selling calls against stock that is owned generates the option premiums, which can be viewed as an enhancement of one's income.
3. The price of the stock at the time the call is sold reflects the opportunity cost of selling the stock rather than holding on to it and selling the call. The original price of the stock is irrelevant. It is a sunk cost.

ESSAY 41

1. A managed futures account typically invests in futures contracts. A hedge fund uses a variety of derivatives as well as investments in the

underlying assets. A hedge fund can typically invest in a broad variety of assets across many global markets.

2. The regulation of mutual funds comes under the 1940 Investment Company Act, which subjects it to regulation but allows funds to offer their products to the general public. Hedge funds are restricted to no more than 100 investors.

3. Hedge fund managers usually receive a management fee of 1% to 3% of assets under management and incentive fees that pay them 20% to 50% of profits, though there are usually no penalties for losses. Sometimes incentive fees have a high-water mark, meaning that they cannot be earned if the fund value is below a previously established high value.

ESSAY 42

1. A call option bull spread consists of a long position in a call with a given strike price and a short position in a call with a higher strike price.

2. A bull spread consists only of options. A risk reversal involves adding the options to a position in the underlying asset. It effectively places upper and lower limits on the effective sale price of the asset.

3. A zero-cost collar is a transaction executed by someone who owns the asset and wants protection. That person buys a put with an exercise price lower than the asset price and sells a call with an exercise price higher than the asset price. The put strike is usually chosen based on the investor's tolerance for downside risk. The call strike is chosen such that the premium on the call precisely offsets the premium on the put, thereby resulting in no net cash cost for the options.

4. A prepaid forward is a collar with an added position in a loan. The investor can borrow the present value of the lower exercise price. It then often would invest those borrowed funds into a diversified portfolio of other assets. The loan is effectively secured by the fact that the underlying asset will be sold for the lower exercise price or more.

ESSAY 43

1. Given exercise prices X_1 and X_2 with $X_1 < X_2$, a long box spread consists of a long call struck at X_1, a short call struck at X_2, a long put struck at X_2, and a short put struck at X_1.

2. In all outcomes at expiration, you will end up buying the asset at X_1, either by exercising the call or having the put exercised on you, and selling the asset at X_2, either by exercising the put or having the call

exercised on you. Thus, you know that you will net a value of $X_2 - X_1$ at expiration.

3. If you have a long box spread, early exercise is never a problem because, at worst, you would receive $X_2 - X_1$ earlier than expected. But if you have a short box spread, you will have to pay out $X_2 - X_1$ earlier than expected.

ESSAY 44

1. An "in" barrier option is one in which the underlying price must breach the designated barrier in order for the option to start. Thus, if the barrier is never breached, any apparent payoff at expiration will not be made. An "out" barrier option is one that dies if the barrier is breached. Thus, if the barrier is breached, any apparent payoff at expiration will not be made.

2. An "up" barrier option is one in which the barrier is above the current level of the underlying. A "down" barrier option is one in which the barrier is below the current level of the underlying.

3. In an up-and-out put, if the underlying rises and reaches the barrier, the option dies. But if there is also an up-and-in put that activates when the underlying rises and reaches the same barrier, the dead option is effectively replaced by a live option. The end result is that the overall combination is equivalent to a standard European option.

ESSAY 45

1. The underlying must move up or down from the exercise price by the sum of the premiums on the call and the put.

2. If the underlying has high volatility, other investors in the market are aware of that fact. The options will therefore be priced accordingly, and it will be difficult to make the strategy succeed. If, however, the investor believes that volatility will be higher than other investors believe, the straddle will be priced lower to reflect the common beliefs of other investors and not the volatility that one believes will be true.

3. A chooser option enables the investor to decide during the option's life if it will be a call or a put. A straddle gives the investor both a call and a put. With a straddle, it is almost certain that either the call or the put will expire in-the-money. With a chooser option, the investor could choose to make it a call (put) and afterward the stock falls (rises) such that the option expires out-of-the-money.

ESSAY 46

1. An ordinary option is the right to buy (call) or right to sell (put) an underlying asset. In a compound option, the underlying asset is another option, either a call or a put. In a sense, a compound option is just a special case of an ordinary option, but the pricing is more complicated because the stochastic process for the underlying is more complex than when an ordinary asset is the underlying. In particular, the volatility of an option is not constant even if the volatility of an underlying asset is constant.

2. The bivariate normal probability in a compound option reveals the joint probability that the compound option will be exercised to acquire or sell the underlying option and the underlying option will be exercised to acquire or sell its underlying asset. The probability is the risk-neutral probability, however, and not the true probability.

3. An installment option is one in which the premium is paid in a series of installments over time. At any premium payment date, the option holder can decide not to pay the premium, which terminates the option. The installment premiums can be equated to multiple compound options, that is, an option on an option on an option, and so on. Pricing is done by a numerical solution that forces the strikes to be equal and to equal the installment premium.

4. The most important contribution of compound option theory is to facilitate the pricing of American options.

ESSAY 47

1. The asset-or-nothing option pays the holder the asset if it expires in-the-money. The cash-or-nothing option pays a fixed amount of cash if it expires in-the-money.

2. As the essay discusses, a long asset-or-nothing call with exercise price of X can be combined with X short cash-or-nothing calls each paying one unit of currency if they expire in-the-money to produce a standard European call struck at X. Hence, you can combine a long asset-or-nothing call with a short European call to produce a long cash-or-nothing call. This result is obtained by rearranging the terms in the Black-Scholes-Merton formula that represent the asset-or-nothing call, the cash-or-nothing call, and the ordinary call.

3. As with ordinary options, digital puts differ from digital calls in that they pay off if the option expires with the asset price below the exercise price.

ESSAY 48

1. A geometric average price option is much easier to price because the distribution of the product of a series of lognormally distributed variables is lognormal. The distribution of the average of a series of lognormally distributed variables is not lognormal and, in fact, is very complex.
2. The average price in an Asian option can be used as either the price of the underlying or the strike price in the option payoff formula.
3. A Bermuda option is an option that can be exercised early but only at limited times during the option's life.

ESSAY 49

1. An option to exchange a random asset, say Y, for another random asset, say X, is the same thing as an option on X with a random exercise price, the randomness of which is being determined by asset Y. The payoff at expiration is the greater of the value of X minus the value of Y or zero. This is the same as an option with a random exercise price in which the randomness is the value of asset Y.
2. An option on the max is an option that starts with two underlying assets. At expiration, you determine which of the two assets has the greater value. Then you compare that asset's value to the exercise price to determine whether the option should be exercised.
3. It would make little sense to have an option on the max if one asset had significantly greater value at the start and was therefore likely to have significantly greater value at expiration. Thus, the option is usually structured so that the payoff is determined by which of the two assets performed better than the other. Performance reflects the rate of return on the asset over the option's life, not just the value of the asset at expiration. In effect, the values of the underlying assets are normalized to a unit value at the start.

ESSAY 50

1. A range forward is a forward contract with maximum and minimum values. It is constructed by going long a forward contract, hedging the downside with a put that is financed by selling a call for the same premium. The call results in the forfeiture of gains on the upside beyond the call strike.

2. The two similar strategies are collars and bull spreads. Both provide a maximum and minimum value and a range with the maximum and minimum in which the position gains with increases in the underlying asset value and loses with decreases in the underlying asset value.
3. A break forward is essentially a call option in which the option premium is borrowed. Thus, there is no initial cash outlay, which makes it appear like a forward contract.

ESSAY 51

1. A standard lookback option allows purchase of the underlying at the lowest price (if a call) or sale of the underlying at the highest price (if a put) of the asset during the option's life. In an extremum lookback, the holder can buy the asset for a fixed price but sell it at the highest price (if a call) or sell the asset for a fixed price and buy it for the lowest price (if a put).
2. A standard lookback call and standard lookback put if combined allow the purchase of the asset at the lowest price (using the call) and sale of the asset at the highest price (if a put). Thus, the investor "buys low and sells high." But the profit earned from doing so is not guaranteed to cover the cost of the two options.

ESSAY 52

1. Holding $c(1, \alpha, T - t)$ units of the asset worth S_t will precisely replicate the forward start option that starts in $T - t$ years and has moneyness of α. This result occurs because of the linear homogeneity of the value of an option.
2. The premium is paid if the option is exercised. But the option might expire in-the-money by an insufficient amount to cover the full premium.
3. The challenge in understanding this option is merely to remember that if the option expires in-the-money by less than the premium, it would not be worthwhile to exercise it. Thus, it must be in-the-money by more than the premium to justify your exercising it.

ESSAY 53

1. Duration measures the sensitivity of a bond price to the yield. It also measures the weighted-average time to all of the payments are made on the bond.

2. If the holding period is set equal to the duration, the bond will be protected against changes in interest rates. This type of strategy is called immunization.

ESSAY 54

1. Convexity is a second-order effect that measures several things. It measures the speed at which duration changes. It also measures the curvature of the line that reflects the relationship between price and yield. As such, it can serve to supplement duration as a measure of the sensitivity of a bond price to its yield.
2. Duration and convexity assume parallel shifts in interest rates, which means that all interest rates are assumed to change by the same amount. This is not only unlikely, but it also admits arbitrage.
3. Duration and convexity are similar but not identical to delta and gamma.

ESSAY 55

1. The basic building block instrument is the zero-coupon bond or loan. This is an instrument in which you pay a fixed amount of money today and receive a fixed amount at a future date. There is no interim payment of interest.
2. Spot rates represent the rates at which zero-coupon bonds and loans are made when a transaction begins today. Forward rates are the rates on zero-coupon bonds and loans that are agreed on today but do not start until a later date. The forward rates are implied by the spot rates and arise from the assumption that arbitrage opportunities are not permitted.

ESSAY 56

1. If the forward rate is higher (lower) than the current spot rate, the market would be predicting that future spot rates will be higher (lower) than current spot rates. Thus, an upward- (a downward-) sloping term structure implies a forecast of rising (falling) spot rates.
2. Forward prices would equal expected spot prices if people are risk neutral.
3. Forward prices would equal expected spot prices if there were no uncertainty about interest rates.

4. The other two explanations are the liquidity preference theory and the market segmentation or preferred habitat theory. The market segmentation theory is contradicted by the existence of arbitrageurs that trade across the spectrum of maturities of bonds.

ESSAY 57

1. A one-factor model of the term structure specifies that all zero-coupon bonds are perfectly correlated. Their prices are driven by a single force or factor.
2. The risk-free bond can be represented only by the bond that has the shortest maturity. A longer-term zero-coupon bond does pay back a sure return, but its price can fluctuate during the interim period.
3. The local expectations hypothesis describes the relationship between bonds on the term structure in which there are no opportunities to earn arbitrage profits. It implies that the expected returns on all bonds under risk neutrality will equal the shortest rate, which represents the risk-free rate. It also implies that under risk neutrality, forward prices equal expected spot prices looking out over the shortest possible holding period.

ESSAY 58

1. "Simple" models, as the term is used here, refer to equilibrium models that produce the term structure as an output. Because of that, the prices of zero-coupon bonds in the model might not match the actual prices of zero-coupon bonds in the market. Thus, it could be possible for an arbitrage to be executed against the party using such a model. "No-arbitrage" models use the actual term structure as an input to the model. Thus, they will prohibit arbitrage against the user of the model.
2. "Mean reversion" refers to the phenomenon that something cannot consistently move upward or downward without limit. In a mean-reverting interest rate model, such as Vasicek, a positive drift in the interest rate would mean that the interest rate would move upward over time without any upper limit, which is an unreasonable assumption. A mean-reverting model pulls the rate down when it is above the long-run average rate and pulls it up when it is below the long-run average rate.
3. The Vasicek model assumes a normal distribution of interest rates, which can cause the interest rate to be negative. The Cox-Ingersoll-Ross model solves this problem by building in a square root term applied

to the volatility. This term goes to zero when the rate goes to zero. As such, when the interest rate is at zero, volatility disappears and the positive drift is the only effect that applies to the change in rates. Thus, the interest rate can then only go up.

ESSAY 59

1. The Ho-Lee model was the first model to take the term structure as an input and to derive a model that assured the absence of arbitrage opportunities.
2. A recombining tree is one in which an up move followed by a down move leaves the underlying at the same place as a down move followed by an up move. A tree that does not recombine will have many branches, will be characterized as bushy, and will be hard to work with. A recombining tree eliminates that problem.
3. In a one-factor model, only one source of uncertainty drives the evolution of interest rates. In a multifactor model, multiple sources of uncertainty drive interest rates. In a one-factor model, all rates are perfectly correlated and any two bonds can be combined to serve as a perfect substitute for a third bond.
4. The evolution of interest rates in the Heath-Jarrow-Morton model is captured by the forward rate.
5. To prevent arbitrage in the Heath-Jarrow-Morton model, the drift or expected change in the interest rate must be constrained to a specific value.

ESSAY 60

1. To model interest rate movements over a binomial time period, it is necessary to have at least one bond whose price can vary due to uncertainty in interest rates. There are n bonds able to fit a model of $n-1$ periods. At the end of each period, one bond matures. Thus, at the end of the last period, there will be one bond left and that bond will mature. Thus, the bond has no price uncertainty, meaning that there is no interest rate uncertainty, so it would be impossible to extend the model to another period.
2. A binomial term structure does not capture actual movements in interest rates. It takes the existing term structure and models movements that prohibit arbitrage. The interest rates in the tree, thus, do not represent real interest rate movements, and their probabilities are not the actual

probabilities. The probabilities are the risk-neutral probabilities, which are weights applied to hypothetical prices to prevent arbitrage and ensure that the prices in the model agree with those trading in the market and do not allow arbitrage trading.

ESSAY 61

1. The price is found as a probability-weighted average of the next two possible prices plus the coupon.
2. A callable bond is a bond in which the issuer can pay off the bond before its maturity. The issuer will do so if the value of the callable bond exceeds the amount that must be paid to call the bond, which is known as the call price. At each node of the binomial tree, the value of the bond is compared to the call price. If the value of the bond exceeds the call price, the bond is treated as called and the value of the bond is replaced by the call price. This operation can occur at any point in the tree. Thus, the bond price at any point is found in the normal manner but could be superseded by the call price.
3. A futures contract requires no outlay of funds. Thus, there is no opportunity cost. The futures price is thus the expected future payoff not discounted.

ESSAY 62

1. In each period there is a single one-period bond. The return on that bond is the one-period rate.
2. An FRA pays off the difference in the interest rate and the fixed rate on the FRA. Pricing the FRA means finding the fixed rate that gives the contract an initial value of zero. The fixed rate solves an equation that forces the expected payoff at expiration to equal zero.
3. An interest rate option (caplet or floorlet) expires at a given time point, but the payoff occurs one period later.

ESSAY 63

1. To price a swap, we require only the prices of the zero-coupon bonds. Thus, it is not necessary to model the evolution of the interest rate. Having a binomial model, however, enables us to determine the value of the swap as it evolves through time.

2. A swap can be priced as a combination of FRAs with different maturities, though each FRA must be treated as having the same fixed rate, whereas FRAs of different maturities would ordinarily have different rates.

ESSAY 64

1. Exercise of a swaption creates a series of payments equal to the difference in the fixed rate on the underlying swap at expiration and the strike rate of the swaption. Of course, if the appropriate difference is not positive, then the swaption is not exercised. This series of payments is discounted to the swaption exercise date. The payoffs for each outcome are then probability weighted and discounted back to the present.
2. An American swaption might be exercised at any time point. If the swaption is exercised, a new swaption is created. Its value must be compared to the value of the swaption if not exercised, and the greater of these two values is used as the value of the swaption. Valuation then proceeds in the same manner as usual: Find the probability-weighted average of the next two payoffs and discount back to the present.

ESSAY 65

1. The differences are largely semantic. The term "executive stock options" refers to options awarded to senior-level officers and board members. The term "employee stock options" refers to options awarded to anyone other than senior-level officers and board members. The options themselves are almost always essentially the same. The term "employee stock options" is the more general term.
2. Stock options generally have a vesting period, during which the employee cannot exercise the options. Because the options cannot be sold, they are less desirable to hold than exchange-listed or over-the-counter options, which can usually be sold or offset to generate cash. To the issuing company, the inability to sell or exercise the options provides the incentive for employees to remain with the company and work hard.
3. Prior to the release of FAS 123R in 2004, the cost of stock options did not have to be recorded as an expense provided the options were not in-the-money. Thus, companies could essentially hide the cost by making sure that the exercise price was no lower than the stock price at the time of issuance.
4. Two recent controversies have been repricing and backdating. The former refers to the practice of lowering the exercise price of out-of-the-money options at some point during the option's life. "Backdating"

refers to the practice of issuing an option on one day but setting the exercise price to the lowest stock price observed on a previous date.

ESSAY 66

1. Value at Risk measures the *minimum* amount of money that will be lost over a defined period of time a certain percentage, usually 1% or 5%, of the time.
2. The three methods of measuring Value at Risk are the historical method, the analytical method, and the Monte Carlo method.
3. The analytical method and the Monte Carlo method require the assumption of a specific probability distribution. The analytical method assumes the normal distribution. The Monte Carlo method can assume the normal distribution but is not required to do so.
4. Stress testing and analysis of a portfolio under hypothetical scenarios can tell how the portfolio will perform in unusual but plausible circumstances.

ESSAY 67

1. Although equity can be modeled as a call option, the limited liability feature is equivalent to a put option. A put gives the right to sell something for a fixed price. In the context of equity on a firm with debt, the stockholders have the analogous right to fully discharge their liability by turning over the assets to the creditors.
2. In conventional put-call parity, the terms are the call price, exercise price, underlying price, risk-free rate, time to expiration, and volatility of the underlying. The corresponding terms are (respectively) the value of the stock, the face value of the debt, the value of the underlying assets, the risk-free rate, the time to maturity of the debt, and the volatility of the underlying assets.
3. A bond subject to default is equivalent to a default-free bond and a short put written by the creditors to the stockholders. This put is the same as the put explained in question 1 that represents the stockholders' right of limited liability.

ESSAY 68

1. In an option, the buyer pays a premium at the start and has the right to exercise the option later. The buyer is under no obligation to exercise

the option, and even if she does exercise the option, she never owes the seller anything beyond the initial premium.

2. In an interest rate swap, the notional principal is never exchanged. Thus, the amount of money represented by the notional principal is never paid. The parties simply pay the difference in two interest rates applied to the notional principal.

3. The primary means is to diversify, that is, not to concentrate too much business with a single party. The secondary means is to use collateral.

4. Close-out netting, whereby the two parties agree that in a bankruptcy, the overall net value is determined and one party owes the other only the net avoids the practice of cherrypicking. Cherrypicking is when one party walks away from some of its obligations. For a defaulting party, this could mean declaring default on contracts in which it owes more than the counterparty and demanding payment on contracts in which the counterparty owes it more.

ESSAY 69

1. Operational risk is difficult to measure because the events are infrequent and each event is different.

2. Rogue trader risk, which was made famous by Nick Leeson's trading that destroyed Barings Bank, is the risk that an isolated individual can destroy an organization by trading.

3. The principal means of managing operational risk are insurance, outsourcing, and setting aside additional capital.

ESSAY 70

1. Risk management can be structured as decentralized risk management, centralized risk management, and enterprise risk management.

2. Enterprise risk management, the most concentrated form of risk management, encompasses centralized risk management but also includes the management of risks that are typically controlled through insurance.

3. The person in charge of risk management should not be the person taking the risk.

ESSAY 71

1. A fair value hedge is a hedge of the value of an asset held by a company. Under FAS 133, a fair value hedge requires recording the gains and

losses on the derivative and the asset being asset hedged while the hedge is alive.

2. In a cash flow hedge, the transaction is designed to protect a future cash flow. While the hedge is in place, the gains and losses from the derivative are recorded but they appear on the balance sheet, not the income statement, in an account called Other Comprehensive Income. Thus, the gains and losses on the derivative are reported but do not lead to volatility in reported income.

3. There is no official standard for gauging hedging effectiveness, but an informal rule has been developed. A hedge is usually deemed effective if the gain or loss on the derivative is within 80% to 125% of the gain or loss on the position being hedged.

4. Firms can disclose using tables with summaries, sensitivity analysis, or quantitative measures such as value at risk.

ESSAY 72

1. Orange County engaged in reverse repurchase agreements, which entailed purchasing U.S. Treasury notes and then using the notes as collateral to borrow additional funds, with which more Treasury notes could be purchased. Those notes were then used as additional collateral to purchase still more Treasury notes. This strategy had a leverage factor of approximately three, meaning that the portfolio would perform at three times the rate of the underlying notes. When interest rates were flat or falling, the portfolio would do well. When rates rose, the prices of the notes fell, and the leverage amplified the loss to a total of about $2 billion.

2. Leeson was in charge of the back office, meaning the bookkeeping. Thus, he had access to the accounting system, which enabled him to hide his trading losses. That is, he was trading and doing the monitoring of his own trades. Hence, there was no independent risk management oversight.

3. Procter & Gamble had used its treasury department as a profit center. A treasury department is responsible for managing a company's short-term financial resources. It can be a profit center only if it can guess the direction of interest and exchange rates better than the rest of the financial world. This is an unreasonable expectation.

ESSAY 73

1. The four principles are: exceptional performance must be questioned to identify the risk; the people engaged in derivatives transactions must